THE MILITARIA
DIRECTORY AND
SOURCE BOOK
2003

© 2003 Compendium Publishing Ltd

A CIP record for this book is available in the British Library

ISBN   1-902579-39-9

Printed in Hong Kong through Printworks Int. Ltd.

Telephone Dialling Numbers
Remember to add the correct international dialling codes to the phone and fax numbers given in this book. In many cases, when dialling an overseas number, the first 0 of the internal number must be dropped.

* Indicates an entry that has remained the same from the last edition.

The descriptive text entries in this directory have been supplied by the companies and individuals listed. Whilst we try to ensure that these factual details are correct at the time of going to press, we apologise in advance for any changes which may occur during the life of this edition.

Suggestions or applications for inclusion in future editions are always welcome.

The Directory Editor
43 Frith Street
Soho, London, W1D 4SA, UK

CONTENTS

INTRODUCTION

When I landed a job with the Military History and Aviation Book Society, I thought I'd died and gone to heaven. I was going to get to spend all day everyday immersed in the subjects that had previously been crammed into evenings and weekends. In the three years since, there have been two aspects that have really made it enjoyable. The first is the constant sense of sharing my enthusiasm for all things military with tens of thousands of like-minded individuals scattered across the British Isles, many of whom have become good friends. The sheer number of entries in this excellent directory show just how many of us there are out there and will put the reader in touch with somebody else, probably many somebodies, who shares their passions or at least has what they need to indulge them.

The second thing I find constantly refreshing is the sheer diversity brigaded together under the supposedly 'specialist' military interest area. Firstly of course there is the whole chronological and geographical sweep of history to choose from, from ancient Sumeria to current global developments. The Book Society consciously tries to cover this whole vast field as far as books in print are concerned, and the ever growing membership suggests we don't badly at all, but we simply can't go into every niche. Where we can't go, some of the many other specialist booksellers listed in these pages will be able to.

But beyond books there are all those other outlets the military enthusiast finds for his or her energies. Model making is a phenomenally popular hobby (who among us has not lost skin from the fingers to polystyrene cement?) yet really good model shops have been increasingly hard to find; unless you know where to look that is—and now you do. The same goes for wargaming (and I have as many unpainted armies under the bed as the next man). Thousands queue up in any weather for the big conventions that happen several times a year, but it can be hard to find clubs or stockists of figurines to pursue the hobby in between. Well this directory will solve that for you too. Personally, I have always fancied trying re-enactment but didn't know how to get into it. If I had owned a directory like this ten years ago, I would probably be writing this from a muddy field somewhere, with a replica sword in my hand. Hmmm, perhaps I'll just give them a ring. . .

Philip Sidnell
Editor
Military History & Aviation Book Society

AUCTION HOUSES

BERLINER AUKTIONHAUS FÜR GESCHICHTE
Motzstrasse 22, 10777 Berlin, Germany
Tel/Fax: 302119538
Email: geboeter@berliner-auktionhaus.com
Website: www.berliner-auktionhaus.com

BONHAMS/PHILLIPS
65–69 Lots Road, Chelsea, London SW10 ORNH
Contact: Liegh Gotch
Tel: 020 7393 3951
Email: i.gotch@bonhams.com
James Opie Tel: 020 7794 7447
Website: www.bonhams.com
Specialist auctioneers since 1795, Bonhams & Brooks offer over 300 auctions each year in over 40 categories including militaria and sporting guns. Free auction valuations and advice on insurance, probate and all aspects of buying and selling at auction.

BUCKLAND DIX & WOOD
1 Old Bond Street, London W1X 3TD
Tel: 020 7499 5022
Fax: 020 7499 5023
Email: auctions@dnw.co.uk
Specialist auctions of orders, decorations and war medals.

CHRISTIE'S
85 Old Brompton Road, London SW7 3LD
Head Office: 8 King Street, St James's, London SW1
Tel: 020 7839 9060
City Office: 50–60 Gresham Street, London EC2
Tel: 020 7588 4424
Email: sgoodman@christie's.com

GLENDINNING'S
101 New Bond Street, London W1Y 9LG
Contact: Andrew Litherland; Chris Allen
Tel: 020 7493 2445
Fax: 020 7491 9181
Email: phillips_glendinnings@hot.com
Auctioneers and valuers of all orders, decorations and medals, as well as rise arms, armour and militaria. Three sales a year. Valuations for insurance,probate, etc. Catalogues by subscription.Open Monday to Friday 8.30am to 5.00pm.

HERMANN HISTORICA OHG
Sandstrasse 33, Munich 80335, Germany
Tel: 89 5237296
Fax: 89 5237103
Specialist international auctioneers of arms, armour, historic militaria, orders, medals, uniforms etc.

JAN K KUBE
Altes Schloss, 91484 Sugenheim, Germany
Tel/Fax: 91 65650
Email: info@kube.de
Website: www.kube.de

ONSLOWS
2 Michael Road, London SW6 2AD
Contact: Patrick Bogue
Tel: 020 7371 0505
Fax: 020 7384 2682
Email: bogue.onslows@btinternet
Website: www.onslows.co.uk
WWI and WWII propaganda posters.

PHILLIPS
7 Blenheim Street, New Bond Street, London W1Y OAS
Contact: Christopher Allen
Tel: 020 7629 6602
Fax: 020 7495 3536
Email: Info@philmark.demon.co.uk
Phillips hold regular specialised sales of arms, armour and militaria which include all types of antique edged weapons, antique and modern firearms uniforms etc.

PHILLIPS BAYSWATER
10 Salem Road, Bayswater, London W2 4DL
Contact: James Opie
Tel: 020 7229 9090
Fax: 0207 792 9201
Phillips Bayswater continues a 27-year series of specialist toy soldier and figure auctions held four times a year under the guidance of world expert James Opie.

SOTHEBY'S
34–35 New Bond Street, London W1A 2AA
Tel/Fax: 020 7293 5000
Email: see below

SOTHEBY'S/BILLINGSHURST
Summers Place, Billinghurst, W. Sussex RH14 9AD
Contact: Gordon Gardiner
Tel: 01403 833500
Fax: 01403 785153
Email: gordon.gardiner@sothebys.com
Regular auctions of militaria, antique firearms, air pistols and rifles, edged weapons, aeronautical medals, orders and decorations. Free auction valuations and advice.

SPINK & SON
69 Southampton Row, Bloomsbury, London WC1B 4ET
Contact Lucy Formosa
Tel: 020 7563 4055
Fax: 020 7563 4068
Email: lformosa@spinkandson.com
Website: www.spink-online.com
Visit our web site at http://www.spink-online.com to view our virtual gallery of hundreds of coins, banknotes, medals and stamps for sale direct, details of forthcoming auctions. Search our auction catalogues online, look up prices realised at auction and read the latest news from Spink. You can also register with us to receive regular updates on your specific area of interest.

STEWART'S MILITARY ANTIQUES & 19TH CENTURY PHOTOGRAPHY
108 W. Main St, Mesa, AZ 85201, USA
Contact: Larry & Terri Stewart
Tel: 480 834 4004
Fax: 480 834 3380
Email: Lstew14244@aol.com
Website.www.stewartsmilitaryantiques.com
We specialize in military collectables from WWII with a heavy emphasis on American and German interests. We feature equipment, bayonets, uniforms, headgear, and some insignia. A specialty item are WWII German equipment boxes. We offer a lifetime guaranty of originality for our customers.

WALLIS & WALLIS
West Street Auction Galleries, BN7 2NJ
Contact: Roy Butler
Tel: 01273 480208
Fax: 01273 476562
Email: auctions@wallisandwallis.co.uk
Website: www.wallisandwallis.co.uk
Militaria, medals, arms and armour auctions held every six weeks throughout the year. Connoisseur collectors auctions held in the spring and autumn.

WARWICK & WARWICK
Chalon House, Scar Bank, Millers Road, Warwick, Warwickshire CV34 5DB
Tel: 01926 499031
Fax: 01926 491906
Auction sales of medals and militaria held three times a year. Phone or send for free specimen catalogue.

WELLER & DUFTY LTD
141 Bromsgrove Street, Birmingham, W. Midlands
Contact: M R Scott
Tel: 0121 692 1414
Fax: 0121 622 5605
Specialist auctioneers of antique and modern arms, armour, militaria and ammunition. Normally about ten sales annually; catalogues available by annual subscription.

BOOK PUBLISHERS

AFTER THE BATTLE
Church House, Church Street, London E15 3JA
Contact: Winston Ramsey
Tel: 020 8534 8833
Fax: 020 8555 7567
Email: afterthebattle@mcmail.com
Website: www.afterthebattle.mcmail.com
Quarterly magazine and full feature books covering WWI & WWII history through presentation of the battlefields in 'Then and Now' photographs. Also posters and postcards.

AIR DATA PUBLICATIONS
Southside Manchester Airport, Wilmslow, Cheshire SK9 4LL
Tel: 0161 499 0023
Fax: 0161 499 0298
Email: books@airplan.u-net.com
Publishers of military and aviation books, mostly in hard-back. Also of the 'Pilots' Notes' series. Distributors of American Flight Manuals and Flugzeug.

AIRLIFE PUBLISHING
101 Longden Road, Shrewsbury, Shropshire SY3 9EB
Tel: 01743 235651
Fax: 01743 232944
Email: editor@airlifebooks.com
Website: www.airlifebooks.com
Airlife is a specialist publisher covering all aspects of aviation both contemporary and historical, military and civil. Proposals for new books welcomed.

AMBER BOOKS
Bradley's Close, 74–77 White Lion Street, London N1 9PF
Contact: Sara Ballard
Tel: 020 7520 7600
Fax: 020 7520 7606
Email: amber.books@dialpipex.com
Publishers of military books ranging from highly illustrated general histories, personalities, battles, units and equipment to fact-filled yearbooks.

*ANDREW MOLLO
10 Rue Jean Juares, 03320 Lurcy-Levis, France.
Tel/Fax: 04 70679183
Military consultant to film and TV production companies; author and collector, specialising in German and Russian subjects; publisher of Historical Research Unit books.

ANGLO-SAXON BOOKS
Frithgarth, Thetford Forest Park, Hockwold-cum-Wilton, Norfolk IP26 4NQ
Contact: Tony Linsell
Tel/Fax: 01842 828430
Email: anglosaxon@compuserve.com
'The English Warrior from earliest times to 1066', examines strategy, tactics, weapons and the attitudes and rituals of warriors. 'English Martial Arts' deals mainly with 15th and 16th century fighting techniques. Contact us for a catalogue or see it at http://anglo-saxon.demon.co.uk/asbooks/.

ARMY BOOKS
Email: belfire@armybooks.com
Website: www.armybooks.com

A S B L LA PORTE D'HOVES
Esselaer 22, B-1630 Linkebeek, Belgium
Contact: Eric Mombeek
Tel/Fax: 3223810003
Email: eric.mombeek@village.uunet.be
Website: www.multimania.com/mombeek/
We are a small company publishing the books written by Eric Mombeek and covering the history of various Luftwaffe fighter units. The second activity (see our web site) is trying to solve fates of Luftwaffe pilots missing in action.

ATHENA PUBLISHING
34 Imperial Crescent, Town Moor, Doncaster, S. Yorkshire
DN2 5BJ
Tel: 01302 322913
Fax: 01302 730531
Website: athenamilitarybooks@btinternet.com
Publishers of Napoleonic facsimiles and UK distributor for
Ryton Publishing and Cannon Books.

AUSTRALIAN MILITARY EQUIPMENT PROFILES
Email: amep@bigpond.com.au

**AUSTRALIAN MILITARY HISTORY
PUBLICATIONS**
Email: warbookshop@bigpond.com

AXIS EUROPA BOOKS
Email: axiseuropa@erols.com

BARRIE & JENKINS LTD
Random House, 20 Vauxhall Bridge Road, London W11 2QA
Tel: 020 77840 8777
Fax: 020 7233 6057
Email: flaurent@random.co.uk

BEAUMONT PUBLISHING
1st Floor Adelphi Mill, Bollington, Cheshire SK10 5JB
Contact: Irene Moore
Tel/Fax: 01625 575700
Email: editor@armourer.co.uk
Website: www.armourer.co.uk
Publishers of both the Armourer and Skirmish magazines.

BERGHAHN BOOKS
Email: publisher@berghahnbooks.com

BLACKWELL PUBLISHERS
108 Cowley Road, Oxford, Oxfordshire OX4 1JF
Contact: Paul Millicheap
Tel: 01865 382200
Fax: 01865 381200
Email: pmillich@blackwellpublishers.co.uk
Academic publisher with some military history titles
including Civil War and World War I. Information sheets
and current titles available.

BERG PUBLISHERS
150 Cowley Road, Oxford, Oxfordshire OX4 1JJ
Contact: Kathryn Earle
Tel: 01865 245104
Fax: 01865 791165
Email: enquiry@berg.demon.co.uk
Website: www.berg.demon.co.uk
Academic publisher with a strong list in European—
especially German—military studies.

BORDER PRESS
Unit 27, Monument Industrial Park, Chalgrove, Oxfordshire
OX44 7RW
Contact: Alan Badger
Tel: 01293 772496
Fax: 01965 400257
Email: info@outdoorsman.co.uk
Specialist firearms books and manuals; trade enquiries
welcome.

BOYDELL & BREWER LTD.
PO Box 9, Woodbridge, Suffolk LP12 3DF
Tel: 01394 411320
Fax: 01394 411477
Website: http://www.boydell.co.uk
Publish medieval history including warfare, arms and
armour, tournaments, battles and modern military history.
Military History catalogue. Mastercard & Visa accepted;
direct orders welcome.

BRASSEY'S
9 Blenheim Court, Brewery Road, London N7 9NT
Tel: 020 7471 1100
Fax: 020 7471 1101
Email: brasseys@chrysalisbooks.co.uk
Website: www.brassey.com
Publishers of a wide range of highly acclaimed titles on
military history, military hobbies, and technology, defence
and international affairs; free catalogue on request.

BRITISH MUSEUM PRESS
46 Bloomsbury Street, London WC1B 3QQ
Tel: 020 7436 7315
Website: www.britishmuseum.co.uk
Books covering many subjects.

CAMBRIDGE UNIVERSITY PRESS
The Edinburgh Building, Shaftesbury Road, Cambridge,
Cambridgeshire CB2 2RU
Tel/Fax: 01223 312393
Email: wdavies@cup.cam.ac.uk
The world's oldest press. Academic books on military
strategy and history.

CASEMATE
2114 Darby Road, Havertown, PA 19083, USA
Tel: 610 8539131
Fax: 610 8539146
Casemate@verizon.com
Publishers and distributors of military books.

CASSELLS
Wellington House, 125 Strand, London WC2R 0BB
Tel: 020 7420 5555
Fax: 020 7240 7261
Website: www.cassell.co.uk
An active military book imprint, producing over 50
titles each year on military, naval and aviation history,
collectables, uniforms etc.

CAXTON PUBLISHING
20 Bloomsbury Street, London WC1B 3QA
Tel: 020 7636 7171
Fax: 020 7636 1922
Email: office@caxtonpublishing.com
Website: www.caxtonpublishing.com

CHATHAM PUBLISHING
99 High Street, Rochester, Kent ME1 1LX
Contact: Julian Mannering
Tel: 01634 810760
Fax: 01634 810761
We specialise in books on most historical maritime
themes, ranging from ship design to life at sea, in varied
formats from highly illustrated technical reference books to
reprints of classic narratives.

CLASSIC ARMS & MILITARIA
Peterson Publications Ltd, Peterson House, Berryhill Ind Est,
Droitwich, Worcs WR9 9BL
Contact: Bruce Ayling
Tel: 01905 795564
Fax: 01905 795905
Classic Arms & Militaria, incorporating Gun Collecting—
is the only publication dedicated to the classic shooter,
military historian and collector. Packed with authoritative
articles on edged weapons, vintage military and sporting
arms, military history, medals, uniforms and a host of
features not often found in other magazines.

CLASSIC PUBLICATIONS
Friars Gate Farm, Mardens Hill, Crowborough, E. Sussex
TN6 1XH
Contact: Robert Forsyth
Tel: 01892 610490
Fax: 01892 610842
Email: classic@classic-books.co.uk
Website: www.classic-books.co.uk
Classic Publications are specialist publishers of lavishly
illustrated, deeply researched quality military aviation books
dealing with all aspects of World War II.

CHAMPLIN FIGHTER MUSEUM PRESS
Email: salesinfo@cfm-press.com

COMBAT PATHS
Email: combatpath@aol.com

COMPENDIUM PUBLISHING
43 Frith Street, London W1D 4SA
Contact: Alan Greene
Tel: 020 7287 4570
Fax: 020 7494 0583
Email: compendiumpub@aol.com
A leading international publisher of books on all aspects of
modelling, including military models and related subjects.
New publications include the new series Compendium
Modelling Manuals which are practical step-by-step guides
for modellers.

CONSTABLE & ROBINSON
3 The Lanchesters, 162 Fulham Palace Road, London W6
9ER
Tel: 020 8741 3663
Fax: 020 8748 7562
Email: enquiries@constablerobinson.com
Website: www.constablerobinson.com

CONWAY MARITIME PRESS
9 Blenheim Court, Brewery Road, London N7 9NT
Tel: 020 7471 1100
Fax: 020 7471 1101
Email: brasseys@chrysalisbooks.co.uk
Website: www.brassey.com
The world's leading publisher of authoritative, highly
illustrated reference books on maritime history. Free
catalogue available.

CRAIG R CROFOOT
Email: orderofbattle@juno.com

CRÉCY PUBLISHING LIMITED
1A Ringway Trading Estate, Shadowmoss Road, Manchester
M22 5LH
Contact: Jeremy M Pratt
Tel: 0161 499 0024
Fax: 0161 499 0298
Email: books@airplan.u-net.com
Crécy publish a range of World War II aviation books, in
cased and paperback formats, under our imprints Crécy,
Goodall and Air Data. Also act as distributors for Air
Research Publications, Independent Books, Cirrus
Associates, Airplan Flight Equipment, Airworthy Publications
and Pacific Century.

CROWOOD PRESS
The Stable Block, Crowood Lane, Ramsbury, Marlborough,
Wiltshire SN8 2HR
Contact: Ken Hathaway
Tel: 01672 520320
Fax: 01672 520280
Email: enquiries@crowood.com
Website: http//:www.crowood.com
Publishers of books on military history and aviation,
including uniforms, weapons, vehicles and equipment, from
Roman times to modern.

DARR PUBLICATIONS
Thorshof, 106 Oakridge Road, High Wycombe,
Buckinghamshire HP11 2PL
Contact: Thorskegga Thorn
Tel: 01494 451814
Fax: 01494 784271
Email: thorskegga@calltoarms.com
Large number of historical booklets, both theoretical stud-
ies and 'how-to-do-it' manuals. Heavily researched but
inexpensive, practical and easy to read. SAE for details.

DATAFILE BOOKS
10 White Hart Lane, Wistaston, Crewe, Cheshire CW2 8EX
Contact: Malcolm Bellis
Tel: 01270 663296
Specialist military sourcebooks, e.g. World War II & post-war British Army orders of battle, etc.

DAVID & CHARLES PUBLISHERS
Brunel House, Newton Abbot, Devon TQ12 4PU
Tel: 01626 61121
Fax: 01626 42904
http://www.davidandcharles.co.uk
Publishers of aviation art books including those of Robert Taylor, Frank Wooton, Gerald Coulson and John Young. Mail order available.

EDITIONS HEIMDAL
Chateau de Damigny, 14400 Bayeux, France
Contact: Georges Bernage

*ERMANNO ALBERTELLI EDITORE
Via S Sonnino 34, 43100 Parma, Italy
Contact: Ermanno Albertelli

*EXCELSIOR PUBLICATIONS
1 Rue du Col Pierre Avia, 75015 Paris, France

FIELDBOOKS
c/o 'Fieldhead', The Park, Mansfield, Notts
Contact: Paddy Griffith
Tel/Fax: 01203 350763
Email: 113131.453@compuserve.com
Website:
www.ourworld.compuserve.com/homepages/paddygriffith
Also incorporating Paddy Griffith Associates, the company publishes a range of military books.

FIREBIRD BOOKS LTD
PO Box 327, Poole, Dorset BHI5 2RG
Contact: Chris Lloyd
Tel: 01202 715349
Fax: 01202 736191
Email: chrlloyd@globalnet.co.uk
Publishers of illustrated military history books including 'Heroes and Warriors' series. Free illustrated catalogue on request. Mail order.

FLICKS BOOKS
29 Bradford Road, Trowbridge, Wiltshire BA14 9AN
Tel: 01225 767728
Fax: 01225 760418
Email: flicks.books@dial.pipex.com
Publishers of books on film and cinema, e.g. Imperial War Museum Film Catalogue, The First World War Archive; The Biograph in Battle (Boer war filming).

FLINTLOCK PUBLISHING
10 Westbourne Road, Walsall, W. Midlands WS4 2JA
Contact: Rob Chapman
Tel: 01922 644078
Fax: 01922 629145
Email: mrflintloc@aol.com or
info@flintlockpublishing.co.uk
Website: www.flintlockpublishing.co.uk
Publishers of postcards, prints and exhibition materials from original artwork by leading artists in costume and military history. Commissions/collaborations welcomed.

FRANK CASS
Newbury House, 890–900 Eastern Avenue, Newbury Park, Ilford, Essex IG2 7HH
Tel: U20 8599 8866
Fax: 020 8599 0984
Email: info@frankcass.com
Website: www.frankcass.com

FRANK SMITH MARITIME AVIATION BOOKS
98/100 Heaton Road, Newcastle-on-Tyne NE1 5HL
Contact: Alan Parker
Tel: 0191 265 6333
Fax: 0191 224 2620
Email: books@franksmith.freeserve.co.uk
Large stocks of books and magazines covering all aspects of aviation and naval history. Monthly catalogues on each subject issued.

GREENHILL BOOKS/LIONEL LEVENTHAL LTD
Park House, 1 Russell Gardens, London NW11 9NN
Contact: Lionel Leventhal
Tel: 020 8458 6314
Fax: 020 8905 5245
Email: lionelleventhal@compuserve.com
Website: www.greenhill.books.com
Publishers of books on military history. The Napoleonic Library now has 33 volumes, including reprints of classic books by Sir Charles Oman, etc.

GREENWOOD PUBLISHING GROUP
3 Henrietta Street, London WC2E 8LU
Tel: 020 78450810
Fax: 02073793313
Email: webmaster@greenwood.com

GRUB STREET
The Basement, 10 Chivalry Road, London SW11 1HT
Tel: 020 7924 3966, 020 7938 1008
Fax: 020 7738 1009
Email: milhis@grubstreet.co.uk
Website: www.grubstreet.co.uk

HAYNES & Co Ltd
Sparkford, Yeovil, Somerset, BA22 7JJ
Tel: 01963 440635
Fax: 01963 440001
Website: http://www.haynes.co.uk

HALSGROVE
Halsgrove House, Lower Moor Way, Tiverton Business Park,
Tiverton, Devon EX16 6SS
Tel: 01884 243242
Fax: 01884 243 325
Email: sales@halsgrove.com
Website: www.halsgrove.com

HELION & COMPANY
26 Willow Road, Solihull, W. Midlands B91 1UE
Tel: 0121 705 3393
Fax: 0121 711 1315
Email: books@helion.co.uk
Website: http://www.helion.co.uk

HELLGATE PRESS
Email: harley@psi-research.com

HISTOIRE & COLLECTIONS (UK)
463 Ashley Road, Parkstone, Poole, Dorset BH14 0AX
Tel: 01202 715349
Fax: 01202 736191
Email: chrlloyd@globalnet.co.uk
Paris-based publisher of military books, now publishing in
English. Full colour illustrated books on historical and
contemporary militaria and World War II.

IAN ALLAN PUBLISHING LTD
Riverdene, Molesey Road, Hersham, Surrey KT12 4RG
Contact: W Y Myers
Tel: 01932 266600
Fax: 01932 266601
Email: info@ianallanpub.co.uk
Website: www.ianallanpub.co.uk
Publishers of military, aviation and transport subjects,
including the 'Collectors' Guides' and 'ABC' series.
Specialist bookshops near Waterloo, Manchester Piccadilly
and Birmingham New Street stations.

INTERNATIONAL SPECIALIZED BOOK SERVICES, INC
Email:orders@isbs.com

I S O PUBLICATIONS
137 Westminster Bridge Road, London SE1 7HR
Tel: 020 7261 9588
Fax: 020 7261 9179

JANE'S INFORMATION GROUP LTD
Sentinel House, 163 Brighton Road, Coulsdon, Surrey
CR5 2NH
Contact: Claire Brunavs
Tel: 020 8700 3700
Fax: 020 8763 1006
Email: info@janes.co.uk
Website: www.janes.com
Jane's is the world's leading provide of defence,
aerospace, geopolitical and transportation related informa-
tion to governments, militaries, businesses and universities.

J J FEDOROWICZ PUBLISHING INC
Email: jjfpub@escape.ca

JOHN DONALD
Unit 8, Canongate Venture, 5 New Street, Edinburgh EH8 4BH
Tel: 0131 556 6660
Fax: 0131 557 6250

KIPLING & KING
3 Saxon Croft, Farnham, Surrey GU9 7QB
Contact: H L & P King
Tel: 01252 710303
Head-dress badges of the British Army. The definitive work
on the subject: Volume One 1800–1920, £65.00; Volume
Two 1920–1998, £45.00. Totalling 3,000 illustrations on
730 pages.

KNIFE WORLD PUBLICATIONS
PO BOX 3395, Knoxville, TN 37927, USA
Tel: 865 397 1955
Fax: 865 397 1969
Email: knifepub@knifeworld.com
Website: www.knifeworld.com
Booksellers and publishers of books about knives and other
cutlery. Also, Publishers of Knife World magazine, the only
publication covering the world of knives. Visit our website.

MACMILLAN
The Macmillan Building, 4 Crinan Street, London N1 9XW
Tel: 020 7833 4000
Fax: 020 7843 4640
Website: www.macmillan.com

MAJOR BOOK PUBLICATIONS
'Hougoumont', Maxworthy, Launceston, Cornwall
PL15 8LZ
Contact: H W or C P Adams
Tel: 01566 781422
Email: hougoumont@freeuk.com
British Regular Army; Napoleonic Period; regimental foot-
prints. We publish our own research on these subjects by
campaign periods (currently Waterloo). Cavalry and Infantry
Regimental research in book or data sheet format at each
campaign period. Footprint data extends to disbandment.
Dates up to 1821. SAE for details.

MANCHESTER UNIVERSITY PRESS
Oxford Road, Manchester, Greater Manchester M13 9PL
Contact: Catherine Whelan
Tel: 0161 273 5539
Fax: 0161 274 3346
Email: mup@man.ac.uk
Publisher with thriving list in military studies including
'War, Armed Forces and Society' series, and the new
series 'Manchester History of the British Army'. A listing of
all titles is available on request.

MALVERN PUBLISHING
Email: orders@malvernfirst.com

MCFARLAND & COMPANY
Email: info@mcfarlandpub.com

MERRIAM PRESS
Email: ray@merriam-press.com

MIDLAND PUBLISHING
See Ian Allan Publishing
Aviation, railway and military publishers now owned by Ian Allan Publishing. Associated with Midland Counties Publications, see entry in Booksellers section.

MILITARY PRESS
1 Gallagher Close, Milton Keynes MK8 0LQ
Email: MilitaryPress@BTInternet.com
Website: www.militarypress.com
Military History: World War I & II, Boer War, British Regimental Lineage Series, Indian Military Campaigns Series, Indian Army VCs & GCs, Indian Army Buttons Series Insurgency & Counter Insurgency Series, German Army World War II Series, Knight's Cross Series, Panzer & Panzer Grenadier Formations Series.

MINISTERE DE LA DEFENSE
27 rue Charles-Michels, 91740 Pussay, France
Contact: Monsieur le directeur de la librairie de l'Armée
Tel: 1 69955221
Fax: 1 69955227
Official French military histories.

MINISTERO DELLA DIFESA
Stato Maggiore dell'Esercito, Ufficio Storico, Roma, Italy
Italian official histories.

THE NAFZIGER COLLECTION
Email: nafziger@fuse.net

NAVAL INSTITUTE PRESS
291 Wood Road, Annapolis, MD 21402, USA
Tel: 410 295 1082
Fax: 410 269 7940
Email: customer@usni.org

NORMAN D LANDING PUBLISHERS
216 Lightwoods Hill, Warley Woods, Warley, W. Midlands B67 5EH
Tel/Fax: 0121 434 4580
Publishers of the US Army uniform reference book 'Doughboy to GI: US Army Uniforms and Equipment 1900–1945'. Trade enquiries welcomed; 24-hour fax.

NEW CAVENDISH BOOKS
3 Denbigh Road, London W11 2SJ
Tel: 020 7229 6765
Fax: 020 7792 0027
Email: narisa@new-cav.demon.co.uk
Specialist publishers of quality illustrated books on toys and other collectables.

OSPREY PUBLISHING LTD
Elms Court, Chapel Way, Botley, Oxford OX2 91LP
Tel: 01865 727022
Fax: 01865 727017
Email: info@ospreypublishing.com
Website: www.osprey-publishing.co.uk
Publishers of authoritative and highly acclaimed series of military and aviation books. Series include Men at Arms, Elite, New Vanguard, Campaign, Warrior, Aircraft Cutaways, the Osprey 20th Century Armour and Transport Library and the new Order of Battle and Production Line to Front Line brands. Catalogue available upon request. Individual orders and Messenger subscription enquiries: Osprey Direct, 27 Sanders Road, Wellingborough, Northants NN8 4NL. Tel: 01933 443862; Fax: 01933 443849.

OXFORD UNIVERSITY PRESS
Walton Street, Oxford, Oxfordshire OX2 6DP
Tel: 01865 556767
Fax: 01865 556646
Email: enquiry@oup.co.uk
International publishing house with titles on strategic studies, war studies, peace studies, current affairs and political economy. Also distribute titles on behalf of the Stockholm International Peace Research Institute—including SPRI Yearbook, reviewing developments in nuclear weapons, world military expenditure and international arms trade.

PACIFICA MILITARY HISTORY
Email: hammel@pacificamilitary.com

PENTLAND PRESS
Email: sales@pentlandpress.co.uk

PEN AND SWORD BOOKS
47 Church Street, Barnsley, S. Yorkshire S70 2AS
Tel: 01226 734222 / 734555
Fax: 01226 734438
Email: design@pen-and-sword.co.uk
Military history publishers including battlefield guidebook series 'Battleground Europe'.

PERSEUS BOOKS
10 East 53rd Street, 23rd Floor, New York 10022-5299, USA
Tel: 212 207 7600
Fax: 212 207 7703
Publishing group of military books including Combined Books, Sarpedon and Presidio.

PICTON PUBLISHING (CHIPPENHAM) LTD
Queensbridge Cottages, Patterdown, Chippenham, Wiltshire SN15 2NS
Contact: David Picton-Phillips
Tel/Fax: 01249 443430
Email: pictonpd@oup.co.uk
Publishers of regimental histories, reprints of classic military histories and allied subjects, military biographies and autobiographies. Booklist and sales leaflets available on request. No callers, please.

PITKIN GUIDES LTD
Healey House, Dene Road, Andover, Hampshire SP10 2AA
Contact: Ian Corsie
Tel: 01264 334303
Fax: 01264 334110
Email: guides@pitkin.u-net.com
Highly-illustrated souvenir guides for tourists. List includes subjects of military interest–battlefields, campaigns, etc.

THE POMPADOUR GALLERY
PO Box 11, Romford, Essex RM7 1HY
Contact: George Newark
Tel/Fax: 01375 384020
Email: christopher.newark@virgin.net
Publishers and distributors of military books, postcards, reproduction cigarette cards. Books: 'Kipling's Soldiers', 'Uniforms of the Foot Guards' and our latest book 'Uniforms of the Royal Marines 1664 to the Present Day'. Send SAE for full details of all our publications.

*R I G O / LE PLUMET
Louannec, 22700 Perros-Guirec, France

PUBLIC RECORDS OFFICE
Ruskin Avenue, Kew, Surrey TW9 4DU
Tel: 020 8392 5271
Fax: 020 8392 5266
Email: webmaster@pro.gov.uk or enquiry@pro.gov.uk
Website: www.pro.gov.uk/bookshop

RAMROD PUBLICATIONS
Email: anita@ramrodbooks.u-net.com

R J LEACH MILITARY PUBLISHERS
73 Priory Grove, Ditton, Aylesford, Kent ME20 6BB
Contact: R J Leach
Tel: 01622 791243
Email: richardleach@cablenet.co.uk
Military publishers covering Napoleonic, British, Colonial, WWII and modern conflicts.

ROBERT HALE LTD
Clerkenwell House, Clerkenwell Green, London EC1R 0HT
Tel: 020 7251 2661
Fax: 020 7490 4958

ST ERMIN'S PRESS
Email: p.p@bookbag.demon.co.uk

SCHIFFER MILITARY HISTORY
4880 Lower Valley Road, Atglen, PA 19310, USA
Tel: 610 593 1777
Fax: 610 593 2002
Email: schifferbk@aol.com
Website: www.schifferbooks.com
Distributed in Europe & the UK by Bushwood Books.

SHIRE PUBLICATIONS LTD
Cromwell House, Church Street, Princes Risborough, Aylesbury, Buckinghamshire HP27 9AA
Contact: Sue Ross
Tel: 01844 344301
Fax: 01844 541080
Website: www.shirebooks.co.uk
Paperbacks on aspects of military history.

SHELF BOOKS
Email: eqn@shelf.dircon.co.uk

SELOUS BOOKS LTD
40 Station Road, Aldershot, Hampshire GU11 1HT
Contact: Trevor Hudson
Tel: 01252 333611
Fax: 01252 344337
Email: 1100307.1735@compuserve.com
Specialist book dealers in military history, historic travel and ethnographic books. Subjects covered include military histories, regimental histories, uniforms, insignia, medal rolls, firearms and equipment.

SIDGWICK & JACKSON LTD
18–21 Cavaye Place, London SW10 9PG
Tel: 020 7373 6070
Fax: 020 7370 0746
We publish mainly on major commanders, battles and campaigns but also specialist publishing in the areas of elite forces.

SOUVENIR PRESS LTD
43 Great Russell Street, London WC1B 3PA
Contact: Ernest Hecht
Tel: 020 7580 9307
Fax: 020 7580 5064

SPECIALTY PRESS
Email: SpecPress1@aol.com

SPELLMOUNT LTD PUBLISHERS
The Old Rectory, Staplehurst, Kent TN12 0AZ
Contact: Jamie Wilson
Tel: 01580 893730
Fax: 01580 893731
Email: enquiries@spellmount.com
Military history publishers specialising in ancient history, 17th and 18th century Napoleonic, Victorian, both World Wars, plus general military topics. Send for free catalogue.

STACKPOLE BOOKS
5067 Ritter Road, Mechanicsburg, PA 17055, USA
Tel: 717 796 0411
Fax: 717 796 0412
Email: stackpoleedit@paonline.com
Website: www.stackpolebooks.com

THE STATIONERY OFFICE BOOKS
St Crispins, Duke Street, Norwich, Norfolk NR3 IPD
Tel: 01603 694723
Fax: 01603 696784
Email: matt.brady@theso.co.uk
Website: www.national-publishing.co.uk
An annually updated collection of military history titles covering land, sea and air interests, written by some of the most distinguished authors.

STUART PRESS
117 Farleigh Road, Backwell, Bristol, Avon BS19 3PG
Contact: Stuart Peachey
Tel/Fax: 01275 463041
Email: stuart@hmaltd.freeserve.co.uk
Publish and sell books on the English Civil War and civilian topics of the period 1580-1660. Send SAE for catalogue. Also banquets and lectures.

STONE & STONE
Email: bstone@sonic.net
Books on World War II.

SUTTON PUBLISHING LID
Phoenix Mill, Far Thrupp, Stroud, Gloucestershire GL5 2BU
Contact: R Schinner
Tel: 01453 751114
Fax: 01453 731117
Email: sales@sutton-publishing.co.uk
Sutton Publishing are leading book publishers specialising in: archaeology, aviation, classic fiction, history (national, regional, social), military (Roman, Medieval, 16th-19th centuries, WWI and WWII), transport.

THE BATTERY PRESS INC
PO Box 198885, Nashville, TN 37219, USA

Contact: Richard S Gardiner
Tel/Fax: 615 298 1401
Email: batterybks@aol.com
Website: www.batterypress.com
The Battery Press publishes 19th and 20th century military history. Our special areas of interest are WWI and II official histories and military unit histories.

THE DEFENCE PICTURE LIBRARY
Sherwell House, 54 Staddiscombe Road, Plymouth PL9 9NB
Tel/Fax: 01752 401 800
Email: pix@defencepicture.com
Website: www.defencepictures.com
The Defence Picture Library is Britain's leading source of military photography. Its photographers were among the first into liberated Kuwait city, Kosovo, East Timor and Sierra Leone to cover the actions of British troops. The agency has images of units across the world, including a unique collection of the PLA.

386TH BOMB GROUP ASSOCIATION, INC
Email: skip386@aol.com

T L O PUBLICATIONS
Longclose House, Common Road, Eton Wick, Nr Windsor, Berkshire SL4 6QY
Contact: Tony Oliver
Tel: 01753 862637
Fax: 01753 841998
Email: mark.tlofilms@virgin.net
Reference books on German subjects for collectors, eg. 'German Order, Decoration and Medal Citations', and DDR subjects.

TOKEN PUBLISHING
Orchard House, Duchy Road, Heathpark, Honiton, Devon EX14 1YD
Tel: 01404 46972
Fax: 01404 44788
Email: info@medal-news.com
Website: www.tokenpublishing.com
Publishers of Medal News magazine, the highly acclaimed Medal Yearbook and a host of other military titles. Medal News is the world's only magazine devoted to medals, battles and the history of heroes. It is also invaluable in tracing lost medals through the renowned Medal Tracker service.

TURNER PUBLISHING
Email: editors@turnerpublishingco.com

UPTON & SONS
917 Hillcrest Street, Segundo, California 90245, USA
Tel: 800 959 1876 or 310 322 7202
Fax: 310 322 4739
Email: richardupton@worldnet.att.net
Please call to speak to a representative. We work by mail order and by appointment. Lay-over at LAX? Call us and visit us while waiting. We are right next to Los Angeles International Airport.

US ALLEGIANCE PUBLISHERS
Tel: 800 327 1402
Email: sc@ipledge.com

VANDAMERE PRESS
PO Box 17446, Clearwater, FL 33762
Tel: 727 556-0950
Fax: 727 556-2560
email: webmaster@vandamere.com

VIKING
27 Wright's Lane, London W8 5TZ
Tel: 020 7416 3000
Fax: 020 7416 3099
Contact: Lynn Royden
Email: lynn.royden@penguin.co.uk

VILMOR PUBLICATIONS
Morton Villa Farm, Misson Springs, Doncaster, S. Yorkshire DN10 6ES
Contact: Philip Baker
Tel/Fax: 01302 770295
Publisher and stockholder of Philip Baker's 'Youth led by Youth'. Three volumes covering most aspects of the Hitler Youth. Hundred of b/w and coloured illustrations. Also hold large archive of Hitler Youth related photographs.

V S-BOOKS
PO Box 20 05 40, D 44635 Herne, Germany
Contact: Torsten Verhülsdonk
Tel: 232573818
Fax: 4325792311
Email: vs.books@cityweb.de
Publishers of books on military history, uniforms and weapons from ancient times to the present day Potential authors welcome.

WARGAMES RESEARCH GROUP
The Keep, Le Marchant Barracks, London Road, Devizes, Wiltshire SN10 2ER
Tel/Fax: 01380 724558
Email: keepwrg@talk21.com
Publisher of wargame rules and reference books; also wholesaler of some allied products, publications, and imported books and rules.

WAREHOUSE PUBLICATIONS
5 Rathbone Square, Tanfield Road, Croydon, Surrey CR0 1BT
Tel: 020 8681 3031
Fax: 020 8686 2362
Mail order military vehicle book specialists. Phone for free catalogue.

W L GRIGGS
Email: bgchops@earthlink.net

WINDRUSH PRESS
Little Window, High St, Moreton-in-Marsh, Glos GL56 0LL
Tel: 01608 652012
Fax: 01608 652125
Email:info@windrushpress.com

W S CURTIS (PUBLISHERS)
PO Box 493, Rhyl, Denbighshire, Wales LL18 5XG
Contact: W S Curtis
Tel/Fax: 01745 584 981
Email: wsc@wscurtis-books.demon.co.uk
Specialising in the reprints–with new researched Introductions–of rare 19th century books on shooting, firearms and artillery for the modern shooter and collector.

BOOKSELLERS

AAC BOOKS BY POST
Email: sales@aacbooks.co.uk

AARDVARK BOOKS
50 Bratton Road, Westbury, Wiltshire BA13 3EP
Contact: Clive Williams
Tel: 01226 867723
Fax: 01225 8634/9
Email: aardvarkbooks@compuserve.com
Website: www.sonic.net/~bstone/aardvarkbooks
We are military bookdealers with a stock of 10,000 books. We have a particular emphasis on World War I and World War II.

A&C LIBRAIRIE
19 Avenue de la République, 75011 Paris, France.
Tel: 01 49237222
Fax: 0140219755
Premier French bookshop specialising in military titles.

ADRIAN FORMAN BOOKS
PO Box 25, Minehead, Somerset TA24 8YX
Contact: Adrian Forman
Tel/Fax: 01271 816177
Distributor and agent for Bender Books USA. Free illustrated book list of German Third Reich new books including many out-of-print titles and Bowen's classic Iron Cross book, plus Forman's Guide series on German Third Reich awards and documents (with values).

AHRENS & HAMACHER
Email: ahha@online-club.de

ALDERSHOT MILITARY HISTORY TRUST
Evelyn Woods Road, Queens Avenue, Aldershot, Hampshire GU11 2LG

ANDREW BURROUGHS BOOKS
34 St Martins, Stamford, Lincolnshire PE9 2LJ
Contact: Andrew Burroughs
Tel/Fax: 01780 765140
Email: militarybooks@andrewburroughs.co.ok
Naval and military specialities: 20th century British naval and military history, in particular World War II. Catalogues issued.

ANGELRAY BOOKS
Email: info@angelraybooks.com

*ANTIK 13
Pieperstrasse 13, Bochum D-44789, Germany
Contact: Peter Nachtigall
Tel: 234 300289
Fax: 234 330919
Antiquarian and secondhand books on militaria and weapons; Osprey Men at Arms series, V S-Books; also 20th century collectables including militaria.

*ANTIQUARIAT BUCHVERTRIEB & VERLAG
Oselbachstrasse 72, 6660 Zweibrucken, Germany
Contact: Heinz Nickel-Verstand

*ARNOLD BUSCK
49 Kobmagerade 1150, Copenhagen K, Denmark

ARTEMIS ARCHERY
29 Bately Court, Oldland, S. Glos BS30 8Y2
Contact: Veronica Soar
Tel/Fax: 0117 932 3276
Email: vee_artemis@yahoo.co.uk
Longbow/archery specific: books by post; historical research, lectures, consultancy, coaching. Also longbow presentations, static exhibitions and longbow and arrow manufacture. SAE for booklist or other details. Archery collection viewing strictly by appointment only.

ARTICLES OF WAR LTD
8806 Bronx Avenue, Skokie, Illinois 60077-1896, USA
Contact: Robert Ruman
Tel: 847 674 7445
Fax: 847 674 7449
Email: warbooks@aol.com
Website: http://www.sonic.net/~bstone/articles
New and secondhand military history books, all eras
ancient to modern; over 20,000 titles. Catalogues issued;
open Tues–Sat.

ATHENA BOOKS
34 Imperial Crescent, Town Moor, Doncaster, S. Yorkshire
DN2 5BU
Contact: Les Thomas
Tel: 01302 322913
Fax: 01302 730531
Email: athenamilitarybooks@btinternet.com
UK's largest stuckists of military history, 3000BC to WW3.
Monthly catalogue of over 1,000 books. SAE for sample.
50,000 books in stock. Normal shop hours.

ATTIC BOOKS
Nilcoptra, 3 Marine Road, Hoylake, Wirral, Cheshire L47 2AS
Tel: 0151 632 5365
Fax: 0151 632 6472
Email: attic@naval.globalnet.co.uk
Antiquarian and out-of-print books. Military and aviation
specialists; general subjects, booksearch service.

AVIATION BOOKSHOP
656 Holloway Road, London N19 3PD
Tel: 020 7272 3630
Fax: 020 7272 9761
Large new and secondhand stock of books, magazines,
posters, videos, CD Roms. Speciality: aviation in all its
aspects.

AVIATION BOOKS
St Catherines, The Green, Hickling, Norwich NR12 0XR
Contact: Roger Billings
Tel/Fax: 01692 598183.
Email: airbooks@aol.com
Website: www.aviation-bookshelf.com
New and used books on military aviation by mail order.
Free quarterly catalogues. PBFA member.

AVIATION SHOP
Kajanukset-ikatu 12A, 00250 Helsinki, Finland
Email: shop@aviationshop.fi

BARBAROSSA BOOKS
14b Maldon Road, Tiptree, Essex CO5 0LL
Contact: Russell Hadler
Tel: 01621 810810
Fax: 01621 810888
Email: barbbook@dircon.co.uk
Military, aviation, naval, modelling books and videos. Titles
from UK, USA, Japan, France, Russia, Poland. Free
quarterly catalogue with SAE/IRC. Mail order to the world.

BATTLEFIELD BOOKS
Email: Battlefield@aol.com

BEHIND THE LINES
Basement Unit, 18 Cambridge Street, Aylesbury,
Buckinghamshire HP20 1RS
Contact: Graham Harrison
Tel/Fax: 01296 423118
Email: behindthelines@3uk.com
Shop with large stocks of secondhand military books,
wargames figures and accessories. All scales and periods.
Also stock paints, brushes and games. Open
10.30am–5.00pm.

BOOKSHELF AVIATION BOOKS
Email: airbooks@aol.com

BOOKS INTERNATIONAL
101 Lynchford Road, Farnborough, Hampshire GU14 6ET
Tel: 01252 376564
Fax: 01252 370181
Email: booksinter@aol.com
Subjects: general military, uniforms, badges & insignia,
weapons, armour and artillery, world wars, Napoleonic period. American wars, civil and military aircraft, warships,
merchant and passenger ships. Suppliers of wide range of
titles published around the world. Leading distributors of
books from Eastern Europe.

BOOKSEARCH LTD
Ten Steps, Church Street, Seagrave LE12 7LT
Contact: Melanie Wilson
Tel/Fax: 01509 812806
Email: melaniewilson@compuserve.com
Free worldwide booksearch for any book in or out of print.
No obligation to buy.

BOOKS OF WAR
Email: info@booksofwar.com

BRANDENBURG HISTORICA
Email: info@brandenburghistorica.com

*BRENTANO'S
37 Avenue de L'Opera, 75002 Paris, France

BROWSERS
10 Theatre Square, Swindon, Wiltshire SN1 1QN
Contact: Janet Terry
Tel: 01793 523170
Fax: 01793 432070
Email: booksinter@aol.com
Specialist bookshop for all military publications. Large
range of military figures. Worldwide mail order service.

*BUCHHANDLUNG STOHR GMBH
Lerchenfelderstrasse 78-80, A-1080 Wien, Austria
Contact: Martin Stohr
Tel: 1 4061349
Fax: 1 431349
Email: slswolfr@ping.at
Website: http://www.page.at/stoehr
We specialise in military books and publish
'Österreichische Militargeschichte' (Austrian military history
to 1938). Also old German language military books.

BUFO BOOKS
32 Tadfield Road, Romsey, Hampshire SO51 5AJ
Contact: Peter Hubbard
Tel/Fax: 01794 517149
Email: bufo@bufobooks.demon.co.uk
Website: http://www.bufobooks.demon.co.uk
We are members of the PBFA, specialising in military
books, maps and ephemera, mainly relating to wars of
20th century. We issue 3/4 catalogues a year and attend
military book fairs. Private premises, visits by appointment
only. Changing selection of stock on the net—see our web
page.

BUSHWOOD BOOKS
6 Marksbury Avenue, Kew Gardens, Surrey TW9 4JF
Contact: Richard Hansen
Tel: 020 8392 8585
Fax: 020 8392 9876
Email: bushwd@aol.com
Exclusive UK distributor for Schiffer Publishing military list,
and also distribute for S S Fedorowicz.

CALIVER BOOKS/PARTIZAN PRESS
816–818 London Road, Leigh-on-Sea, Essex SS9 3NH
Contact: David Ryan
Tel/Fax: 01702 473986
Email: dave@caliverbooks.demon.co.uk or
ask@caliverbooks.com
Website: www.caliverbooks.com
Publishers of: Valkyrie, English Civil War Times, The Age of
Napoleon, The Age of Empires, Battlefields: C18th.
Bookshop and International Mail Order Service. Notes &
queries welcomes.

CHELIFER BOOKS
Todd Close, Curthwaite, Wigton, Cumbria CA7 8BE
Contact: Mike Smith
Tel/Fax: 01228 711388
Email: militbks@aol.com
Secondhand and antiquarian military books bought and
sold. A5 SAE for catalogue or ask for Email list. Postal
service, visitors by appointment.

CHRIS EVANS BOOKS
Unit 6, 2 Jervoise Drive, Birmingham, W. Midlands B31 2X
Contact: Chris Evans
Tel: 0121 477 6700
New and secondhand military specialist with extra
emphasis on titles for the collectors of military vehicles,
AFVs, small arms and militaria. Always interested in
purchasing your unwanted military books, training manuals
and user manuals. International mail order service plus
regular attendance at arms and militaria fairs, modelling
and wargaming events and military vehicle rallies. Personal
callers strictly by prior arrangement, please. Telephone
enquiries welcome any day 8am till 8pm.

CHRISTIAN SCHMIDT BOOKSTORE
Sauerbruchstrasse 10, 81377 München, Germany
Tel: 89703227
Fax: 897005361
Email: info@christian-schmidt.com
Military, shipping, aviation books; scale models; catalogues
available. Store hours Mon–Fri 9am-6pm, Saturday
9am-12am, closed Sundays. Mail order; Visa, Amex
Euro/Mastercard accepted.

CLASSIC ARMS & MILITARIA
Peterson Publications Ltd, Peterson House, Berryhill Ind Est,
Droitwich, Worcs WR9 9BL
Contact: Bruce Ayling
Tel: 01905 795564
Fax: 01905 795905
Classic Arms & Militaria, incorporating Gun Collecting, is
the only publication dedicated to the classic shooter,
military historian and collector. Packed with authoritative
articles on edged weapons, vintage military and sporting
arms, military history, medals, uniforms and a host of
features not often found in other magazines.

HECTOR COLE
The Mead, Great Somerford, Chippenham, Wiltshire SN15 5JB
Contact: Hector Cole
Tel: 01666 825794.
Email: hectorcole@lineone.net.
Website: hectorcoleironwork.co.uk
Archaeological Ironworker. Specialist in archaeological re-
construction of iron artefacts for museums, collectors and
living history groups. All hand forged items from Early Iron
age to late Medieval periods can be reproduced.

COLLECTORS UK
16 Bridge Street, Carmarthen , Carmarthenshire SA31 3JS
Tel: 01267 223496

*COLLECTIANA (CHRISTINE WIRTZ)
Im Kebergrund 2, 56295 Lonnig, Germany

COLLECTOR LIBRERIA
Pau Clabis 168, Barcelona 08037 Spain
Contact: E Broto
Tel/Fax: 93 2158115
Email: collectur@collector-libreria.com
Website: collector-libreria.com
Specialising in military books.

COMBAT PATHS
1037 Chickasaw Trail, Frankfort, KY 4061, USA
Contact: Jim Clark
Tel: 502 695 0521
Fax: 502 564 2124
Email: comabatpath@aol.com
Day by day chronology of the 1st US Armored Division in
WWII. Other chronologies covering US divisions in ETO
being compiled. These are NOT narratives, but day-by-day
listings of locations and units.

CRUSADER TRADING
Email: info@crusaderbooks.com.au

*DANYELA PETITOT
54 bis Avenue de la Motte Picquet, Paris 75015, France
Tel/Fax: 145674435
Auction adviser; we act as counsellor for our customers.
Sale, purchase, research on old and ancient books covering
history, military art, costumes and uniforms.

DEREK HAYLES BOOKS
35 St Marks Road, Maidenhead, Berkshire SL6 6DJ
Tel: U1628 39535
Fax: 01628 788377
Email: derekhaylesmilitarybooks@msn.com
Website: www.militarybooks.co.uk/dhmb
Secure site for credit card details. Postal only. 5,000 scarce
and out-of-print books on land forces. Specialising in
Campaigns, Battles, Regiments, Uniforms, Militaria and person-
alities of the British Army. Current catalogue always available
includes selected new books. Wants lists welcomed.

DEREK VANSTONE AVIATION BOOKS
Email: derek.vanstone@lineone.net

D P R MARKETING & SALES
37 Heath Road, Twickenham, Middlesex TW1 4AW
Tel/Fax: 020 8891 3169

DYFI VALLEY BOOKSHOP
6 Heol Y Doll, Machynlleth, Montgomeryshire SY20 8BQ
Tel: 01654 703849
Send SAE for Bullets & Bows—our catalogue of collectable
books on archery, arms, armour and firearms.

FALCONWOOD TRANSPORT & MILITARY BOOKSHOP
5 Falconwood Parade, The Green Welling, Kent DA16 2PL
Contact: Andy Doran
Tel/Fax: 020 8303 8291
Email: falconw@globalnet.co.uk
Open Thurs, Fri, Sat 9.30-5.30. Second hand books on
motoring, motorcycling, buses, railways, aviation, shipping,
canals, military, engineering etc sold, bought and
exchanged.

FOYLES
113-119 Charing Cross Road, London WC2H 0EB
Tel: 020 7437 5660
Large military, aviation and naval department on second
floor, and transport department on first floor, of London's
most famous bookshop.

FRANCIS EDWARDS (LONDON)
13 Great Newport Street, London WC2 4JA
Contact: Alex Lamb
Tel: 020 73797669
Fax: 020 7836 5977
Email: sales@febooks.demon.co.uk
secondhand and antiquarian booksellers covering all
aspects of military history including naval and aviation.
Open Monday to Saturday, 9.30am to 6.30pm. Catalogues
issued yearly.

FRANK SMITH MARITIME AVIATION BOOKS
100 Heaton Road, Newcastle upon Tyne, Northumberland
NE6 5HL
Contact: Frank Smith
Tel: 0191 265 6333
Fax: 0191 224 2620
Large stocks covering all aspects of aviation and naval his-
tory. Shop opening times: 10.00am 4.00pm Mon-Fri, Sat
10.00am-1.00pm. Free monthly catalogues; please state
subject required.

G C ROBBINS MARITIME & MILITARY BOOKS
Email: grobbins@nbnet.nb.ca
G & D MARRIN & SONS
1-19 Sandgate Road, Folkestone, Kent CT20 2DA
Tel: 01303 253016
Fax: 01303 850956
Email: marrinbook@clara.co.uk
Opening times: Tuesday-Saturday 9.30am-5.30pm. Regular
catalogues issued. Large stock of rare and secondhand
books covering the history and literature of World War I.
Including posters and original works of art. Specialities:
literature, poetry, regimental histories, trench maps,
posters, drawings and manuscript letters and diaries.

G HARRIS MILITARY BOOKS
Heathview, Habberley Road, Bewdley, Worcs DY12 1JH
Contact: George Harris
Tel: 01299 402413
All military conflicts covered, from the English Civil War
to Korea. Specialising in Napoleonic, Victorian and WWI
battles. Bookfairs and catalogues produced annually.

THE GARTER
228 Sydenham Road, Croydon, Middlesex CR0 2EB
Contact: Frances Tucker
Tel/Fax: 020 8684 1095
The directory and sourcebook for costuming. Fabric shops,
booksellers, costumers, accessory makers, haberdashery,
material suppliers and much more.

THE GENERAL STAFF LIBRARY
Email: info@generalstafflibrary.com

GRAHAM PILGRIM
15 Ticehurst Close, Worth, Crawley RH10 7GN
Tel: 01293 885388
Automobile historian. Specialist in automobile literature.
Sales brochures and catalogues dating from the early
1900s to the present day.

GREAT WAR BOOKS 1914–1918
Email: mikestedman@csi.com

HARTSHILL BOOKSHOP
439 Hartshill Road, Stoke-on-Trent, Staffordshire ST4 6AB
Contact: John Green
General bookshop with wide range secondhand military books. open Mon–Sat, 10.00am–6.00pm.

HELION & COMPANY
26 Willow Road, Solihull, W. Midlands B91 1UE
Contact: Duncan Rogers
Tel: 0121 705 3393
Fax: 0121 711 1315
Email: books@helion.co.uk
Website: http://www.helion.co.uk
Over 14,500 in-print books listed in catalogues: antiquity, 1700AD/1700–1914/WWI/Post-1945/Maritime/Aviation. Free book search.

HERSANTS MILITARY BOOKS
18 Herne Gardens, Rustington, W. Sussex BN16 3EF
Contact: Steve Mankelow
Tel/Fax: 01903 770123
Email: herbooks@dircon.co.uk
Website: www.herbooks.dircon.co.uk

H P BOOKFINDERS
22 Fords Close, Bledlow Ridge, Buckinghamshire HP14 4AP
Contact: M Earl
Tel/Fax: 01494 481118
Email: martin@hp-bookfinders.co.uk
Website: www.hp-bookfinders.co.uk
An established and professional service that will locate and supply all out-of-print military titles. No obligation or SAE required. Phone, fax, write, Email.

HOBBYBOKHANDELN AB
Box 8153, Pipersgatan 25, S-10420 Stockholm, Sweden
Contact: Bjorn Alnebo
Tel: 8 6548455
Fax: 8 7590490
Email: order@hobbybooks.se
Website: http://www.hobbybook.se
Shop stocking books and magazines on military, aviation, transport, modelling; unusual and secondhand plastic kits. Open Mon–Fri, 12 noon–6pm; Sat, 11am–2pm.

*HOBBYBUCH
Morgartenstrasse 22, CH-8004 Zurich, Switzerland

*HOUTSCHILD INTERNATIONAL BOOKSELLERS
Papestraat 13, PO Box 30716, 2500 GS Den Haag, Netherlands
Contact: A Houtschild
Tel: 703467949
Fax: 703452881
Email: abouts@inter.nl.net
Website: www.boutschild.com
Dutch, German, French, English and American books on all aspects of militaria; only new. Also modern history and politics. Mail order.

*INTERNATIONAL ARMS LITERATURE
PO Box 10 04 20, Siegen D-57004, Germany
Contact: Manfred Weber Snr
Large stock of books (on Waffen-SS edged weapons; militaria; guns; military history); magazines; posters; videos. World wide mail order. Please write/fax for more details.

J B BOOKS
PO Box 386, Bothell, WA 98041-0386, USA
Contact: Joseph Bishop
Voicemail and fax: 707 929 8417
Email: JBBooks5000@aol.com
Website: www.jbbooks.com
Rare, out of print, collectable books, all fields. Webstore at www.jbbooks.com, searchable by author, title, keywords. All major credit cards accepted.

JOHN LEWCOCK (MARITIME BOOKSELLER)
6 Chewells Lane, Haddenham, Ely, Cambs CB6 3SS.
Contact: John Lewcock
Tel: 01353 741960
Fax: 01353 741710
Email: lewcock@maritime-bookseller.com
Website: www.maritime-bookseller.com or www.ahehooks.com/home/maritime
Specialising in out of print books on maritime subjects. Includes: naval and maritime history, yachts and yachting, naval architecture and marine engineering. Flags and signalling, navigation. Member of the Antiquarian Booksellers Association.

J P BOOKS
Email: j.parker@jpbooks.com

J T READING
101 Alexandra Road, Hasbury, Halesowen, W. Midlands B63 4BP
Contact: Jim Reading
Tel/Fax: 0121 550 6641
Email: jim.reading@btinternet.com
Specialist weaponry books, new and secondhand, including Western Americana.

KEEGAN'S BOOKSHOP
Merchant's Place, Friar Street, Reading, Berkshire RG1 1DT
Contact: John Keegan
Tel: 0118 958 7253
Fax: 0118 958 5220
Secondhand bookshop with good military, aviation, naval and transport sections. BR station and parking nearby. We also buy books. Open 9am–5.30pm Mon–Sat.

KEN TROTMAN LTD
Unit 11, 135 Ditton Walk, Cambridge, Cambridgeshire
CB5 8PY
Contact: Richard & Roz Brown
Tel: 01223 211030
Fax: 01223 212317
Email: trotman@netcomuk.co.uk
Website: http://www.kentrotman.ltd.uk
We are a mail order bookseller issuing 3-4 catalogues a year alternating between new and rare books. We cover military history and uniforms for all periods from ancient civilizations through to the world wars, Napoleonics and American Civil War a speciality, also a large section on ancient armour and firearms.

KLAUS-DIETER GERSON
Militärhistorische Fachbuchhandlung, Bornweg 5a, D-21509 Glinde, Germany
Contact: Klaus-Dieter Gerson
Tel: 40 710 4522
Fax: 40 710 1944
New and secondhand military books from ancient to 1914. Mail order service. Two catalogues issued yearly. Three international reply coupons for list.

KRUPPER INTERNATIONAL BOOKS
Email: bill@krupper.com

LANDMARK BOOKSELLERS
PO Box89, Leatherhead, Surrey KT23
Contact: Douglas Blann
Tel/Fax: 01372 450780
Email: info@landmarkmilitarybooks.com
Website: www.landmarkmilitarybooks.com
We sell a wide range of specialist books for the collector, enthusiast, modeller and re-enactor, covering Imperial and Third Reich uniforms, medals and awards, edged weapons, unit histories and AFVs. Also British and Allies during WWII, plus special forces. Many of these books are not generally available elsewhere.

LIBRAIRIE ARMES ET COLLECTIONS
19 Avenue de la République, 75011 Paris, France
Specialist bookshop for all military publications; the retail branch of the publishers of the leading French magazines 'Militaria', 'Tradition', 'RAIDS', etc. Also stocks a wide range of outdoor clothing, survival equipment, etc.

LA LIBRAIRIE HISTOIRE ET FORTIFICATIONS
8 Rue de Crussol, 75011 Paris, France
Tel: 01 48057039
Website: www.histoire-fortifications.com

*LIBRAIRIE UNIFORMOLOGIQUE INTERNATIONALE
111 Avenue Victor Hugo, Galerie Argentine, 75116 Paris, France
Contact: Thierry Lecourt

LIBROS REYES
Dato 1, 50005 Zaragoza, Spain
Contact: Angel Marti
Tel: 976219443
Fax: 976230179
Email: l.reyes@arrakis.es
Specialists in Spanish military history, Spanish air force, navy, uniforms and weapons, all periods. Send for free catalogue.

LA LIBRERIA MILITARE
Galleria Borella 1, Milan, Italy 20123
Contact: Angelo Pirocchi
Tel/Fax: 02 89010725
Email: libmil@starfarm.iT
Website: www.libreriamilitare.com
Military history, strategy, Intelligence, weapons, tanks, ships, aircraft, uniforms, special forces. Also historical services, Italian Armed Forces and Italian military maps.

*LA MAISON DU LIVRE AVIATION
75 Boulevard Malesherbes, 75008 Paris, France

MARTIN GLADMAN
235 Nether Street, Finchley, London N31NT
Tel: 020 8343 3023
Large stock of military/naval/aviation within a very large history stock. 'Wants' lists welcomed. Individual volumes or collections purchased.

MCGOWAN BOOK CO.
PO Box 4226, Chapel Hill, NC 27515, USA
Tel: 919 968 1121
Fax: 919 968 1644
Email: mcgowanbooks@mindspring.com
Website: www.mcgowanbooks.com
Specializing in Abraham Lincoln and the American Civil War. Please visit our website. Member: Antiquarian Booksellers' Association of America International League of Antiquarian Booksellers International Autograph Collectors Club ALWAYS BUYING quality books, autographs, documents, photographs, postal history items, veterans' memorabilia (U.C.V. and G.A.R.), and objects of the period, especially uniforms, weapons, and flags.

MARITIME BOOKS
Lodge Hill, Liskeard, Cornwall PL14 4EL
Contact: Roger May
Tel: 01579 343663
Fax: 01579 346747
Email: marbooks@aol.com
Website: http://members.aol.com/marbooks/
Specialist publishers of Royal Naval books and bookseller of RN titles. Over 100,000 books in stock. Mail order only; free catalogues.

MICHAEL McLAUGHLIN
BCM CAMPFIRE, London WC1N 3XX
Tel: 0836 384112
Third Reich audio/cassette/CD/video. Repro Third Reich, Folk heritage art posters, postcards, Military and political books.

MIDLAND COUNTIES PUBLICATIONS
Unit 3, Maizefield, Hinckley, Leicestershire LE10 1YF
Contact: Mike Everton
Tel: 01455 233747
Fax: 01455 433737
Email: midlandbooks@compuserve.com
Website: www.midlandbooks.com
Distributors of aviation, military, railway, spaceflight and astronomy books, magazines and videos. Large selection of titles stocked for mail order worldwide. Free catalogue.

MIL-ART
41 Larksfield Crescent, Dovercourt, Harwich, Essex CO12 4BL
Tel: 01255 507440
Producers of metal military figure kits in 54mm, 80mm and 100mm scales. Also retailer of new and out-of-print military books.

*MILITARIA
c/Bailen 120, 08009 Barcelona, Catalonia, Spain
Contact: Xavier Andreu
Tel/Fax: 32075385
Email: militaria@ctv.es
Website: http://www.ctv.es/users/militaria
Buy, sell and exchange militaria, medals, edged weapons, insignia, headgear etc. Also large selection military books in stock.

MILITARY AND AVIATION BOOK SOCIETY
Guild House, Farnsby Street, Swindon, Wiltshire SN99 9XX
Tel: 01793 512100
Fax: 01793 616789
Email: jeverden@bca.co.uk
Website: www.militarybook.co.uk
A book club for military and aviation enthusiasts ancient and modern (membership UK only). Books by post at reduced prices.

THE MILITARY BOOKMAN
Email: history@militarybookman.com

MILITARY BOOKS
3226 Woodley Rd NW, Washington DC, 20008-3334, USA
Contact: Richard Williams
Tel: 202 298 7551
Email: militarybooks@earthlink.net
Buying and selling used, out of print and rare books and printed materials relating to military history including unit histories, official histories, studies of battles and campaigns, studies of weapons and other military equipment, biographies etc. Covering all periods and nations but especially from 1600 to present in Europe and America.

MILITARY BOOKWORM
PO Box 235, London SE23 1NS
Contact: David W Collett
Tel/Fax: 020 8291 1435
Email: david@militarybookworm.co.uk
Website: www.militarybookworm.co.uk
Secondhand books on British military history, school registers and other publications for family research. Mail Order only. Stock listed on website. Payment taken on Visa or Mastercard if preferred.

THE MILITARY COLLECTOR.
The Manse, East Lee Lane, Todmorden, W. Yorkshire OL14 8RW
Contact: Ian Wilkinson
Tel/Fax: 01706 839690
Email: military.collector@virgin.net
Website: www.sonic.net/~bstone/military
A stock of 11,000 mainly secondhand military, naval and aviation books covering all periods. Postal only. Credit cards accepted or payment by us dollar or sterling cheques.

MILITARY HISTORY BOOKSHOP
77–81 Bell Street, London NW1 6TA
Contact: K W Barber
Tel: 020 7723 2095
Fax: 020 7723 4665
Email: milhist@mint.net
Specialist in military history. Large stock of new and secondhand books including many imported titles, on uniforms, weapons, unit histories, biographies, battles, campaigns, espionage and terrorism. Annotated catalogues issued, each over 1000 titles. Catalogues £1 (stamps). Credit cards accepted. Visitors welcome: 10am-5pm Monday to Friday-10am-to 2pm Saturday.

MILITARY HISTORY BOOKSHOP
PO Box 97, Postcode 04921, USA
Contact: Ray and Andrea McGuire
Tel: 207 722 3620
Fax: 413 556 8094
Email:milhist@mint.net
Website: www.abebooks.com/home/militaryhistory
Out of print and rare books on military, naval, aeronautics, China and the Far East.

MILITARY PARADE BOOKSHOP
The Parade, Marlborough, Wiltshire SN8 1NE
Contact: Peter Kent
Tel: 01672 515470
Fax: 01980 630150
Email: enquiry@militaryparadebooks.com
Military warfare from the Crusades to the Gulf. Specialises in regimental histories, Napoleonic, World War I and World War II. Over 5,000 titles available; send SAE for catalogue. Open Mon–Sat, 10.00am–5.00pm.

MILITARY SERVICES
87 Ellacombe Road, Longwell Green, Bristol BS30 9BP
Contact: T S Walsh
Tel: 0117 932 4085
New and secondhand military books and magazines.

MILITARY SUBJECTS
2 Locks Road, Locks Heath, Southampton, Hampshire SO3 6NT
Contact: C Pearce
Tel: 01489 572582
Books, models and militaria. Private premises; visitors by prior appointment only, please.

MILITARY VEHICLE TRUST
PO Box 102, Whitefield, Manchester M45 6ET
Tel: 0161 798 7877
Fax: 0161 773 3731
Email: neilweiner@mvt.org.uk

MOTOR BOOKS
Military Department
London: 36 St Martin's Court, St Martin's Lane, London
WC2N 4AN.
Tel: 020 7836 5376   _Justin Bayley._
Fax: 020 7497 2539
Email: motorbooks.military@virgin.net
Website: www.motorbooks.co.uk
Motor Books specialises in transport and military history.
Established since 1957 in the heart of London's busy West
End, selling books, videos and CDs. Opening times:
9.30am-6pm. Late night Thursday till 7pm. Saturday
10.30am-5.30pm.

NAVAL AND MILITARY PRESS
PO Box 61, Dallington, Heathfield, E. Sussex TN21 9JS
Tel: 01435 830111
Fax: 01435 830623

THE NEW POSTMASTER
Bwlch House, Beguildy, Radnorshire LD7 1U9
Contact: B Carter
Tel: 01547 510 289
Original 19th century newspapers, containing despatches
and reports from the Napoleonic wars, the Crimea,
American Civil War, European and Colonial conflicts, the
Anglo-Boer War, etc. Also available: Titles for WWI and II.

OSRIC BOOKS
116 Charles Street, Oxford OX4 3AT
Contact: Simon Chadwick
Tel: 01865 722126
Authentically constructed manuscript books.

OUTDOORSMANS BOOKSTORE
22-24 High Street, Horley, Surrey RH6 7AB
Contact: R Vithlani
Tel: 01293 772496
Fax: 01293 431286
Email: sales@outdoorsmans.co.uk
Website: www.outdoorsmans.co.uk

OLD ARMY BOOKS INC
4516 Mandeville Way, Lexington, KY 40515, USA
Contact: Bruce Halsted
Tel: 859 273-5614
Fax: 859 272-3319
Email: bhalstead@infi.net
Website: www.sonic.net/~bstone/oldarmy/
New, used and out of print military history. All periods, all
countries.

PAUL MEEKINS
34 Townsend Road, Tiddington, Stratford upon Avon,
Warwickshire CV37 7DE
Tel/Fax: 01789 295086
Email: paul.meekins@ecws.co.uk
Secondhand, out of print and new. Covering ancient, medieval,
16th/17th/18th/19th centuries, Napoleonic, English and
American civil wars, WWI & II, uniforms, costume, arms &
armour. Wants lists welcome. Free book search. Books bought.

PATTON
PO Box 862, Acworth, GA 30101, USA
Contact: Terry Patton
Tel: 770 529 0307
Fax: 770 529 2848
Email: pattont@mindspring.com
German and US militaria, specializing in signatures, auto
graphs, documents and rare books in all fields, military,
political, aviation, etc.

*PELTA
16 Swietokrzyska Street, 00 Warsaw 050, Poland
Contact: Mark Machala
Tel: (+48-22) 8276614
Fax: (+48-22) 8269186
Leading distributor of Polish, Russian and Czech books on
aviation, vehicles, AFVs, naval and militaria subjects (eg
uniforms), covers all historical periods. Also military models, plastic kits, vacuforms, figures (30mm, 54mm) painted
and unpainted. The widest selection in the world, available
for trade and mail order. Free catalogues and super prices.

PEN AND SWORD BOOKS
47 Church Street, Barnsley, S. Yorkshire S70 2AS
Tel: 01226 734222 or 734555
Fax: 01226 734438
Email: design@pen-and-sword.co.uk
Military history publishers.

PETTY CHAPMAN
18 Armitage Road, Huddersfield, W. Yorkshire HD2 2UB
Contact: David Rushworth or Lindy Pickard
Tel: 01484 512968
Email: info@pettychapman.co.uk
Illustrated costume handbooks covering various periods.
£3.50 each. SAE for list.

P G de LOTZ
20 Downside Crescent, Hampstead NW3 2AP
Tel: 020 7794 5709
Fax: 020 7284 3058
Books on military history covering all countries and
periods.

PHOENIX BOOKS
Email: phoenixbuk@aol.com

POCKETBOND LTD
PO Box 80, Welwyn, Hertfordshire AL6 0ND
Contact: Phillip Brook
Tel: 01707 391509
Fax: 01707 327466
Website: http://www.btinternet.com/-pocketbond
Exclusive importer for: Squadron Signal Publications and
Squadron products: Testors, Toko, ICM, Tauro, Hobbycraft,
AFV Club and Emhar plastic kits and Imex Civil War
figures.

*PREUSSISCHES BUCHERKABINETT
Knesebeckstrasse 88, 10623 Berlin, Germany
Contact: Stefan Muller
Tel: 315 7000
Fax: 315 70077
Specialists in military books from around the world. Mail
order catalogue available. Shipping anywhere.

PROSPECT BOOKS
18 Denbigh Street, Llanwurst, Conwy, Wales LL26 0LL
Tel/Fax: 01492 640111
Email: prospect@books.demon.co.uk
Website: www.books.demon.co.uk
Rare, new and collectable books, covering artillery, ammu-
nition, pistols, rifles, gunsmithing, game shooting, antiques,
armour, edged weapons and ephemera.
Free mail order catalogue. All major credit cards accepted.

R M ENGLAND
4 Baker House, Darien Road, Battersea, London SW11 2EQ
Tel: 020 7738 1304
Old newspapers, books and prints wide selection of original
newspapers, books and newspaper prints on Napoleonic
and Victorian campaigns.

RAY WESTLAKE MILITARY BOOKS
53 Claremont, Malpas, Newport, Gwent NP9 6PL, Wales
Tel: 01633 854135
Fax: 01633 821860
A mail order business supplying new and secondhand
books. Most at below publishers prices. Send large SAE
(31p stamps) for latest 46-page catalogue.

ROBINSON IMPORTS
25 Princetown Road, Bangor, Co. Down BT20 3TA,
N. Ireland
Contact: Cameron or Hilary Robinson
Tel/Fax: 01247472860
Email: irish@brigade28.freeserve.co.uk
ACW Society Magazine 'Zouave', American Civil War books
and related items. Irish and Irish Brigade books. Also re-
enactment services.

ROBIN TURNER
30 Great Norwood Street, Cheltenham, Glos GL50 2BH
Tel/Fax: 01242 234303
Email: robinturner@robamol.fsnet.co.uk
Small stock of military books (pre 1914). Specialising in
Napoleonic period. Lists/catalogues issued two or three
times a year.

ROTTERDAMSE SCHEEPVAART BOEKHANDEL
Email: sjardijn@xs4all.nl

RUNELORE BOOKS
Flat 12, 10 Queens Gardens, Eastbourne, E. Sussex
BN21 3EF
Contact: Sean Bradley
Tel: 01323 412694

SCHULL BOOKS
Ballydehob, Co Cork, Ireland
Tel/Fax: 3532837317
Email: schullbooks@eircom.net
Website: www.schullbooks.com
We are out of print/antiquarian booksellers, specialising in
Irish interest and military history. We have also re-
published volumes of the histories of the disbanded Irish
regiments of the British Army, and on the involvement of
the Irish in the Great War. We also sell military prints.

SELOUS BOOKS
40 Station Road, Aldershot, Hants GU11 1HT
Contact: Jeremy Tenniswood
Tel: 01252 333611
Fax: 01252 342 339
Email: trevor_n@militaria.co.uk
Website: www.militaria.co.uk
Suppliers and retailers of specialist publications, including:
technical firearms, edged weapons, history of warfare, col-
lecting militaria, coins & medals. Original and reproduction
of scarce books on travel, exploration, archeology, natural
and cultural history of India, South East and Central Asia.

SENTIMENTAL JOURNEY
35–37 Chapelgate, Sutton St James, Lincolnshire PE12 0EF
Contact: Ian Durrant
Tel/Fax: 01945 440289
Email: sales@sentimentaljourney.co.uk
Website: www.sentimentaljourney.co.uk
Specialist supplier of items relating to Britain's military and
civilian services 1914–1965. We sell uniforms, maps,
manuals, ephemera, 78s, books and webbing. As collectors
ourselves we provide a service by collectors for collectors.
Our shop should open this year.

SERVICE PUBLICATIONS
Email: sales@servicepub.com

SPINK & SON
69 Southampton Row, Bloomsbury, London WC1B 4ET
Contact: Lucy Formosa
Tel: 020 7563 4055
Fax: 020 7563 4068
Email: lformosa@spinkandson.com
Website: www.spink-online.com
Spink is a leading dealer and auctioneer in orders,
decorations, campaign medals and militaria, encompassing
all countries and all periods. As the specialist company in
the Christie's group, Spink offers an exceptional selection
of material, and impartial and confidential advice, whether
you are looking to buy or sell.

*STENVALL'S
Foreningsgatan 12, S-21144 Malmo, Sweden
Tel: 40 127703
Fax: 40 127700
Sweden's best stocked bookshop for military and transport subjects. Mail order catalogue issued periodically. Shop open Mon–Fri 9am–6pm.

STEPHEN E TILSTON
37 Bennett Park, Blackheath, London SE3 9RA
Tel/Fax: 020 8318 9181
Email: tilston@attglobal.net
Secondhand and out-of-print military, maritime and naval books bought and sold; WWI a speciality. Lists issued; booksearch service; postal business only.

STEVEN J HOPKINS
Court Farm, Kington, Flyford Flavell, Worcs WR7 4DQ
Contact: Steven Hopkins
Tel/Fax: 01386 793427
Email: tokyngton@aol.com
Napoleonic and Victorian campaign histories, particularly African wars. Send SAE for catalogue. Good military books and Zulu memorabilia purchased.

STUART PRESS
117 Farleigh Road, Backwell, Bristol BS48 3PG
Contact: Stuart Peachey
Tel: 01275 463041
160 titles, most 1580–1660, some earlier, on war, food, farming, medicine, sex and more.

TERENCE WISE MILITARY BOOKS
Pantiles, Garth Lane, Knighton, Powys LD7 1HH, Wales
Contact: Terence Wise
Tel/Fax: 01547 529160
Mail order only. Out-of-print, secondhand and antiquarian military books, specialising in regimental and divisional histories. Annual catalogue of wargames figures and model soldiers.

*THIERRY LECOURT
31 Rue Berthollet, 94110 Arcueil 94110, France
Tel/Fax: (0033) 47353158

THIN RED LINE MILITARY BOOKS
11 St Andrews Road, Prenton, Wirral CH43 1TB
Contact: Dr R A Dutton
Tel/Fax: 0151 652 4483
Out of print books on military subjects including WWI & II, Special Forces, Victorian campaigns, collectables, weaponry, manuals, Napoleonic and earlier. Free book search services. Militaria fairs attended. Mail order only.

THIRD REICH BOOKS
Email: trbooks@aol.com

TOMAHAWK FILMS WW2 GERMAN ARCHIVE
PO Box 279 Winchester Hampshire SO21 1XT
Contact: Brian Matthews or Stan Googe
Tel: 01962 714989
Fax: 01962 713966
Email: Brian.tomahawk@btinternet.com
Website: www.tomahawkfilms.com
The Tomahawk Films Archive is the world's leading producer of original pre-1945 German military marching music on CD/Cassette to historians, collectors, enthusiasts, schools & colleges via our mail-order division. We also supply, original German combat film, sound effects and documentary voice-overs to film & television production companies

THE TOY SOLDIER BOOK SHOP
PO Box 62514, Sharonville, Ohio 45262, USA
Contact: Robert Wagner
Tel: 513 554 1162
Fax: 513 554 1162
Email: rrwagner@earthlink.net
Mail order bookseller specialising in toy soldier/model soldier books, and the painting and modelling of toy and model soldiers. List free with large SAE.

TRAPLET PUBLICATIONS LIMITED
Traplet House, Severn Drive, Upton upon Severn, Worcs
WR8 0JL
Tel/Fax: 01684 594505
Email: mis@traplet.com

*TRADITION H ZORN
Bettenfeld 21, 9154-1 Rothenburg, Germany
Tel/Fax: 986121611

*TRAEME SELECTION
62 Boulevard Jean-Jaures, 92100 Boulogne, France

T R ROBB
17 Thoriey Bay Road, Canvey Island, Essex SS8 0HG
Contact: Terry Robb
Tel: 01268 696054
Fax: 01268 681068
Email: terry.robb@pop3.hiway.co.uk
Airgun tuning books, range targets and airgun tuning parts, tuning kits.

TURNER DONOVAN MILITARY BOOKS
1132 London Road, Leigh on Sea, Essex SS9 2AJ
Contact: Brian Turner
Tel: 01702 478771
Fax: 01702 714278
Email: tom@turner-donovan.co.uk
Website: http://www.turner-donovan.co.uk

*TUTTOSTORIA
Via S Sonnino 34, 43100 Parma, Italy

UNIVERSAL SOLDIER
10 Old Rectory Close, Instow, Bideford, Devon EX39 4LY

ULRIC OF ENGLAND

PO Box 55, Church Stretton, Shropshire SY6 6WR
Contact: Ulric
Tel/Fax: 01694 781354
Email: mail@ulricofengland.com
Website: www.ulricofengland.com
Specialist dealers in Kaiser Reich and Third Reich
antiquities, established for over 25 years. Catalogue issued
twice a year, with over 1000 original artefacts for sale. Or
visit our website.

*VAN NIEUWENHUIJZEN MODELSHOP

Oude Binnenweg 91, 3012 JA Rotterdam, Netherlands
Contact: Mike Lettinga
Tel: 10 41535923
Fax: 10 4141324

VICTOR SUTCLIFFE

36 Parklands Road, London SW16 6TE
Contact: Victor Sutcliffe
Tel: 020 8769 8345
Fax: 020 8769 6446
Email: v@victorsutcliffe.demon.co.uk
Website: www.victorsutcliffe.demon.co.uk
Secondhand books bought and sold on all aspects of mili-
tary history before 1914, Napoleonic Wars and British India
especially.

VALERIE MICHAEL

37 Silver Street, Tetbury, Glos GL8 8DL
Tel/Fax: 01666 502179
The Leatherworking Handbook—£15.99 (inc. p&p).

VILMOR PUBLICATIONS

Morton Villa Farm, Misson Springs, Doncaster, S. Yorkshire
DN10 6ES
Contact: Philip Baker
Tel/Fax: 01302 770295
Publisher and stockholder of Philip Baker's 'Youth Led by
Youth'. Three volumes, covering most aspects of the Hitler
Youth. Hundreds of B/W and colour illustrations.

VOLUME CONTROL

Email: Ww2volcont@aol.com

THE WAR ROOM BOOKSHOP

Email: warrm@webspan.net

WORDSWORTH MILITARY LIBRARY

A Guide to the Battlefields of Europe by Dr David Chandler.

WOOLCOTT BOOKS

Kingston House, Higher Kingston, Nr Dorchester, Dorset
DT2 8QE
Contact: H M, J R or J A St Aubyn
Tel: 01305 267773
Fax: 01305 751899
Military history including: 17th & 18th century campaigns,
Napoleonic era, Crimean War, WWI & II, India, Gurkhas,
Africa, Malaya, Korea, Ireland. Regimental histories, military
medicine, miscellaneous.

WORLD OF WARFARE

106 Browhead Road, Burnley, Lancs BB10 3BX
Contact: Arthur Thornton
Tel/Fax: 01282 420541
Specialising in German and early American history.

WORLD WAR BOOKS

Oaklands Camden Park, Tunbridge Wells, Kent
TN2 5AE
Contact: Tim Harper
Tel/Fax: 01892 538465
Email: wwarbooks@btinternet.com
Specialist booksellers dealing in out of print military, naval
and aviation books. Manuscripts, photo albums and maps
are also stocked. Wants list welcomed and catalogues
issued. We also organise world war bookfairs and specialist
fairs held in London, Marlborough and Kent (Chatham and
Tunbridge Wells).

WORLD WAR 2 BOOKS

PO Box 55, GU22 8HP
Contact: Graham Parker
Tel: 01483 722 880
Fax: 01483 721 548
Email: ww2books@churchill.net.uk
Website: www.worldwarbooks.co.uk
Secondhand books on WWII.

HISTORICAL SOCIETIES

*A C M N

11 Rue Alexis Quirin, (Bat.AI), 94350 Villiers sur Marne,
France
Contact: Daniel Poisson

A I F REMEMBRANCE PROJECT

75B Clova Road, Forest Gate, London E7 9AG
Contact: Matt Smith
Tel: 020 8534 4996
Email: matts_smith@hotmail.com
Website: www.aifrememranceproject.com
An Internet project dedicated to the memory of Australia's
war dead from two world wars.

ALDERSHOT MILITARIA SOCIETY

1 Littlefield Gardens, Ash, Aldershot, Hampshire GU12 6LN
Contact: H W Glover
Tel: 01252 321931
Email: sales@authenticmilitaria.com
Website: www.milweb.net/dealers/Dealerindex.htm
AMS meets last Thursday each month at Aldershot Library
at 7.30pm; visitors welcome. Interests include medals,
insignia, weapons, and all aspects of military history.

AMERICAN CIVIL WAR ROUND TABLE (UK)
41 Templemere, Oatlands Drive, Weybridge, Surrey
KT13 9PA
Contact: Paul Pilditch
Tel/Fax: 01932 846150
Email: Cwshistory@aol.com
Society for the study of the military, naval and civil history
of the American Civil War 1861–65. Formed 1953;
affiliated to CVMT Associates USA. Meetings', talks,
newsletter, library. Membership for amateur/ professional
historians/ researchers £5 p.a. UK, £6 overseas.

AMERICAN CIVIL WAR SOCIETY
PO Box 52, Brighouse, Yorkshire HD6 1JQ
Contact: Philip Clark
Tel: 01625 431500
Fax: 01625 435036
Email: pbilipcarswell@compuserve.com
Website: www.acws.demon.co.uk
For 'living history' and re-enactment country-wide of the
American Civil War 1861–1865.

AMICI (Association Militaria Italian Collectors International)
c/o James Burd, 177 Palmetto Drive, Rincon, Georgia 31326
USA
Contact: James Burd
Email: jsb715@aol.com
Website: http://members.aol.com/jsb715/index.htm
AMICI is an Italian militaria collectors association which
publishes a bimonthly newsletter. Its goal is to further the
knowledge of Italian military history through collecting. Its
primary time period is WWI to WWII. It includes historical
reviews of battles and campaigns and detailed articles on
insignia, uniforms, headgear, and weapons.

ARMY RECORDS SOCIETY
National Army Museum, Royal Hospital Road, Chelsea,
London SW3 4HT
Contact: Professor I F W Beckett
Tel: 01582 489043
Fax: 01582 489014
Email: ian.beckett@luton.ac.uk
Publishes annual volume illustrating some aspect of the
Army's past. Subscription only £15.00 per annum, although
the volumes retail commercially at £40.00 or more.

ASSOCIATION OF FRIENDS OF WATERLOO COMMITTEE
2 Coburn Drive, Four Oaks, Sutton Coldfield, W. Midlands
B75 5NT
Contact: John S White
Tel/Fax: 0121 308 4103
Email: jwhite02@globalnet.co.yk
Website: www.afc.1c24.net
Founded by the eighth Duke of Wellington in 1922, the
Association promotes study and research into Waterloo and
the events of the Napoleonic War. The Waterloo Journal is
published three times a year and a programme of visits,
talks and lectures is promoted.

AXHOLMR & THE DANNAE
15 Mond Avenue, Goole, East Yorkshire DN14 6LQ
Contact: Matt Jones
Tel: 01405 763550
Email: axholmruik@aol.com
Website: www.axholmr.co.uk
Historical re-enactment society covering 3rd–11th
centuries. Anglian, Saxon, Viking and Norman periods
covered. Also 3rd century BC–3rd century AD Celtic.
Combat, living history, research, family friendly, archery,
crafts, TV/film and photographic.

BARMY ARMY FILM CLUB
Contact: John Simpson
Fax: 01322 616 305

BATTLEFIELDS TRUST
Meadow Cottage, 33 High Green, Brooke, Norfolk NR15 1HR
Contact: Michael Rayner
Tel/Fax: 01508 558145
Email: BattlefieldTrust@aol.com
The Trust has been formed to help save battlefield sites
from destruction and to preserve them for posterity as
educational and heritage resources.

BIRMINGHAM WAR RESEARCH SOCIETY
43 Norfolk Place, King Norton, Birmingham B30 3LB
Contact: Alex Bulloch
Tel: 0121 459 9008
Fax: 0121 459 8128
Battlefield tours, cemetery visits Northern Europe.

BRITISH MILITARY RECORDS
Website: www.genuki.org.uk

*BRITISH MILITARIA COLLECTORS COMMUNITY
Gutenbergstrasse 32, D-90766 Fuerth, Germany
Contact: Robert Schorr
Tel: 911 973 2631
Fax: 911 860 6255
British Militaria Collectors' Community of Germany estab-
lished 1991. Members throughout Germany. Main focus on
19th/20th century. Regular newsletter published. New
members welcome.

BRITISH FEDERATION FOR HISTORICAL SWORDPLAY
15 Halmyre Street, Edinburgh, Scotland EH6 8QA
Contact: Paul Macdonald
Tel: 0131 538 0745
Email: macdonaldacademy@aol.com
Website: www.bfhs.co.uk
The British Federation for historical swordplay is a national
umbrella organisation for UK societies practicing historical
fencing workshops as well as offering an extensive library
of facsimile historical treatises.

BRITISH PLATE ARMOUR SOCIETY
82 Skinner Street, Poole, Dorset BH15 1RJ
Contact: David Barnes

CHANNEL ISLANDS OCCUPATION SOCIETY: JERSEY
Les Geonnais de Bas, Rue de Geonnais, St Ouen, Jersey
JE3 2BS
Tel: 01534 482089
Email: mcostard@localdial.com
A non-profit organisation dedicated to the preservation and
recording of all aspects of the German Occupation, includ-
ing bunkers and coastal defences.

CHARLES II SOCIETY
The Whitemoor, Codsall Wood, Wolverhampton, Staffordshire
WV8 1RA
Contact: M Whittaker
Tel/Fax: 01902 850363
A society formed to promote interest, at all levels, in the
life and times of Charles II in particular, and the Stuart
dynasty in general.

*CHUTE AND DAGGER/EUROPE
Bordes de Riviere, 31210 Montrejeau, France
Contact: A P Gaudet
We are 250 collectors of elite unit insignia from around
the world. Subscription $19 US or equivalent for non-
Europeans, 75 French francs or equivalent for Europeans.
For a free sample copy of Chute and Dagger/Europe
illustrated newsletter, apply in writing.

COMMONWEALTH FORCES HISTORY TRUST
37 Davis Road, Acton, London W3 7SE
Contact: Shamus Wade
Tel: 020 8749 1045
Provides a history of the Defence Forces of the British
Commonwealth and Empire from 1066 to 1945.
Information on 10,459 different units from 82 countries.

CONFEDERATE STATES NAVY
HQ Redoubt Fortress, Royal Parade, Eastbourne, E. Sussex
BN20 8BB
Tel/Fax: 01343 410300
Email: eastbourne_museums@breathemail.net
Archives and library. 1858-1870. Great Britain and
America. Navies and blockade running. Artefacts. Lectures.
'Living history' section with howitzer. Secretary call 01273
400037.

CONFEDERATE UNION RE-ENACTMENT SOCIETY (CURS)
13 Amythyst Road, Fairwater, Cardiff, South Wales CF5 3MS
Contact: Phil Buck Day
Tel: 02920 317980
Email: p.day@ntlworld.com
Website: www.homestead.com/curs1/index.html
We recreate American Civil War infantry units 23rd VA,
97th NY, Medical Corps and Artillery, and participate in
battle re-enactments and living history displays
1860-1865. Soldier and civilian impressions at their best.
New members welcome. Also postal members. The Society
was founded in 1997.

CORPS OF DRUMS SOCIETY
62 Gally Hill Road, Church Crookham, Hampshire GU13 0RU
Contact: Reg Davies
Tel/Fax: 01252 614852
Email: soc@corpsofdrums.softnet.co.uk
Website: http://www.softnet.uk/corpsofdrums
The Corps of Drums Society for anyone who plays military
drum or fife, or who wishes to study their history and pre-
serve their future.

CRIMEAN WAR RESEARCH SOCIETY
4 Castle Estate, Rippunden, Sowerby Bridge, W. Yorkshire
HX6 4JY
Contact: David Cliff
Tel/Fax: 01422 823529
Email: colinrobins@withycut.demon.co.uk
The society encourages research into every facet of the
war; and has a quarterly journal 'The War Correspondent'.
New members are always welcome.

CROWN IMPERIAL
37 Wolsey Close, Southall, Middlesex UB2 4NQ
Contact: Lt Cdr Maitland Thornton
Tel/Fax: 020 8574 4425
This society was formed in 1973, to study traditions and
regalia of the forces of the crown. Four journals circulated
annually.

THE DARK AGES CHARITABLE TRUST
Rosemary Cottage, Camp Road, Canwell, Sutton Coldfield
B75 5RA
Contact: Paul Craddock
Tel: 0121-323-4309
Fax: 0121-323-4309
Email: MerciaS@hotmail.com
Website: DarkAgesTrust.org.uk
An historical and nature conservation charity, near
Birmingham, specialising in the period 500-1500 AD. We
have our own seven-acre site with a re-constructed ringfort
and lake. We have planted about 200 rare fruit trees and
are looking for more volunteers. We run groups for The
Vikings and Regia Anglorum.

DAWN DUELLISTS SOCIETY
15 Halmyre Street, Edinburgh, Scotland EH6 8QA
Contact: Paul Macdonald
Tel: 0131 538 0745
Email: macadonaldacademy@aol.com
The Dawn Duellists Society practices historical fencing and
duelling styles from C13th to C19th. Training is held weekly and open to all. Demonstrations of historical fencing can
be offered, outlining the development of European swords
and swordsmanship.

DEUTSCHES ATLANTIK WALL ARCHIV
Schmittgasse 151, D-51143 Köln-Zündorf, Germany
Contact: Harry Lippmann
Tel: 477816504
Historical society regularly publishing archive material
covering all countries whose coastline made up the Atlantic
Wall.

EASTERN FRONT ASSOCIATION 1914-21
165 Marlborough Avenue, Kingston upon Hull, England
HU5 3LG
Contact: Martin Clarke
Tel: 01482 447188
International newsletter-linked society. Has 'living history' section which comes together twice a year. Has access to reconstructed WW I trench and Russian type village.

88th FOOT CONNAUGHT RANGERS
12 Hale Road, Farnham, Surrey GU9 9QH
Contact: Robert Anderson
Tel: 01252 726258
Email: robanderson@ukonline.co.uk
Website: www.88thfoot.co.uk
Our club based in Farnham, Surrey, depicts the 88th Foot on campaign in the Peninsular War in 1812. We participate in Napoleonic battle re-enactments in the UK and Europe, and organise our own battle display annually at Farnham Castle Park. We plan to organise another battalion in the west of Ireland.

THE ERMINE STREET GUARD
Oakland Farm, Dog Lane, Witcombe, Gloucester, Glos
GL3 4UG
Contact: Chris Haines
Tel: 01452 862235
Fax: 01452 862235
Email: theESG@aol.com
Website: www.ESG.ndirect.co.uk
Roman re-enactment society formed in 1972. We have a worldwide reputation for authenticity, with displays for English Heritage and others. Film work also undertaken.

THE ESSEX MILITIA
27 Shalford Road, Billericay, Essex
Contact: Dennis Ward
Tel: 01277 655612
Email: dennis@essex1648.freeserve.co.uk
The Militia covers the period from the English Civil War through to the restoration of Charles II (1640s–1660s). We can people a castle, stately home or encampment, as well as give civil or corporate presentations.

509TH COMPOSITE GROUP
366 E. Wagner Road, Buchanan, MI 49107, USA
Contact: Robert Krauss
Email: rwkrauss@hotmail.com
509th Composite Group, 1st Atomic Bombardment (1944–1945), source for photographs, documents, and reunion information and products.

FORTRESS STUDY GROUP
The Severals, Bentleys Road, Market Drayton, Shropshire
TF9 1LL
Contact: B C Lowry
Email: bclowryfsg@aol.com
An international group aiming to advance the education of the public in all aspects of fortifications and their armaments, especially works constructed to mount and resist artillery. Founded in 1975, we have 700+ members.

42ND ROYAL HIGHLAND REGIMENT OF FOOTE–THE WATCH
26 Brighton Road, Horley, Surrey RH6 7HD
Contact: Keith Jepson
Tel: 0797 971 8367
A military and civilian re-enactment group covering mid to late 18th century life in Europe and North America. We cover the War of the Austrian Succession, the French and Indian Wars and the American Revolution.

FRIENDS OF WAR MEMORIALS
4 Lower Belgrave Street, London SW1W 0LA
Tel: 020 7259 0403
Fax: 020 7259 0296
Email: fowm@eidosnet.co.uk
Website: www.war-memorials.com
To maintain and explain. Newsletter published quarterly.

THE FRONTLINE ASSOCIATION
3 Plym Grove, Longhill, Hull, E. Yorkshire HU8
Contact: Andy Marsh
Tel: 01482 811569
A growing re-enactment/living history society in the North re-enacting 1914 to 1945–German, Russian, British–military and civilian. Can convert uniforms and provide tailoring/helmet conversion as well as static displays and pyro-filled battles and most things in between. Looking for recruits–especially British infantry.

THE GENERALL'S MUSICK AND PLAYERS
150 St Pancras, Chichester, W. Sussex PO19 7SH
Contact: Alison Wiley
Tel: 01858 565537
Fax: 01858 565392
Email: alisowiley@compuserve.com
The group encompasses the years 1590-1660, the period of Netherland Independence, Huguenot-Catholic, Thirty Years War and English Civil War, reflecting the period's musical experience. Using early violins, 'cello, lute, harpsichord, recorders, shawms, crumhorns, racket and sordunes, the group perform the songs, dances and instrumental music of the european capitals.

GUERNSEY ARMOURIES
Sans Souci, Le Villoccq, Castel, Guernsey, CY5 7SA
Fax: 01481 46325
Collectors and restorers of historic arms, vehicles and fortifications on the Island.

THE HAWKER HURRICANE SOCIETY
Hurri.proto@virgin.co

THE HERALDRY SOCIETY
PO Box 32, Maidenhead, Berkshire SL6 3FD
Contact: Marion Miles
Tel/Fax: 0118 932 0210
Email: heraldry-society@ewcom.net
The Heraldry Society extends interest and knowledge in heraldry, armour, chivalry, genealogy, and allied subjects. It is a non-profit making registered charity. New members welcome.

HOLTS, TOURS (BATTLEFIELDS & HISTORY)
15 Market Street, Sandwich, Kent CT13 9DA
Contact: John Hughes-Wilson
Tel: 01304 612248
Fax: 01304 614930
Website: www.battletours.co.uk
Europe's leading military historical tour operator, offering annual worldwide programme spanning history from the Romans to the Falklands War. Holts' provides tours for both the Royal Armruries Leeds and the IWM. Every tour accompanied by specialist guide-lecturer. Send for free brochure.

INDIAN MILITARY HISTORICAL SOCIETY
37 Wolsey Close, Southall, Middlesex LTB2 4NQ
Contact: Lt Cdr Maitland Thornton
Tel/Fax: 020 8574 4425
Formed in 1983 to study the military history of the Indian sub-continent. Subjects include medals, uniforms, insignia of all forces including police. Four journals are published annually.

KENTWELL HALL
Kentwell Hall, Long Melford, Sudbury, Suffolk CO10 9BA
Contact: Alex Scott
Tel: 01787 310207
Fax: 01787 379318
Email: info@kentwel.co.uk
Website: www.kentwell.co.uk
Mellow redbrick Tudor manor famed for award-winning recreations. Volunteer groups and individuals always welcome to apply to take part in WWII and Home Front events. Must have own uniform/costume and be prepared to assume 'first person' role and authenticity. Phone (in office hours) for form. Public and groups welcome to visit.

*KURATORIUM ZUR HIST. WAFFENSAMMLUNGEN
Staudenweg 28, 44265 Dortmund, Germany

LAWRENCE WOODCOCK MILITARY RESEARCH
30 Sheen Gate Gardens, London SW14 7NY
Tel: 020 8878 9828
Email: lawrence.woodcock@btinternet.com
Were your ancestors in the British Army, Navy or Air Force? Personnel and operational research undertaken.

LEGIO IX HISPANA
87 Langland Drive, Burton, Stoke-on-Trent, Staffs ST3 2ET
Contact: Mark Shore
Website: megamoose@cwctv.net
Academic research into the history of the 9th Legion Hispana.

LEGIO SECUNDA AUGUSTA
61 Totland Road, Cosham, Hants PO6 3HS
Contact: David Richardson
Tel/Fax: 02392 369970
Email: legiiaug@cwcom.net
Website: www.legiiaug.org.uk
Roman living history society, depicting the life and times of mid 1st and 2nd Century Roman Britain. Military and civilian aspects covered. We now present gladiators—as they should be shown!

LONGSHIP TRADING COMPANY
342 Albion Street, Wall Heath, Kingswinford, W. Midlands DY6 0JR
Contact: Ivor Wilcox
Tel: 01384 292237
Email: info@longship.org.uk
Website: www.longship.org.uk
Viking & Saxon education days in schools and museums, corporate entertainment, displays, banquets, craft displays, costume hire, film, TV and theatre work. Prop weapon and armour hire.

MACDONALD ACADEMY OF ARTS
15 Halmyre Street, Edinburgh, Scotland EH6 8QA
Contact: Paul Macdonald
Tel: 0131 538 0745
Email: macdonaldacademy@aol.com
The Macdonald academy of arts is a historical fencing academy offering professional tuition in historical swordsmanship and European martial arts from 13th to 19th centuries, presently offering open classes twice weekly. The academy also offers weapons workshops, bespoke private tuition and informative talks and demonstrations on the history of European swordsmanship.

THE MAPLE LEAF LEGACY
c/o 22 Southdown Road, Tadley, Hampshire RG26 4BT
Contact: Steve Douglas
Tel/Fax: 0118 957 6452
Email: sdouglas2001@hotmail.com
Website: www.mllp.demon.co.uk
A Millennium project in remembrance of Canada's War Dead.

MEDIEVAL COMBAT SOCIETY
Flat 2, 93 Surbiton Road, Kingston, Surrey KTI 2HW
Contact: David Debono
Tel/Fax: 020 8974 8101
Email: david@nouarltd.demon.co.uk
We are a society made up from all ages and walks of life and recreate the period of Edward III, one of England's greatest kings.

MEDIEVAL SUPPLIES
20 Weaver Drive, Western Downs, Stafford, Staffs ST17 9DD
Contact: Neil Butler
Tel/Fax: 01785 243637
Email: butlerneil@aol.com
Hand made padded jacks, gambasons, akatons, coates of plates, and brigandines for full contact fighting, from the 5th to the 15th century. We also make clothing for the same period.

MERCIA MILITARY SOCIETY
17 Barne Close, Nuneaton, Warwickshire CV11 4TP
Contact: Joe Lawley
Meets at 7.30pm on the second Monday in every month, at Nuneaton Chilvers Coton Liberal Club, for lectures/discussions on military subjects. Membership @5.00 p.a.

MILITARY HERALDRY SOCIETY
37 Wolsey Close, Southall, Middlesex UB2 4NQ
Contact: Lt Cdr Maitland Thornton
Tel/Fax: 020 8574 4425
The society specialises in researching and exchanging
cloth military insignia worldwide. These include formation
signs, shoulder titles and other cloth items. Four journals
published annually.

MILITARY HISTORICAL SOCIETY
National Army Museum, Royal Hospital Road, London
Contact: Philip Jobson
Email: pjjobson@hotmail.com
A society for all interested in the Armed Forces of the
Crown.

MINISTRY OF DEFENCE
Ministry of Defence, Horse Guards Avenue, London
SW1A 2HB
MOD Public Enquiry Office Tel: 0870 607 4455
Press Office Tel: 0870 607 4455
Email: webmaster@dgics.mod.uk
If you wish to make a general telephone enquiry to the
MOD, please contact the MOD Public Enquiry Office. This
service is available from Monday-Friday, 9am-5pm.
Defence journals, Service records, veterans advice, surplus
military equipment, links, archives, history and museum
listings.

THE NAME SHOP
Unit 28, Parade Shops, St Mary's Place, Shrewsbury,
Shropshire SY1 1DL
Tel: 01743 270220
Fax: 01952 410689
Email: gary.huston@cableinet.co.uk
Website: www.family-name.co.uk/history
Free name search.

NAPOLEONIC SOCIETY
157 Vicarage Road, Leyton, London E10 5DU
Contact: Ronald King
Tel/Fax: 020 8539 3870
Historical Society—not modelling or re-enactment.

NAVAL HISTORICAL COLLECTORS & RESEARCH ASSOCIATION,
81 Mountbatten Avenue, Sandal, Wakefield, W. Yorkshire
WF2 6HE
Contact: Richard Taylor
Tel: 01924 256644
Email: richard.j.taylor@talk21.com

1940 ASSOCIATION
43 The Drive, Ilford, Essex IG1 3HB
Contact: Michael Conway
Tel: 020 8554 8169
The Association brings together all those interested in
Britain's Home Front 1939-45. Membership includes
individuals, museums, libraries, specialist groups, etc.
Magazine.

95TH RIFLES LIVING HISTORY GROUP
10 Park Hill, Awsworth, Nottingham, Nottinghamshire
NG16 2RD
Contact: William Whitlam
Educational displays of weapons, equipment and tactics of
riflemen employed by His Majesty King George III. Private
lectures/publicity venues by appointment. Beware of
imitations.

THE NORMANDY ARNHEM SOCIETY
22 Cousin Lane, Illingworth, Halifax, W. Yorkshire HX2 8AF
Contact: David P Mitchell
Tel/Fax: 01422 250891
The Normandy Arnhem Society is a living, breathing muse-
um of remembrance dedicated to keeping history alive by
recreating, as accurately as possible, the life and times of
German and British soldiers during the latter half of WWII.
Comprises 9./SS-Pz Gr.Rgt.20 and 9 Field Company RE.
Specialises in 'living history' displays for museums.

NORTH EASTERN MILITARIA SOCIETY
2 Meadowgate, Eston under Nab, Middlesbrough, Cleveland
TS6 9JD
Contact: Amanda Luker
Tel/Fax: 01642 454609
Meetings first Thursday each month at Eaglescliffe Hotel,
Stockton. Varied interests—raffles—quarterly newsletter. New
members welcome.

ORDERS & MEDALS RESEARCH SOCIETY
123 Turnpike Link, Croydon, Surrey CR0 5NU
Contact: N G Gooding
Tel/Fax: 020 8680 2701
Website: www.omrs.org.uk
Researchers' and collectors' organisation. Quarterly journal,
annual convention.

THE ORDNANCE SOCIETY
3 Maskell Way, Farnborough, Hants GU14 0PU
Contact: Ian Mckenzie
Tel: 01252 521201
Website: www.freespace.virgin.net/ordnance.society/index.htm
An international society concerned with all aspects of the
history of ordnance and artillery. It publishes quarterly
newsletters containing shorter articles, notes, reviews,
inquiries etc. Also an annual journal of a much higher
standard with longer more scholarly papers. Several visits
are organised each year to various military establishments.

PA ENGLISCAN GESIPAS
Gerefa, 38 Cranworth Road, Worthing, W. Sussex BN11 2JF
Contact: Janet Goldsbrough-Jones
Tel: 01903 207485
Society for the study of Dark Ages' subjects.

THE RAVEN
35 Carnarvon Road, Leyton, London E10 6DW
Contact: Morgana
Tel/Fax: 020 8539 3569
Email: Caduceus@talk21.com
Historical re-enactment group. Medieval13th–15th century.
Full contact sword fighting. Approx 20 members.

REGIA ANGLORUM
9 Durleigh Close, Headley Park, Bristol BS13 7NQ
Contact: Jim K Skiddorn
Tel/Fax: 0117 964 6818
Email: 101364.35@compuserve.com
Website: http://www.ftech.net/-regia
An international society of over 500 people, dedicated to
the authentic recreation of the life of the folk who lived in
the Islands of Britain around the turn of the first millennium. Specialists in Viking, Saxon, Norman and Cwmru life
in forty different local UK groups research all aspects of
that far-off time. At public and private events and for film
and TV, they provide extensive living history, crafts and
battle re-enactment and replica equipment for museums
and others. Six period ship replicas are owned and
operated by the society, which also has specialist teams
performing school visits.

RICHARD III SOCIETY
4 Oakley Street, Chelsea, London SW3 5NN
Contact: E M Nokes
Website: http://www.r3.org
The society promotes research and interest in the field of
15th century history in general, and the life of King
Richard III in particular.

THE RINGWOODS OF HISTORY
34 Sandford Road, Mapperley, Nottingham NG3 6AL
Contact: Ralph Needham
Tel: 0115 9692922
Accurately costumed historical presentations from Viking to
WWII Home Guard. Specialist subject 17th century military
surgery. We provide lectures for schools, historic sites and
history groups anywhere in the UK. For further details
please contact us at the above.

ROMAN RESEARCH SOCIETY
8 Leechmere Way, Ryhope, Sunderland, Tyne & Wear
SR2 0DH
Contact: Eddie Barrass
Tel/Fax: 0191 523 6377

ROSA MUNDI
53 Dene Street, Silksworth, Sunderland, Tyne & Wear
SR3 1DA
Tel: 0191 522 0903
Email: scroopisec@hotmail.com
Rosa Mundi works to the highest standards of research
and practical skills to present all aspects of military and
domestic life of the late fifteenth century (1475–1500). Our
hierarchical military structure demonstrates the skills and
technologies of late Medieval warfare using authentic
period fighting techniques

ROYAL MARINES HISTORICAL SOCIETY
c/o RM Museum, Eastney, Southsea, Hants POH 9PX
Contact: Membership Secretary
Membership is open to anyone interested in the history of
the Royal Marines, on payment of an annual entrance fee
and annual subscription by standing order.

LA SABRETACHE
7 Rue Guersant, 75017 Paris, France
Tel/Fax: 01 45726410
Long-established society for specialists of military history,
uniforms and tin soldiers. Quarterly bulletin issued.
Membership carries free admission to Paris army and navy
museums.

SALISBURY MILITARIA SOCIETY
Red Lion Hotel, Milford Street, Salisbury, Wiltshire SP1 2AN
Contact: M Maidment
Tel: 01722 323334
Fax: 01722 325756
Email: reception@the-redlion.co.uk
Meets third Wednesday of each month at above address
for talks and discussion on all aspects of military history
and memorabilia.

SCOTTISH MILITARY HISTORICAL SOCIETY
4 Hillside Cottages, Glenboig, Lanarkshire ML5 2QY, Scotland
Contact: Tom Moles
Email: scottish.military@btinternet.com
The Society exists to encourage the study of Scottish
military history and publishes its own illustrated journal
covering the collecting of badges, headdress, uniforms,
medals, photographs, postcards, prints, watercolours,
equipment, pistols, powderhorns etc. The SMHS has a
worldwide membership.

SHRAPNEL'S BATTERY
9 Firgrove Hill, Farnham, Surrey GU9 8LH
Contact: Brian Miller
Tel: 01252 721332
1770s British Royal Artillery. Fully uniformed demonstrations of flintlock pistol, musket, mortar and field guns,
along with explanations of technical details and the
lifestyle of the men who served with the guns. Also tactics
used by infantry, cavalry and artillery explained—ammunition used—its range and effects. Demonstrations of casting,
linstock, quill making and flint knapping.

SOCIETY OF ARCHER-ANTIQUARIES
61 Lambert Road, Bridlington, E. Yorkshire YO16 5RD
Contact: Douglas Elmy

*SOCIÉTÉ DES AMIS DU MUSÉE DE L'ARMÉE
Musée de l'Armee, Hotel National des Invalides, 75007
Paris, France
Contact: Mlle Pierron

SOCIETY FOR ARMY HISTORICAL RESEARCH
c/o National Army Museum, Royal Hospital Road, London
SW3 4HT
Contact: Derek A Mumford
Tel/Fax: 020 7730 0717
Email: info@national-army-museum.ac.uk
The Society of Friends of the Nation Army Museum assists
the museum in the acquisition of significant militaria and
members enjoy lectures, private views, battlefield and Army
establishment excursions, and newsletters. Annual subscription £8.00; contact Secretary/Treasurer above.

SOKE MILITARY SOCIETY
45 Warwick Road, Walton, Peterborough, Cambridgeshire
PE4 6DE
Contact: Roger Negus
Varied membership of historians, collectors, modellers and
wargamers Monthly meeting every second Wednesday at
the Peterborough Museum, with guest speaker. A monthly
newsletter is also distributed. Subscription £3.00.

SOUTH & CENTRAL AMERICAN MILITARY SOCIETY
27 Hallgate, Cottingham, E. Yorkshire HU16 4DN
Contact: Terry D Hooker
Tel/Fax: 01482 84708
Website: http://www.magweb.com
Publishers of quarterly journal 'El Dorado' covering from
pre-Columbian times to present day; English and Spanish
text, with illustrations and book reviews, all areas of
military history.

SUBTERRANEA BRITANNICA
G5 Trindles Road, South Nuffield, Redhill, Surrey RH1 4JL
Contact: Malcolm H Tadd
Tel/Fax: 01737 823456
Website: http://www.stonix.demon.co.uk/sub-brit
Historic redundant underground defence structures
(especially Cold War) are frequently the subject of our
newsletters. Conferences and field studies. New members
welcome.

TRAILBLAZERS WESTERN RE-ENACTORS ASSOCIATION
38 Harewood Road, Harrogate, N. Yorkshire
HG3 2TW
Contact: Tony Rollins
Tel: 01423 502442
Website: www.4thcavalry.co.uk
We are a Western re-enactment and living history
association who enjoy researching and recreating all
aspects of 19th Century American life. Based in Yorkshire
we can often be seen at the Yorkshire Farming Museum,
York, as 4th Cavalry. Available for shows as a means of
raising funds for charity.

THE TREBUCHET SOCIETY
23 Viewside Close, Corfe Mullen, Dorset BH21 3ST
Contact: R Barton
Tel/Fax: 01202 090224
Email: richardbarton@msn.com
Research into the trebuchet and other siege weaponry.
Design, construction and experimentation with working
reproduction weapons, using authentic materials, and in
further modern technological evolution.

23rd FOOT, ROYAL WELCH FUSILIERS RE-ENACTMENT SOCIETY
c/o 15 Llancaiach View, Nelson, Treharris CF46 6EW
Contact: Colin Rogers
Tel: 01443 451 754
Email: colrogers@lineone.net
Website: www.kingsgrenadiers.co.uk
The Kings Grenadiers (23rd Foot) RWF re-enact the
Regiment's history during the Peninsular War against
Napoleon from 1809–1814., and the Waterloo Campaign of
1815. Members reside anywhere in the UK and families are
most welcome as part of our large living history campsite.
The Unit has appeared on television and videos, including
the BBC's Vanity Fair and the Cromwell video series.

33rd WEST YORKSHIRE REGIMENT OF FOOT
42 Woodside Road, Halifax, W. Yorkshire HX3 6EL
Contact: J Eeles
Email: tapper@tiscali.co.uk
The 33rd Foot are a re-enactment/living history group of
British Redcoats and their families circa1812–1816. We
portray a battalion company of a line regiment, the empha-
sis being on the life of a private soldier. Based in
Yorkshire, we attend events across the UK and in Europe.

VICTORIAN MEDICAL SOCIETY
17 Park Road, Southville Road, Bristol BS3 1PU
Contact: Chris Jordan
Tel: 0117 953 8710
Vicmed@hotmail.com
We are a small group of enthusiasts who portray in
costume (English Navy and Confederate), a small Victorian
field hospital. Most of our medical and pharmaceutical
equipment is original from the period. We give talks to the
public on conditions of the period and the use of the
equipment.

VICTORIAN MILITARY SOCIETY
3 Franks Road, Guildford, Surrey GU2 6NT
Contact: Ralph Moore-Morris
Tel/Fax: 01483 560931
Email: rmoore-morris@hotmail.com
The society encourages original research of the Victorian
era, has specialists study groups, journals, newsletters,
annual fair and comprehensive expert advice to help
members.

VICTORIAN NAVAL BRIGADE
7 Markstakes Corner, South Chaley, E. Sussex BN8 4BP
Contact: Commander K Fry
Tel: 07773 886957
Victorian Naval Brigade reflects all aspects of its original in
a living history format. Library research, navigation and
seamanship, black powder cannon and weapons. Family
section will be formed in support crews for original vessels
of the period.

VIETNAM
Dresdener Strasse 46, 91058 Erlangen, Germany
Contact: Arne Beerhold
Tel: 0913114847
Email: t.froemel@gmx.de

THE VIKINGS (N F P S) (ADMIN BODY)
2 Stanford Road, Shefford, Bedfordshire SG17 5DS
Contact: Sandra Orchard
Tel/Fax: 01462 812208
Email: SANDRA.ORCHARD@roche.com
As the original re-enactment society, the Vikings–Norse Film and Pageant Society–captures the atmosphere of the Dark Ages with a unique blend of authenticity and humour. Our Vikings, Celts, Saxons and Normans encapsulate the whole flavour of Medieval life, from the simple craftsman to the professional warrior. We have performed at home and abroad, and with equal ease for film crews and schoolchildren. Contact your local Hird now.

WATERLOO STUDY GROUP
Scharnhorststrasse 4, Kiel D-24105, Germany
Contact: Mathias Wiegert MA
Tel/Fax: 431335535
Email: roewie@t-online.de
Enthusiasts of Napoleonic military history, promotes interest in the Waterloo Campaign of 1815. WSG comprises both researchers and modellers, publications projected. English spoken, enquiries welcome.

WESTERN FRONT ASSOCIATION (1914–1918)
PO Box 1914, Reading, Berkshire RG4 7YP
Contact: Paul Hanson
Tel: 01203 415161
Fax: 01203 415201
Email: Hanso2@aol.com
Formed to perpetuate the memory of the courage and comradeship of all who served in France and Flanders. Open to members of all ages and both sexes.

WELSH MARITIME ASSOCIATION
257 Clydach Road, Morriston, Swansea, W. Glamorgan Wales SA6 6QJ
Contact: Robert Morgan
Tel/Fax: 01792 797185
Formed in 1982 to promote and encourage all aspects of maritime research and hobbies in Wales. Corresponding members throughout Europe and the world.

WW II RAILWAY STUDY GROUP
17 Balmoral Crescent, West Molesey, Surrey KT8 1QA
Contact: Greg Martin
Group for promotion and research into all aspects of railways during the war. A bimonthly bulletin is published. Send SAE for details.

ILLUSTRATORS, ARTISTS & DISPLAY FIGURES

ADMIRALTY HOUSE PUBLICATIONS
PO Box 6253, Los Osos, California 93412, USA
Contact: Beth Queman
Tel: 805 534 9723
Fax: 805 534 9127
Email: lbjgreene@thegrid.net
Computer-generated maps and artwork for both books and games. All military topics.

C & C MILITARY FINE ART
Prince St Station, PO Box 441, New York, NY 10012, USA
Contact: Mark Churms
Tel: 212 229 0159
Fax: 212 229 1480
Website: www.markchurmsmilitaryart.com
Military and equestrian art, original oil paintings by Mark Churms (commissions and image licences available). Full range of Cranston Fine Arts prints. Visa/Mastercard accepted.

ROB CHAPMAN
10 Westbourne Road, Walsall, W. Midlands WS4 2JA
Contact: Rob Chapman
Tel/Fax: 01922 644078
Specialising in campaign dress and action 18th–20th centuries; postcards, prints and original artwork. Represented in private museum and regimental collections.

CHRISTOPHER COLLINGWOOD
1 Barton Cottages, Monkleigh, Bideford, Devon EX39 5JX
Tel/Fax: 01805 623023
England's foremost military artist–work includes ECW, American Civil War, Roman and Norman, Medieval, Jacobite, Napoleonic, World War I and II. Private commissions undertaken.

CLIVE FARMER
6 Churchway, Faulkland, Bath, Somerset BA3 5US
Tel/Fax: 01373 834752
Accurately researched artwork in most media, for publication or fine art collectors. Specialising in 19th century. Regimental and private commissions undertaken.

DAVID CARTWRIGHT
Studio Cae Coch Bach, Rhosgoch, Anglesey, Gwynedd, Wales LL66 0AE
Contact: David Cartwright
Tel: 01407 710801
Military artist specialising in Napoleonic and Crimean scenes on canvas. Commissions undertaken. Contact for further details of original as limited prints.

DAVID ROWLANDS
6 Saville Place, Clifton, Bristol, Avon BS8 4EJ
Contact: David Rowlands
Tel/Fax: 0117 9731722
Email: djrowlands@supanet.com
Military artist. Military prints. War artist in the Gulf War and Bosnia. Many paintings commissioned by the Army. Historical and modern subjects.

DOUGLAS N ANDERSON
37 Hyndland Road, Glasgow, Strathclyde G12 9LTY, Scotland
Contact: Douglas N Anderson
Tel: 0141 339 8381
Professional artist specialising in military and historic costume, male and female, particularly of Scotland, Wide knowledge of Scottish/Highland regiments and Highland dress ancient and modern.

GALLERY MILITAIRE
1 Hoistock Road, Ilford, Essex IG1 1LG
Contact: Rodney Gander
Fine and investment art dealers and publishers, supplying original paintings, limited edition prints, reproductions, plates and postcards. All types of framing and art commissions undertaken. European dealers and distributors for major military artists. Gallery viewing by appointment. Mail order. Large A4 illustrated catalogue £3.00 UK, £4.00 Europe, $10.00 USA Airmail.

GEOFF SUMPTER
Barton End House, Bath Road, Nailsworth, Glos GL6 0QQ
Contact: Geoff Sumpter
Email: sumptergr@hotmail.com
Website: www.geoffsumpter.tripod.com

*HEINZ RODE
Karl-Marx-Allee 141, 10243 Berlin, Germany

IAN WHITE MODELS
238 Taunton Avenue, Whitleigh, Plymouth, Devon PL5 4EW
Contact: Ian White
Tel: 01752 768507
Completely new figures. Large scale (1:5.5) historical and modern military uniform figurines. Available complete or as kits. Resin and white metal. Easy assembly. Larger commissions accepted.

JOHN WYNNE HOPKINS
Dept. MD, Gatooma, 58 Queen Victoria Road, Llanelli, Carms SA15 2TH, Wales
Contact: John Wynne Hopkins
Tel/Fax: 01554 750761
Artist specialising in 20th century military and aviation paintings in oils. Regularly commissioned by British Army. Rhodesian Fireforce and Army Air Corps limited edition prints available. Commissions accepted. Presently researching Dark Ages and Medieval periods and Battle of Bosworth for a series of Welsh history paintings. SAE for free details.

*MILITARY HISTORY WORKSHOP INTERNATIONAL
cp 231, 36078, Valdagno, VI, Italy
Contact: Alessandro Massigani.

MORRISON FREDERICK (TABLEAUX)
Studio 5D, 1 Fawe Street, London E14 6PD
Contact: Jasper Lyon
Tel/Fax: 020 7515 4110

OSSIE JONES TECHNICAL ORIGINATION
135 Ashbourne Road, Liverpool, Merseyside L17 9QQ
Tel: 0151 727 3661
Superb maritime, aviation and military transport drawings and paintings to commission from this up-and-coming artist. Research undertaken. Contact for details and samples.

OIL PAINTINGS TO ORDER/TANKS FOR SALE
26 Peartree Road, Croston, Preston, Lancashire PR5 7HX
Contact: Duncan Nicholson
Tel/Fax: 01772 601214
Email: duncan@tanksforsale.co.uk
Website: www.tanksforsale.co.uk
Your cherished vehicle painted. See website from examples.

PAN EUROPEAN ART
Lansbury Business Estate, Lower Guildford Road, Knaphill, Woking, Surrey GU21 2EP
Contact: Clive Jackson
Tel: 01483 799550
Fax: 01483 799660
Producers of fine art oil paintings, primarily from customers' photographs/artwork. Specialists in the area of uniformed personnel, often with spouse and modes of transportation that represent their profession. Company also paint special limited editions in oils or watercolour of specific events in military, regimental or public service history. Commission a fine work of art at affordable prices.

PATRICE COURCELLE
38 Avenue Des Vallons, B-1410 Waterloo B-1410, Belgium
Contact: Patrice Courcelle
Tel/Fax: 322 354 3607
Email: courcelle@linkline.be
Illustrator and painter. Main periods: American Revolution, French Revolution & Napoleonic wars. Publisher of the plate series 'Ceux Qui Bravaient l'Aigle' and of the 'Waterloo' prints.

PIERRE CONRAD
Residence Mozart, 691 Avenue de la Liberation', 77350 La Mee sur Seine, France

RAY KIRKPATRICK
57 Hookfield, Epsom, Surrey KT19 8JQ
Tel: 01372 727513
Email: rkirkpatriack@talk21.com
Website: www.arms-and-armour.co.uk
Military illustration.

ROB CHAPMAN
10 Westbourne Road, Walsall, S Midlands WS4 2JA
Contact: Rob Chapman
Tel: 01922 644078
Fax: 01922 629145
Email: robpics@aol.com
Specialising in campaign dress and action 18th–21st centuries. Postcards, prints and original artwork. Represented in private museum and regimental collections. Collaborations welcomed.

*TIME MACHINE GA
La Chaine 15, 2515 Preles, Switzerland
Contact: Gerry Embleton
Tel: 32 315 2393
Fax: 32 315 1793
Realistic, accurately costumed life-size mannequins for museum and other exhibition settings. Specialist in military and other historical costumes, arms and armour; research for TV and film productions, etc., to the most exacting standards. See our work in the National Army Museum, London (Napoleonic and 19th century galleries).

LIBRARIES & RESEARCH SERVICES

ALEX & MEGAN ROBERTSON
12 Bude Close, Crewe, Cheshire CW1 3XG
Tel: 01270 504992 or 504994
Email: arobertson@cix.compulink.co.uk
Uniforms and medals research service.

*ANDREW MOLLO
10 rue Jeanjuares, 03320 Lurcy-Levis, France
Military consultant to film and TV production companies; author and collector, specialising in German and Russian subjects; publisher of historical Research Unit books.

ARMY MUSEUMS OGILBY TRUST
58 The Close, Salisbury, Wiltshire SP1 2EX
Contact: Antony Makepeace-Warne
Tel: 01722 332188
Fax: 01722 334211
Registered charity (No. 250907) supporting all Regimental and Corps Museums of the British Army; focus on research and education; publishers of military reference works.

ARTEMIS ARCHERY
29 Bately Court, Oldland, S. Glos BS30 8Y2
Contact: Veronica Soar
Tel/Fax: 0117 932 3276
Email: vee_artemis@yahoo.co.uk
Longbow/archery specific: books by post; historical research, lectures, consultancy, coaching. Also longbow presentations, static exhibitions and longbow and arrow manufacture. SAE for booklist or other details. Archery collection viewing strictly by appointment only.

AWICS
New House, Murton, Appleby in Westmoreland, Cumbria CA16 6ND
Contact: Adrian Waite
Tel: 017683 52165
Email: awaite@ukonline.co.uk
Website: www.awics.co.uk
Working in schools and museums. Presenting and planning events, presentations, demonstrations and lectures. Publications and historical research. Supply of reproduction costume, weapons, tents and artifacts.

B D I C–MUSÉE D'HISTOIRE
Hotel National des Invalides, 75007 Paris, France
Tel: 144425491
Fax: 144189384
Email: mhc_bdic@club_internet.fr.
Important documentary, art and photo archives both World Wars; limited space so partial displays only, though occasional special exhibitions. Closed Sun, Mon, and August.

B K WEED MILITARIA AND HISTORICAL FLAG RESEARCH
Email: b.k.weed@worldnet.att.net

BRITANNIA ROYAL NAVAL COLLEGE
Dartmouth, Devon TQ6 0HJ
Contact: R J Kennell
Tel: 01803 832141
Fax: 01803 837015

BRITISH FEDERATION FOR HISTORICAL SWORDPLAY
15 Halmyre Street, Edinburgh, Scotland EH6 8QA
Contact: Paul Macdonald
Tel: 0131 538 0745
Email: macdonaldacademy@aol.com
Website: www.bfhs.co.uk
The British Federation for historical swordplay is a national umbrella organisation for UK societies practicing historical fencing workshops as well as offering an extensive library of facsimile historical treatises.

CANTIACI
24 Johnson Avenue, Gillingham, Kent ME7 1FD
Contact: Christine Toomey
Tel: 01634 58170
Email: cantiaci.livinghistory@virgin.net
Cantiaci Iron Age living history group offer a range of fully researched craft displays that we can tailor to the requirements of the client. We have extensive experience of reconstruction acting, for film and television, research and consultation services, school visits and festival organisation. Versatile, professional and archeologically correct.

HELION & COMPANY
26 Willow Road, Solihull, W. Midlands B91IUE
Contact: Duncan Rogers
Tel: 0121 705 3393
Fax: 0121 711 1315
Expert bibliographic research for all periods of military history.

INTERNATIONAL INSTITUTE FOR STRATEGIC STUDIES
23 Tavistock Street, London WC2E 7NQ
Contact: Hilary Oakley
Tel: 020 7379 7676
Fax: 020 7836 3108
Email: oakley@iiss.org.uk
Open 10am–5pm Mon to Thurs; 10am–12pm Fri; no appointment necessary; entry fee £2.00 per day (students), £5.00 per day all other categories. Subject coverage: security arms control, international relation Services: research facilities incl. 6,000 books, 12,000 pamphlets, press library, CD-Roms and on-line services. Enquiries by phone or let please.

[handwritten: conyers-silverthorn e iiss.org. Tanya]

THE IRISH HISTORY COMPANY
Northside Resource Centre, Forthill, Sligo, Ireland
Contact: Kay Erb
Tel: 353 7147616
Email: info@irishhistoryco.com
Website: www.irishhistoryco.com
Providers of quality historical garments at reasonable prices.18th and 19th centuries are a specialty as are 17th century Irish garments. Research services are also offered.

MACDONALD ACADEMY OF ARTS
15 Halmyre Street, Edinburgh, Scotland EH6 8QA
Contact: Paul Macdonald
Tel: 0131 538 0745
Email: macdonaldacademy@aol.com
The Macdonald academy of arts is a historical fencing academy offering professional tuition in historical swordsmanship and European martial arts from the 13th to 19th centuries, presently offering open classes twice weekly. The academy also offers weapons workshops, bespoke private tuition and informative talks and demonstrations on the history of European swordsmanship.

MAJOR BOOK PUBLICATIONS
Hougoumont, Maxworthy, Launceston, Cornwall PL15 8LZ
Contact: H W or C P Adams
Tel/Fax: 01566 781422
Napoleonic research. Essential, statistically based data sheet system for British regiments. First dossier 'Waterloo Campaign and Army of Occupation 1814 to 1820'. SAE for details.

MUSEE DE L'ARMÉE
Hotel National des Invalides, 75 Paris, France
Tel/Fax: 145559230
The French national museum of military history; not to be missed by any Paris visitor.

NATIONAL ARMY MUSEUM READING ROOM
Royal Hospital Road, Chelsea, London SW3 4HT
Contact: Michael Ball
Tel: 020 7730 0717
Fax: 020 7823 6573
Email: nam@enterprise.net
Website: www.failte.com/nam/
About 40,000 books; over 200 current historical and regimental journals; archives; prints and drawings; photographs. Normally open Tues-Sat, 10am–4.30pm, to holders of readers' tickets, for which application must be made in advance on forms available from the Museum's Department of Printed Books.

NATIONAL MARITIME MUSEUM
Park Row, Greenwich, London SE10 9NF
Tel/Fax: 020 8858 4422
Email: Amcloud@nmm.ac.uk
Britain's national museum of naval and maritime history, set in magnificent surroundings by the Thames at Greenwich. Historic exhibits, models, art collection, documentary and pictorial archives. Open September to April, Mon-Sat 10am–5pm, Sun 12am–5pm; May-October, closes 6pm.

THE NEW POSTMASTER
Bwlch House, Beguildy, Radnorshire LD7 1U9
Contact: B Carter
Tel: 01547 510 289
Original 19th century newspapers, containing despatches and reports from the Napoleonic Wars, the Crimea, American Civil War, European and Colonial conflicts, the Anglo-Boer War, etc. Also available: Titles for WWI and II.

PRINCE CONSORT'S LIBRARY
Knolly's Road, Aldershot, Hampshire GU11 1PS
Tel/Fax: 01252 349381
Email: pcl@dera.gov.uk

PUBLIC RECORD OFFICE
Ruskin Avenue, Kew, Richmond, Surrey IW9 4DU
Contact: The Keeper
Tel: 020 8876 3444
Fax: 020 8878 8905
Website: http://www.pro.gov.uk
The national archive; contains records of the British Army and its personnel from 1660, naval, air archives, etc. Open Mon-Sat, 9.30am-5pm, admission free.

RAY WESTLAKE MILITARY BOOKS
53 Claremont, Malpas, Newport, Gwent NP9 6PL, Wales
Tel: 01633 854135
Fax: 01633 821860
The Ray Westlake Unit Archives hold files dealing with the histories, uniforms, badges and Organisation of some 6,000 units of the British Army.

ROYAL AIR FORCE MUSEUM
Grahame Park Way, Hendon, London NW9 5LL
Tel: 020 8205 2266
Fax: 020 8200 1751
Email: henry.hall@rafmuseum.org.uk
Website: www.rafmuseum.org.uk
Britain's National Museum of Aviation, displays 70 full size
aircraft. Open daily. Extensive library research facilities
(weekdays only). Large free car park. Licensed restaurant.
Souvenir shop with extensive range of specialist books and
model kits.

ROYAL COLLEGE OF DEFENCE STUDIES
Seaford House, 37 Belgrave Square, London SW1X 8NS
Contact: Cdr T Binney
Tel/Fax: 020 7915 4800
Email: Webmaster@rcdsone.demon.co.uk

ROYAL ENGINEERS LIBRARY
Brompton Barracks, Chatham, Kent ME44UG
Contact: Maggie Magnuson
Tel: 01634 822416
Fax: 01634 822419
Founded in 1813, this remarkable archive contains printed
books, manuscripts, maps, plans and photographs. A
unique source for scholars and family history. Open by
appointment.

ROYAL MARINES MUSEUM
Southsea, Portsmouth, Hampshire PO4 9PX
Contact: Jorj Jarvrie
Tel: 01705 819385
Fax: 01705 838420
Email: info@royalmarinesmuseum.co.uk
The history of the Royal Marines from 1664 to the present.
Open seven days a week. Library and archives by
arrangement.

ROYAL MILITARY ACADEMY SANDHURST
Central Library, Camberley, Surrey GU15 4PQ
Tel/Fax: 01276 63344 x2041
Email: Ac.HQRMAS@dial.pipex.com

SUNSET MILITARIA
Dinedor Cross, Herefordshire HR2 6PF
Contact: David Seeney
Tel/Fax: 01432 870420
Email: sunsetmilitaria@btinternet.com
Military research. Medal card and computer check
1914–1922 for £4.00 + SAE when number, regiment
known, £6.00 + SAE when details vague. For details of
this and other research, all periods, send SAE.

SUSSEX HISTORICAL NAVAL UNIT
Redoubt Fortress, Royal Parade, Eastbourne, E. Sussex
BN22 7AQ
Tel: 01323 410300
Email: redoubt@breathmail.net
The history of the Royal Navy in Sussex. Our section is
part of the military living history at the fortress. We also
research all maritime subjects that relate to Sussex.

TIME MACHINE GA
La Chaine 15, 2515 Preles, Switzerland
Contact: Gerry Embleton
Tel: 32 315 2393
Fax: 32 315 1793
Realistic, accurately costumed life-size mannequins for
museum and other exhibition settings. Specialist in military
and other historical costumes, arms and armour research
for TV and film productions, etc., to the most exacting
standards. See our work in the National Army Museum,
London (Napoleonic and 19th century galleries).

TOMAHAWK FILMS WWII GERMAN ARCHIVE
PO Box 279 Winchester Hampshire SO21 1XT
Contact: Brian Matthews or Stan Googe
Tel: 01962 714989
Fax: 01962 713966
Email: Brian.tomahawk@btinternet.com
Website: www.tomahawkfilms.com
The Tomahawk Films Archive is the world's leading
producer of original pre-1945 German military marching
music on CD/Cassette to historians, collectors, enthusiasts,
schools & colleges via our mail-order division. We also
supply, original German combat film, sound effects and
documentary voice-overs to film & television production
companies.

T R MILITARY SEARCH
65A Wix's Lane, London SW4 0AH
Contact: Talbot Rich
Tel: 020 7228 5129
Expert research into the military records of the British, the
EIC's and the Indian armies held by the Public Record
Office, the Oriental and India Office Library, the Liddell Hart
Library and the National Army Museum.

UNIFORMS & MEDALS RESEARCH SERVICE
Phoenix Enterprises (Crewe), 12 Bude Close, Crewe,
Cheshire CWI 3XG
Contact: Megan Robertson
Tel/Fax: 0127 504994
Email: mcrobertson@phoenix.co.uk
Research into military and other uniforms, medals, insignia,
ceremonial &c. of all nations, all periods, for modellers,
re-enactors, historians, film makers, museums. SAE for
individual quote.

VITAE LAMPADAE
25 Rowan Close, Scarborough, N. Yorkshire YO12 6NH
Contact: G Hughes
Tel: 01723 367746
Fax: 01743 342111
Historical education services to schools, libraries and
museums, with full coverage of the national curriculum.
Costumed interpreters, artefacts, work sheets. SAE for
further details.

WARSHIP PRESERVATION TRUST
HMS Plymouth, Dock Road, Birkenhead, Merseyside
PI41 1DJ
Tel: 0151 650 1573
Fax: 0151 650 1473
Email: manager@warships.freeserve.co.uk
Historic warships at Birkenhead Falklands War veterans, the form Royal Navy frigate 'Plymouth' and submarine 'Onyx' are open to the public daily from 10am. New German U-Boat U-534 now open.

WATERLOO STUDY GROUP
Scharnhorststrasse 4, Kiel D-24105, Germany
Contact: Mathias Wiegert MA
Tel/Fax: 0049 431 335535
Email: roewie@t-online.de
Enthusiasts of Napoleonic military history, promotes interest in the Waterloo Campaign of 1815. WS comprises both researchers and modellers, publications projected English spoken, enquiries welcome.

MAGAZINES

*A B M MAGAZINE
96 Rue de Paris, 92100 Boulogne, France
Contact: Nicolas Draeger

AAC JOURNAL
RHQ AAC Middle Wallop, Stockbridge, Hants SO20 8DY
Contact: Col (Retd) G R Mallock AFC
Tel: 94329 4384
Fax: 94329 4146
Email: editoraac@gtnet.gov

AFF FAMILIES JOURNAL
Trenchard Lines, Upavon, Pewsey, Wilts SN9 6BE
Contact: Sue Bonney
Tel: 01980 615517
Fax: 01980 615526
Email: editor.afj@care4free.net

AGC JOURNAL
RHQ AGC, Gould House, Worthy Down, Winchester, Hants SO21 2RG
Contact: Lt Col (Retd) G B Meekin
Tel: 94271 2435
Fax: 942712590
Email: agc.regtsec@virgin.net

AIR INTERNATIONAL
PO Box 100, Stamford, Lincolnshire PE9 1XQ
Contact: Malcolm English
Tel: 01780 755131
Fax: 01780 757261
Email: english@keymags.demon.co

AIRCRAFT ILLUSTRATED
Riverdene Business Park, Molesey Road, Horsham, Surrey KT12 4RG
Contact: Ian Allan
Tel: 01932 266600
Fax: 01932 266601
Email: info@ianallanpub.co.uk

ARMOURER MAGAZINE
1st Floor Adelphi Mill, Bollington, Cheshire SK10 5JB
Contact: Irene Moore
Tel/Fax: 01625 575700
Email: editor@armourer.co.uk
Website: www.armourer.co.uk
The Armourer Magazine for militaria collectors and military enthusiasts is published bi-monthly and available on subscription and through selected newsagents. All aspects of military antique collecting are covered and there is a UK militaria fair/event diary as well as hundreds of contacts for buying and selling.

ARMÉES D'AUJOURD'HUI
6 Rue St Charles, 75015 Paris, France
Contact: Bruno Nielly

ARMES MILITARIA MAGAZINE/STEEL MASTERS
Histoire & Collections, 5 Avenue de la République, 75541 Paris cedex 11
Tel: 01 40 21 18 20
Fax: 01 47 00 51 11
Email: militaria@histecoll.com and abonnements@histecoll.com
Website: www.militariamag.com
French militaria magazine.

ARMY CADET
E Block, Duke of York's HQ, Chelsea, London SW3 4RR
Contact: Kevin Traverse-Healy
Tel: 020 7730 9733 or 9734
Email: editor@armycadets.co

ARMY QUARTERLY & DEFENCE JOURNAL
1 West Street, Tavistock, Devon PL19 8DS
Contact: T D Bridge
Tel: 01822 613577
Fax: 01822 612785
Email: aqdj.publications@virgin.net
International military journal containing articles and features on current defence matters worldwide, accounts of historic campaigns, personality profiles, book reviews, etc.

BATTLEFIELDS REVIEW
Freepost NEA 5274, Barnsley, S. Yorkshire S70 2BR
Tel: 01226 734627
Fax: 01226 734343
Website: www.yorkshire-web.co.uk/battlefields-review/
Archeological discoveries, visitor attractions, museum events, anniversaries, battlefields at risk, high quality maps, specially commissioned photos, in depth analysis.

BLACKTHORN
(Journal of the Royal Irish Regiment)
HQ The Royal Irish Regt, Saint Patrick's Barracks, Ballymena,
Ireland
Contact: Capt (Retd) J Knox MBE
Tel: 028 2566 1355
Fax: 028 2566 1378

THE BRITISH ARMY REVIEW
Trenchard Lines, Upavon, Pewsey, Wiltshire SN9 6BE
Contact: Col (Retd) W M Crawshaw
Tel: 94344 5056
Fax: 9344 5310
Email: ba-review@ukf.net

CALL TO ARMS
1 Lyng Lane, North Lopham, Norfolk IP22 2HR
Contact: Duke Henry Plantagenet
Tel/Fax: 01953 681676
Email: duke@calltoarms.com
The Worldwide Directory of Historical Re-enactment Societies
and Traders. Published once a year with continuous updating
service—fax and email supported—entry in our listings is free.
For sample copy send £2.50 (UK), £3.00 (airmail Europe), or
£3.50 (airmail rest of world)—sterling only. Listings are unique
ly annotated with society size / activity data. Also contains
high quality articles of news, research and development. Free
and friendly advice on-line to subscribers, a 'to-your-door'
update service planned. W W Web pages planned. Email for
details. To find out anything about Historical Re-enactment and
Living History, first you buy 'Call to Arms'. Get your copy now.

*CASUS BELLI
Excelsior Publications, 1 Rue du Colonel Pierre Avia, 75015
Paris, France

THE CASTLE
(Journal of the Royal Anglian Regt)
HQ Royal Anglian Regt, The Keep, Gibraltar Barracks, Bury St
Edmunds, Suffolk IP33 3RN
Contact: Col (Retd) A C Tayler
Tel: 01248 752394
Fax: 01284 752026

CHIRON CALLING
RHQ RAVC, Defence Animal Centre, Melton Mowbray LE13 0SL
Contact: Lt Col (Retd) P Roffey
Tel: 01664 411811 extn 8626
Email: dac.hq@dialpipexcom

CLASSIC ARMS & MILITARIA
Peterson Publications Ltd, Peterson House, Berryhill Ind Est,
Droitwich, Worcs WR9 9BL
Contact: Bruce Ayling
Tel: 01905 795564
Fax: 01905 795905
Classic Arms & Militaria, incorporating Gun Collecting—is
the only publication dedicated to the classic shooter,
military historian and collector. Packed with authoritative
articles on edged weapons, vintage military and sporting
arms, military history, medals, uniforms and a host of
features not often found in other magazines.

CLASSIC MILITARY VEHICLE
Kelsey Publishing Group, Cudham Tithe Barn, Berry's Hill,
Cudham, Kent TN16 3AG
Tel: 01959 541444
Fax: 01959 541400
Email: cmv.ed@kelsey.co.uk
Website: www.kelsey.co.uk

THE CRAFTSMAN
Journal of REME
PO Box H075, Isaac Newton Road, Arborfield RG2 9NJ
Contact: Cpl D J Wright
Tel: 94251 2221
Fax: 94251 2467
Email: craftsman@rhqreme.demon.co.uk

CROWN & CORONET
RMLY, Bridgeman House, Cavan Drive, Dawley Bank, Telford,
Shropshire TF4 2 BQ

DEFENCE MANAGEMENT JOURNAL
Petersgate House, St Petersgate, Stockport SK1 1HE
Contact: Dr M Harte

THE DELHI SPEARMAN
(Journal of the 9/12 Royal Lancers)
RHQ 9/12L, TA Centre, Saffron Road, Wigston, Leics LE8 2TU
Contact: The Editor

DEUTSCHES WAFFEN-JOURNAL
Schmollerstrasse 31, 74523 Schwabisch Hall, Germany
Tel: 791494515
Fax: 791404505
Email: info@dwj.de
Europe's premier magazine for collectors, hunters and
marksmen.

DRAGOON
Potters Hill, Wrotham Heath, Sevenoaks, Kent TN15 7SX
Editor: Martin Sankey
Tel: 01732 883212
Fax: 01732 886044
Journal of the Westminster Dragoons.

THE EAGLE
(Journal of the Essex Regt)
47 Acorn Avenue, Cowfold, W. Sussex RH13 8RR
Contact: Gordon Wren
Tel: 01403 864182
Email: gwren75257@aol.com

THE EAGLE AND CARBINE
(Journal of the Royal Scots Dragoon Guards)
The Castle, Edinburgh, Scotland EH1 2YT
Contact: Maj J L Melville
Tel: 0131 310 5100
Fax: 0131 310 5101

*EDITIONS HEIMDAL
Chateau de Damigny, 14400 Bayeux, France
Contact: Georges Bernage

*FIGURINES
Histoire & Collections, 5 Avenue de la République, 75011
Paris, France
Contact: Jean-Marie Mongin

FIRST EMPIRE LTD
1st Floor, 21 Whitburn Street, Bridgnorth, Shropshire XW6 4QN
Contact: David Watkins
Tel: 01746 765691
Fax: 01746 768820
Email: enquiries@firstempire.ltd.uk
Website: www.firstempire.ltd.uk
Publishers of the Napoleonic magazine 'First Empire'. Also
available: books, prints, wargames figures & software.
Send SAE for details and subscription information.

FIRM & FORESTER
(Journal of the Worcestershire & Sherwood Foresters)
RHQ WFR, Norton Barracks, Worcester, Worcs WR5 2PA
Contact: Maj (Retd) D W Reeve
Tel: 01905 354359
Fax: 01905 353871
Email: rhq-wfr@lineone.net

1st GURKHA RIFLES REGT ASSOCIATION NEWSLETTER
15 Church Lane, Darley Abbey, Derby DE22 1EX
Contact: Maj T Wells MBE
Tel: 01332 557121
Fax: 01332 559358

THE FUSILIER
RHQ RRF, HM Tower of London, Tower Hill, London
EC3N 4AB
Contact: Lt Col (Retd) W J Williams
Tel: 020 7488 5609
Email: rhq@thefusiliers.org

THE GARTER
Redcote, 228 Sydenham Road, Croydon, Surrey CR0 2EB
Contact: Frances E Tucker
Tel/Fax: 0181 684 1095
Email: thegarter@fsnet.co
The directory that supports costuming. The first source book
containing a list of fabric shops, booksellers, costumers,
accessory makers, materials suppliers, associated societies,
pattern makers etc.

THE GLOBE AND LAUREL
HMS Excellent, Whale Island, Portsmouth, Hampshire
PO2 8ER
Tel: 01705 651305
Fax: 01705 547212
Email: GL97@aol.com
Bimonthly journal of the Royal Marines. 12000 copies are sent
worldwide, keeping past and present RMs up to date.

THE GREEN HOWARDS GAZETTE
RHQ The Green Howards, Trinity Church Square, Richmond,
N. Yorkshire DL10 4QN
Contact: Lt Col (Retd) N D McIntosh MBE
Tel: 01748 822133
Fax: 01748 826561

GRENADIER GAZETTE
c/o CIE (MOD), Vauxhall House, Vauxhall Barracks, Didcot,
Oxon OX11 7ES
Contact: Henry Hanning
Tel: 94234 3243
Fax: 94234 3151

THE GUARDS MAGAZINE
(Journal of the Royal Household Division)
Church Farm, Beer Hackett, Sherborne, Dorset DT9 6QT
Contact: Col O J M Lindsay CBE
Tel/Fax: 01935 872287

THE GUNNER
Artillery House, Front Parade, RA Barracks, Woolwich, London
SE18 4BH
Contact: Maj (Retd) J W Timbers
Tel: 94691 3703
Fax: 94691 3706
Email: gunnermag@aol.com

HCAV JOURNAL
(Household Cavalry)
HQ HCAV, Horse Guards, Whitehall, London SW1A 2AX
Contact: The Editor

THE HIGHLANDER
RHQ The Highlanders, Cameron Barracks, Inverness,
Scotland N2 3XD
Contact: Lt Col A M Cumming OBE
Tel: 01463 224 4380

HISTOIRE & COLLECTIONS
Histoire & Collections, 5 Avenue de la République, 75541
Paris cedex 11
Tel: 01 40211820
Fax: 01 47005111
Website: www.abcollection.com

*HISTORIA
18 Rue Neuve des Bois, 75011 Paris, France

INVESTOR
Defence School of Transport, Normandy Barracks, Leconfield,
E. Yorkshire HU17 7LX
Contact: Maj A A Couper
Tel: 94775 5304 or 01904 665304

I P M S (UK) MAGAZINE
26 Sandygate Road, Marlow, Buckinghamshire SL7 3A2
Contact: Edgar Brooks

IRISH GUARDS REGIMENTAL JOURNAL
RHQ IG, Wellington Barracks, London SW1 6H
Contact: Lt Col R J S Bullock-Webster
Tel: 020 7414 3293

THE IRON DUKE
(The Duke of Wellington's Regt Journal)
53 Church Avenue, Farnborough, Hants GU14 7AT
Contact: Brig (Retd) G J Denholm
Tel/Fax: 01252 514786

JEEP WORLD MAGAZINE
54 High Street, Beighton, Sheffield, S Yorkshire S20 1ED
Contact: Mark Askew
Tel/Fax: 0114 26924450
Mobile: 0589 516401
Website: www.jeepworld.co.uk
Jeep World Promotions organise Jeep Fest, Jeep Off-Road
Days and publish Jeep World magazine–a glossy full
colour bi-monthly magazine with over 70 pages covering
all Jeeps–and the Jeep Directory.

JOURNAL OF THE DEVONSHIRE & DORSET REGIMENT
RHQ D&D, Wyvern Barracks, Exeter, Devon EX1 6AE
Contact: Maj C L Pape MBE
Tel: 94348 2436
Fax: 94348 2469
Email: regtsec@supanet.com

JOURNAL OF MILITARY ORDNANCE
PO Box 5884, Darlington, USA
Tel: 410 457 5400
Fax: 410 457 5400
Email: dpi14@aol.com
Website: www.darlingtonproductions.com
Independently run by Darlington Productions. Six issues a
year.

JOURNAL OF THE HONOURABLE ARTILLERY COMPANY
Hon Artillery Company, Armoury House, City Road, London
EC1Y 1JY
Contact: Peter Patrick
Tel: 020 7382 1537
Fax: 020 7382 1538

JOURNAL OF THE PRINCESS OF WALES ROYAL
REGIMENT
(Queen's and Royal Hampshires)
RHQ PWRR, Howe Barracks, Canterbury, Kent CT1 1JY
Contact: Maj A J Martin
Tel: 01227 818050

JOURNAL OF THE ROYAL ARMY MEDICAL CORPS
RHQ RAMC, Keigh Barracks, Ash Vale, Aldershot, Hants,
GU12 5RQ
Contact: Maj Ian Greaves
Tel: 01733 875806
Email: ramcjournal.editor@virgin.net

JOURNAL OF THE ROYAL HIGHLAND FUSILIERS
RHQ RHF, 518 Sauciehall Street, Glasgow Scotland
G2 3LW
Contact: Lt Col J L Kelly MBE

KARFUNKEL
Haupstrasse 85, 69483 Schönmattenwag, Germany
Contact: Sabine Wolf
Tel: 06207 920191
Fax: 06207 920990
Email: karfunkel@karfunkel.de
Dates of historical festivals and events Europe-wide. 1,000s
of addresses of actors, re-enactors and performers.

THE KEY
PO Box 135, Alton, Hants GU34 2WA
Contact: Mark Seymour
Tel: 01420 84260
Fax: 01420 84627
Email: keymagazine@talk21.com

THE KINGSMAN
RHQ King's Regt, Graeme House, Derby square, Liverpool
L2 7SD
Contact: Col (Retd) M G C Amlot OBE
Tel: 94552 2417
Fax: 94552 8260
Email: rhqkings@northwest.co.uk

THE KING'S ROYAL HUSSARS REGIMENTAL JOURNAL
RHQ KRH(S), Peninsula Barracks, Winchester, Hants SO23 8TS
Contact: The Editor

KNIFE WORLD PUBLICATIONS
PO BOX 3395, Knoxville, TN 37927. USA
Tel: 865-397-1955
Fax: 865-397-1969
Email: knifepub@knifeworld.com
Website: www.knifeworld.com
Booksellers and publishers of books about knives and other
cutlery. Also, Publishers of 'knife world' magazine, the only
publication covering the World of knives. Visit our website
at www.knifeworld.com.

LIVING HISTORY REGISTER
56 Wareham Road, Lytchett Maltravers, Poole, Dorset
BH16 6DS
Contact: Roger Emmerson
Tel/Fax: 01202 622115
Email: lhrbangman@aol.com
This international magazine covers all periods of re-enactment and 'living history'; promoting research and contact
between groups and interested parties; a networking aid.
Published biannually, annual subscription, posted direct
available. 'The Register' developed from a list of partici-
pants and their skills into a magazine, written by partici-
pants, to fill a need for all.

THE LANCASHIRE LAD
(Journal of the Queen's Lancashire Regt)
RHQ QLR, Fulwood Barracks, Preston, Lancs PR2 8AA
Contact: Lt Col (Retd) E J Downham
Tel: 94554 2426
Fax: 94554 2583

JOURNAL OF THE LIGHT DRAGOONS
RHQ LD, Fensham Barracks, Barrack Road, Newcastle upon
Tyne NE2 4NP
Contact: The Editor

THE LINK
RAC Trg Regt, Bovington Camp, Wareham, Dorset UK
BH20 6JA
Contact: Lt Col (Retd) Brian Bell
Tel: 94374 3708
Fax: 94374 3218

THE LION AND THE DRAGON
(Journal of the King's Own Royal Border Regt)
KORB Regt, The Castle, Carlisle, Cumbria CA3 8UR
Contact: Maj (Retd) J A Farrell
Tel: 01228 521275

LIONESS
(Journal of the Women's Royal Army Corps)
Worthy Down, Winchester, Hants SO21 2RG
Contact: Maj (Retd) D M McElligott

LONDON SCOTTISH REGIMENTAL GAZETTE
RHQ London Scottish, 95 Horseferry Road, London SW1P 2DX
Contact: Clem Webb
Tel: 020 7630 1639

[handwritten: RW Harmond regimental see]

THE MASCOT
(TA, OTC, Cadets magazine)
HQ2 Div, Annandale Block, Craigiehall, South Queensferry,
West Lothian, Scotland EH 30 9TN
Contact: The Editor
Tel: 0131 310 2091 or 2092
Fax: 0131 310 2058

THE MEN OF HARLECH
(Journal of the Royal Regiment of Wales)
RHQ RRW, Maindy Barracks, Cardiff, Wales CF14 3YE
Tel: 94355 8207
Fax: 94355 8357

MILITARY PROVOST STAFF CORPS JOURNAL
RHQ MPSC, Berechurch Hall Camp, Colchester, Essex
CO2 9NU
Contact: aj (Retd) C N Bunbury
Tel: 01206 783494
Fax: 01206 783527

M H Q (MILITARY HISTORY QUARTERLY)
741 Miller Drive SE, Suite D-2, Leesburg, VA 20175, USA
Contact: Christopher J Anderson
Tel: 703 779 8557
Fax: 703 779 8545
Email: chrisa@cowles.com
Fully illustrated hardcover magazine devoted to military
history from ancient times to present day. One year
subscription $70.00 US. Back issues from 1988 available.

MAQUETTES MODELES ACTUALITES
Sevart, BP 3067, 78130 Les Mureaux, France
Contact: Didier Lefevre
Tel: (0033) 134748080
Fax: (0033) l347140405
Email: 106636.2506@compuserve.com
Kit modellers' magazine covering aircraft, ships, vehicles,
and figures.

MEDAL NEWS
Token Publishing Ltd, PO Box 14, Honiton, Devon EX14 9YP
Contact: Carol Hartman
Monthly magazine for the collector of medals and the military historian; regular features, articles, book reviews, competitions and display advertising; classified advertising and
medal tracker service now free to all subscribers.

MILITARIA
Histoire et Collections, 5 Avenue de la République, 75011
Paris, France
Contact: Philippe Charbonnier
The world's leading magazine for 20th century uniform,
insignia, and equipment collectors and enthusiasts. Colour
illustrated throughout, including many expert photographic
reconstructions of the soldiers, sailors, and airmen of the
two world wars.

MILITARY ARMOR INTERNATIONAL
Rear of the Talbot Hotel, Iwerne Minster, Blandford Forum,
Dorset DT11 8QN
Email: military-armor@wanadoo.fr
Website: www.military-armor.com
Magazine published by modellers for modellers, dealing
exclusively with vehicles and figures from 1914 up to now,
in various scales: 1/72, 1/76, 1/35, 54mm, 1/15 1/9.

MILITARY ILLUSTRATED
43 Museum Street, London WC1A 1LY
Contact: Tim Newark
Tel: 020 76922900
Fax: 020 7242 0702
Email: mailbox@publishingnews.co.uk
Monthly magazine covering all periods and nationalities,
strong emphasis on uniform and equipment history but
also articles on weapons, vehicles, medals, etc.

[handwritten: Tim Newark @ publishingnews.co.uk]

MILITARY IN SCALE
Traplet Publications Ltd, Traplet House, Severn Drive,
Upton-upon-Severn, Worcestershire WR8 OJL
Contact: Andrea Mann
Tel: 01684 594505
Fax: 01684 594586
Email: general@traplet.co.uk
Website: http://traplet.co.uk
Full colour, informative magazine for plastic modellers.
Covers everything from tanks to aircraft. Regular features
offer constant flow of info; military kits, books and decals.

MILITARY MODELLING
PO Box 6017, Leighton Buzzard, Hertfordshire LU7 7FA
Contact: Ken Jones
Tel/Fax: 01525 370389
Email: milmodmag@compuserve.com
The monthly magazine for modellers, military enthusiasts
and wargamers of all persuasions. This international maga-
zine is a trend-setter and forum for everything military.

NATO REVIEW
Communication Planning Unit, MOD, Room 0370 Main
Building, London SW1A 2HB
Website: www.nato.int/
Published under the authority of the Secretary General, this
magazine is intended to contribute to a constructive
discussion of Atlantic issues.

NAUTICAL MAGAZINE
Brown, Son and Ferguson Ltd., 4-10 Darnley Street, Glasgow,
Strathclyde G41 2SD, Scotland
Tel/Fax: 0141 429 1414
Email: info@skipper.co.uk

NAVAL ENGINEERS JOURNAL
Hunter's Moon, Exford, Minehead, Somerset TA24 7PD
Contact: Bryan H Jackson
Tel: 01643 831695
Fax: 01643 831576
The Journal dealing with naval design, weapons, electronic
warfare, propulsion, construction, in fact all that goes to
make up the fighting ship.

NEXUS SPECIAL INTERESTS
Nexus House, Boundary Way, Hemel Hempstead, Hertfordshire
HP2 7ST
Contact: Ken Jones
Publishers of 'Military Modelling' the world's best selling
military modelling magazine, and 'Practical Wargamer'.
Organisers of Europe's premier military modelling show—
Euromilitaire'. Publish numerous military modelling books.

THE OAK TREE
(Journal of The Cheshire Regiment.)
RHQ The Cheshire Regt, The Castle, Chester, Cheshire CH1
2DN
Contact: Maj J Ellis
Tel: 94555 2926
Fax: 01244 327 617

OFFICERS' PENSIONS SOCIETY
68 South Lambeth Road, Vauxhall, London SW8 1RL
Contact: D Marsh RN
Tel: 020 7820 9988
Fax: 020 7820 9948
Email: lettersags@officerspensionsoc.co.uk
Membership Organisation protects pension interests of ex-
Service people and gives members pension advice.
Magazine is 'Pennant'—print run 37,000, biannual.

PARTIZAN PRESS
816–818 London Road, Leigh-on-Sea, Essex SS9 3NI
Contact: David Ryan
Tel/Fax: 01702 473986
Email: dave@caliverbooks.co.uk
Publishers of books, magazines, ECW Times, Age of
Napoleon, Age of Empires; 18th Century and Renaissance
Notes & Queries, Battlefields. Sole European distributor of
major international wargaming magazines.

PEGASUS
(Journal of the Parachute Regiment)
RHQ The Parachute Regt, Browning Barracks, Aldershot,
Hants GU11 2BS
Tel: 01252 349624
Fax: 01252 349203

PETERSON PUBLICATIONS
Peterson House, North Bank, Berryhill Industrial Estate,
Droitwich, Worcestershire WR9 9BL
Contact: Geoffrey Hudson
Tel: 01905 795564
Fax: 01905 7954905
Publishers of 'Classic Arms & Militaria', the definitive mag-
azine for enthusiasts and collectors, as well as 'Target
Sports', the journal for all competitive shooters.

PIREME PUBLISHING LTD
Suite 10, Wessex House, St Leonard's Road, Bournemouth,
Dorset BH88QS
Contact: Iain Dickie
Tel: 01202 297344
Fax: 01202 297345
Email: iaindickie@freeuk.com
Publishers of 'Miniature Wargames' magazine—covers all
periods of history and all theatres of conflict. Also the
Miniature Wargames Starter Packs for Ancients, Pirates,
Napoleonic and World War 11, plus inexpensive military
prints, booklets and 15mm Waterloo card buildings.

THE PRESTON KINGSMAN
3 Valley View, Fulwood, Preston, Lancashire PR2 4HP
Contact: Peter Golding
Tel/Fax: 01772 718357
Monthly newsletter of the King's and Manchester
Regiments' Association. Events, news, views, pictures,
poems, searchline, postbag, minutes, adverts memorabilia,
meetings. Annual subscription.

Q A R A N C GAZETTE
Keogh Barracks, Ash Vale, Aldershot, Hants
GU 12 5RQ
Contact: Lt Col (Retd) M M Mumford-George
Military medical journal—Queen Alexandra's Royal Army
Nursing Corps.

THE QUEEN'S DRAGOON GUARDS JOURNAL
RHQ QDG, Maindy Barracks, Cardiff, Wales CF4 3YE
Contact: The Editor

RDG REGIMENTAL JOURNAL
(Journal of The Royal Dragoon Guards)
RHQ RDG, 3 Tower Street, York, Yorkshire YO1 1SB
Contact: The Editor

THE RED HACKLE
(Regimental magazine of the Black Watch)
RHQ The Black Watch, Balhousie Castle, Perth, Scotland
PH1 5HR
Contact: Lt Col (Retd) S J Lindsay
Tel: 0131 310 8530
Fax: 01738 643245

RAIDS
Histoire et Collections, 5 Avenue de la République, 75011
Paris, France
Leading monthly magazine of current military news, with
colour photo features from today's best correspondents
with the world's elite forces and front line reports.

REVIVAL
PO Box 168, Wellington Street, Leeds, W. Yorkshire LS1 1RF
Tel: 0113 238 8818
Fax: 0113 238 8962
Email: amand.marshall@ypn.co.uk
International bi-monthly magazine of military re-enactment,
civilian living history and historical interpretation.

ROSE & LAUREL
(Journal of the Intelligence Corps)
ICA DISC,Chickensands, Nr Shefford, Beds SG17 5PR
Contact: Lt Col (Retd) J D Woolmore OBE
Tel: 94649 2340
Fax: 94649 2297

ROYAL ARMY CHAPLAINS JOURNAL
RAChD, Amport House, Amport, Andover, Hants
SP11 8BG
Contact: Maj (Retd) M A Easey
Tel: 01246 773144 Extn 248
Fax: 01246 771042

ROYAL ARMY MEDICAL CORPS MAGAZINE
AMS Museum Keogh Barracks, Ash Vale, Aldershot, Hants
GU12 5RQ
Contact: Capt (Retd) P H Starling
Tel: 94222 5320
Fax: 94222 5332
Email: museum@keogh72.freeserve.co.uk

ROYAL ENGINEERS JOURNAL
Institution of Royal Engineers, Ravelin Building, Brompton
Barracks, Chatham, Kent ME4 4UG
Contact: Lt Col D N Hamilton MBE
Tel: 94661 2298
Fax: 94661 2397
Email: corps.secretary@inst-royal-engrs.co.uk

ROYAL HIGHLAND FUSILIERS MAGAZINE
RHQ RHF, 518 Sauciehall Street, Glasgow, Scotland
G2 3LW
Contact: Lt Col (Retd) R E M Thorburn

ROYAL MILITARY POLICE JOURNAL
RHQ RMP, Rousillon Barracks, Chichester, W. Sussex
PO19 4BN
Contact: Maj (Retd) R A Peedle
Tel: 01323 899985
Email: bobpeedle@supanet.com

THE ROYAL LOGISTIC CORPS JOURNAL
RHQ RLC, Dettingen House, The Princess Royal Barracks,
Deepcut, Camberley Surrey GU16 6RW
Contact: Maj (Retd) D J Glossop
Tel/Fax: 01252 340875

SCOTTISH MILITARY HISTORICAL SOCIETY
4 Hillside Cottages, Glenboig, Lanarkshire ML5 2QY
Contact: Tom Moles
The Society exists to encourage the study of Scottish
military history and publishes its own illustrated journal,
covering the collecting of badges, headdress, uniforms,
medals, photographs, postcards, prints, watercolours,
equipment, pistols, powderhorns etc. The SMHS has a
worldwide membership.

THE SILVER BUGLE
(Journal for Cadets)
RHQ LI, Peninsula Barracks, Winchester, Hants
SO23 8TS
Contact: Lt Col (Retd) P J Wykeham
Tel: 01962 828529
Fax: 01962 828534
Email: pj-wykeham@which.org

SOLDIER MAGAZINE
Parsons House, Ordnance Road, Aldershot, Hampshire
GU11 2DU
Contact: Chris Horrocks
Tel: 01252 347355
Fax: 01252 347358
Email: solmag@btinternet.com
Published by the Ministry of Defence, Soldier is the official
magazine of the British Army and circulates worldwide. It
is aimed at serving and retired soldiers and their families
as well as civilian enthusiasts. it was the only British
Service publication with combat reporting teams covering
the Gulf War.

SOUTH & CENTRAL AMERICAN MILITARY SOCIETY
27 Hallgate. Cottingham, E. Yorkshire HU16 4DN
Contact: Terry D Hooker
Tel/Fax: 01482 847068
Email: scambs@enterprise.net
Website: http://www.magweb.com

STAFFORD KNOT
(Journal of the Staffordshire Regiment)
RHQ Staffords, Whittington Barracks, Lichfield, Staffs WS14 9PY
Contact: Maj (Retd) E Green
Tel: 0121 311 3240
Email: museum@rhqstaffords.fsnet.co.uk

STEEL MASTERS
Histoire & Collections, 19 Avenue de la République, 75011
Paris, France
Contact: Didier Chomette

SKIRMISH MAGAZINE
1st Floor Adelphi Mill, Bollington, Cheshire SK10 5JB
Contact: Irene Moore
Tel/Fax: 01625 575700
Email: editor@skirmishmagazine.co.uk
Website: www.skirmishmagazine.co.uk
Skirmish is a bi-monthly magazine for re-enactors and military history enthusiasts available on subscription or through selected newsagents. It features UK and worldwide re-enacting societies and lists forthcoming events.

SOLDIER OF FORTUNE
18 Tyn-y-Llidart Ind Est, Corwen, North Wales LL21 9RQ
Contact: Peter Kabluczenko
Tel/Fax: 01490 412225
Email: sof@chesternet.co.uk

TANK
RHQ RTR, Staley Barracks, Bovington, Dorset BH20 6JA
Contact: George Forty
Tel: 01929 403444
Email: rhqrtr@cwcom.net or forty@clara.net
Journal of the Royal Tank Regiment.

TANKETTE
45 Balmoral Drive, Holmes Chapel, Cheshire CW4 7JQ
Contact: G E G Williams
Tel: 0147753537,3
Fax: 01477535892
Email: mafvahq@aol.com
Website: http://www.geocities.com/pentagon/5437/mafva/.html
The bimonthly magazine of the Miniature AFV Association; contains plans, articles, reviews and photographs of military vehicles and equipment. Includes members' want ads and information.

THE THIN RED LINE
(Regt Journal of the Argyll & Sutherland Highlanders)
RHQ A&SH, The Castle, Stirling, Scotland
Contact: Maj (Retd) C A Campbell
Tel: 01786 475165
Fax: 01786 446038
Email: regtsec@argylls.co.uk

THE THISTLE
(Journal of the Royal Scots Regiment)
RHQ The Royal Scots, The Castle, Edinburgh, Scotland EH1 2YT
Contact: Maj (Retd) R Mason
Tel: 0131 310 5014
Fax: 0131 310 5019

*39/45 MAGAZINE
Editions Heimdal, BP 320, Chateau de Damigny, F-14400
Bayeux, France
Contact: Bernard Paich
Tel: 231516868
Fax: 231516860

TOKEN PUBLISHING
Orchard House, Duchy Road, Heathpark, Honiton, Devon
EX14 8YD
Contact: Philip Mussell
Tel: 01404 831878
Fax: 01404 831895
Publishers of Medal News, the world's only magazine devoted to medals and battles. Also The Medal Yearbook, the definitive guide to British orders and medals.

TRACKLINK
Newsletter of the Friends of the Tank Museum, published Jan, May & Sept.

TRACTOR & MACHINERY MAGAZINE
Kelsey Publishing, Cudham Tithe Barn, Berry's Hill, Cudham,
Kent TN16 3AG
Tel: 01959 541444
Fax: 01959 541400
Email: tm.mag@kelsey.co .uk

TRADITION MAGAZINE
25 Rue Bargue, 75015 Paris, France
Contact: Corrine Jarque
Monthly colour magazine of pre-1870 uniforms, weapons, military history 1st and 2nd Empire.

TRIDENT PRESS
PO Box 8704, Birmingham B25 8UW
Tel: 0800 138 8989
Website: www.secondworldwar.net
Publishers of 'The Second World War' illustrated series.

THE VEDETTE
(Regimental magazine of the Queen's Royal Lancers)
RHQ QRL, Prince William of Gloucester Barracks, Grantham,
Lincs NG31 7TJ
Contact: The Editor

WELSH GUARDS REGIMENTAL MAGAZINE
Welsh Guards Assoc, Maindy in Barracks, Cardiff, Wales
CF14 3YE
Contact: Capt (Retd) D M Davies
Tel: 024207 8219

THE WIRE
(Journal of the Signal Corps)
RHQ Royal Corps of Signals, Blandford Camp, Blandford,
Dorset DT11 8RH
Contact: Adam Forty
Tel: 01258 2079
Fax: 01258 2084

THE WHITE ROSE
(Regt journal of The Prince of Wales Own Regiment of Yorkshire)
RHQ PWORY, 3 Tower Street, York, N. Yorkshire YO1 9SB
Contact: Lt Col (Retd) T C Vines
Tel: 01904 662 790

WARBIRDS WORLDWIDE LTD
PO Box 99, Mansfield, Nottinghamshire NG18 2BF
Contact: Paul Cogan
Tel: 016Z3 624288
Fax: 01623 6220-59
Email: edit@warbirdsww.com

WARGAMES ILLUSTRATED
Stratagem Publications Ltd, 18 Love Lane, Newark, Nottinghamshire NH24 1HZ
Contact: Duncan McFarlane
Tel/Fax: 01636 71973

WARSHIP WORLD
Lodge Hill, Liskeard, Cornwall PL14 4EL
Contact: Roger May
Tel: 01579 343663
Fax: 01579 346/47
Email: marbooksc@aol.com
Website: http://members.aol.com/marbooks/
Quarterly magazine covering both current Royal Navy and Auxiliary scene and naval history. Subscription £12 p.a. ($14 overseas). SAE for details.

WW II MILITARY JOURNAL
PO Box 28906, San Diego CA 9219 USA
Tel: 001 619 884 3483
Fax: 001 619 471 7406
A quarterly magazine concerned the history of WWII (1931–1945).

WINDSCREEN
PO Box 6, Fleet, Hants GU13 9PE
Editor: Andy Jones
Tel: 01489 881646
Fax: 01489 881696
Email: andyjones@mvt.org.uk
Website: www.mvt.org.uk
The magazine of the Military Vehicle Trust.

Y DDRAIG GOCH
(Journal of the Royal Welch Fusiliers)
RHQ RWF, Hightown Barracks, Wrexham, Clwyd, Wales, LL13 8RD
Contact: Maj (Retd) R P Lake
Tel: 01978 264521
Fax: 01978 316121

MEDAL DEALERS & SERVICES

ALEX & MEGAN ROBERTSON
12 Bude Close, Crewe, Cheshire CW1 3XG
Tel: 01270 504992 or 504994
Email: arobertson@cix.compulink.co.uk
Uniforms and medals research service.

ANTIQUE MILITARIA & SPORTING EXHIBITIONS
PO Box 194, Warwick CV34 5ZG
Contact: C P James
Tel/Fax: 01926 497340
Email: user@chrisjames.slv.co.uk
Website: www.medalsandmilitaria.co.uk
'The International'—the National Motorcycle Museum, Birmingham (on J6/M42 motorway) is the UK's largest militaria fair. Send SAE for dates and location map.

A D HAMILTON & CO.
7 St. Vincent Place, Glasgow, Strathclyde, Scotland G1 2DW,
Tel: 0141 221 5423
Fax: 0141 248 6019
Email: jeffery@hamiltons.swinternet.co.uk

BRANDENBURG HISTORICA
346 B Winchester Street, Ste. 121 W, Keene, New Hampshire NH 0343 1, USA
Contact: Diane M Schreiber
Tel: 603 352 1961
Fax: 603 357 5364
Email: preussen@top.monad.net
Brandenburg Historica mail order catalogue of books, military music and militaria; Imperial, Third Reich, DDR: uniforms, insignia and medals. Bi-monthly listings. Ship worldwide. US$4.00.

BRIC-A-BRAC
16A Walsingham Place, Truro, Cornwall TRI 2AG
Contact: Richard Bonehill
Tel/Fax: 01872 225200
Email: richard@bonehill3.freeserve.co.uk
One of the few shops left in Cornwall dealing in medals, badges, helmets, swords and a range of militaria. We specialise in the weird and wonderful (when we can get it!). Original 3rd Reich and DCLI items wanted.

BRYANT & GWYNN ANTIQUES
8 Drayton Lane, Drayton Bassett, Staffordshire B78 3TZ
Contact: David Bryant
All types of military uniforms, medals, swords and militaria supplied. Also deactivated military arms and muskets. Items not stocked can be ordered and traced.

C & J MEDALS
14 Fairford Road, Tilehurst, Reading RG 6QB
Contact: John G Southern
Tel/Fax: 0118 942 5356
Email: southern@cjmedals.co.uk
Website: www.cjmedals.co.uk
Military medal specialists. Medals mounted ready to wear.
Replacement medals. Miniatures supplied. Framing service.
Regimental blazer badges, ties, cufflinks, cap badges, tie
pins, lapel badges, key rings and coasters.

C F SEIDLER
Stand G12, Grays Antique Mkt, 1–7 Davies Mews, Davies
Street, London W1V 1AR
Contact: Christopher Seidler
Tel/Fax: 020 7629 251
Email: tomus@tinyworld.co.uk
American, British, European, Oriental edged weapons,
antique firearms, orders and decorations, uniform items-
watercolours, prints; regimental histories, army lists; horse
furniture, etc. We purchase at competitive prices and will
sell on a consignment or commission basis. Valuations for
probate and insurance. Does not issue a catalogue but will
gladly receive clients' wants lists. Open Mon–Fri,
11.00am–6.00pm. Nearest tube station Bond Street.

C J & A DIXON LTD
23 Prospect Street, Bridlington, E. Yorkshire
Tel: 01262 676877
Fax: 01262 606600
Email: chris@dixonmedals.fsnet.co.uk
Specialist dealers in war medals and decorations. Dixons
Gazette contains over 1,000 priced medals–3 a copy, sub-
scription 4 issues UK £8, overseas £12.

COTREL MEDALS
7 Stanton Road, Bournemouth, Dorset BH10 5DS
Contact: Peter Cotrel
Tel/Fax: 01202 388367
Mail-order company dealing in medals and related accessories. SAE for list. Callers by appointment. Offers made on
surplus medals. Mounting service.

D & R MILITARIA
1700 Preston Drive, Tarboro, NC 27886-4716, USA
Contact: Don Pixley
Tel: 252 823 1671
Email: pixddrcol1@aol.com
Website..http://hometown.aol.com/pixddrcol1/index.htm
General Militaria of WWII Germany and East Germany to
include insignia, uniforms, medals, and similar items.

E G FRAMES MILITARIA UK
7 Saffron, Amington, Tamworth, Staffordshire B77 4EP
Contact: Tony Cooper
Tel/Fax: 01827 63900
Email: tony@egframes.oo.uk
Website.http://www.egframes.co.uk
We specialise in military framing, in addition we sell British
Army badge, museum quality reproduction medals, Third
Reich Insignia and MOD issue pace sticks and canes.

GEORGE RANKIN COIN COMPANY LTD
325 Bethnal Green Road, London E2 6AH
Contact: George Rankin
Tel: 020 7729 1280
Fax: 020 7729 5043
Buyers and sellers of all coins, banknotes, military and
civilian medals, jewellery, scrap gold and silver, antiques
and collectables.

GIUSEPPE MICELI COIN & MEDAL CENTRE
173 Wellingborough Road, Northampton NN1 4DX
Contact: Giuseppe Miceli
Tel: 01604 639776
Coins and medals bought and sold.

GORDONS MEDALS LTD
Stand G 16- t7, Grays in the Mews Antique Centre, Davies
Mews, Davies Street, London W1V 1AR
Contact: M R Gordon
Tel: 020 7495 0900
Fax: 020 7495 0115
Email: gordons_medals@compuserve.com
Specialising in campaign medals, German military collecta-
bles, Third Reich documents and awards. Comprehensive
catalogue issued every two months–£6.00 UK & BFPO,
£12.00 overseas. Shop hours 10.30am–6pm, Mon–Fri.

GREAT WAR MEDALS
22 Selbourne Road, London N14 7DH
Contact: M A Law
Tel: 020 8886 4120
Email: malaw@gwmedals.freeserve.co.uk
Established 1985 by collectors for collectors. Catalogues
typically list 500 interesting groups and singles, plus new
& secondhand books. Medals fully described under unit
headings. Effective advertising gives first refusal on specific
wants. Inexpensive Research Service. Member OMRS &
WFA. Credit cards accepted. Six issues £7.50 UK/£11.00
Overseas.

HANOVER TRADING
32 Birch Way, Chesham, Bucks HP5 3JL
Contact: Ian or Catherine Tindle
Tel: 0800 731 1201

HISTORY, BY GEORGE!
129 W. Main Street, Mesa, AZ 85201, USA
Contact: George Notarpole
Tel: 480 898 3878
Fax: 480 668 2721
Email: gnotarpole@historybygeorge.com
Website: historybygeorge.com
Militaria, stamps, coins and general antiques. Specializing
in fine medals and orders. We buy, sell and trade. Let us
know what you have!

INTERNATIONAL COLLECTIBLES, BELTS AND MILITARIA
44 Bliss Mine Road #1, Middletown, RI, 02842, USA
Contact: Don Palen
Tel: 401-848-7252
Fax: 401-849-7440
Email: don@icbm.com.
Website: www.icbm.com
Icbm.com website has a variety of military qualification insignias from around the world (para/pilot/submarine/ship/special forces), watches, submarine clocks, books, binoculars, all sorts of other related goodies and even KGB stuff! A fun website with lots of good natured humour, worth a stop even if you don't buy anything.

JAMIE CROSS
PO Box 73, Newmarket, Suffolk CB8 8RY
Contact: Jamie Cross
Tel/Fax: 01638 750132
Email: jamiecross@aol.com
Specialist dealer in Third Reich medals and badges; Axis-related awards also. Good selection always available. All guaranteed 100% original. 'Wants' lists a speciality.

JEREMY TENNISWOOD
PO Box 73, Aldershot, Hampshire GU11 1UJ
Contact: Jeremy Tenniswood
Tel: 01252 319791
Fax: 01252 342339
Email: 100307.1735@compuserve.com
Established 1966, dealing in collectable firearms civil and military, de-activated and for shooters; also swords, bayonets, medals, badges, insignia, buttons, headdress, ethnographica; and books. Regular lists of Firearms and Accessories; Medals; Edged Weapons; Headdress, Headdress Badges and Insignia; comprehensive lists Specialist and Technical Books. Office open 9am–5pm, closed all day Sunday. Medal mounting service.

JOHN D LOWREY MILITARIA
PO Box 7928, Fremont, California 94537-7928, USA
Tel/Fax: 510 657 7957
Medals and related books. six price lists per year (£2.50) includes US and foreign. Will consider exchanges. Accepts Visa/Mastercards/cheques.

JONATHAN COLLINS MEDALS
17 Queens Road, Warsash, Hampshire, SO31 9JY
Contact: Jonathan & Susan Collins
Tel/Fax: 01489 582222
Email: jonathan@jcollinsmedals.co.uk
Websites: www.jcollinsmedals.co.uk for medal sales
www.militaryresearchon.com for research services.
www.bids-on.com for militaria auction site
Jonathan & Susan Collins offer a good selection of British & commonwealth Decorations and medals for sale, sales site updated daily. A full Naval, military & Air Force research service is offered for medal collectors and family historians. A fully automated auction site for medals and militaria is offered to sell items surplus to your requirements. In business 25 years.

JUST MILITARY
701 Abbeydale Road, Sheffield, S. Yorkshire S7 2BE
Tel: 0114 255 0536
Dealers in all types of military memorabilia and collectables. Full medal mounting and framing service including the supply of miniature and replacement medals.

KAMPFGRUPPE MEDALS & BADGES
28–380 Framosa Road, Suite 242, Gublh, Ontario, N1E 7E1
Tel/Fax: 519 823 8249
Email: info@kampfgruppemedals.com
Website: www.kampfgruppemedals.com
Collecting for 20 years. Dealer of authentic Third Reich militaria.

LIVERPOOL MEDAL COMPANY LTD
42 Bury Business Centre, Kay Street, Bury, Lancs BL9 6BU
Tel: 0161 763 4610 or 4612
Fax: 0161 4963
Email: liverpoolmedals@online.rednet.co.uk
The largest and best selection of orders, medals and decorations of the world on offer four times a year. Buyers and sellers, single pieces or entire collections.

MEDALS & MILITARIA CO UK
Warwick Antique Centre, 22–24 High Street, Warwick
CV34 4AP
Contact: Chris James
Tel: 07710 274452
Email: user@chrisjames.siv.co.uk
Website: medalsandmilitaria.co.uk
We buy and sell British, Soviet, German and Japanese medals and decorations, Japanese and European swords, bayonets and military badges. Imperial and Third Reich militaria, flying log books and aviation collectables, German passes, documents, daggers etc. Edged weapons of the world, uniforms headgear and militaria.

MEDALS OF WAR
Email: egu@magma.ca

MEDAL SOCIETY OF IRELAND
32 Clonmacate Road, Birches, Portadown, Co.Armagh,
N. Ireland
Contact: Jonathan Maguire
Collector of medals and books relating to The Royal Dublin Fusiliers and their predecessors, research undertaken, very modest fees.

MILITARY ANTIQUES
11 The Mall Antiques Arcade, 359 Upper Street, Islington,
London N10PD
Contact: Robert Tredwen
Tel: 020 7359 2224
Fax: 020 8467 7027
Email: milantique@tredwen7.freeserve.co.uk
Website: www.militaryantiques.co.uk
We supply a large selection of WWI and WWII uniforms, headdress, arms and armour and other items of interest. Our shop is open Wednesday, Friday and Saturday from 11–4pm.

MILITARIA
C/Bailen 120, 08009 Barcelona, Catalonia, Spain
Contact: Xavier Andreu
Tel/Fax: 32075185
Email: militaria@ctv.es
Website: http://www.ctv.es/users/militaria
Buy, sell and exchange militaria, Medals, edged weapons, insignia, headgear etc. Also large selection of military books in stock.

M J & S J DYAS COINS & MEDALS
Sandy Hill Industrial Estate, Unit 3, 42 Stratford Road, Shirley, Solihull, W. Midlands B90 3LS
Contact: M J Dyas
Tel: 0121 733 2225
Fax: 0121 733 1513
We sell all types of medals, worldwide & British. We issue six lists per year on WWI medals, three lists on campaign medals and one list on foreign medals. We also sell regimental history books for WWI only.

NEATE MILITARIA & ANTIQUES
PO Box 3794, Preston St Mary, Sudbury, Suffolk CO10 9PX
Contact: Gary C Neate
Tel: 01787 248168
Fax: 01787 248363
Email: gary@neatemedals.fsnet.co.uk
Specialists in worldwide orders, decorations and medals. Catalogues available, five per annum: £6 UK, £10 rest of world. Stamped SAE for sample copy.

NICHOLAS MORIGI–THE REGALIA SPECIALIST
PO Box 103, Newmarket, Suffolk CB3 3WY
Contact: Nicholas Morigi
Tel: 01440 821245
Fax: 01440 821246
Email: nmorigi@nascr.net
Website: www.nicholasmorigi.com
Britain's premier supplier of cloth and metal military insignia from WWI and II through to the present day, including the finest collection of replica Third Reich items for collectors and re-enactors currently available. Special 25th Anniversary Catalogue £10.50 (£13 Overseas) or sample literature selection at no charge.

NORMAN W COLLETT
PO Box 235, London SE23 1NS
Contact: Norman W Collett
Tel/Fax: 020 8291 1435
Email: norman@medalsonline.co.uk
Website: www.medalsonline.co.uk
British orders, decorations and campaign medals. Unusual combinations and interesting research. Mail Order only. Stock listed on our website, with many illustrations. Payment taken on Visa or Mastercard if preferred.

THE OLD BRIGADE
10A Harborough Road, Kingsthorpc, Northampton, Northamptonshire NN2 7A7
Contact: Stewart Wilson
Tel: 01604 719369
Fax: 01604 712489
Email: theoldbrigade@easynet.co.uk
Website: www.theoldbrigade.co.uk
Specialist dealer in Third Reich militaria, daggers, uniforms, medals, badges, flags, helmets, etc also a good selection of Imperial German items and militaria from other countries. Please visit our web site or visit our shop in person,visitors by appointment only please.

ORDERS, MEDALS, & DECORATIONS
PO Box 890190, Temecula, CA 92589-0190, USA
Contact: Tim Eriksen
Tel: 909 699 5826
Fax: 909 699 3623
Email: timeriksen@msn.com
Worldwide orders, medals, and decorations, dealing in rare and quality items.

PETER MORRIS COINS & MEDALS
1 Station Concourse, Bromley North BR Station, Kent
Postal: PO Box 233, Bromley, Kent BR1 4EQ
Contact: Peter Morris
Tel: 020 8313 3410
Fax: 020 8466 8502
Email: info@petermorris.co.uk
Website: www.petermorris.co.uk
Large stock of medals, militaria, cap badges, medal groups mounted. Retail sales lists issued quarterly; valuations given. Open Mon, Tues, Thurs, Fri, 10am–6pm; Sat, 9am–2pm.

PETER COTREL MEDALS
7 Stanton Road, Bournemouth, Dorset BH10 5DS
Contact: Peter Cotrel
Tel/Fax: 01202 388367
Mail order company dealing in medals and accessories, mostly British Ribbons stocked. Callers by appointment only. Medal mounting and engraving service available. Undamaged British medals bought and sold. SAE for list.

PHILIP BURMAN MEDALS
Email: Freddy@military-medals.co.uk

PICWELL MEDALS
Email: colourpatch@hotmail.com

*POUSSIERES D'EMPIRES SARL
33 Rue Brezin, 75014 Paris, France
Poussieres d'empires sells badges, orders, decorations and military items, particularly French Indochina and other Colonial. Open 11am–7pm; catalogue available for mail order service; Visa and Access accepted.

R H SMART
39 Mount Lane, Kirkby-la-Thorpe, Sleaford, Lincolnshire
NG34 9NR
Contact: Roy Smart
Tel: 01529 304236
Medal ribbons, specialising in former Soviet Union, United
Nations, Imperial Germany and GB. Full size and miniature
medals. Medal mounting service.

ROMSEY MEDALS
5 Bell Street, Romsey, Hampshire SO51 8GY
Tel: 01794 512069
Fax: 01794 830332
Website: www.romseymedals.co.uk

RAYMOND D HOLDICH INTERNATIONAL
7 Whitcomb Street, Trafalgar Square, London WC2H 7HA
Contact: Raymond D Holdich
Tel: 077741 33493
Fax: 020 7930 1152
Email: rdhmedals@aol.com
Website: www.rdhmedals.com
A selection of British campaign and gallantry medals,
British cap badges, Third Reich badges and medals, orders,
medals and decorations from around the world. Full medal
mounting and framing service. Court style of swing-style
mounting. Replacement and veterans medals supplied.
Open Mon–Fri 10am–4.30pm.

ST PANCRAS ANTIQUES
150 St Pancras, Chichester, W. Sussex PO19 7SH
Contact: Ralph Willatt
Tel: 01243 787645
An antique business, established for 20 years, specialising
in high quality arms and armour, militaria and medals,
early furniture, pre-1820 fine glassware and ceramics.

SOUTHERN MEDALS
16 Broom Grove, Knebworth, Hertfordshire SG3 6BQ
Contact: John Williams
Tel: 01438 811657
Fax: 01438 813320
Website: www.dalehamhouse.com/southernmedals
Dealers in orders, decorations and medals. Regular lists
issued. Subscription (four issues): £3.00 UK, £4.00 Europe,
£6.00 elsewhere. Send SAE for sample copy.

SPINK & SON LTD
5 King Street, St James's, London SW1Y 6QS
Contact: David Erskine-Hill
Tel: 020 7930 7888
Fax: 020 7839 4853
Email: derskine-hill@spinkandson.com
Spink buy and sell orders, decorations and medals of the
world. A retail list, 'The Medal Circular' is published three
times a year and available by subscription. Also three
specialist auction catalogues per annum. Open Monday to
Friday, 9am to 5.30pm.

III ARM MILITARIA
PO Box 121, Market Rasen, Lincolnshire LN8 3GF
Contact: Duncamb Lamb
Tel/Fax: 01673 828159
British Victorian medals and Soviet documented awards a
speciality. Lists published periodically throughout the year.
SAE for free sample copy.

T L O MILITARIA
Longclose House, Common Road, Eton Wick, Nr Windsor,
Berkshire SL4 6QY
Contact: Tony Oliver
Tel: 01753 862637
Fax: 01753 841998
Email: tlo.militaria@virgin.net
Specialists in DDR collectables at all levels of scarcity and
price. Mail order; callers welcome seven days a week, BY
PRIOR APPOINTMENT.

TOAD HALL MEDALS
Toad Hall, Newton Ferrers, Devon PL8 1DH
Tel: 01752 872672
Fax: 01752 872723
Email: th.medals@virgin.net
Established mail order medal business producing five lists
annually each with several hundred constantly changing
items, including British Gallantry singles and Foreign
sections. Also includes Nazi award documents and military
miscellania. SAE for latest list.

THE TREASURE BUNKER
21 King Street, Glasgow, Scotland G1 5QZ
Contact: Kenny Andrew
Tel: 0141 552 8164
Fax: 0141 552 4651
Email: info@treasurebunker.com
Website: www.treasurebunker.com
We specialise in British and German militaria from WWI
and WWII. We also stock items from before this period
and have a stock of most nationalities from all conflicts.
We offer a mail order catalogue @ £4.00. UK and £6
overseas. We also offer a state of the art e-commerce
website and high street retail premises.

MILITARY VEHICLES

A C MILES (INSURANCE CONSULTANTS) LTD
663 High Road, Leytonstone, London E11 4RD
Contact: Alan & Moira Cogdell
Tel: 020 8989 9595
Specialists in historic military vehicle and militaria
insurance.

*A C V M A
79 Avenue de la Premiere Armée, 63300 Thiers, France
Contact: Joel Dosjoub

*A N A C A
La Gerbe de Ble, Place J.Guihard, 44130 Blain, France

AEROSPACE & VEHICLE CLUB
163 Bells Lane, Stourbridge, W. Midlands DY8 5DS
Contact: J van Leerzem

A F BUDGE (SALES) / RYTON ARMS
West Carr Road, Retford, Notts DN22 7SR
Contact: Tony Budge
Tel: 01977 860222
Fax: 01909 530231
Email: afb@btinternet.com
Wide range of deactivated weapons from WWI and II
always available. Suppliers and dealers in armoured
military vehicles from the 1940s–1970s, principally
ex-British Army: Stalwarts, Ferrets, 432 APCs, Abbot
SPG, Centurion and Chieftain tanks.

ALLIED FORCES
York Cottage, Old Gloucester Road, Alveston, Bristol
BS35 3LQ
Contact: Jim Clark
Tel: 0117 9247945
Mobile: 0831 378904
Contact: Martin Hammond
Tel: 01454 415575
Military vehicle restorers and canvas manufacturers.

ANCHOR SUPPLIES LTD
Peasehill Road, Ripley, Derbyshire DE5 3JG
Contact: Barbara Merrett
Tel: 01773 570139
Fax: 01773 570537
Also:
The Cattle Market, Nottingham, NG2 3GY
Tel: 0115 9864902 or 9864041
Fax: 0115 9864667
Email: sales@govsurplus.co.uk
Website: www.govsurplus.co.uk
Anchor Supplies is one of Europe's largest genuine
government surplus dealers. Specialising in clothing,
tools, electronics, domestic ware, furniture, watches,
military vehicles, you name it! Goods are available mail
order, or visit our Derbyshire or Nottingham depots.
Please ring for directions.

ARMOUR AND SOFTSKIN LTD
Unit 5, Brandon Business Centre, Putney Close, Brandon,
Suffolk IP27 0PA
Tel: 01842 819430
Fax: 01462 819429
Mobile: 07711 516152
Email: sales@armourandsoftskin.com
Website: www.armourandsoftskin.com
We specialise in sales, spares and repairs of all British
military vehicles.

*ASSOCIATION DE VEHICULES MILITAIRES
Automobile Club du Rhône, 7 Rue Grolek, 69002 Lyon, France

C & C MILITARY SERVICES LTD
Based at Aylesbury, Bucks and Newmarket and Suffolk
Tel/Fax: 01296 658761
Mobile: 07889 127720
Email: ccmilitaryservices@btinternet.com
Many vehicles for sale. Full workshop facilities available.
Any vehicle catered for–soft skin or armour.

*C L V M A
51 Rue Daubree, 57245 Peltre, France
Contact: Isabelle Mann

CHAMP SPARES UK
Woodgate Farm, Stubby Lane, Draycott in the Clay,
Staffordshire DE6 5HA
Tel/Fax: 01283 820050
The specialist dealer in British WWII and postwar military
vehicle spare parts.

CLEMENTS TRADING
Rijksweg Zuid 44, 6662 KE Elst (Gld), The Netherlands
Tel: 481352460
Fax: 481352470
Mobile: 655885206
Email: clements.trading@worldonline.nl
Military Surplus and collectables; military vehicles, Harley
Davidson parts (WLA & WLC).

*CLUB D'AMATEURS DE MATERIEL MILITAIRE
B.P.508, 77304 Fontainebleau Cedex, France

*CLUB DE L'EST DE VEHICULES MILITAIRES
Musée de l'Automobile, Bainville aux Miroirs, 54290 Bayon,
France

*CLUB EUROPEEN DE MATERIEL MIL HIST
65 Avenue de Versailles, 75016 Paris, France
Contact: Christine Verrier

*CLUB LORRAIN DE VEHICULES MIL ALLIES
Impasse Didier Leroy, 57159 Morenchy Marauges, France
Contact: Alain Bertelotti

COBBATON COMBAT COLLECTION
Chittlehampton, Umberleigh, Devon EX37 9RZ
Contact: Preston Isaac
Tel/Fax: 01769 540740
Email: preston@cobattoncombat.co.uk
Private collection of about 50 vehicles, tanks and artillery,
British, Canadian, some Warsaw Pact, fully equipped. Home
Front section. Militaria shop. Open daily April–November,
Winter Mon–Fri.

COLIN WATERWORTH
125 Ashton Road, Newton le Willows, Lancs WA12 0AH
Tel: 01925 226186
Email: orion323@tinyworld.co.uk
Collector of Boeing B-17 Flying Fortress parts and aviation
equipment.

COLLS DES VEHICULES MILITAIRES/OUEST
Le Quebec, 72330 Cerans-Foulletourte, France
Contact: Jean Royer

DALLAS AUTO PARTS
Cold Ash Farm, Long Lane, Hermitage, Newbury, Berkshire
RG18 9LT
Contact: Stephen Rivers
Tel: 01635 201124
Fax: 01635 202479
Website: www.dallasautoparts.com
WWII Dodge and Jeep specialist. Military vehicles for sale.
Servicing, spares and accessories also available, including
mail order.

ERIK HAXE
Leeuwerikstraat 22, 2802 GG Gouda, Holland
Tel: 0182 582345
German vehicles, engines and parts.

ESCADRON DE L'HISTOIRE
35 Avenue des Gobelins, 75013 Paris, France
Contact: Andre Lecocq

FALLINGBOSTEL WWII & 2RTR REGT. MUSEUM
MBB3 Lumsden Barracks, Fallingbostel BFPO 38, Germany
Contact: Kevin Greenhalgh
Museum of WWII relics/items recovered from the actions
around Fallingbostel, including the POW camps 11B and
326. 2RTR Regimental Museum covers regimental history
1916 to the Gulf War; uniforms, large collection of WWII
RTR items, photos, books, etc.

FOOTMAN JAMES
Tel: 0121 561 4196
The vehicle enthusiast's insurance broker

FSU CONNECTIONS LTD
9 Heatherlands, Sunbury-on-Thames, Middlesex TW16 7QU
Contact: Oleg Savochkin
Tel: 01932 770836
Fax: 01932 786257
Email: fsu@rusmilitary.com
Website: www.rusmilitary.com
Russian military & outdoor clothing and equipment. Plus
2WD Ural Army combinations, night vision goggles, binocu-
lars, sights, rifle scopes, deactivated AKs, air rifles, assault
vests, insignia etc. Manufacturer's catalogues available.

GOTT & WYNNE
11 Madoc Street, Llandudno, North Wales LL30 2TH
Tel: 01492 870991
Fax: 01492 878600
Email: enquiries@ottandwyne.co.uk
Website: www.gottandwynne.co.uk
Specialist insurance for the classic and military vehicle.
Policies based on a limited mileage—comprehensive—
agreed value. Phone for a quote.

GRAHAM PILGRIM
15 Ticehurst Close, Worth, Crawley RH10 7GN
Tel: 01923 885388
Automobile historian, specialising in sales brochure and
catalogue dating, from the early 1900s to the present day.

HISTORY ON WHEELS MOTOR MUSEUM
Longclose House, Little Common Road, Eaton Wick,
Nr.Windsor, Berkshire
Contact: Tony L Oliver
Tel/Fax: 01753 862637

HUMMER UK OWNERS CLUB
Contact: Patrick Kear
Tel: 01924 249261
Fax: 01924 249006
Mobile: 07775 863506
Email: patrick@jeepclub.prestel.co.uk

IMPERIAL WAR MUSEUM DUXFORD
Duxford Airfield, Cambridge, Cambridgeshire CB2 4QR
Contact: Frank Crosby
Tel: 01223 835000
Fax: 01223 837267
Email: mail@iwm.org.uk
Website: www.iwm.org.uk
Houses the largest collection of military and civil aircraft in
the country, totalling over 140. Also exhibiting over 100
military vehicles, artillery, and much more.

INVICTA MILITARY VEHICLE PRESERVATION TRUST
The Old Rectory, Sandwich Road, Ash, Canterbury, Kent CT3 2 AF
Contact: Rex Cadnam
Tel: 01304 813128
Fax: 01304 812422
Email: rex@warandpeace.uk.com
Website: www.warandpeace.uk.com
Invicta runs the military vehicle preservation society show
at Beltring.

LEJEUNE JEEP MONS
St Maccaire 1, 7034 Obourg, Belgium
Tel/Fax: 003265364117
Specialising in MB/GPW/CJ parts and accessories

JEEPARTS UK
The Old Station, Broome, Craven Arms, Shropshire SY7 0NX
Contact: Amanda or Graham
Tel: 01588 660400 or 660700
Fax: 01588 660777
Mobile: 0410 837577

JEEP SUD EST
Village d'Entreprises ERO, RN 7 Vaucluse, 84700 Sorgues,
France
Tel: 04 90395627
Fax: 04 90398629
Specialising in Jeep, Dodge, GMC. Parts and accessories etc.

LINCOLNSHIRE MILITARY PRESERVATION SOCIETY
Memories, 20 Market Place, Alford, Lincolnshire LN13 9EB
Contact: Trevor Budworth
Tel/Fax: 01507 462541
Established 1981, and dedicated to WWII social, dances, military vehicles, battle re-enactment. British, American, German units with own field HQ at former RAF station. New recruits, ex-service, and associated groups welcome. Charity events undertaken.

LYS TOUT TERRAIN
Route de Clarques, 62129 Thérouanne, France
Tel: 03 21934378
Fax: 03 21380475
Email: lys.tout.terrain@wanadoo.fr
Website: www.lys-tout-terrain.com
Specialising in Jeep, Berliet, Renault, Simca, Mercedes, MAN, Reo, Dodge and GMC.

MARCUS GLEN
Hope House, Hundreds Lane, Little Sutton, Nr Spalding, Lincolnshire PE12 9AJ
Contact: Marcus Glen
Tel: 01406 364753
Fax: 01406 364745
Email: marcus.glenn@btinternet.com
Website: www.marcusglenn.com
We carry large stocks of spare parts for most postwar British armoured and soft skinned vehicles. Call for a quote.

MB/GPW
Henley House, Wadhurst Road, Frant, Tunbridge Wells, Kent TN3 9EJ
Contact: Dick Pettman
Tel: 01892 750249
Jeep parts and accessories.

M & C MOTORCYCLES
110 Cricklewood Broadway, London NW2
Tel: 020 8450 0505
Europe's largest ex-military motorcycle specialists, dealers in Can-Am & Armstrong. Repairs and servicing.

*MILITARY CLUB DE NORMANDIE
Chateau de l'Abbaye, 27230 Le Theil Molent, France
Contact: Michel de Montrion

MILITARY VEHICLE CLUB OF IRELAND
Dresden House, Ballyshannon, Curragh, Co Kildare, Ireland
Contact: Seoirse Devlin
Tel/Fax: 045 485473
A club for people who are interested in the restoration and preservation of military vehicles.

MILITARY VEHICLE MUSEUM
Exhibition Park Pavillion, Newcastle-upon-Tyne, Tyne & Wear NE2 4PZ
Tel/Fax: 0191 281 7222
Website: http://llris.n199.org.uk/museums/milvehl.htm
The museum houses up to 50 military vehicles, mainly WWI, and 60 cabinets displaying WWI, WWII and postwar memorabilia plus WWI mock up trench.

MVPA
PO Box 520378, Independence, Missouri 64052-0378, USA
Tel: 816 833 6872
Fax: 816 833 5115
Email: CMV@mvpa.org
Website: www.mvpa.org
Established in 1976 as an international organisation dedicated to the restoration and preservation of historic military vehicles and host to the largest annual swap meet and vehicle display in the USA.

MVR LTD
Oak Business Park, Wix Road, Beaumont, Essex CO16 0AT
Tel: 01255 871113
Fax: 01255 871109
Email: mvr@mil.com
Website: afvupgrades.com
Specialists in automotive upgrades and refurbishments for a wide range of tracked and wheeled AFVs.

MILITARY VEHICLE TRUST
96 Gawsworth Road, Macclesfield, Cheshire SK11 8UF
Contact: T R Hayter
Tel: 01625 23353
Vehicle Verification Officer. Provides help to obtain civilian registrations from D.V.L.A. at Swansea.

MILITARY VEHICLE TRUST
PO Box 6, Fleet, Hampshire GU13 9PE
Contact: Nigel Godfrey
Tel/Fax: 01264 392951
Email: nigelgodfrey@)mvt.org.uk
Website: http://www.mvt.org.uk
Website: http://www.mvt.org.uk/contacts.html
The Trust is an international group which supports the military vehicle enthusiast. There is a quarterly magazine 'Windscreen' and a bimonthly newsletter, club shop etc.

MVT BERKS & OXON AREA
White Cottage, Nunhide Farm Lane, Sulham, Pangbourne, Berks
Contact: Sheila Ward
Tel: 01189 303141
Meet 2nd Wednesday in the month, 8.00pm: The Plough, Long Wittenham.

MVT BIRMINGHAM & WEST MIDLANDS
46 Harvest Road, Smethwick, Warley, W. Midlands B67 6NH
Contact: Bob Davies
Tel: 0121 429 7606
Meet 1st Tuesday in the month, 8.00pm
United Services Club, Gough Street, Birmingham.

MVT BLETCHLEY PARK
The Bungalow, Bletchley Park, Wilton Avenue, Bletchley, Milton Keynes MK3 6EF
Contact: Gordon Beale
Tel: 01908 322578

MVT BRITISH FORCES, GERMANY
Klinter Kirch Weg 6, Adolphsheide, 29683 Fallingbostel, Germany
Contact: Herr Kev Greenhalgh

MVT CHESHIRE & MERSEYSIDE
6 Grasmere Road, Ellesmere Port, South Wirral L65 9BR
Contact: Alex Jenkins
Tel: 0151 356 3330
Meet 8pm 2nd Tuesday in the month at The Shell Club,
Dunkirk Lane, Ellesmere Port, South Wirral.

MVT CORNWALL
Bissom Cottage, Mylor, Nr. Penryn, Cornwall. PR10 9LJ
Contact: Adrian Snell
Tel: 01326 374984

MVT CUMBRIA
7 Bowlands Drive, Kendal, Cumbria, LA9 6LT
Contact: Jimmy Miller
Tel: 01539 732931
Meetings held on last Tuesday in month. General Woolfe
Pub, Little Dockray in the centre of Penrith.

MVT DALES
94 Burnside Avenue, Skipton, N. Yorkshire BD23 2DA
Contact: Glynn Beresford
Tel: 01756 794849
Meet 2nd Wednesday of Month at the Tarn House Hotel,
Stirton, Nr Skipton, North Yorkshire.

MVT DEVON
Meet 3rd Wednesday in month at the Smugglers Inn,
Steamer Quay, Totnes.

MVT DORSET
35 Purbeck Close, Wyke Road, Weymouth, Dorset DT4 9QU
Contact: John Butcher
Tel: 01305 778444
Meet 3rd Tuesday of the month at the Parley Sport Club,
Christchurch Road, Parley Cross, Bournemouth, Dorset.

MVT EAST MIDLANDS
Falcon House, Leverton Road, Sturton le Steeple, Retford
DN22 9HE
Contact: Robert Fleming
Meet 2nd Monday of the month (except January) at Hop
Pole Hotel, Ollerton, Notts.

MVT ESSEX
Contact: Colin Tebb
60 Molrams Lane, Gt. Baddow, Chelmsford, Essex CM2 7AJ
Tel: 01245 476249
Meet 4th Thursday in month at the The Crown, Sandon,
Chelmsford, Essex

MVT GUERNSEY
Contact: Deborah Doherty
Passchendaele, Rue des Pointues Rocques, St Sampson,
Guernsey GY2 4HW
Tel: 01481 249227
Meet 2nd Tuesday in month at The Harton Lodge Hotel,
Rue du Galaad, Castel, Guernsey.

MVT HEATHROW & WEST LONDON
50 Harlington Road, East Feltham, Middlesex TW13 5BN
Contact: Roger Jerram
Tel: 020 8890 2714
Meet 3rd Monday of month at the Railway Club, Harlington
Road East, Feltham, Middlesex.

MVT HERTFORDSHIRE
'Glenthorn', Hempstead Road, Hunton Bridge, Watford, Herts.
WD1 3NH
Contact: Andy Camp
Tel/Fax: 01923 269026
Meet 2nd Wednesday of the month at The Kings Head,
Bridge Road, Hunton Bridge, Herts.

MVT IRELAND
Contact: Seoirse Devlin
Dresden House, Ballyshannon, Curragh, County Kildare,
Ireland
Tel: 045 485473
or
Contact: John Anderson
Ballyrickard Road, Raloo, Larne, County Antrim, Northern
Ireland BT40 3EQ
Tel: 01574 277350

MVT ISLE OF WIGHT
'The Dell', The Causeway, Freshwater, Isle of Wight
PO40 9TN
Contact: Derek Harvey
Tel: 01983 753208
Meet 3rd Friday of Feb, April, June, August, October,
December at Yafford Mill.

MVT JERSEY
La Chasse, Le Chemin, De L'Eglise, St Ouen, Jersey JE3 2HG
Contact: Richard Le Brocq
Tel: 01534481748
Meet 1st Wednesday of month, 7.30. at Jersey Rugby Club,
St. Peter.

MVT KENT
80 Cornwall Road, Herne Bay, Kent, CT6 7SX
Contact: Anne Phillips
Tel: 01227 367662
Meet 2nd Monday of month at the Share and Coulter Pub,
Owls Hatch Road, Greenhill, Herne Bay.

MVT MID HANTS
6 Hawthorne Road, Denmead, Hants PO7 6LJ
Contact: John Lines
Tel: 01705 268318
Meet 2nd Thursday of month at the Chairmakers Pub,
Worlds End, near Portsmouth.

MVT NORFOLK
Rowan Lodge, Dareham Road, Yaxham, Norfolk NR19 1RF
Contact: Terry Quinn
Tel: 01362 691985
Meet 1st Thursday of month at the Wensum Lodge, King
Street, Norwich.

MVT NORTH EAST
Contact: Jon Kerr
22 Castleton Road, Seaton Carew, Hartlepool, Cleveland
TS25 1EF
Tel: 01429 275408
Meet 2nd Tuesday of month at the Seaton Social Club,
Station Lane, Seaton Carew.

MVT NORTH LONDON
64 Brunswick Park Road, New Southgate, London NW11 1JJ
Contact: Pam Church
Tel: 0181 361 1524
Meet 2nd Tuesday in month at the 'Oakmere House' Pub,
High Street, Potters Bar.

MVT NORTH STAFFORD
1 High St, Wood Lane, Nr Audley, Staffs ST8 9PB
Contact: Mark Simmons
Tel: 01782 723852
Phone Mark for details of meetings.

MVT NORTH WEST
Contact: Peter Cartner
12 Limefield, off Kings Drive, Middleton, Manchester
M24 4ED
Tel: 0161 643 4534
Meet 1st Thursday of month at the British Rail Staff
Association Club, Edgeley Road, Stockport.

MVT NORTHUMBRIA AND TYNE TEES
7 Cragside Farm, Rothbury, Morpeth, Northumberland
NE65 7PX
Contact: Denny Thompson
Tel: 01669 620233
Meet 1st Friday in the month at Bridge Hotel, Croxdale,
South of Durham on old A1.

MVT POWYS AND MID WALES
23 Garden Village, St. Martins, Oswestry, Shropshire
SY11 3AU
Contact: Mrs. Williams
Tel: 01691 778147
Meet the Last Monday in month at the Four Crosses public
house, Four Crosses, Powys (between Oswestry &
Welshpool).

MVT SCOTLAND
Contact: John Webster
2 Knockniddeling Cottages, Maybole, Ayrshire KA19 8LB
Tel: 01655 760215
Meetings not held due to distances involved.

MVT SEVERNSIDE
The Armoury, 130, Stapleton Road, Easton, Bristol BS5 0PH
Contact: Steve Curtis
Tel: 01179 510915
Meet last Thursday in month at the Rnyal British Legion,
Regent Street , Kingswood, Bristol.

MVT SHROPSHIRE & BORDER COUNTIES
Darn-O-Dir, Green End, Presteigne, Powys, LD8 2DT
Contact: Mike Edwards
Tel: 01544 267114
Meet 2nd Wednesday in month at the The Wroxeter Hotel,
Wroxeter, nr Shrewsbury.

MVT SOLENT
7 Hart Plain Avenue, Cowplain, Waterlooville, Hants. PO8
8RP
Contact: Lesley Taylor-Cram
Tel: 01705 250463
Meet 3rd Weds in month at the Royal British Legion Hall,
Forest End, Waterlooville.

MVT SOUTH CUMBRIA & NORTH LANCASHIRE
3 Bell Hill, Levens, Kendal, Cumbria, LA8 8NQ
Contact: Tony Martin
Tel. 01539 561329
Phone for details.

MVT SOUTH EAST MIDLANDS
7 Highfield Street, Market Harborough, Leicestershire
LE16 9AL
Contact: Tim Webster
Tel: 01858 433355
Meet 1st Thursday in month at the T.A. Drill Hall, Clare
Street, Northampton.

MVT SOUTH MIDLANDS
12, The Ridgeway, Astwood Bank, Redditch, Worcs B96 6LT
Contact: Neil Wedgbury
Tel: 01527 892282
Meet 2nd Monday in month at the Strawberry Field pub
(on the A46 Evesham bypass).

MVT SOUTH WALES
Contact: Ernie Williams
46, Tydraw Street, Port Talbot, West Glamorgan SA13 1BT
Tel: 01639 770946
Meet 2nd Tuesday in month at Taibach Rugby Club,
Commercial Road, Taibach, Portalbot (on A48 one mile
east of Portalbot town centre).

MVT SUFFOLK
Cherry Tree Cottage, The Street, Stoke Ash, Eye IP23 7EW
Contact: Quentin Brundle
Tel: 01379678119
Meet 2nd Tuesday in month at the Royal British Legion
Club, Tavern Street, Stowmarket, Suffolk.

MVT SURREY & HAMPSHIRE BORDERS
272 Mytchett Road, Mytchett, Camberley, Surrey
Contact: Wayne Boroman
Tel: 01252 546238
Meet 1st Wednesday in month at The Normandy Cricket
Club, Hunts Hill Road, Normandy, Guildford, Surrey.

MVT SUSSEX
PO Box 12, Peacehaven, E. Sussex BN10 8RA
Contact: David King
Tel/Fax: 01273 579727
Contact David for meeting details.

MVT WESSEX
Contact: Richard (Dick) Fryer
10, Easthams Rd, Crewkerne, Somerset TA18 7AQ
Tel: 01460 74250
Meet 3rd Saturday in month at The Windwhistle Inn
(on A30 between Crewkerne & Chard).

MVT WEST LANCASHIRE
21 Bath Street, Waterloo, Liverpool L22 5NY
Contact: Dave De Roos
Tel: 0151 928 1703
2nd Wednesday in month at The Kicking Donkey, Ormskirk.

MVT WILTSHIRE
Wren Cottage, Silverless Street, Marlborough, Wilts SN8 1JQ.
Contact: Clive Stevens
Tel: 01672 515030. mbl.0498 921992
Meet every 3rd Wednesday in month at The Bear, High
Street, Marlborough, Wilts. (Eastern end of High Street,
A4).

MVT YORKSHIRE
24, Cranbrook Avenue, Acomb, York YO26 5JF
Contact: Nick Butler
Tel: 01904 330684
Meet 1st Wednesday in month at the The Crown Hotel,
Boston Spa.

*MUSÉE DE LA BATAILLE DES ARDENNES
08270 Novion-Porcien, France
Tel/Fax: 24232013
1870, World War I, but particularly important World War II
vehicle, uniform, and weapon collection.

*MUSÉE DE LA CAVALERIE
Ecole d'AABC, 49409 Saumur, France
Tel/Fax: 41510543
Open by appointment, afternoons except Fridays; closed
August. All periods, but important World War 11 AFV col-
lection, housed at French Army Armoured Cavalry School.

*MUSEUM OF ARMY TRANSPORT
Flemingate, Beverley, Humberside (N.) HU17 ONG
Tel: 01482 860445
Fax: 01482 866459
History of Army transport from the Boer War to the present
day. Over 110 vehicles; archives, workshops, restoration,
Sir Patrick Wall model collection, Blackburn Beverley air-
craft, book/gift shop. Open daily 10am–5pm, free parking;
cafeteria.

*MEMORIAL DE VERDUN
Fleury-devant-Douaumont, 55100 Verdun, France
Tel/Fax: 29843534
Important WWI collection including uniforms, equipment,
artillery, dioramas, etc.

MVR (MILITARY VEHICLE REPAIRS)
Oak Business Park, Wix Road, Beaumont, Essex CO16 0AT
Contact: Iain Greenwood
Tel: 01255 871113
Fax: 01255 871109
Email: mvr@mil.com
Website: www.afvupgrades.com
MVR was formed to maintain support and supply mili-
tary and ex-military vehicles from around the world.
With a 10,000sq foot workshop complex near
Thetford, we can cater for any vehicle from a Ferret or
Jeep to Main Battle Tanks. We provide spares, servic-
ing, maintenance, fabrication, restoration, painting and
technical assistance worldwide and quotations; our
website contains example of projects that we have
recently completed.

*M V C G AQUITAINE
3 Quai Hubert Prom, 333000 Bordeaux, France
Contact: Jean Gomis

*M V C G ARTOIS
La Charite, 62400 Bethune, France
Contact: Dr Frederic Rey

*M V C G CENTRE
40 Rue de la Gare, 36120 Ardentes, France
Contact: Eric Boussardon

*M V C G CHARENTE
La Tenaille, 17240 St Denis de Saintonge 17240, France
Contact: Francois Begouin

*M V C G COTE D'AZUR
Imm. Les Marguerites, 65 Avenue Raoul Dufy, 06200 Nice, France
Contact: Michel Caligaris

*M V C G EST
5 Rue du Roerthal, 68530 Buhl, France
Contact: Bernard Rost

M V C G FRANCE
BP 24, 79201 Parthenay, France
Contact: J C L Fillon
Tel/Fax: 549943945
Email: FILLONJ@district.parthenay.fr
French federation of military vehicle collectors' clubs, 700
members, 120 vehicles.

*M V C G GASCOGNE
Chcmin de Gaouere, 32000 Auch, France
Contact: Alfred Algeri

*M V C G GRAND RHONE-ALPES
16 Place du Commerce, 71250 Cluny France
Contact: M Noel

*M V C G ILE DE FRANCE
78 Rue de la Roquette, 75011 Paris, France
Contact: Jean Pisapia

*M V C G MIDI-PYRENEES
Locadour, RN 113, 47420 Bon Encontre, France
Contact: Thierry Jacques

*M V C G NORMANDIE
25 Rue de l'Observatoire, 76600 Le Havre, France
Contact: M Sautreuil

*M V C G PAYS DE LOIRE
Les Esnauderies, Douille Menard, 49520 Combrecy, France
Contact: Alain Quemener

*M V C G SIXTEENS CLUB
42 Rue Victor Hugo, 16600 Magnac sur Tourve, France
Contact: Gilles Ducouret

*M V C G VALLEE DU RHONE
Quartier Saint Laurent, 84350 Courthezon, France
Contact: Alain Gomez

NATIONAL MUSEUM OF MILITARY HISTORY
10 Bamertal, PO Box 104, L-9209 Diekirch, Luxembourg
Contact: Roland Gaul
Tel: 808908
Fax: 804719
Email: mnhdiek@pt.lu
Important collections from Battle of the Bulge 1944–45, life-size dioramas, uniforms, vehicles, weapons, equipment. Open from January 1–March 31: daily 14.00–18.00hrs; April 1–November 1: daily 10–18hrs; November 2–December 31: daily 14.00–18.00hrs; last ticket sold 17.15hrs.

PAUL GANDY
Email: Paul.gandy@btinternet.com
S Wales MAFA.

REGIA ANGLORUM
9 Durleigh Close, Headley Park, Bristol BS13 7NQ
Contact: J Kim Siddorn
Tel/Fax: 0117 964 6818
Email: 101364.35@compuserve.com
Website: http://www.ftech.net/-regia
From lean, predatory sea raiders and deep-sea traders to inshore fishing boats, Regia Anglorum has a range of six ship replicas from the Viking countries and early Norman times. Available for public events, private functions and film & TV work, these vessels add a whole new dimension to re-enactment. Regia Anglorum is the only re-enactment society in any period to own and operate ship replicas.

RELICS
20 St Wilfrid's Green, Hailsham, E. Sussex BN27 1DR
Contact: Colin Hodgson
Tel/Fax: 01323 842234
Website: www.relicsarmsandarmour.co.uk
Film prop quality replica 'Guns, Grenades, Missiles and Mines'. International mail order catalogue to current day. 'Flying Flags & Banners' national and military catalogue £2. 'Auld Arms' display quality arms and armour, including wild-west guns, scale model cannons, swords, pikes, axes, daggers, crossbows, flintlock muskets & pistols, and Nazi daggers: colour catalogue £4. 'Relics Arms & Armour' quality stage and living history pieces: catalogue £3.

R E M E MUSEUM OF TECHNOLOGY
Isaac Newton Road, Arborfield, Nr Reading, Berkshire
RG2 9LN
Tel/Fax: 01734 760421

RR MOTOR SERVICES LTD
Bethersden, Kent TN26 3DN
Contact: Tim Fuggle
Tel: 01233 820219
Fax: 01233 820494
Email: tim@rrservices.co.uk
Website: www.rrservices.co.uk

STAMAN INTERNATIONAL TRADING
Transportweg 4, 7442 CT Nijverdal, Holland
Contact: Joop Staman
Tel: 0548 613446
Fax: 0548 613446
Army trucks and parts.

TANK MUSEUM
Bovington Camp, Wareham, Dorset BH20 6JG
Tel: 01929 405096
Fax: 01929 405360
Email: admin@tankmuseum.co.uk
The world's most comprehensive collection of AFVs. Free 'Firepower & Mobility' displays Thursdays 12 noon, July, August, September. Open daily 10am–5pm.

THOMAS TERRANG
Post Box 2102, S-433 02 Partille, Gothenburg, Sweden
Tel: 4631264848
Fax: 4631264849
Mobile: 46708264848
Jeeps. Mini-jeeps

T S AUTO'S
Contact: Tony Sudds
Tel: 01474 703131
Fax: 01322 861191
European agents for M V Spares. Uniquely Jeep and Jeep parts.

*U S TANK CORPS
5bis Rue des Iris, 52000 Chaumont,
France

WILLIAM GALLIER'S SPORTS CARS
Tel: 01694 731373
Fax: 01694 731746
Email: info@willysjeeps.com
Website: www.willysjeeps.com
Classic car and ex-military vehicles. Sales, repair, restoration, hire, export, import.

W F WELLS & SON
410/411 High Street, Brentford, Middlesex TW8 0DU
Tel: 020 8047 2109 or 020 8568 8889
Fax: 020 8568 3656
Ex-Government surplus and secondhand vehicles. Builders plant and machinery.

YANKEE JEEP CLUB
112 Plainthorpe Lane, Crigglestone, Wakefield, W. Yorkshire
WH4 3HE
Contact: Patrick Kear
Tel: 01924 249261
Fax: 01924 249006
Mobile: 07775 863506
Email: patrick@jeepclub.prestel.co.uk
American Jeep enthusiasts club.

THE VW 181/182 REGISTER
40 Chelmsford Road, South Woodford, London E18 2PP
Contact: Ian Harrison
Tel: 020 8504 9834
Fax: 020 8262 5752
Email: iandharrison@lineone.net
Listing of all known British 181s and 182s.

WARSAW PACT FORCES GROUP
Contact: David Brennan
Email: dave@iconism.net
We are a group of collectors who respectfully and correctly depict the forces of the Eastern Bloc during the Cold War period of the last century. The WPFG is a non-political organisation which wishes to advance living history through the enthusiasm and enjoyment of its members.

WILLIAM GALLIERS
Tel: 01694 731373
Fax: 01694 731746
Website: www.willysjeeps.com
Classic car and ex-military vehicles. A good selection of military jeeps always in stock.

JOHN & MARY WORTHING
Spout House, Orleton, Ludlow SY8 4JG
Tel: 015 84 83 12 39
Fax: 015 84 83 15 54
Email: canvasco@aol.com
Website: www.canvasco.com
23 years making canvas for military vehicle enthusiasts, manufactured in England from top quality US canvas and hardware. Canvas parts for all major vehicle types. See our online catalogue.

MODELLING CLUBS & SOCIETIES

BRITISH MODEL SOLDIER SOCIETY (BMSS)
44 Danemead, Hoddesdon, Hertfordshire EN11 9LU
Tel: 01992 441078
Email: model.soldiers@btinternet.com
Website: www.model.soldiers.btinternet.co.uk
The UK's leading society for military modellers, painters, and collectors. Regular meetings held in London and around the country (see branch list below). Members receive the quarterly 'Bulletin' magazine, additions to the 'BMSS Handbook' and 'Bulletin Extra' newsletters. Events include the BMSS Annual Show, Competitions, and the Society Auction.

BMSS BRISTOL
The Old Coach House, 18 York Place, Clifton, Bristol BS8 1AH
Tel: 0117 973 2067

BMSS DEVON
Warleigh Avenue, Keyham, Plymouth, Devon PL2 1NP
Tel: 01752 556811

BMSS DORSET
20 Crusader Road, Bearwood, Poole, Dorset BH11 9TZ
Tel: 01202 573553

BMSS EAST MIDLANDS
7 Arran Close, Stapleford, Notts NG9 8LT
Tel: 01159 170511

BMSS GRAMPIAN
Findon Croft, Findon, Portlethen, Aberdeen AB12 3RT
Tel: 01224 780606

BMSS LONDON (NORTH)
Stoneyfields Lane, Edgware, Middlesex HA8 9SL
Tel: 020 8959 3176

BMSS LONDON (SOUTH)
125 Lethbridge Close, Lewisham Road, London SE13 7QW
Tel: 020 8691 1746

BMSS LONDON (EALING/WEST)
93 Leighton Road, West Ealing, London W13 9DR
Tel: 020 8840 2284

BMSS NORFOLK & SUFFOLK
11 Fulmar Way, Oulton Broad, Lowestoft, Suffolk NR33 8PL.
Tel: 01502 581131

BMSS NORTHANTS
35 St. Barnabas Street, Wellingborough, Northants, NN8 3HA
Tel: 01933 383018

BMSS NORTH EAST ENGLAND
7 Hever Close, Etherley Dene, Bishop Auckland DL14 0LW
Tel: 01388 606141

BMSS NORTHERN
24, Broad Oak Lane, Penwortham, Preston, Lancashire
PR1 0UX
Tel: 01772 745952

BMSS NORTH HERTS
Oakwell Close, Bragbury End, Stevenage, Herts SG2 8UG
Tel: 01438 814225

BMSS OXFORD
17 Cary Close, Newbury, Berkshire RG14 9QT
Tel: 01635 820168

BMSS SHROPSHIRE
2 Holland Drive, Muxton, Telford, Shropshire TF2 8RA.
Tel: 01952 676822

BMSS SOUTH HANTS
6 Anderson Close, Woodley, Romsey, Hampshire SO51 7UE
Tel: 01794 501770

BMSS SUSSEX
78 Deerswood Road, West Green, Crawley, W. Sussex RH11 7JR
Tel: 01293 442850

BMSS WALES
305, Chepstow Road, Newport, Gwent, Wales NP9 8HJ
Tel: 01633 272579

BMSS WILTSHIRE
Apple Garden, Corsley, Warminster, Wiltshire BA12 7QL.
Tel: 01373 832323

*AMIS D'HISTOREX & FIGURINES HISTORIQUES
75 Rue Henri Barbusse, 77290 Mitry-Mory, France
Contact: M Hanin

AEROSPACE & VEHICLE CLUB
163 Bells Lane, Stourbridge, W. Midlands DY8 5DS
Contact: J Van Leerzem
Annual show and competition.

CITY & EAST LONDON MODEL MAKING CLUB
St John Ambulance Hall, East Avenue Walthamstow,
London E17
Contact: Paul Melton
Tel/Fax: 020 8559 0189 (pm)

CORNWALL MILITARY MODELLING SOCIETY
24 Central Avenue, St.Austell, Cornwall PL25 4JG
Contact: T Grainger-Allen

DARLINGTON MILITARY MODELLING SOCIETY
127 Dinsdale Crescent, Darlington, Co Durham DL1 1EZ
Contact: Colin Holmes
Tel/Fax: 01325 489801
Meetings on second Friday of each month at 7.30pm in the
Arts Centre, Vane Terrace, Darlington. Figures, vehicles, air-
craft etc. Subscription 110 per year.

*DE TINNEN TAFELRONDE
Jan van Nassau Str 10f, 2596 BIZ Den Haag, Netherlands
Contact: J R Mengarduque

EAST MIDLANDS MODEL CLUB
65 Shilton Road, Barwell, Leicestershire LE9 8HB
Contact: Gordon Upton
Tel: 01455 848772
Fax: 01455 230952
Scale model club for AFV, figure, marine and aircraft mod-
ellers. Meets first Monday of each month at the RAFA Club,
Lancaster Road, Hinckley, Leics. at 7.30pm. Subscription
£5.00.

ESSEX SCALE MODEL SOCIETY
151 Pollards Green, Chelmer Village, Chelmsford, Essex
CM2 6UX
Contact: David Ball
Tel/Fax: 01245 004552
Figure, vehicle and aircraft modelling. Meetings at The
Cricketers, Moulsham Street, Chelmsford, Essex, at
19.30hrs on the first Wednesday of each month.

*FIGURINA HELVETICA
Postfach 649, CH-8025 Zurich, Switzerland

GLASGOW MINIATURE ARMOUR GROUP
15 Mill Street, Bridgeton, Glasgow, Strathclyde, Scotland
G40 1LT
Contact: Robert Burns

*GROUPEMENT DES CLUBS DE FIGURINES
75 Rue Henri Barbusse, 77290 Mitry Mory, France
Contact: M Hanin

HALESOWEN MILITARY MODELLING SOCIETY
45 Comberton Avenue, Kidderminster, Worcs DY10 3EQ
Tel/Fax: 01562 8.Z3829

IPMS
51 Richmond Road, Lincoln, Lincolnshire LN1 1LH
Contact: Ian Crawford
E-mail: liaison@ipms-uk.co.uk
Details of your local branch will be provided when joining the
Society, however a full list of over 60 Local Branches is
provided on our website. Many branches have local exhibitions
in libraries and model shops. Some branches develop liaisons
with international IPMS branches/chapters, most notable with
our neighbours on the other side on the English Channel.
Several shows and exhibitions throughout the year, including
the IPMS/UK Nationals (Scale Modelworld), many modellers
are drawn towards the competition table, but there is no undue
emphasis on competing against other modellers, should you
prefer not to compete, you are just as welcome.

IPMS Abingdon
1 Argentan Close, Abingdon, Oxon OX14 5QW
Contact: Tony Clements

IPMS Air Cadet Group
(Thames Valley Wing)
2 Headley Close, Woodley, Berkshire RG5 4SF

IPMS Avon
Contact: Mike Chilestone
143 Brockworth Yate, S. Glos BS37 8SP

IPMS Avro Lancs
243 Helmshore Road, Haslingden, Lancashire BB4 4DJ
Contact: Ian Southwood

IPMS Barnet
47 Dales Path, Borehamwood, Hertfordshire WD6 2SF
Contact: Les Rawlins

IPMS Birkenhead & District
15 Castleton Rise,, Moreton, Wirral, Merseyside L46 3SP
Contact: Geoff Sullivan

IPMS Birmingham
7 Lansdowne Road, Erdington, Birmingham B24 8AR
Contact: Rowland Turner

IPMS Bolton
6 Sandringham Road, Horwich, Bolton, Lancashire BL6 6NX
Contact: David Swift

IPMS Brampton
39 Ermine Way, Sawtry, Huntingdon PE28 5UQ
Contact: Sam Bratby

IPMS Bridlington & Wolds
31 Elm Road, Driffield, E. Yorkshire YO25 7SQ
Contact: Kevin Dolman

IPMS Chiltern
26 Leaves Spring, Stevenage, Hertfordshire SG2 9BH
Contact: Dave Burlison

IPMS Clacton
Contact: Peter Terry
42 Valley Road, Clacton-on-Sea, Essex CO15 4AJ

IPMS Cleveland
49 Runswick Avenue, Acklam, Middlesbrough, N. Yorkshire
TS5 8HY
Contact: Mike Burns

IPMS Country Members
3 Sandown Close, Seaton Delaval, Northumberland NE25 0NX
Contact: Paul Lloyd

IPMS Coventry & Warwickshire
15 Severn Road, Lower Stoke CV1 2BD
Contact: Carl Lewis

IPMS Cumbria
4 Orsova Gardens, Barrow-in-Furness, Lancashire
LA14 3HJ
Contact: Dave Stowell
Tel: 01229 470442

IPMS Derby & District
8 Oakwood Close, Stenson Fields, Derby DE24 3ET
Contact: Nick Allen

IPMS Dorset
8 Martins Way, Ferndown, Dorset BH22 9SJ
Contact: Graham Young

IPMS Durham
38 Caversham Road, Chapel House, Newcastle-upon-Tyne NE5 1JP
Contact: Brian Watt

IPMS East Neuk
6 Drybriggs, Balgarvie Road, Cupar, Fife, Scotland KY15 4AJ
Contact: Brian Murray

IPMS Edinburgh
10 Milton Bridge, Penicuik, Edinburgh EH26 0RD
Contact: Phil Spencer

IPMS Essex
70 Coopers Close, Chigwell, Essex IG7 6EY
Contact: Ken Johnson

IPMS Essex–South East
15 Wild Close, Hutton, Shenfield, Essex CM13 1JQ
Contact: Brian Thomas

IPMS Farnborough
6 Purslane, Wokingham, Berkshire RG40 2DD
Contact: Pete Readman

IPMS Fenland
73 Pilgrims Way. Spalding, Lincolnshire PE11 1LJ
Contact: Bill Pickering

IPMS Glasgow
33 Overlee Road, Clarkston, East Renfrewshire, Scotland
G76 8BY
Contact: Richard Dorward

IPMS Gloucester
123 Pheasant Way, Beechers Park, Cirencester, Glos GL7 1BJ
Contact: Jeff Brown

IPMS Grantham
The Old Sidings, Sewstern Lane, Harston, nr Grantham,
Lincolnshire NG32 1PL
Contact: John Tinkler

IPMS Hornchurch
5 Roslyn Gardens, Gidea Park, Essex RM2 5RH
Contact: Alan Carr

IPMS Keighley
13 Station Road, Denholme, W. Yorkshire BD13 4DE
Contact: Steve Gibbins

IPMS Kent
77 Sutherland Avenue, Petts Wood, Kent BR5 1QY
Contact: Jim Chapman

IPMS Leeds
Squirrel Cottage, Squirrel Ditch, Newsome, Huddersfield
HD4 6QF
Contact: Mike Robson

IPMS Leicestershire
6 Kestrel Close, Broughton Astley, Leicestershire LE9 6RX
Contact: Martin Connolly

IPMS Lincoln
4 Eastfield Street, Lincoln LN2 5ES
Contact: Ian Da Silva

IPMS London
14 Link Way, Hornchurch, Essex RM11 3RW
Contact: Wally Arrowsmith

IPMS London (SE)
100 Culverley Road, Catford, London SE6 2JY
Contact: Alan Patington

IPMS Manchester
49 Furnace Avenue, Ashton-under-Lyne, Lancashire OL7 9JL
Contact: Karen Cunliffe

IPMS Medway
4 Florence Street, Strood, Rochester, Kent CV11 4FT
Contact: Kevin Knowles

IPMS Mercia
7 Pembroke Way, Nuneaton, Warwickshire CV11 4FT
Contact: Simon Mepstead

IPMS Merseyside & District
Dunmail, Heswall, Wirral, Merseyside CH60 1XG
Contact: W. D. Carruthers

IPMS Mid-Sussex
7 Prospect Place, West Green, Crawley, Sussex RH11 7BA
Contact: Dave Allen

IPMS Milton Keynes
26 Treborough, North Furzton, Milton Keynes,
Buckinghamshire MK4 1LR
Contact: Phil Smith or Derek Barret

IPMS Miniature Armour Group
12 Merrygreen Place, Stewarton, Ayrshire, Scotland KA3 5EJ
Contact: Geoff Crow

IPMS Nene Valley
24 Field Rise, Yaxley, Peterborough PE7 3YT
Contact: Roger Bolt

IPMS Newark
40 Hykeham Road, Lincoln LN6 8AB
Contact: Fred Hempsall

IPMS Norfolk
Three Gables, Clint Green, Norwich Road, Yaxham
Dereham, Norfolk NR19 1AB
Contact: Graham Crisp

IPMS Northern Ireland
6 Rostrevor Close, Bangor, Northern Ireland BT19 1AF
Contact: Roger Andrews

IPMS North Somerset
15 Priory Road, Weston-Super-Mare, Somerset BS23 3HU
Contact: Fred Tooke

IPMS North West
Car & Motorcycle Club
19 Tannery Lane, Penketh, Warrington, Cheshire WA5 2UD
Contact: Paul McCracken

IPMS Nottingham
17 Quantock Close, Nottingham NG5 9QA
Contact: James Downham

IPMS Portsmouth
17 Victory Avenue, Horndean, Waterlooville, Hampshire PO8 9PH
Contact: Richard Parkhurst

IPMS Rotherham
42 Thicket Drive, Maltby, S. Yorkshire S66 7LB
Contact: Dave Neale

IPMS Rutland
25 Nene Crescent, Oakham, Rutland, Leicestershire
LE15 6SG
Contact: Jeremy Hall

IPMS Salisbury
'Lothlorien', 18 Llynton Avenue, Firsdown, Salisbury,
Wiltshire SP5 1SH
Contact: Peter James

IPMS Sheffield
57 Hemsworth Road, Norton, Sheffield, S. Yorkshire S8 8LJ
Contact: Dickon Green

IPMS Southampton
7 Litchfield Road, Midanbury, Southampton SO18 2BH
Contact: Nigel Robins

IPMS Stafford
3 Leedham's Croft, Walton on Trent, Swadlincote, Derbyshire
DE12 8NW
Contact: Terry Campion or John Tapsell

IPMS Stirling & District
30 Woodavens, Tullibody, Clackmannanshire, Scotland
FK10 2XA
Contact: Ernie Romer

IPMS Swindon
22 Thames Avenue, Greenmeadow, Swindon, Wiltshire
SN2 3NW
Contact: Dave Theobald

IPMS Tayside
46 Scott Street, Dundee, Scotland DD2 2AJ
Contact: Ron Mitchell

IPMS Telford
8 Whitemere Road, Mount Pleasant, Shrewsbury, Salop
Shropshire SY1 3BT
Contact: Gary Stevens

IPMS Thames Valley
72 Grosvenor Road, Caversham, Reading, Berkshire RG4 5ES
Contact: Hugh Beyts

IPMS Torbay & South Devon
17 Helford Drive, Broadsands, Paignton, S. Devon TQ4 7NL
Contact: Les Wells

IPMS Tyneside
9 Uplands Road, Darlington, County Durham DL23 7SZ
Contact: Andrew Harbron

IPMS Wakefield
3 Crescent Avenue, Rothwell, Leeds, W. Yorkshire LS26 0JT
Contact: Adrian Laycock

IPMS Wallingford
6 Saxons Way, Millbrook, Didcot, Oxon OX11 9RA
Contact: Steven Lovelock

IPMS Warrington
32 Mallard Lane, Birchwood, Warrington, Cheshire WA3 6NZ
Contact: Dave Foxall

IPMS Wessex
7 Litchfield Road, Midanbury, Southampton, Hampshire SO18 2BH
Contact: Karen Robins

IPMS West Glamorgan
4 Meol Bedwas, Birchgrove, Swansea, Wales SA7 9LF
Contact: Keith Ryder

IPMS West Riding
48 Shakespeare Grange, Harehills, Leeds, W. Yorkshire LS9 7UA
Contact: Chris Norfolk

GRAVESHAM MILITARY MODELLING SOCIETY
Tel: 01474 327003

LSA MODELS
151 Sackville Road
Email: lsamodels@mcmail.com

MINIATURE ARMOURED FIGHTING VEHICLE ASSOCIATION
45 Balmoral Drive, Holmes Chapel, Cheshire CW4 7JQ
Contact: Gary Williams
Tel: 01477 535373
Fax: 01477 5358892
Email: garywilliams@mafva.com
Website: www.mafva.com
MAFVA is a worldwide organisation of mainly modelmakers interested in military vehicles of all types. The
operation of the association revolves around the
dissemination of information, plans, photographs and news
through our magazine Tankette which is published six
times per year. Further information is posted on our website.

MAFVA BRANCHES AND REPRESENTATIVES
MAFVA Bristol
4 Greenfield Ave, Westbury-on-Trym, Bristol, Avon BS10 5LN
Contact: Dave Molyneaux

MAFVA Bedfordshire
53 Cambridge Rd, Langford, Biggleswade, Beds SG18 9PS
Contact: Barry Wood

MAFVA Cambridgeshire
21 The Wayback, Saffron Walden, Essex CB10 2AX
Contact: Steve Schwab
Email: bkp1956@cs.com
Monthly meetings at The George Inn, Babraham,
Cambridge, first Tuesday of each month 19.30hrs onwards.

MAFVA Cheshire
10 White Hart Lane, Wistaston, Crewe, Cheshire CW2 8EX
Contact: Malcolm Bellis

MAFVA Derbyshire
100a Whitemoor Lane, Belper, Derbyshire DE56 0HD
Contact: Ralph Page

MAFVA Devon
'Rosencombe', Inwardleigh, Okehampton, Devon EX20 3AZ
Contact: Edwin Adcock

MAFVA E. Sussex
1 Harebeating Drive, Hailsham, E. Sussex BN27 1HP
Contact: Tony Roberts

MAFVA Essex (Central)
50 Victoria Crescent, Chelmsford, Essex CM1 1QF
Contact: Tony Surridge

MAFVA Essex (East)
404 Main Road, Dovercourt, Harwich, Essex CO12 4DN
Contact: Ivan Airey

MAFVA Gloucestershire
158 Field Court Gardens, Quedgeley, Gloucester, Glos
GL2 4UA
Contact: Robert Griffin
Email: rob@griffin42.fsnet.co.uk

MAFVA Hampshire
15 Pine Manor Road, Ashley Heath, Ringwood, Hants
BH24 2EZ
Contact: Richard Lane

MAFVA Hampshire (South)
7 Litchfield Road, Midanbury, Southampton, Hants
SO18 2BH
Contact: Nigel Robins

MAFVA Hertfordshire (South)
9 Belswains Lane, Frogmore End, Hemel Hempstead, Herts
HP3 9PN
Contact: Chris Lloyd-Staples
Email: lloydstaples@btopenworld.com
Monthly meetings at the above address.

MAFVA Lincolnshire
23 Brinkhall Way, Welton, Lincoln, Lincs LN2 3NS
Contact: Mick Bell
Email: mick@the-belfry.demon.co.uk

MAFVA London
8 Vicarage Drive, Northfleet, Kent DA11 9HA
Contact: Peter Bailey
Tel: 01474 536232 (evenings)
Bi-monthly meetings in central London.

MAFVA Northumberland
5 Brinkburn Place, Amble, Northumberland NE65 0BJ
Contact: Barry Wright
Email: bwmodels@aol.com

MAFVA Nottinghamshire
22 Swallow Close, Basford, Nottingham, Notts NG6 0NF
Contact: David Johnson
Email: davidpmj1@aol.com

MAFVA Shropshire
20 Moreton Crescent, Belle Vue, Shrewsbury, Shropshire SY3 7BZ
Contact: Tim Roberts
Email: kempsfield@tagdigs.demon.co.uk
or:
MAFVA Shropshire
22 Springfield Avenue, Newport, Shropshire TF10 7HW
Contact: Andrew Tomlinson
Tel: 01952 825 629
Email: atomlinson@blueyonder.co.uk

MAFVA Somerset (South)
38 Sandringham Road, Yeovil, Somerset BA21 5JF
Contact: Mark Hazzard

MAFVA Somerset
22 Briar Close, Burnham-on-Sea, Somerset TA8 1HU
Contact: Shaun Matthews

MAFVA Southport
22 Kent Road, Birkdale, Southport, Merseyside PR8 4BJ
Contact: Stefan Switala
Email: stef@switala.freeserve.co.uk

MAFVA Staffordshire
53 Chapel St, Bignall End, Stoke-on-Trent, Staffs ST7 8QD
Contact: Alan Boughey

MAFVA Suffolk
10 Clements Way, Beck Row, Bury St Edmunds, Suffolk IP28 8AB
Contact: Gary Wenko
Email: gswenko@btopenworld.com

MAFVA Sussex
2 Green Close, Southwick, Brighton, W.Sussex, BN42 4GR
Contact: Richard Allebone
Email: sussex.mafva@ntlworld.com

MAFVA Tyne & Wear
14 Kensington Gardens, Parklands Estate, Wallsend, Tyne & Wear NE20 0UW
Contact: Gordon Rose

MAFVA Thames Valley
77 Armour Road, Tilehurse, Reading, Berkshire RG31 6HB
Contact: Mike Cooper
Email: coopmik1@hotmail.com

MAFVA W. Yorkshire
3 Wrenbury Cres, Cookridge, Leeds, W. Yorkshire LS16 7EF
Contact: Tony Chuter
or:
MAFVA W. Yorkshire
3 Silver Street, Newton Hill, Wakefield, W. Yorkshire WF1 2HZ
Contact: Karl Grubb
Email: karlgrubb@blueyonder.co.uk

MAFVA Wiltshire (West)
45 The Downlands, Warminster, Wiltshire BA12 0BD
Contact: Rick Hone

MAFVA Wirral
30 Dee Park Rd, Gayton, Heswall, Wirral, CH60 3RQ
Contact: Reg Schofield
Email: dr@dorreg.freeserve.co.uk

MAFVA York
24 Ullswater, York, N. Yorkshire YO2 2RS
Contact: Mike Welch

MAFVA Scotland (Glasgow)
15 Mill St, Bridgeton, Glasgow G40 1LT
Contact: Rab Burns

MAFVA Scotland (Grampian)
105 Craigiebuckler Avenue, Aberdeen AB1 8PB
Contact: Allen Davidson

MAFVA Scotland (Lothian)
Musselburgh, E.Lothian
Contact: Ian Hanratty
Email: ian@hanra.freeserve.co.uk
Monthly meetings in Edinburgh.

MAFVA South Wales
2 Maes Y Grug, Foxfields, Upper Church Village, Pontypridd, Mid-Glamorgan CF38 1UN
Contact: Paul Gandy
Email: Paul.Gandy@btinternet.com
Monthly meetings.

MAFVA AUSTRALIA (ACT)
PO Box 1281, Woden, ACT, 2606, Australia
Contact: Michael Grieve

MAFVA AUSTRALIA (NSW)
229 St.James Rd, New Lambton, NSW, 2305, Australia
Contact: Greg Douglas

MAFVA AUSTRALIA (Tasmania)
Antarctic Division, Channel Highway, Kingston, Tasmania, 7050, Australia
Contact: David Watts

MAFVA AUSTRALIA (WA)
29a Owston St, Mosman Park, W.A. 6012, Australia
Contact: Peter Ware
Email: Peter.Ware@eddept.wa.edu.au

MAFVA AUSTRALIA (PERTH)
33 Boronia Avenue Nedlands WA 6009 Australia
Contact: Jon Bailey.
Meets as members of Perth Military Modelling Society.

MAFVA AUSTRIA
Tivoligasse 69 / Top 14, Wien, A-1120, Austria
Contact: Karl Brandel

MAFVA BELGIUM
Rue de le Fraternité, 10 Braine-L'Alleud, B-1420, Belgium
Contact: Paul Binard

MAFVA CANADA (Alta)
9137 151st St. Edmonton (AB), T5R 1J5, Canada
Contact: Roy Reid

MAFVA CANADA (Ontario)
446 Lynd Ave, Mississauga (ON), L5G 2L6, Canada
Contact: Sandy McRorie

MAFVA FRANCE (SW)
1 Rue Ramparts, St.Jacques, Perpignan, F-66000, France
Contact: Gérard Vernet
Email: gvernet6@hotmail.com

MAFVA FRANCE (NW)
5 Rue de la Fontaine, Champigny, Saumur, F-49400, France
Contact: Spike Judd
Email: Tanketteed@hotmail.com

MAFVA FRANCE (C)
BP34, Valence d'Agen, F-82400, France
Contact: Alain Laffargue

MAFVA GERMANY
Mainstrasse 14, Mürfelden, D-64546, Germany
Contact: Ulrich Rohrbach

MAFVA GREECE
11 Polemonos Str., Pagrati, Athens, GR-116 35, Greece
Contact: Fyll Metsovitis
Email: torpy@e-free.gr

MAFVA HONG KONG
Flat 2B, Princes Garden, 284 Prince Edward Rd, West
Kowloon, Hong Kong
Contact: David Kan Che Leung

MAFVA ITALY
Via dei Tigli, 41, Calenzano, (FI) I-50041, Italy
Contact: Daniele Guglielmi
Email: dguglielmi@iol.it

MAFVA NETHERLANDS
Overtoom 244-3, Amsterdam, NL-1054 JA,
The Netherlands
Contact: Henk Visschers

MAFVA POLAND
Robotnicza 10m14, Pabianice, PL-95-200, Poland
Contact: Jerzy Hanczka

MAFVA PORTUGAL
Rua Dr. Ricardo Jorge, Venda Nova Amadora, P-2700-301,
Portugal
Contact: José Ventura

MAFVA ROMANIA
Str.Cameliei Nr 24, Bloc 114, Ap.78, Sc.D, Ploesti, 2000,
Romania
Contact: Dan Silvestru

MAFVA USA (CALIFORNIA)
9633 La Nuez Drive, Elk Grove, California, 95624, USA
Contact: Ken Brown

MAFVA USA (CALIFORNIA)
Rhino Models, 7317 Walnut Rd, Fair Oaks, California, 95628-
6725, USA
Contact: David Runkle

MAFVA USA (INDIANA)
5201 Canterbury Drive, Muncie, Indiana, 47304, USA
Contact: Poitr Kubiczek

MAFVA USA (INDIANA)
Harrier Court, Durham, North Carolina, 27713, USA
Contact: Adam Armstrong

MAFVA USA (INDIANA)
PO Box 189, Hasbrouck Heights, New Jersey, 07604-0189,
USA
Contact: Bill Postman

MAFVA USA (PENNSYLVANIA)
RD1, Box 397, Lock Haven, Pennsylvania, 17745, USA
Contact: Nickolas Walkowiak

MAFVA USA (TEXAS)
3413 Monte Vista Dr, Austin, Texas, 78731-5722, USA
Contact: Edward Poole

MAFVA USA (VIRGINIA)
14200 Foliage Ct, Midlothian, Virginia, 23112-4126, USA
Contact: Leo Johns

IRISH MODEL SOLDIER SOCIETY
12 Kingsland Parade, Portobello, Dublin 8, Ireland
Contact: Shane McElhutton
Tel/Fax: 1453917
IMSS welcomes modellers from all disciplines—figures,
vehicles, aircraft and ships. Workshops, trade stands,
monthly and annual competitions. Annual subscription
IM15.00.

K L I O—A G V
Papiererstrasse 34, 84034 Landshut, Germany
Contact: Fritz Neureuther

K L I O ARBEITSGRUPPE SHOGUN
Sperberweg 33, D-50997 Cologne, Germany
Contact: Axel Bücher
Tel/Fax: 243321379
Society of Japanese military history enthusiasts, manufacturing 30mm flat tin figures, organizing exhibitions in museums and annual sessions in Goslar. English spoken, enquiries welcome.

*L I H M C S
PO Box 118, Wantagh, New York 11793, USA
Contact: Kevin W Dunne
Tel: 516 764 7104
Long Island Historical Miniature Collectors Society–the major figure modelling club in the North-East USA–holds an annual exhibition and competition in November.

THE LEICESTER MODELLERS
Thurmaston Working Men's Club, Old Melton Road, Thurmaston, Leicestershire
Tel/Fax: 0116 2671057

LETCHWORTH & N HERTS MILITARY MODEL CLUB
6 Casion Way, Letchworth, Hertfordshire SG6 4QL
Contact: Frank Henson
Tel/Fax: 01402 685039
Incorporating North Herts BMSS branch. Meetings held at Plinston Hall, Letchworth, on third Wednesday each month at 7.30pm.

*MILITARY MINIATURE SOCIETY OF ILLINOIS
PO Box 394, Skokie, Illinois 60077, USA

M & P MODELS
1 Amwell Road, Kings Hedges, Cambridge CB4 2ULI
Tel/Fax: 01223 315101
Email: maurice@nobbybeth.demon.co.uk

RUDI GOOSSENS
Minksbossenstraat 13, 2220 Heist-op-den-Berg, Belgium
Tel/Fax: 32 015 251337
Mobile: 32 075 802606

*MINIATURE FIGURE COLLECTORS OF AMERICA
19 Mars Road, North Star, Newark, Delaware 19711, TJSA
Contact: Alban P Shaw

NORTH EAST MODELLERS
6 Jude Place, Peterlee, Co. Durham SR8 5JW
Contact: Len Swaisland
Tel/Fax: 0191 5867139

NORTH LONDON MILITARY MODELLING SOCIETY
4 College Court, Cheshunt, Hertfordshire EN8 9NJ
Contact: Jack Snary
Tel/Fax: 01992 038046
Members' interests include figures, AFVS, aircraft, naval and fantasy. Meetings 1900hrs first Friday of the month at Millfield House, Silver Street, Edmonton, London N18.

NORTH SURREY MILITARY GROUP
5 Flimwell Close, Bromley, Kent BR1 4NB
Tel/Fax: 020 8698 0890

*OSTERREICHISCHER ZINN-CLUB
Postfach 59, A-110 1 Wien, Austria

PETERBOROUGH MODEL MAKERS SOCIETY
58 Station Road, Nassington, Peterborough, Cambridgeshire PE8 6QB
Contact: Nick Tebbs
Tel/Fax: 01780 782274

PLYMOUTH MODEL SOLDIER SOCIETY
102 Warleigh Avenue, Keyham, Plymouth, Devon PI2 1NP
Contact: Harry Miller
Tel/Fax: 01752 556811

POOLE VIKING MODEL CLUB
20 Crusader Road, Bearwood, Poole, Dorset BH11 9TZ
Contact: Ian Groves
Tel/Fax: 01202 573553
Meetings held at the Civic Centre Social Club, Municipal Buildings, Poole, at 19.30hrs on the first Wednesday of each month. Covers all aspects of modelling. (Includes BMSS and IPMS branches.)

*S C A M M S
11456 Broadmead South, El Monte, California 91733, USA
Southern California Area Military Miniature Society hosts major exhibition / competition annually in March for figure and associated models. With seminars, auction, etc. International entries and attendance.

SOUTH HANTS MILITARY MODELLING SOCIETY
38 The Spinney, Fareham, Hampshire PO16 8QB
Contact: Terry Nappin
Tel/Fax: 01329 36365
Meetings held at Staff Club House, University of Southampton, University Road, Highfield, Southampton at 20.00hrs. on the first Wednesday each month.

SUTTON COLDFIELD MODEL MAKERS SOCIETY
Ashgrove, Didgley Lane, Fillongley, Coventry, Warwickshire CV7 8DQ
Contact: Robert Day
Tel/Fax: 01676 540469
The club caters for modellers of all kinds and ages. We hold competitions, workshops, social evenings and trips; entertain guest speakers; and display at shows.

SWEDISH MODEL FIGURE SOCIETY (CAROLINEN)
Alvkarleovagen 25, S-115 43 Stockholm, Sweden
Contact: Henrik Moberg
Tel/Fax: 6644024
Association for collectors of old toy soldiers, plastic figures, flats and model figures. We publish a magazine twice a year. Meetings are held regularly.

SWINDON MILITARY MODELLERS
20 Bryanston Way, Nythe, Swindon, Wiltshire SN3 3PG
Contact: Michael Copland
Tel/Fax: 01793 642020
Modelling group meets fortnightly (Sun). All standards and age groups.

UNIVERSAL MODELLING SOCIETY
Midland Adult School Union Ctrl, Gaywood Croft, Cregoe Street, Lee Bank, W. Midlands B45 2ED
Contact: Den Karsey
Tel/Fax: 0121 7054085
Over fifty members whose interests cover a wide range of modelling including military figures, ships, planes, armoured fighting vehicles, space and science fiction. Participates in major shows and holds own annual show. Meetings weekly, Mon 7.30pm-10.00pm.

WEST SCOTLAND MILITARY MODELLING CLUB
Koorydoon, Hollybush by Ayr, Ayrshire, Scotland KA6 7EA
Tel/Fax: 0129256 763
Scotland's largest figure modelling club covers all aspects and periods. Based in Glasgow; monthly meeting on Sundays; and hosts annual two-day show 'Suldiers'. Contact Secretary at above address for details.

WIRRAL MODELLING CLUB
10 Beaumaris Road, Wallasey, Merseyside L45 8NH
Contact: Ian Weir
Tel/Fax: 0151 639 3636
A club of widespread interests and abilities, meeting on the evening of the last Wednesday each month.

MODELLING EQUIPMENT & SERVICES

ALEC TIRANTI LTD
70 High Street, Theale, Reading, Berkshire RG7 5AR
Contact: J Lyons
Tel: 01189 302775
Fax: 01189 323487
Email: enquiries@tiranti.co.uk
Website: www.tiranti.co.uk
Sculptors' tools, materials and equipment, including silicone rubbers, white metals, centricast machines, fine modelling tools and materials, Milliput.
London branch: 27 Warren Street, W1P 5DG (020 7636 8565), open Mon-Fri 9am-5.30pm, Sat 9.30am-1.00pm. Theale: Mon-Fri 8.30am-5.00pm, Sat 9.30am-1.00pm (mail order). Access, Switch and Visa.

*ASSEMBLEUR MULTIFONCTION
5 Ruelle du Colombier, 78410 Nezel, France
Contact: M Dussieux

BASES AND CASES
308 Church Road, Kessingland, Lowestoft, Suffolk NR33 7SB
Tel: 01502 740791
Hardwood and MDF bases for figures, vehicles, planes and ships. Figure clamps and painting aids. Sculpture tools, button and rivet punch. Panel scribing tool. Diorama boxes and aids for flats painting. 32nd Street building components and miniature structural timber elements. Free brochure.

CAER CASTELL MILITARY MINIATURES
25 Two Stones Crescent, Kenfig Hall, Bridgend CF33 6DZ
Tel: 01656 743744
Contact: Anthony Arcari or Sally Quinton
Mail order suppliers of military miniatures and plastic figures and kits. Old and new 54mm, 1/32, 1/72. Many makes and models. We also have a shop at: Unit 9, High Street Arcade, Swansea–opposite Argos.

CARN METALS LTD
8 Carn View Terrace, Pendeen, Cornwall R19 7DU
Tel/Fax: 01736 787343
Email: info@carnmetals.co.uk
Manufacturer of high quality pewters, whitemetal casting alloys and soldiers from 250gms to 250kg.

*LE CIMIER
38 Rue Ginoux, 75015 Paris, France
Contact: Jacques Vuyet
Military figurines, plates of uniforms; books and documentation; working material. Exhibition of nearly 1,000 painted figurines.

COCKTAIL JOUETS
32 Rue Becquerel, 78130 Les Mireaux, France
Tel: 34743399
Fax: 3091461
Models and kits, including Historex, Nemrod, Fenryll, Des Kit, Nimix, Somov, Eduard, Classic Airframes, Special Hobby, Verlinden, Alexander.

C R CLARKE & CO (UK)
Unit 3, Betws Industrial Park, Ammanford, Carmarthenshire Wales SA18 2LS
Contact: Christoher Clarke
Tel: 01209 593860
Fax: 01209 591890
Email: sales@crclarke.co.uk
Website: http://crclarke.co.uk
Vacuum Forming equipment for model making, starting at 9 X 10in cut sheet size. Able to form acrylic, polystyrene, polycarbonate, etc to high definition.

CRAFT SUPPLIES LTD
The Mill, Miller's Dale, Nr. Buxton, Derbyshire SK17 8SN
Tel: 01298 871636
Fax: 01298 872263
Email: sales@craft-supplies.co.uk
Supplier of glass domes and bases to display and protect models. Catalogue available on request. Shop and mail order.

DAYLIGHT STUDIOS
223a Portobello Road, London W11 1LU
Contact: Matthew Briggs
Specialists in daylight lighting, magnification and visual accessories, including two very popular modellers' tools –a special rimless 5-inch flexiarm magnifier, and clip-on spectacle magnifiers.

DEAN FOREST FIGURES
62 Grove Road, Berry Hill, Coleford, Glos GL16 8QX
Contact: Philip & Mark Beveridge
Tel: 01594 836130
Wargame figure painting, scratch-built trees, buildings and terrain features. Large scale figure painting and scratch-building to any scale. SAE for full lists.

DIECAST INTERNATIONAL LTD
Website: www.diecast-international.com

*DIOSTAR
9 Grand Rue, 11400 Villeneuve la Comptal, France
Contact: Patrice Raynaud

D K L METALS LTD
Avontoun Works, Linlithgow, Lothian Scotland EH49 6QD
Tel/Fax: 01506847710
Email: dklmetals@aol.com

ENSIGN HISTORICAL MINIATURES
32 Scaitcliffe View, Todmorden, Lancashire OL14 8EL
Contact: Paul Wood
Tel/Fax: 01706 818203
Email: paul.wood@zen.co.uk
Suppliers of a wide range of 54mm traditional toy soldiers. Castings and painted figures available. English Civil War, Zulu Wars, Medievals, ancients, Indian Army, Cavalry, Infantry and artillery. Send £1 Cheque/Postal Order for illustrated lists made out to Paul Wood.

GEO W NEALE LTD
Victoria Road, London NW10 6NG
Tel: 020 8965 1336
Fax: 020 8965 1725
Email: phil@gwneal.fsnet.co.uk
Manufacturers of white metal casting alloys.

GRAPHIC AIR SYSTEMS
8 Cold Bath Road, Harrogate, N. Yorkshire HG2 0NA
Contact: Doug Taylor
Tel: 01443 522836
Fax: 01423 525397
Email: graphicairuk@btinternet.com
Mail order suppliers of airbrush/compressor & spraybooth equipment. Most makes of airbrush available at discount prices. Send for catalogue. Technical and product advice available.

HISTOREX AGENTS
Wellington House, 157 Snargate Street, Dover, Kent CT17 9BZ
Contact: Lynn Sangster
Tel: 01304 206720
Fax: 01304 204528
Email: sales@historex-agents.demon.co.uk
Website: www.historex-agents.demon.co.uk
Supplier of pyrogravures for plastic work, and punch and die sets, together with the finest Kolinsky sable paint brushes, etc.

HUMBROL LTD
Marfleet, Hull, N. Humberside HU9 5NE
Tel: 01482 701191
Fax: 01482 7-72908
Email: trevorsnowdon@humbrol.com

LANGLEY MODELS
166 Three Bridges Road, Crawley, W. Sussex RH10 1LE
Contact: Ian McLellan
Tel: 01293 516329
Fax: 01293 403955
Email: ian@langley-models.co.uk
Toy soldiers—foot, mounted, bands, gun teams—as castings or hand-painted. Also knights, Romans, mythological. Illustrated catalogue £3.55 post free. Mail order by return.

MAD TOY
11 Rue Oberkampf, 75011 Paris, France
Tel: 01 43555264
Email: madtoy@libertysurf.fr
Website: www.madtoy.ifrance.com
Model and toy soldiers bought sold and exchanged.

MAC WARREN
50 Sunnybank, Hull, N. Humberside HU3 1LQ

*MAQUETTE 21
9 Rue du Chapeau Rouge, Passage Bossuet, 2 1000 Dijon, France

*METAL MODELES
Quartier Engaspaty, Seillans, 83440 Fayence, France
Contact: Bruno Leibovitz

MILITES MINIATURES
Wild Acre, Minchinhampton, Glos GL6 9AJ
Design and manufacture 25mm and 40mm figures'; Seven Years War, Medieval, Plains Indians. Mail order only.

OPTUM HOBBY AIDS
PO Box 262, Haywards Heath, W. Sussex RH16 3FR
Contact: David Bedding
Tel/Fax: 01444 416795
Email: sylmaster@aol.com
Distributor of modelling materials: Sylmasta A+ B, Kneaclatite-Duro, Artificial Water, Superglues, pewter sheet, moulding rubbers, casting resins, No 5 wax carver, modelling tools, Milliput, Swiss Files.

PAINTWORKS
99–101 Kingsland Road, London E2 8AG
Contact: Dorothy Wood
Tel: 020 7729 7451
Fax: 020 7739 0 39
Art materials shop and mail order selling top quality oil and acrylic paints and a comprehensive range of brushes. Opening hours 9.30am–5.30pm Mon–Sat.

PICTURE PRIDE DISPLAYS
17 Willow Court, Crystal Drive, Sandwell Park, Warley,
W. Midlands B66 1RD
Contact: Eileen Bourn
Tel: 0121 544 4946
Fax: 0121 5529959
Email: rpb@picture-pride-displays.co.uk
Website: http://www.picture-pridedisplays.co.uk
Solid wood display cabinets in all finishes for your collect-
ables. Wall mounting, complete with polished edged glass
shelves. Totally dust proof Free colour brochure available.

SDKFZ MODELLBAU ARMOUR VEHICLE MODELS
Email: toshi@sdkfz-modellbau.com

*SOLDATS DE PLOMB
Route de Bourg, 38490 Fittilou, France
Contact: Joany Jabouly

SUMMIT SOLDIER PRODUCTS
Rail Works, Biggleswade, Bedfordshire SG18 8BD
Tel: 01767 318999
Fax: 01767 318912
Email: mountstar@compuserve.com
Manufacturers of high quality tin-lead and lead free pewter
casting alloys. Suppliers to the military modelling industry.

WHITTLESEY MINIATURES
75 Mayfield Road, Eastrea, Whittlesey Peterborough,
Cambridgeshire PE7 2AY
Contact: Keith Over
Tel/Fax: 01733 205131
Email: keith98@aol.com
Manufacturers and suppliers of high quality, painted 'toy'
soldiers. Currently specialising in Medieval and Ancient
subjects in 54mm. Master and mould making services are
available.

MODEL
MANUFACTURERS

*A & F NEUMEISTER (FLATS)
Hauptstrasse 98, 98553 Hirschbach, Germany

AB FIGURES/WARGAMES SOUTH
Ffos yr Eloig, Lianfynydd, Carmarthen SA32 7DD
Contact: Mike Hickling
Tel/Fax: 01558 668771
Email: michael@ab-figures.demon.co.uk
Website: www.ab-figures.demon.co.uk
Manufacturers of the 15mm AB Figure range for
wargamers and collectors; plus 10mm WWII and 19th
century wargames figures. Mail order only, SAE for lists.

ACCURATE ARMOUR LTD
Units 15–16, Kingston Industrial Estate, Port Glasgow,
Inverclyde PA14 5DG, Scotland
Contact: David Farrell
Tel: 01475 743 955
Fax: 01475 743 746
Email: 101363.74@compuserve.com
Website: www.accurate-armour.com
Largest UK producer of specialist 1/35 scale military
models of AFVs and accessories/conversions/decals. All
products available by direct mail order, catalogue £4.95+
postage. Also distributors for Collectors Brass (USA), MR
Models (Germany), FCM Models (Germany) and Kendal
Model Co. (USA), Art Box books (Japan) and Model Kasten
(Japan).

*AL BY MINIATURES
BP 34, Valence d'Agen 82400, France
Contact: Yannick Laffargue
Tel 563 291 122
Fax: 563 393 090
We produce a range of about 200 resin kits and conver-
sion sets to 1:35, 1:72 and 1:87 scales. We also cast for
other manufacturers.

*ALEXANDER WILKEN (FLATS)
Carl-Spitzweg-Platz 3, 85586 Poing, Germany
Tel/Fax: 81211972757

ALL THE QUEEN'S MEN
The Old Cottage, Gilmorton, Lutterworth, Leicestershire
LE17 5PN
Contact: D Cross
Tel: 01455 552653
Fax: 01455 557787
Email: derek@allthequeen'smen.com
Website: www.allthequeen'smen.com
Designers & producers of military miniatures (toy soldiers).
490 sets available. Full colour catalogue with descriptive
lists. Plus unique exquisite interlocking base vignettes.
Visits to our showroom/museum by appointment.

ANCIENT ARTILLERY MODELS
6 Arlington Close, Attleborough, Norfolk NR17 2NF
Contact: Mathew Shearn
Manufacturer of working scale models of Roman and
Medieval catapults, including the mangonel, onager and
ballistae; educational kit of the 13th century trebuchet
siege engine.

*ANNE-MARIE AMBLARD
4 Chemin du Luquet, 80120 Lannoy-les-Rues, France
Tel/Fax: 22250654
Large scale figure models in wax, fabrics, etc.; enquire for
details of one-off and limited edition subjects.

*ARTHUR SPEYER (FLATS)
Taunusstrasse 23, 65345 Eltville-Rauenthal, Germany

*ARTISAN MINIATURES
6 Overstone Court, Westwood, Peterborough, Cambridgeshire
PE3 7E

*AZIMUT PRODUCTIONS
8 Rue Baulant, 75012 Paris, France
Dealer and manufacturer of 1/35th scale military models;
we offer over 60 ranges of vehicles, figures, accessories
and books. Trade enquiries welcome.

AVANT GARDE MODELS
29 Barcaldine Avenue, Glasgow, Scotland G69 9NT
Contact: Derek McCarron
Website: ww.avantgarde2000.freeserve.co.uk
Producers of toy soldiers and military vehicles. Periods
covered include the Balkan wars, world wars, ACW etc.
Check our website for current production list.

*BAHR & SCHMIDTCHEN ZINNFIGUREN (FLATS)
Posnaer Str. 5, 04299 Leipzig, Germany

B & B MILITARY
1 Kings Avenue, Ashford, Kent TN23 1LU
Contact: Len Buller
Tel: 01233 632923
Fax: 01233 642670
Makers of military model vehicles and figures in Dinky
1/60 inch scale. All white metal. Mail order only: send SAE
for list of kits and finished models available. Colour
catalogue £3.50.

BENGURION MODELS
Glebe Farm House, East Keal, Spilsby, Lincolnshire PE23 4HA
Contact: Tim Humphries
Tel: 01790 754630
Manufacturers of white metal and resin military vehicles,
and aircraft to compliment. Toy soldiers 54mm scale. 1914
onwards. Catalogue £2.00 or SAE for details.

*BERLINER ZINNFIGUREN (FLATS)
Knesebeckstrasse 88, 10623 Berlin, Germany
Contact: Hans-Gunther Scholz
Germany's largest manufacturer and shop for flat tin
figures. Illustrated mail order catalogue available. Shipping
anywhere.

BORBUR ENTERPRISES
Unit 220, 62 Tritton Road, London SE21 8DE
Contact: M Borbur
Tel,fax: 020 8766 7227
Email: borburent@btinternet.com
Manufacturers of Steadfast Soldiers and white metal
casters.

BORDER MINIATURES
Fernlea, Penrith Road, Keswick, Cumbria CA12 4LJ
Contact: Peter Armstrong
White metal kits, 80mm, medieval subjects, designed by
Pete Armstrong. Direct mail order or through specialist
shops worldwide. Visitors welcome by appointment, illus-
trated catalogue.

*BRAUNSCHWEIGER ZINNFIGUREN (FLATS)
Schaferteich 4a, 38302 Wolfenbüttel, Germany
Contact: Dr Peter Dangschat
Speciality Victorian period, Regency, maritime figures,
ships, French Revolution, Vendee, Bonapartes, Napoleons,
Prussia, USA, Erotica.

*BREMER ZINNFIGUREN (FLATS)
Enscheder Strasse 13, 27753 Delmenhorst, Germany
Contact: Gunter Scharlowsky

C K SUPPLIES
28 Hillbrow Road, Bromley, Kent BR1 4JL
Contact: Carl Miller
Exclusive European distributors of 'Soldiers of Russia',
54mm lead/pewter models from St Petersburg, Russia.
Also exclusive manufacturers of 280mm bronze resin
military figurines. Mail order only.

*C M S
3 Square Valerie, 95260 Parmain, France

*C P GOLBERG (FLATS)
Christian-Rohlfs-Weg 11, 24568 Kaltenkirchen, Germany
Tel: 41911404
Fax: 419160746
Flats 30mm from Punic wars to Napoleonic, soldiers and
civilians. Dealers for Gottstein-Terana-Sivhed-Kovar-
Schramm. 6800 different items, catalogue available,
worldwide delivery.

B W MODELS
5 Brinkburn Place, Amble, Northumberland NE65 0BJ
Contact: Barry Wright
Tel: 0665 710702
Model kit manufacturers.

CAVENDISH MINIATURES
1 Little Buntings, Windsor, Berkshire
Contact: Tony Kite
Tel: 01753 855474
Fax: 01753 852178
Metal handpainted 54mm models of Marines, Guards,
Scottish and Irish Pipers, Germans, Knights of Garter,
Mounted Lifeguards, Drum Horse, Falkland Par artillery gun
carriage.

CLYDECAST MODELS
97 Fenemere Avenue, Clarkstom, Glasgow, Scotland G76 7RT
Contact: Tom Park
Tel: 0141 638 1904
Fax: 0141 589 4482
Email: clydecast@mtlworld.com
Website: www.homepage.mtlworld.com/clydecast
Designers and makers of military figures for collectors in
75mm/90mm/110mm scales.

COLONIAL SOLDIER

Apt 11, Thames Row, Kew Bridge Road, Middlesex TW8 0HG
Contact: Stewart Tuckniss
Tel/Fax: 020 8580 3945
Email: stewarttuckniss@colonialsoldier.freeserve.co.uk
Exclusive individually hand carved and painted 3.5–4ft,
2–6kg soldiers. 20 different designs.

CONCORDE MODELS

179 Victoria Road, Aldershot, Hampshire GU11 1JU
Contact: Brian Ballard
Tel/Fax: 01252 326825
Collector Model Soldier Kits, Toy soldiers, Plastic Kits,
Books and Accessories.

CONVOY

23 Mare Bay Close, St Leonard's on Sea, E. Sussex TN38
8EQ
Tel/Fax: 01424 854731
Artillery vehicles and equipment in 1/76th scale.

CORTUM FIGUREN (FLATS)

Auf dem Kluschenberg 5, 23879 Mnlln, Germany
Contact: Christian Carl

CORVUS MINIATURES

Bards Hall Cottage, Chignal Smealy, Chelmsford, Essex
CM1 4TL

DEREK CROSS (AQM) (All The Queens Men) LTD

The Old Cottage, Lutterworth Road, Gilmorton, Lutterworth
Leics LE17 5PN
Tel: 01455 552653
Fax: 01455 557787
Email: derek@allthequeensmen.com
Website: www.allthequeensmen.com
Designers and manufacturers of military miniatures.
Extensive Napoleonic range. All armies including vignettes
and limited editions utilising our exclusive interlocking
bases. Comprehensive price list and colour updates
available on request. New catalogue under production.

D M H MODELS

3 Greensand Road, Bearsted, Maidstone, Kent ME15 8NY
Contact: Derek Hansen
Miniature figure designer and manufacturer.

D P & G (MINIATURE HEADDRESS)

PO Box 186, Doncaster, S. Yorkshire DN4 0HN
Miniature headdress, 1/5th scale—British Household
Cavalry, Dragoon, Dragoon Guard, helmets; British and
French Lancer caps, Hussar busbies; infantry blue cloth
helmets; German Pickelhaubes. Special commissions
undertaken; send 3 first class stamps for catalogue.

*DANIEL HOHRATH (FLATS)

Berkheimerstrasse 50, 73734 Esslingen am Neckar, Germany
Editor and engraver of flat figures. Standard size 30mm:
Roman army, Frederick the Great, 18th century civilians-,
special series of 75mm cats. Catalogue DM 6.00.

DARTMOOR MILITARY MODELS

Woodmanswell House, Brentor, Tavistock, Devon PL19 0NE
Tel/Fax: 01822 82250

DAVCO PRODUCTIONS

28 Brook Street, Wymeswold, Loughborough, Leicestershire
LE12 6TU
Produces an extensive range of 1/3000th scale ship mod-
els and harbour accessories for and modern periods. Also
produce a range of 1/300th vehicle and aircraft models for
WWI and modern periods. All ranges, including new
Starguard space fleet model kits, are retailed through
Skytrex Ltd.

*DES KITS

27 Rue des Hauts de Bonne Eau, 94500 Champigny sur
Marne, France

DIECAST INTERNATIONAL LTD

Website: www.diecast-international.com

*DIETER SCHUBERT (FLATS)

Ritterstrasse 71, 79639 Grenzach-Wyhlen, Germany

*DIETER SCHULZ (FLATS)

Weinmeisterhornweg 169, 13593 Berlin, Germany

*DOLP ZINNFIGUREN

Im Paradies 20, 8940 Memmingen, Germany

*DR PETER HOCH (FLATS)

Meistersingerstrasse 8, 14471 Potsdam, Germany
Tel/Fax: 33197388
Artistically crafted models of historical personalities, cast in
metal, in every scale; construction of historically based
dioramas, models for exhibition purposes, replicas of military monuments.

*DR WOLFGANG VOLLRATH (FLATS)

Am Ruhrstein 11, 45133 Essen, Germany

DORSET SOLDIERS

Unit 112, South Way, Southwell Business Park, Portland,
Dorset DT5 2JS
Contact: Giles Brown
Tel: 01305 823003
Fax: 01305 823851
Email: dorset.soldiers@usa.net
Website: www.help-me.to/dorsetsoldiers
We produce a large range of 54mm toy soldiers, civilians
and associated equipment, both painted and unpainted, for
the collector who wants something different. Periods
covered from the Napoleonic Wars (and some earlier) up
to—the Future!

DRUMBEAT MINIATURES
4 Approach Road, Ramsey, Isle of Man IM8 1EB
Contact: Peter Rogerson
Tel/Fax: 01624 816667
Email: dbeatmin@aol.com
A large and rapidly expanding range of toy soldiers covering many periods and unusual subjects. Sets can be varied on request and a sculpting service is offered.

DUCAL MODELS
5 Weevils Road, Eastleigh, Hants SO50 8HQ
Contact: Jack Duke
Tel: 02380 692119
Fax: 02380 602456
Email: jackandthelma@fort-ducal.co.uk
Website: www.fort-ducal.co.uk
Makers and distributors of an international range of hand-crafted and painted 54mm metal mounted and foot ceremonial figures. World wide mail order; colour illustrated catalogue (£4.50) includes badges and postcards. Visitors welcome to see our extensive display weekdays 9am–4.30pm; also some Saturdays–phone for directions.

*E & G TOBINNIIS (FLATS)
Matthaikirchstrasse 58, 30519 Hannover, Germany

*EJ SCHULZE (FLATS)
Haustenbeck 2, 44319 Dortmund, Germany

*E KASTNER (FLATS)
Eichenhain 6a, 90571 Schwaig, Germany

EASTERN IMPORT & EXPORT
35 Kennedy Court, Stonehouse Drive,
St Leonards-on-Sea, E. Sussex TN38 9DH

*EDITH FOHLER (FLATS)
Isoppgasse 6, A-1238 Wien-Mauer, Austria

*EGON KRANNICH (FLATS)
Bergstrasse 6, 04828 Schmolen, Germany

*EFTTINGER ZINNFIGUREN (FLATS)
Bachstrasse 32, 76275 Ettlingen, Germany
Contact: Dieter Schwarz

FIANNA MINIATURES
78 Bridgefoot Street, Dublin 8, Ireland
Contact: Richard Keane
FM.offer a range of busts/figures dealing with the Irish Army and subjects. All figures in the range can be supplied painted and finished.

FORT ROYAL REVIEW
25 Woolhope Road, Worcester, Worcs WR5 2AR
Contact: David Gerrett
Manufacturer and supplier of finooast military figurine kits–format resin and white metal. Suppliers world wide. All enquiries welcome.

FORTRESS MODELS
87 Yew Tree Road, Southborough, Tunbridge Wells, Kent TN4 0BJ

*FRANKFURTER ZINNFIGUREN (FLATS)
Quellenweg 7, 61250 Usingen, Germany
Contact: Helga Lanipert

FRONT RANK FIGURINES
The Granary, Banbury Road, L. Boddington, Daventry,
Northamptonshire NN11 6XY
Contact: Alec Brown
Tel: 01327 262720
Fax: 01327 260569
Manufacturers of 25mm figures.

F & S SCALE MODELS
227 Droylsden Road, Audenshaw, Greater Manchester,
M34 5RT
Tel/Fax: 01613703235
Email: frank/sue@fsmodels.fsnet.co.uk

FUSILIER MINIATURES (MAIL ORDER)
The Command Post, 23 Ashcott Close, Burnham-on-Sea,
Somerset TA8 1HW
Contact: Tony Moore
Tel/Fax: 01278 786858
A wide range of hand-painted, well-detailed figures and guns in 1:32 scale. Sets and single figures available. SAE and £1.50 for current catalogue.

GLEBE MINIATURES
Retreat House, Dorchester Road, Broadwey, Weymouth, Dorset
DT3 5LN
Contact: Peter Turner
Tel/Fax: 01305 815300
Glebe Miniatures, in addition to their original range, now offer marching sets to complement action sets, and action sets to complement marching sets–all in the original Britain's style. The first sets represent the Balkan Wars and the Russian/Japanese conflicts. There are new mounted officers and action artillery sets. Other period sets will follow.

GOOD SOLDIERS
246 Broadwater Crescent, Stevenage, Herts SG2 8HL
Contact: Alan Goodwin
Tel: 01438 354362
A small but well established company. We specialise in Third Reich figures, but many other countries/regiments available. Also a large bank of other characters–Laurel & Hardy, Rupert, Dad's Army, etc. SAE please for a full list.

*GERHARD FETZER (FLATS)
Marktstrasse 761, 89537 Giengen, Germany

*GERLINDE & ULRICH LEHNART (FLATS)
Roulandstr. 41, 54294 Trier, Germany
Tel/Fax: 651 80194
Largest assortment of Medieval figures in 30mm of all periods from 1280 to 1480: military, civil and erotic. Documentation for painting. Catalogue against 5 IRCs.

GERT GROSSE (FLATS)
Salzburgstrasse 8, 73268 Erkenbrechtsweiler, Germany

*GLORIOUS EMPIRES (FLATS)
1 Vicarage Walk, Bray, Berkshire SL6 2AE
Contact: Jacques Vullinghs

G N M MINIATURES
Micawber, Yewbank, Skipton Road, Utley, Keighley,
W. Yorkshire BD20 6H
Contact: Graham Mollard
Tel/Fax: 015350 91587
65mm Napoleonic miniatures created by Graham Mollard,
strongly influenced by the work of Fernande Metayer and
Roger Berdou.

*GUNTER FUHRBACH (FLATS)
Im Himmelreich 4, 59320 Ennigerloh, Germany

G W LACY
315a South Lane, New Malden, Surrey, KT3 5RR
Hundreds of soldiers of all nationalities all 1/76th in scale.

*H D OLDHAFER (FLATS)
Huttfleth 48, 21720 Grunendeich, Germany

*HANS G LECKE (FLATS)
Finkenstrasse 19, 31543 Rehburg, Germany

*HANS JOACHIM REIBOLD (FLATS)
Treuenbrietzener Strasse 14, 13439 Berlin, Germany

HART MODELS LTD
Cricket Green, Hartley Wintney, Hampshire RG27 8QB
Tel/Fax: 01252 842637
Email: hart@asam.co.uk
Manufacturers of the world's largest range of high quality
1/48 scale military models and kits. Send £1 or 3 IRCs for
full list.

*HECKER & GOROS ZINNFIGUREN
Romerhofweg 51c, 8046 Garching, Germany

HECO
23 Addison Road, Brockenhurst, Hampshire SO4 27SD

*HEIDRUM URICH (FLATS)
Guardini-Strasse 139, 81375 München, Germany

*HEINRICH JEISMANN (FLATS)
Münsterstrasse 49, 44145 Dortmund, Germany

*HEINZ TETZEL (FLATS)
Wespenstieg 3, 03090 Magdeburg, Germany

HELMET SOLDIERS
Mundy's Farm, Middle Road, Aylesbury, Buckinghamshire HP21 7AD
Contact: George Hill
Tel/Fax: 01296 415710
Manufacturer of 54mm cavalry and infantry kits. Mainly
Napoleonic. Illustrated spare parts catalogues on request.
Suitable for dioramas, single display figures or wargaming.

*HERBU ZINNFIGUREN (FLATS)
Weidenbruch 15, 21147 Hamburg, Germany

HEROICS & ROS FIGURES
Unit 12, Semington Turnpike, Semington, Trowbridge,
Wiltshire BA14 6LB
Tel: 01380 870228
Fax: 01380 871045
Email: heroics.ros@virgin.net

H ZWICKY AU VIEUX PARIS
1 Rue de la Servette, CH-1201 Geneva, Switzerland
Tel: 227342576
Fax: 227347709
Shop open in 1964: everything for the military modeller.

HINCHCLIFFE MODELS
28 Brook Street, Wymeswold, Loughborough, Leicestershire
LE12 6TU
Cast metal model kits. Extensive range 54mm I/-35th
scale figures and equipment, Medieval to WWII. 20mm
1/76th scale £2 vehicle kits. Mail order available.

*HISTORIA (FLATS)
Lindenstrasse 39, 40789 Monheim, Germany
Contact: Marie-Luise Muller

*HORST TYLINSKI (FLATS)
Achtermannstrasse 53, 13187 Berlin, Germany

HUSSAR MILITARY MINIATURES
3 Third Avenue, Hayes, Middlesex UB3 2EF
Contact: Michael Hearn
Tel: 020 8573 4597
Fax: 020 8573 1414
We manufacture a large range of white metal figures,
mainly Medieval and Samurai in 90mm and 54mm scales.
Colour catalogue available at £4.00.

I/R MINIATURES INC
PO Box 89, Burnt Hills, New York 12027, USA
Contact: William Imrie
Tel: 518 885 6054
Fax: 518 885 0100
Largest manufacturer of 54mm kits supplying the trade in
the USA: over 1,000 subjects from ancient to present mili-
tary, plus literary subjects.

*INGRID TROTHE (FLATS)
Narzissenweg 13, 06118 Halle, Germany

*IRENE & MICHAEL BRAUNE (FLATS)
Dammweg 1, 01662 Miessen, Germany

IRREGULAR MINIATURES
3 Apollo Street, Heslington Road, York YO1 5AP
Contact: I Kay
Tel/Fax: 01904 671101
Ranges of white metal figures in following scales: 2mm;
6mm; 10mm; 15mm; 20mm; 25mm; 42mm; 54mm. Rules,
accessories, award winning rapid mail order service.

IT FIGURES
193 St Margaret's Road, Lowestoft, Suffolk NR32 4JX
All nationalities WWII 1/76th scale.

J B CHUCH
Honrywood, Middle road, Tiptree, Nr Lymington, Hants SO41 6FX
British & American plans in 1/76th scale.

J F BENASSI
55 St Mungo Avenue, Glasgow, Strathclyde G4 0PL, Scotland
Contact: Julian Benassi
Designer of white metal model soldiers, produced in small quantity and available by mail order. Send for catalogue. Painting service also available.

*J PEDDINGHAUS ZINNFIGUREN
Beethovenstrasse 20, 5870 Henner 5870, Germany

*JURGEN SCHMITTDIEL (FLATS)
Postfach 1220, 35276 Neustadt/Hessen, Germany

*KARL ROMUND (FLATS)
Lavesstrasse 19, 30159 Hannover, Germany

*KARL-WERNER REIGER (FLATS)
Melsdorferstrasse 77, 24109 Kiel, Germany

KING & COUNTRY
20 Rockingham Way, Portchester, Fareham, Hampshire PO16 8QS
Contact: Mike Neville
Tel/Fax: 01329 233141
Email: mike@kingandcountry.co.uk
Suppliers of fine quality, all-metal, handpainted 54mm military and civilian figures, plus handcarved 1:32 scale desk top display. Aircraft and vehicles. Mail order our speciality.

*KJELD LULLOFF (FLATS)
Lauravej 14/60, Copenhagen 2000, Denmark
Contact: Kjeld Lulloff
Private collection figures of Danish kings: 8 centimetre.

*KLAUS HOFRICHTER (FLATS)
Gebeschusstrasse 48, 65929 Frankfurt, Germany

*KLAUS KARBACH (FLATS)
Talstrasse 83, 41516 Grevenbroich, Germany

*KLAUS KITTLEMANN (FLATS)
Halleschestrasse 62a, 06366 Kothen, Germany

LANCER
Forest View, Holt Pound, Farnham, Surrey GU10 4SZ
Contact: Margaret Bracey
Tel: 01420 22354
Email: lanmab@aol.com
Website: www.4milmodels.com
Lancer is a small company producing 54mm figures for the collector and modeller. Ranges include Victorian/Edwardian civilians, police figures, American Civil War and War of Independence. Lancers, colonial contingents from the 1953 Coronation and Gurkhas also feature in the catalogue.

*LISELOTTF, MAIER (FLATS)
Steinstrasse 8, 91086 Aurachtal, Germany

*LUBECKER ZINNFIGUREN (FLATS)
Schaarweg 3, D-23683 Scharbeutz, Germany
Contact: Marleen Worbs
Tel/Fax: 450 374488
Prussian 18th century, 'Menzel' figures; War of American Independence 1775-1783; Lubeck State & Militia troops 1750-1900 Hanoverian 1820; complete showcase sets.

MACS MODELS
133-135 Canongate, The Royal Mile, Edinburgh, Lothian EH8 8BP, Scotland

MARKSMEN MODELS
(Dept MDS), 7 Goldsmith Avenue, London W3 6HR
Contact: Michael Ellis
High quality, low cost plastic figures from 25mm to 120mm, most periods from ancient to Korean War. Mostly cast from original Marx and Ideal moulds. Also sculpting and visualising for many leading manufacturers.

*MARTIN ANDRA (FLATS)
Narzissenweg 13, 06118 Halle, Germany

*MARTINA VOGEL (FLATS)
Finkenstrasse 7, 72294 Grombach, Germany

MATADOR MODELS
6 Cliffe Road, Barton-on-Sea, New Milton, Hants BH25 7PB
Fax (only): 01425 628219

M BELL
The Belfry, 23 Brinkhall Way, Welton, Lincs LN2 3NS
All nationalities in 1/76th scale

*MELLITA VON DROSTE (FLATS)
Ulrichsrain 32, 71729 Erdmannshausen, Germany

*METAL MODELES (FLATS)
Quartier Engaspaty, Seillans, 83440 Fayence, France
Contact: Bruno Leibovitz

M & C MODELS
32 London Road, Teynham, Kent ME9 9QN
Mail order distributors of 'Roco' precision plastic semi-assembled H.O. scale (1:87) models of military and civilian models.

*M D M LES GRANDES COLLECTIONS
9 Rue Villedo, 75001 Paris, France
Tel/Fax: (0033) 14261 7601
Manufacturer of tin soldiers, miniatures for collectors; Napoleonics; French Regimental standards of US War of Independence; mail order service.

M P STUDIOS
23 Peregrine Close, Winshall, Burton-on-Trent, Staffordshire DE15 0EB
Professional model maker and figure painter—the finest quality painted figures available, by national competition winner. Commissions undertaken to your own specifications; quality guaranteed—a sure investment. Character figures also available—all we need is a photograph. Write or call for more information.

MIL-ART
41 Larksfield Crescent, Dovercourt, Harwich, Essex
CO12 4BL
Tel/Fax: 01255 507440
Email: mikeduncan_uk@yahoo.com
Producers of metal military figure kit in 54mm, 80mm
and 100mm scales. Also retailer of new and out-of-print
military books.

MICK LUNN METAL MASTERS
46 Staindale, Guisborough, Middlesbrough, Cleveland TS14 8JU
Tel/Fax: 01287 652700

MILICAST
PO Box 711, Glasgow, Strathclyde, Scotland G41 2HX
Contact: Tom Welsh
Manufacturers of authentic scale model military kits in
1:76 scale in polyurethane resin; over 100 kits in the
range. Also specialise in all WWII AFVS, soft-skins, tanks,
armoured landing vehicles etc. Send SAE for free catalogue. Mail order.

MILITARY MOTORS
16 Coolhurst Lane, Horsham, W. Sussex RH 13 6DH
British World War II vehicles in white metal, 1/7600 scale,
hand made and painted for display or wargaming; SAE for
catalogue.

MILITARY PAGEANT
45 Silverston Way, Stanmore, Middlesex RA7 4HS

MILITIA MODELS
Rosedean, Gorsty Knoll, Coleford, Glos GL16 7LR
Contact: Esme Walker
Cottage industry still producing—after sudden death of
founder Ken Walker—small number of new 54mm figures
in limited edition action sets, 1870-1902 period.

MITRECAP MINIATURES
Manorfield House, 46 Main Street, Sheffield, S. Yorkshire
S31 0XJ

MMS MODELS
Unit 23, Uplands Industrial Estate, Sawtry Way, Wyton,
Cambridgeshire
Tel: 01480 414415
Email: mms_models@hotmail.com
MMS models represents the current state-of-the-art in
white metal casting. Three expanding ranges feature the
vehicles, guns and troops of WWII, all in constant 1:76
(20mm) scale. The 'Classic' vehicle and 'Gunpack' towed
gun kits contain full instructions; including general tips, if
you've never worked with white metal before. Robust and
easy to assemble, they are ideally suited to the Wargamer
and yet have the accuracy and a wealth of detail that
gives satisfaction to the serious collector.

*MOPICOM
104 Avenue Pierre Semard, 95400 Villiers le Bell, France
Contact: Rene Henry
Resin-made military scale models at 1/35 and 1/87 (HO)
scale.

NAVWAR PRODUCTIONS LTD
11 Electric Parade, Seven Kings, Ilford, Essex IG3 8BY
Tel/Fax: 020 8590 6731
Manufacturers of 1/3000 and 1/1200 scale ships,
Roundway and Naismith 15mm figures; 1/300 figures,
tanks & aircraft. Closed Thursdays.

NEW CAVENDISH BOOKS
3 Denbigh Road, London W11 2SJ
Tel: 020 7229 6765
Fax: 020 7792 0027
Email: narisa@new-cav.demon.co.uk
Specialist publishers of quality illustrated books on toys
and other collectables.

*NECKEL ZINNFIGUREN (FLATS)
Hattenhoferstrasse 11, 73066 Uhingen, Germany

*NEW CONNECTION MODELS
Dorfgutingen 40, 91555 Feuchtwangen, Germany
Tel: 98 52 4329
Fax: 98 52 3594
High quality conversions and figures in 1/35 scale.

NEW HOPE DESIGN
Rijksweg 42, 6269 AC Margraten, Netherlands
Contact: Josephine Huntjens
Tel: 43458 2211
Fax: 43458 2626
Email: info@nh-design.com or soldier@cobweb.nl
Website: http://www.nhdesign.com
Produces nearly two thousand white metal figure kits in
54mm size. A comprehensive listing/catalogue is available
on request.

OLD GLORY CORPORATION
Institute House, New Kyo, Stanley, Co Durham DH9 7TJ
Contact: Andrew Copestake
Tel: 01207 283332
Fax: 01207 281902
UK and European agents for Old Glory Corp, PO Box 20,
Calumet, PA 15621 USA. Phone 724 423 3580, fax 724
423 6898. Manufacturers of a wide range of 25mm,
15mm and 20mm scale figures in a wide range of periods.
Trade enquiries welcome worldwide.

*ORIGINALHEINRICHSEN-FIGUREN (FLATS)
Marktstrasse 14, 76883 Bad Bergzabern, Germany
Contact: Kurt Wilms

PARADE FIGURES
65 Shilton Road, Barwell, Leicestershire LE9 8HB
Contact: Gordon Upton
Tel: 01455 230952
Fax: 01455 615747
Email: modelspot@dialpipex.com
Distributors of quality Russian-made 54mm figures,
featuring Italian Carabinieri, Russian Napoleonic,
Revolutionary, 17th century, and personality series. SAE
for full list. Trade/mail order welcome.

PARAGON DESIGNS
39 Cantley Lane, Norwich, Norfolk NR4 6TA
Tel: 01603 507152
Fax: 01603 506057
Over 200 conversion and accessory sets available for the
scale aircraft modeller.

PATRICKS TOYS AND MODELS
107–111 Lillie Road, Fulham, London
Tel: 020 7385 9864
Fax: 020 7385 2187
Website: www.patrickstoys.co.uk

*PETER EWALD KOVER (FLATS)
Liechtensteinstrasse 66/5, A-1090 Wien, Austria

*PIERRE BOURRILLY (FLATS)
81 Avenue de Montolivet, 13004 Marseille, France

*PIERRE BRETEGNIER (FLATS)
505 Rue des Moulins, 28260 La Chaussee d'Ivry, France

PIPER CRAFT
4 Hillside Cottages, Glenboig, Lanarkshire ML5 2QY, Scotland
Contact: Thomas Moles
Tel: 01236 873801
Fax: 01236 873044
Manufacturer of white metal military and non-military
figures designed to a general scale of 75mm. Suppliers to
museums, places of historic interest, shops and collectors.
Established 1985. Send SAE or 2 x IRCs for a complete
illustrated list.

POCKETBOND LTD
PO Box 80, Welwyn, Hertfordshire AL6 0ND
Contact: Phillip Brook
Tel: 01707 391509
Fax: 01707 327466
Website: http://www.btinternet.com\-pocketbond
Exclusive importer for: Squadron Signal Publications and
Squadron products: Testors,'fokol, ICM,'Fauro, Hobbycraft,
AFV Club and Emhar plastic kits and Imex Civil War
figures.

POSTE MILITAIRE
Station Road, Northiam, Rye, E. Sussex TN31 6QT
Contact: Ray or Norma Lamb
Tel: 01797 252518
Fax: 01797 252905
Email: sales@postemilitaire.freeserve.co.uk
Comprehensive range of white metal kits–70mm 75mm
90mm 110mm by Ray & Julian Lamb, Stefano Cannone
Julian Hullis, Derek Hansen Mike Good & Keith Durham.
Resin/white metal busts 1/10th scale by Julian Lamb. Full
colour catalogue–£6.50.

RAY BROWN DESIGN
Laundry House, Sowhill, Selkirk, Scotland TD7 5ET
Contact: Ray Brown
Tel/Fax: 01750 20430
Email: ray@raybrowndesign.com
Website: www.raybrowndesign.com and:
www.militarysculptures.com
Designers and manufacturers of precision sculptures,
producing the most detailed and anatomically correct
statuettes currently available to collectors and connoisseurs
alike. Each piece is designed and sculpted by Ray Brown
and produced in-house to maintain continuity of the style
required of a themed range. Sixteen years in the business.

REDOUBT ENTERPRISES
49 Channel View Road, Eastbourne, E. Sussex BN22 7LN
Contact: Peter Helm
Manufacturers and retailers of 25mm figures for Zulu
Wars, Sudan, Napoleonic, ECW, Pirates, AWI, Foreign
Legion, Three Musketeers and others. Send £2 for
catalogue.

REGIMENTAL STATUETTE MANUFACTURERS
Littlebury Hall, Station Road, Kirton, Nr.Boston, Lincolnshire
PE20 1LQ
Contact: Robert & Atitz Roite
Family business providing limited edition, large scale
(11 inches approx), high quality statuettes primarily for
military establishments. Figures are cast in resin with white
metal parts and finished either in bronze or hand painted.
Callers welcomed to discuss requirements.

REPLICA MODELS
40 Durbar Avenue, Foleshill, Coventry, W. Midlands CV6 5LU
Tel: 01203 684338

*RETTER / BRENNER-MAURLE (FLATS)
Kleinhohenheimerstr. 32, 70619 Stuttgart, Germany

*RUDIGER ENGEL (FLATS)
Grundelbach 8, 56329 St Goar, Germany

*RUDOLF GRUNEVALD (FLATS)
Larchenweg 28, 30900 Wedemark-Elze, Germany

SCALE MODELS
c/o Blackwells of Hawkwell, 733–735 London Road,
Westcliffe-on-Sea, Essex SS0 9ST
Tel/Fax: 01702 472248
Email: sales@blackwells/.co.uk

SCIENTIFIC MODELS
Unit 3, Point Pleasant Estate, Hadrian Road, Wallsend, Tyne
& Wear NE28 6HA
Contact: Jason & Martin Purns
Tel: 0191 2340455
Fax: 0191 295 4822
Email: info@scientificmodelsa.com
Website: www.scientificmodels.com
Scientific Models are model makers to the Defence
industry, and our experience as such has allowed us to
produce specialists' 1:35 scale modern armour kits.

SCOTIA MICRO MODELS
Hallgreen Castle, Inerbervie, Scotland DD10 OPE
Tel: 01561 362861
Fax: 01561 362444
Email: scotiagrendel@onet.co.uk
Website: www.lineone.net/-
model.design.craft/modelhome.html
Manufacturers of 1/300th scale vehicles, aircraft and landing craft. Also manufacturers of 25mm science fiction and fantasy figures—Grendel, Leviathan, Kryomek etc.

*SIEGFRIED NONN (FLATS)
Kranzbergstrasse 14, 86316 Friedberg, Germany

*S H A ZINNFIGUREN (FLATS)
Schonblick 3, 74544 Michelbach, Bilz, Germany
Contact: Werner Fechner

SHQ MINIATURES
34 Copland Close, Basingstoke, Hants RG22 4JX
Tel: 013224 47926
!/76 Scale WWII figures and models.

SKYTREX LTD
Unit 3, Canal Bank, Loughborough, Leicestershire
LE12 6TU
Cast metal kits. Extensive armour and vehicles ranges in 1/200th and 15mm (t/100th) scales. WWII and Modern Naval metal model kits in 1/1200 scales, all periods. Mail order available.

*REGINA SONNTAG (ENGRAVER)
Eschenworther Weg 71, 29690 Gilten, Germany
Tel/Fax: 5071 3455
Carl Spitzweg, Jugendstil, Fairies, Laokoon, Teddy Bear's Picnic, Der Abschcid, Zany Zoo, Apokalyptische Reiter, Rubens' fruit angel, Chinese Lady with Dragon.

SOLDIER PAC
2 Holland Drive, Muxton, Telford, Shropshire TF2 8RA
Contact: Mr Chris Bartlett
Tel/Fax: 01952 676822
Producers of re-cast Britain figures (1893-1969): horses, vehicles, guns and wagons. Hundreds of spare parts. Send A5 SAE for listing.

*STARLUX
BP 36, 24021 Perigueux Cedex, France

SUMMIT SOLDIER PRODUCTS
Rail Works, Biggleswade, Bedfordshire SG18 8BD
Contact: Chris Burton
Tel: 01767 318999
Fax: 01767 318912
Email: summit@mountstar.com
Website: www.summitsoldier.com
Manufacturers of white metal and pewter casting alloys for the use in modelling and jewellery production for centrifugal and drop casters. We have a wide choice and an extensive range.

*TAPPERT ZINNFIGUREN (FLATS)
Neckarstrasse 9, 47051 Duisburg, Germany

THISTLE MINIATURES
Findon Croft, Findon, Aberdeen, Grampian AB1 4RN, Scotland
Tel/Fax: 01224 571831
Manufacturer of white metal/resin figures in 1/24th, 1/20th and 1/16th scales. They are mainly Scottish, in ranges: modern barrack dress, The Great War, personalities, and mess dress. Also produce prints depicting the kilts and trews of the British Army. Available by mail or telephone order.

*THORILD SIVHED (FLATS)
Engelbrektsgatan 83, S-23134 Trelleborg, Sweden

TOYWAY
Unit 20 Jubilee Trade Centre, Jubilee Road, Letchworth, Hertfordshire SG6 1SG
Contact: Richard Morriss
Tel: 01462 672509
Fax: 01462 672132
Email: toys@toyway.co.uk
Toyway manufacture and distribute Timpo 54mm figures and accessories.

TRADITION OF LONDON LTD
33 Curzon Street, Mayfair, London W1V 7AL
Contact: Steve Hare
Tel: 020 7493 7452
Fax: 020 7355 1224
Largest range of painted and unpainted figures in 54mm, 90nim, 110mm plus over 300 different 'Toy Soldier' style sets, including 'Sharpe' range. Full mail order, credit cards. Shop open Mon–Fri 9.00am-5.30pm, Sat 9.30am-3.00pm.

TROPHY MINIATURES WALES LTD
Unit 4, Vale Enterprise Centre, Sully, Penarth, S. Glamorgan, Wales CF64 5SY
Tel: 01446 721011
Fax: 01446 732483
Email: sales@trophyminiatures.co.uk
Toy soldier manufacturer—catalogue, mail order. Factory open for visitors—phone for directions and appointment.

TUMBLING DICE MINIATURES/SHIRE DESIGN
96 Sandfield Road, Arnold, Nottingham, Nottinghamshire NG5 6QJ
Contact: Paul Sulley
Designers and manufacturers with extensive ranges of historical 1/72nd scale (20mm) figurines cast in pewter or white metal. Mould making, casting and packing services available.

ULRICH PUCHALA
Zoithausstrasse 14, 7906 Blaustein-Wippingen, Germany

URSULA SCHILLER-RATHKE (FLATS)
Blumenstrasse 56a, 47057 Duisburg, Germany

VENTURA CASTINGS
119 Farnham Road, Guildford, Surrey GU25QE
Contact: Tony Pope
Tel: 01483 300574
Fax: 01483 452374
Email: tonypope@ukonline.co.uk
Manufacturers of Elite Forces, P & B and A.R.T.S. Trade and retail sales. Casting and mould making service available.

VIKING MINIATURES LTD
Littlebury Hall, Station Road, Kirton, Nr Boston, Lincolnshire PE20 ILQ

VINTAGE LTD
104 Stanwell Road, Penarth, S. Glamorgan, Wales, CF64 3LP
Contact: David Vanner
Tel/Fax: 01222 701030
International mail order metal waterline model ship and aircraft business established 15 years. For illustrated lists of stocks and shows attended send S,1.00 plus SAE.

V L S CORPORATION
Lone Star Industrial Park, 811 Lone Star Drive, O'Fallon MO 63366, USA
Contact: Tom Gerringer
Tel: 314 281 5700
Fax: 314 281 5750
Email: vlsmo1@il.net
Manufacturer/distributor of Verlinden Productions. Importer/distributor for over 13,000 hobby products for scale modellers.

W & G S 3D MODELMAKERS
Barton End House, Bath Road, Nailsworth, Glos GL6 0QQ
Contact: Geoff Sumpter
Tel/Fax: 01453 833883
Email: sumptergr@hotmail.com
Models, props, themed special effect dioramas etc. Tiny scale to life-size and beyond. Quality work at sensible prices. Send for free colour literature.

*WALTER ONKEN (FLATS)
Alsterkrugchaussee 312, 22297 Hamburg, Germany

*WERNER KLOTZSCHE (FLATS)
Wilhelm-Pieck-Strasse 88, 01445 Radebeul, Germany

WESTERN MINIATURES (FLATS)
1 Henacre Road, Lawrence Weston, Bristol, Avon BS11 0HB

*WILHELM SCHWEIZER (FLATS)
Herrenstrasse 7, 86911 Diessen/Ammersee, Germany

WOLF MODELS
PO Box 64, Rochester, Kent ME1 3JR
Contact: Nicholas Adams
Tel/Fax: 01634 842523
Range of 1/35 scale WWII resin figures, white metal accessories. American Civil War, Napoleonic and British Empire 1/32 scale (54mm) metal and resin figures. 1/9 scale resin busts. Available direct from Historex Agents (see Section: Modelling Equipment) and Roger Saunders.

*WOLF-DIETER WEIRICH (FLATS)
Goldener-Au-Strasse 34, GG280 Sulzbach, Germany

*WOLFGANG HAFER (FLATS)
Schlangenweg 14, 34117 Kassel, Germany
Tel/Fax: 1561773113
Figurines of antiquity, hunting, civil, military. The catalogue covers 148 pages (A5), price DM48.

*WOLFGANG HODAPP (FLATS)
Sophienstrasse 60, 76133 Karlsruhe, Germany

*WOLFGANG UNGER (FLATS)
Fregestrasse 5a, 04105 Leipzig, Germany
Tel/Fax: 3419800092
Flat 30mm figures: Middle Ages, 18/19th century military and civilians.

*WOLFGANG WOHLMANN (FLATS)
Invalidenstrasse 55a, 10557 Berlin, Germany

WORLD WIDE MILITARIA
PO Box 522, Germantown, MD 20875, USA
Contact: Robert Pitta
Tel: 301 972 3773
Fax: 301 972 3773
Email: bob@worldwidemilitaria.com
Website: www.worldwidemilitaria.com
Dealers in military and police uniforms, insignia, flags, books, field manuals, field gear, WWII and Vietnam reproductions, toys, armor, and all things military from all countries and all periods.

YEOMANRY MINIATURES
10 Dolphin Lodge, Grand Avenue, Worthing, W. Sussex BN11 5AI,
Contact: Brian Harrison
Tel/Fax: 01903 505151
Manufacturers of finely sculpted cavalry figures for the connoisseur. Available hand-painted in the modern toy style to the highest standards or as castings.

MODEL PAINTING SERVICES

A J DUMELOW

53 Stanton Road, Stapenhill, Burton-on-Trent, Staffordshire
DE15 9RP
Tel/Fax: 01283 30556
Dealer and painter of wargames figures in all scales.
Comprehensive stock to supply complete armies or single
figures, painted and unpainted. Mail order welcome.

ACE MODELS

Fountain Arcade, Dudley, W. Midlands DY1 1PG
Contact: Dixon
Tel/Fax: 01384 257045
All branches of military modelling stocked. Professional
building service by award winning modeller.

ALAN E JONES

96 High Avenue, Letchworth, Hertfordshire SG6 3RR
Tel/Fax: 01402 676020
Figures, toy soldiers and military models assembled and
hand-painted to your individual requirements. Personal
service guaranteed. All scales and subjects considered.
Mail order welcome.

ART MILITAIRE

6 Gypsy Lane, Oulton, Leeds, W. Yorkshire LS26 8SA
Contact: A Buttery

B HARRIS PROFESSIONAL FIGURE PAINTING

123 Coverside Road, Great Glen, Leicester, Leicestershire
LE8 9EB
Contact: Barry Harris
Tel: 0116 2592004
Fax: 0116 2593355
Member of the Guild of Master Craftsmen. World-wide mail
order—all types of figures painted. Send seven 1st class
stamps for full colour brochure.

BATH MINIATURES/BONAPARTE'S LTD

1 Queen Street, Bath, Avon BA1 1HE
Stockists of figures, s/h plastic kits, military books, painted
figures incl. chess sets; also glass domes, cases, bases,
etc; buying uniform books, figures, plastic kits. Painting
service offered by winning artist. Mail order available, post
free in UK.

C BALDWIN

4 Cooper Row, Southgate, Crawley, W. Sussex
RH10 6DJ
Contact: Charles Baldwin
Tel/Fax: 01293 521 288
Mobile: 07770 235 301
Traditional toy soldiers and connoisseur figures painted to a
high standard. 54mm and larger. Napoleonic period a
speciality.

CHRIS COLLINGWOOD

1 Barton Cottage, Monkleigh, Bideford, Devon EX39 5JX
Contact: Chris Collingwood
Tel/Fax: 01805 623023
Website: www.chriscollingwood.com
England's foremost military fine artist. All periods from
ancient Greece to WWII covered. Historical portraits.
Private commissions undertaken. Limited edition prints and
book jackets a speciality.

CLIVE FARMER

6 Churchway, Faulkland, Radstock, Somerset BA3 5US
Contact: Clive Farmer
Tel: 01373 834 752
Illustrator and artist. Main periods: Napoleonic and Crimean
wars. Original artwork for resale. Illustrator for Mark Adkins
The Waterloo Companion and Flintlock Publishing's Face to
Face series of postcards. Regimental and private commis-
sions undertaken.

CONFLICT MINIATURES

27 Leighton Road, Hartley Vale, Plymouth, Devon PL3 5RT
Contact: Tim Reader
Tel/Fax: 01 752 770761
Manufacturer of wargaming figures/models. Worldwide
mail order. Stockist of rules, Kreigsspiel, paints, brushes
etc. Painting service available. Trade enquiries welcome.

DEAN FOREST FIGURES

62 Grove Road, Berry Hill, Coleford, Glos GL16 8QX
Contact: Philip & Mark Beveridge
Tel/Fax: 01594 836130
Wargame figure painting, scratch-built trees, buildings and
terrain features. Large scale figure painting and scratch-
building to any scale. SAE for full lists.

DEBRA RAYMOND HAND-PAINTED FIGURES

Catbells, 1 Hilthead Cottages, Rectory Road, Staplegrove,
Taunton, Somerset TA2 6ER
Tel/Fax: 01823 333431
Professional military figure painting service, at sensible
prices. Any scale, period or subject considered. Please ring
with any enquiry (evenings).

FERNANDO ENTERPRISES

107 Galle Road, Walana, Panadura, Sri Lanka
Contact: Sanath Fernando
Tel/Fax: 34 32833
Professional wargaming flat and round figure painting serv-
ice. Any scale, competitive prices and quick delivery.
Contact us with details of your job.

G J M FIGURINES

74 Crofton Road, Orpington, Kent BR6 8HY
Contact:Gerard Cronin
Tel/Fax: 01689 828474
Wargame figures painted £3.95 or £4.95 respectively.
Wargame armies bought/sold. Worldwide mail guaranteed.

G OTTY
50 Willbye Avenue, Diss, Norfolk IP22 3NW
Mail order painting service—all periods and scales undertaken to a high standard. Please write for details.

H Q PAINTING SERVICES
114 Windmill Hill Lane, Derby, Derbyshire DE3 3BP
Contact: Paul Spencer
Tel/Fax: 01332 298519
Specialists in the hand painting of wargames figures and
accessories. All scales from 5mm-120mm. Send SAE
for full details.

HELION & COMPANY
26 Willow Walk, Solihull, W. Midlands B91 IUE
Contact: Duncan Rogers Tel: 0121 705 3393
Fax: 0121 711 13-15
Yourfigures painted down to their lastgaiter button!
Competitive prices—quality and accuracy assured. All
scales and periods catered for. Discounts available.
Vignettes produced to order.

J F BENASSI
55 St Mungo Avenue, Glasgow, Strathclyde, Scotland G4 OPL
Contact: Julian Benassi
Designer of white metal model soldiers, produced in small
quantity and available by mail order. Send for catalogue.
Painting service also available.

THE LAST DETAIL
196 Parlaunt Road, Langley, Slough, Berkshire SL3 8AZ
Contact: David Seagrove
Professional figure painting service producing high quality
artwork on 15-30mm figures for discerning wargamers
and collectors. Figures available from stock. Established
1984. SAE for details.

MP STUDIOS
23 Peregrine Close, Winshall, Burton-on-Trent, Staffordshire
DE15 OEB
Tel/Fax: 01283 37104
Professional model maker and figure painter—the finest
quality painted figures available, by national competition
winner. Commissions undertaken to your own specifications; quality guaranteed—a sure investment. Character
figures also available—all we need is a photograph. Write
or call for more information.

NEIL MULLIS
21 Harvey Road, Meir, Stoke-on-Trent, Staffordshire ST3 6BG
Contact: N C Mullis
Top-class figure painting service providing prompt reliable
delivery, using registered post for added security. Referrals
from many past clients an assurance of efficiency.

THE PAINTED SOLDIER
138 Friern Road, East Dulwich, London SE22 OAY
Contact: Bill Brewer
Tel/Fax: 020 8693 2449
Painting service for wargamers and collectors established
for 25 years. Work on show at studio and has yearly trade
stand at 'Salute', Chelsea and Kensington Town Hall.

RICHARD NEWTH-GIBBS PAINTING SERVICES
59 Victor Close, Hornchurch, Essex RM12 4XH
Tel/Fax: 01708 448765
Any scale from 15mm up, single figures, groups, dioramas,
artillery pieces, mounted gun teams; British and Indian
Army specialist, actual military work oniv. Callers by
appointment.

*LE 11e HUSSARD
15 Rue Trousseau, 75011 Paris, France
Contact: J L Ribot
Tel/Fax: 147007433

MODEL SHOPS
& SUPPLIES

*A D V M
15 Rue Dunoise, 41240 Verdes, France

*ACTRAMAC DIFFUSION
31/33 Rue Esquirot, 75013 Paris, France

THE AIRBRUSH & SPRAY CENTRE LTD
39 Littlehampton Road, Worthing, W. Sussex BN13 1QJ
Contact: Kenneth Medwell
Tel: 01903 266991
Fax: 01903 830045
Email: airbrush@lineone.net
Airbrush and compressor equipment and materials
suppliers. Main agents for Aerograph, Badger, Iwata and
Paasche. Servicing, repairs, spares and technical advice
from factory trained staff.

*ANNI-MINI
22 Boulevard de Reuilly, 75012 Paris, France

ACE MODELS
Fountain Arcade, Dudley, W. Midlands DY1 1PG
Contact: Dixon
Tel/Fax: 01384 257045
All branches of military modelling stocked. Professional
building service by award winning modeller.

A J DUMELOW
53 Stanton Road, Stapenhill, Burton-on-Trent, Staffs DE15 9RP
Tel: 01283 530556
Dealer in wargames figures and equipment. All scales,
painted and unpainted. From complete armies to individual
figures, all historical periods, fantasy and science fiction.
Painting service also available.

ANOTHER WORLD
23 Silver Street, Leicester, Leicestershire
Tel/Fax: 0116 2515266
Website: www.anotherworld.co.uk

ANTICS (BRISTOL)
8 Fairfax Street, Bristol, Avon BS1 3DB
Contact: Alan
Tel/Fax: 01453 764487
Email: antics@lineone.net
Stockists of modelling accessories and military items.

ANTICS (GLOUCESTER)
79 Northgate St, Gloucester, Gloucestershire GL1 2AG
Tel/Fax: 01452 410693
Email: antics@lineone.net
or:
89E Woodbridge Rd, Guildford, Surrey GU1 4QD
Tel/Fax: 01483 39115
Email: antics@lineone.net
Both: stockists of modelling accessories and military items.

ANTICS (PLYMOUTH)
30 Royal Parade, Plymouth, Devon PL1 1DU
Tel/Fax: 01752 221851
Email: antics@lineone.net
Stockists of modelling accessories and military items.

ANTICS (STROUD)
49 High Street, Stroud, Gloucestershire GL5 1AN
Contact: Alan Tyndall
Tel: 01453 764487
Fax: 01453 752845
Email: antics@lineone.net
Stockists of modelling accessories and military items.

ANTICS (SWINDON)
8 Regent Circus, Swindon, Wiltshire SN1 1JQ
Tel/Fax: 01793 340417
Email: antics@lineone.net
Stockists of modelling accessories and military items.

ANTICS (WORCESTER)
16 St Swithin Street, Worcester, Worcs WR1 2PS
Tel/Fax: 01905 22075
Email: antics@lineone.net
Stockists of modelling accessories and military items.

*ARHISTO
p/a Office du Tourisme, CH-1530 Payerne, Switzerland

AUTO CONCEPT BIGAUDET
23, Avenue Carnot, 75017 Paris, France
Tel: 01 56689975
Fax: 01 56689976
Email: acbparis@compuserve.com
Website: www.acbparis.com
Action figure maquettes and models up to 30cm in height.
WWII, Vietnam, modern uniforms.

*AU PARADIS DES ENFANTS
3bis Grande Rue, 91260 Juvisy-sur-Orge, France

*AU SANCTUAIRE DE LA MINIATURE
7 Boulevard de l'Observatoire, 34000 Montpellier, France

*AU TAPIS VERT
40 Rue Voltaire, 47000 Agen, France

AWFUL DRAGON MANAGEMENT
3 Ransome's Dock, 35-37 Parkgate Road, London
SW11 4NP

AZIMUT PRODUCTIONS
8 Rue Baulant, 75012 Paris, France
Tel: 143070616
Fax: 143471193
Dealer and manufacturer of 1/35th scale military models;
we offer over 60 ranges of vehicles, figures, accessories
and books. Trade enquiries welcome.

B & B MILITARY
1 Kings Avenue, Ashford, Kent TN23 1LU
Contact: Len Buller
Tel/Fax: 01233 632923
Makers of military model vehicles and figures in Dinky
1/60 inch scale. All white metal. Mail order only: send SAE
for list of kits and finished models available. Colour
catalogue £3.50.

BATTLEFIELD MODEL SUPPLIES
12 Delta Drive, Musselburgh, Lothian, Scotland EH21 8HR
Contact: Ian Hanratty
Mail order company specialising in AFV models in plastic,
resin and metal. Stock includes: Roco, Trident, M.A.A.G.,
C.M.S.C., Model Transport, J.B. Models, M.M.S., Trux, S & S
Models, Strong-Point, Custom Miniatures. Send large SAE
for list.

BATH MINIATURES/BONAPARTE'S LTD
1 Queen Street, Bath, Avon BA1 1HE
Tel/Fax: 01225 423873
Email: david@bonaparte's.co.uk
Website: www.banaparte's.co.uk
Stockists of figures, s/h plastic kits, militarybooks, painted
figures incl. chess sets; also glass domes, cases, bases,
etc; buying uniform books, figures, plastic kits. Painting
service offered by winning artist. Mail order available, post
free in UK.

BRADFORD MODEL CENTRE
1 Ivegate, Bradford
Tel: 01274 306668

BRIGADE MODELS
Beaney's Model Hobbies 55 West Street Sittingbourne Kent
Tel: 01795 472815

BLUESTAR MODELS
42 Westgate, Cleckheaton
Tel: 01274 851589

LES BROWN MODELS
12a Bond Street, Birstall, Batley
Tel: 01924 441991

BROWSERS
10 Theatre Square, Swindon, Wiltshire SN1 1QN
Contact: Janet Terry
Tel: 01793 523170
Fax: 01793 432070
Specialist bookshop for all military publications. Large
range of military figures. Worldwide mail order service.

*CARL GRUEN (FLATS)
PO Box 2019, Remsenburg, New York 11960-2019, USA

C & B Models
103 Normanton Road Derby
Tel: 01332 367506

*CENTRAL LOISIRS
83 Rue du President Wilson, 92300 Levallois Perret, France

*CHATELET MINIATURES
15 Place du Chatelet, 45000 Orleans, France

CHELTENHAM MODEL CENTRE
39 High Street, Cheltenham, Glos GL50 IDY

*CHRISTIAN SCHMIDT FACHBUCHHANDLUNG
Sauerbruchstrasse 10, 81377 München, Germany
Tel: 8970322 7
Fax: 897005361
Military, shipping, aviation books; 1/1250 scale models; catalogues
available. Store hours Mon–Fri 9am–6pm, Saturday 9am–12am,
close Sundays. Mail order; Visa, Amex Euro/Mastercard accepted.

*CHRISTIAN TERANA
31 Boulevird Kellerman, 75013 Paris, France

*LE CIMIER
38 Rue Ginoux, 75015 Paris, France
Contact: Jacques Vuyet
Tel/Fax: (0033) 01 45789428
Military figurines; plates of uniforms' books and
documentation; working material. Exhibition of nearly 1,000
painted figurines.

CASTOFF
Wayside, 16 Driffield Road, Nafferton, E. Yorkshire YO25 4JL
A range of 1/35 armoured cars, with accessories plus
resin figures sets and pewter.

CONCORDE MODELS
179 Victoria Road, Aldershot, Hampshire GU11 1JU
Contact: Brian Ballard
Tel/Fax: 01252 326825
All prominent makes of figures, military kits and toy
soldiers stocked. Osprey, Verlinden, Kalmbach,
Compendium books. Mail order.

CONFLICT MINIATURES
27 Leighton Road, Hartley Vale, Plymouth, Devon PL3 5HT
Contact: Tim Reader
Manufacturer of wargaming figures/models. Worldwide
mail order. Stockist of rules, Kreigsspicl, paints, brushes
etc. Painting service available. Trade enquiries welcome.

CONVOY
23 Mare Bay Close, St Leonards-on-Sea, E. Sussex
TN38 8EQ
Tel/Fax: 01424854731
1/76 scale resin or metal kits and accessories.

*CONTACT MODELISME
183 Grande Rue, 86000 Poitiers, France

COVE MODELS
119 Lychford Road Farnborough Hampshire
Tel: 01252 544532

D HEWINS MODELS & HOBBIES
7B East St Mary's Gate, Grimsby, S. Humberside DN31 1LH
Stockists of 'Men at Arms' books, plastic kits, fantasy
figures, general modelling accessories, fantasy board/role
playing games. Open Mon–Wed Fri-Sat, 9.00am-5.30pm.

D J S MILITARIA
Contact: Dave Storey
Tel: 01268 777381
Action men, toys, models.

DOMINOES
66 High Street, Leicester
Tel: 0800 5423071

DORKING MODELS
12–13 West Street, Dorking, Surrey RH41 1BL
Tel/Fax: 01306 881747
One of the finest ranges of model kits in the south of
England. Hornby and Scalextric main agents. International
Mail Order service available.

*LES DRAPEAUX DE FRANCE
34 Gallerie Montpensier, Palais Royal, 75001 Paris, France

THE DUNGEON / MODELLER'S NOOK
15-17 Winetavern Street, Belfast, Co.Antrim BT1 1JQ,
N. Ireland
Contact: Joseph F Barlow
Non radio control. Specialising in military, aircraft, fantasy
modelling, manufacturing fantasy wargaming, scenery &
figures, new range of 'Hairball' figures. Send £1.50 for
catalog and figure.

*ÉCOLE MODELISME SA
70 Boulevard St Germain, 75005 Paris, France

E D MODELS
64 Stratford Road, Shirley, Solihull, W. Midlands B90 3LP
Tel: 0121 744 7488
Fax: 0121 7332591
Email: airwaves@ultramail.co.uk
Model kits and accessories–extensive range. International
mail order; catalogue available. Manufacturers/distributors
of Airwavoc, K K Castings, Scaleplanes. Shop open
Mon-Sat 9.15am-6.00pm.

*ELECTRO JOUETS
18 Vue Gougeard, 72000 Le Mans, France

*ESDEVIUM GAMES
2 Morley Road, Farnham, Surrey GU9 8LY

*FANAKITS 37
109 Rue Colbert, 37000 Tours, France

*FANATIC MODELE REDUIT
17bis Rue Roger Collerve, 89000
Auxerre, France

FANTASY AND MILITARY WORLD (now ANOTHER WORLD)
10 Market Square Arcade, Hanley, Stoke-on-Trent, Staffs
Tel/Fax: 01782 279294
Email: sales@anotherworld.co.uk

*FIVE EASY PIECES
102 Grande Place, 38100 Grenoble, France

*FONDERIE MINIATURE
36 Rue Charron, 93300 Aubervilliers, France

FORBES & THOMSON
Burgate Antiques Centre, 10c Burgate, Canterbury, Kent
Contact: Rowena Forbes
Specialist dealers in old toy soldiers by Britain's, Johillco etc.
and related lead and tinplate toys. Model soldiers & kits by
Rose Models and Chota Sahib. Painted military miniature fig-
ures. Mail order and office address, PO Box 375, South
Croydon, CR2 6ZG. Open Mon-Sat 10.00am–5.00pm.

G K's MODEL CENTRE
390 Holdenhurst Road, Bournemouth, Dorset BH8 8BL
Contact: Frank Parsons
Tel: 01202 394007
Fax: 01202 251260
Email: frank@gk-models.demon.co.uk
Website: www.gk-models.demon.co.uk
Stockists of all leading manufacturers; Tamiya, Dragon, etc.
Specialist kits & accessories by Verlinden, Accurate
Armour etc; also books and magazines.

*GAITE CONFORT
63 Boulevard Philippe August, 75011 Paris, France

THE GAMES ROOM
29A Elm Hill, Norwich, Norfolk
Tel/Fax: 01603 628140
Email: mike@thegamesroom.fsnet.co.uk

GAUGEMASTER CONTROLS PLC
Gaugemaster House, Ford Road, Arundel, W. Sussex
BN18 0BN
Tel: 01903 884488
Fax: 01903 884321
Email: gaugemaster@gaugemaster.co.uk
Website: www.gaugemaster.co.uk
Distributors of Preiser and Elastolin figures and accessories.
Catalogue/price lists available and mail order/retail shop open
Mon-Sat 9am–5.30pm.

G B MODELS
185 Woodland Road, Stanton
Tel: 01283 845585

GEE DEE MODELS
21 Heathcoat Street, Nottingham
Tel: 01159 412211
G W LACEY
315a South Lane, New Malden, Surrey KT3 5RR
Hundred of British, American, German, French, Italian,
Israeli, Russian, Polish and Japanese plans, all in 1/76
scale.

H ZWICKY AU VIEUX PARIS
1 Rue de la Servette, CH-1201 Geneva, Switzerland
Tel: 22 7344576
Fax: 22 734779
Shop open in 1964: everything for the military modeller.

HALIFAX MODELLERS WORLD
55 The Arcade, The Piece Hall, Halifax, W. Yorkshire
HX1 1RE
Contact: David Smith
All types of model kits, figures, paints, accessories. Open
seven days a week, Mon-Fri 10.30am-5pm, Sat 9am-5pm,
Sun 10.30am-4.30pm. Visa/Access accepted.

HANNANT'S MAILORDER
Harbour Road, Oulton Broad, Lowestoft, Suffolk NR32 3LZ
Tel: 01502 517444
Fax: 01502 500521
Email: sales@hannants.co.uk
Website: www.hannants.co.uk
Retailer and mail order suppliers of plastic and resin model
figures, tanks, aircraft, ships, cars etc.

HANNANT'S MODEL SHOP
Colindale Station House, 157-159 Colindale Avenue, London
NW9 5HR
Tel: 020 8205 6697
Fax: 020 8205 6691
Email: Sales@hannants.co.uk
Website: www.hannants.co.uk
Retailers of plastic and resin model figures, tanks, aircraft,
ships, cars etc. Decals, paints, accessories, books.

HENLEY MODEL MINIATURES
24 Reading Road, Henley-on-Thames, Oxfordshire RG9 LAB
Contact: David Hazell
Tel/Fax: 014915720-84
Email: enquiries@toysoldier.co.uk
We stock the widest range of painted toy soldiers available
in the UK, together with castings, paints and modelling
materials. Mail order a pleasure.

HISTOREX AGENTS
Wellington House, 157 Snargate Street, Dover, Kent
CT17 9BZ
Contact: Lynn Sangster
Tel: 01304 206720
Fax: 01304 206528
Email: sales@historex-agents.demon.co.uk
Website: www.historex-agents.demon.co.uk
Mail order and wholesale distributor of model soldier and AFV
kits. We represent the following UK and overseas manufacturers: Historex, Vertinden, Le Cimier, Fonderie Miniature, Metal
Mod&les, Puchal Hecker-Goros, Bencito, Andrea, Pegaso,
Soldiers Luchetti, Friulmodellismo, Wolf, Hornet, P Militaire, Tiny
Troopers, Sovereig Tomker, Fort Royal Review, Azimut, Mil-Art,
Mascot, Starlight, Ridwulf, Trophy.

HOBBINS MODELS
6 Portland Street, Lincoln
Tel: 01522 531084

HOVELS LTD
18 Glebe Road, Scartho, Grimsby, S. Humberside DN33 2HL
Contact: Dennis Coleman
Tel/Fax: 01472 750552
Email: sales@hovelsltd.co.uk

IT FIGURES
193 St Margaret's Road, Lowestoft, Suffolk NR32 4HN
A range of 20mm figures, artillery and cavalry of WWI.
Figures of WWII covering most theatres plus Napoleonic
figures, artillery and cavalry.

*IDEAL MODELS
67 Boulevard Carnot, 31000 Toulouse, France

ILKLEY MODEL CENTRE
15 Grange Avenue, BenRhydding, Ilkley, W. Yorkshire

*J E HANCOCK
19 Sydenham Road South, Cheltenham, Glos GL52 6EF

*JE M'AMUSE
3 Rue Saint Michel, 84000 Avignon, France

*JEUX DE GUERRE DIFFUSION
6 Rue Meissonier, 75017 Paris, France

*JOANNY JABOULEY
Route de Bourg, 38490 Fittilieu, France

KINGSGRAND MINIATURES
Prinny's Gallery, The Lanes, Brighton, E. Sussex BN1 1HB

KIT BITS—THE MODEL STORE
Market House, Market Hill, St Austell, Cornwall PL25 5QB
Contact: M L Squire
Tel: 0172G 72018
Fax: 01726 65424
We stock a varied selection of paints, glues, models,
including cars, Warhammer, tanks, kites, boats, planes,
Star Trek, fantasy militaria. Open 9am–5pm Mon-Sat.

KEITH'S CARS
Unit 11a Eagle Centre
Tel: 01332 380598

KIT'N'DOC
144 Rue Martre, 92110 Clichy, France
*LE KANGAROU
58 Grande Rue C de Gaulle, 92600 Asnieres, France

K M B MODELS
56a Alexandra Road Swadlincote
Tel: 01283 215138

L S A MODELS
151 Sackville Road, Hove, Sussex BN3 3HD
Contact: J Lake
Tel/Fax: 01273 705420
Suppliers/importers of a wide range of military-related
models in plastic and resin. Figures, tanks, soft-skins and
accessories. Phone for more details.

J B CHUCH
Honeywood, Middle Road, Tiptoe, Nr Lymington, Hants
SO41 6FX
British & American plans in 1/76 scale.

KEEP WARGAMING
The Keep, Le Marchant Barracks, London Road, Devizes,
Wiltshire SN10 2ER
Contact: Paul & Teresa Bailey
Tel/Fax: 01380 724558
Email: keepwarg@talk21.com
Shop and mail order service; stockists of wargames
figures, books and equipment; some military models and
plastic kits. Shop open Tues-Sat 10am–6pm.

KIT KRAZY
303 The Broadway, Bexleyheath, Kent DA6 8DT
Contact: L or S Clarke
Tel/Fax: 020 8298 7177
Plastic and metal kit retailers. Hobby and pastime
materials.

LANGLEY MODELS
166 Three Bridges Road, Crawley, W. Sussex RHIO 1LE
Contact: Ian McLellan
Tel: 01293 516329
Fax: 01293 403955
Email: ian@langley-models.co.uk
Toy soldiers—foot, mounted, bands, gun teams—as castings
or hand-painted. Also knights, Romans mythological.
Illustrated catalogue £3.55 post free. Mail order by return.

LEEDS MODEL CENTRE
Merrion Centre, Leeds
Tel: 01132 455432

LES WRIGHT MODELS
72 Horninglow Road, Burton-on-Trent
Tel: 01283 515440

*LELCHAT FILS
35 Rue Porte aux Saints, 78200 Mantes la jolie, France

*LE KANGAROU
58 Grande Rue C de Gaulle, 92600 Asnieres, France

LITTLE SOLDIER
58 Gillygate, York, N. Yorkshire
Tel: 01904 642568

MAD 4 MODELS
3 Hasgill Close, Oakwood
Tel: 01332 680086
M BELL
The Belfry, 23 Brinkhall Way, Welton, Lincs LN2 3NS
British, Belgian, French, Dutch, Russian, German, Polish,
Canadian, South African, American and Czech plans in
1/76 scale.

*LES LUTINS
78 Boulevard Marechaljoffre, 92340 Bourg-la-Reine, France

*M J N MAQUETTES
9 Rue Boirot, 63000 Clermont-Ferrand, France

MACS MODELS
133135 Canongate, The Royal Mile, Edinburgh, Lothian,
Scotland EH8 8BP
Tel/Fax: 0131 557 5551

*LA MAISON DU LIVRE AVIATION
75 Boulevard Malcshcrbes, 75008 Paris, France

*MARC TOLOSANO
Val du Carei, 06500 Menton, France

*MAURICE VERDEUN
1 bis, Rue Piliers de Tutelle, 33000 Bordeaux, France

MAXIMUM EFFORT
4 Cornhill, Spilsby
Tel: 01790 754700

MEDWAY GAMES CENTRE
294-296 High Street, Chatham, Kent
Tel/Fax: 01634 847809

*MICRO-MODEL
Rue Percheret, La Visitation, 83000 Toulon, France

MILITARY AND MYTHS
61a St Johns Hill, Sevenoaks, Kent TN13 3NY
Contact: John Ewing
Tel: 01732 463800
Model kits, toy soldiers, Warhammer, Sci-Fi, chess sets,
militaria, books, videos, Marvel-DC comics, painting
service, prints, LRP equipment, re-enactment weapons.

MILTON KEYNES METALS
(Dpt WG) Unit A2, Ridge Hill, Farm, Little Horwood Rd, Nash,
Milton Keynes, Buckinghamshire MK17 0GH
Contact: Vivian Wilson
Tel: 01296 713631
Fax: 01296 714155
Email: miltonkeynesmetals@compuserve.com
White metal, silicone rubber, vulcanised rubber, centrifugal
casting machines and equipment, model metals and
engineers' tools. Mon-Fri 9am-5pm. Access & Visa
accepted. Consultancy service.

MILITÄRMODELLBAU
Eichgasse 13, D-52393 Hürtgenwald Strasse
Tel/Fax: 024292086

MILNSBRIDGE MODELS
77 Market Street, Milnsbridge, Huddersfield
Tel: 01484 655276

*MINIATURE 2000
63 Avenue Philippe-Auguste, 75011 Paris, France

*MINIMODELS 87
11 bis Rue Jean Jaures, 87000 Limoges, France

*MINIMODELS TERNOIS
29-31 Rue du Quai, 27400 Louviers, France

*MITREGAMES
77 Burntwood Grange, Wandsworth Common, London SW18

*MODEL & HOBBY
Fredriksborgade 23, DK-1360 Copenhagen, Denmark

*MODEL 25 SARL
24 Rue des Febvres, 25200 Montbeliard, France

HQ MODEL AERODROME
Fax: 019037 536643

MODEL AERODROME
Unit 223, Stoneborough Centre, Maidstone, Kent
Tel/Fax: 01622 691184

MODEL AERODROME
36 The Boulevard, Crawley, W. Sussex RH10 1XP
Tel/Fax: 01293 540331

MODEL AERODROME
37 West Street, Brighton, E. Sussex BN1 2RE
Tel/Fax: 01273 26790

MODEL AERODROME
68 Seaside Road, Eastbourne, E. Sussex BN21 3P9
Tel/Fax: 01323 644001

MODEL AIRCRAFT KITS
28a The Market Place, Melbourne
Tel: 01332 864916

MODEL IMAGES RETAIL
56 Station Road, Letchworth, Hertfordshire

MODEL NATION
Merideth Road, Clacton on Sea
Tel: 01255 222931

THE MODEL SHOP
209 Deansgate, Manchester, Greater Manchester, M3 3NW
Tel: 0161 8343972
Fax: 0161 831 7459
Stockist of Dragon, Kirin, Academy, A.U-V Club, Tamiya,
Italeri, Wolf, Hornet, Revell, etc. Comprehensive range of
books, paints, airbrushes and accessories. Open 7 days.

THE MODEL SHOP
190–194 Station Road, Harrow, Middlesex
Tel: 020 8863 9788
Fax: 020 8863 3839

THE MODEL SHOP
25 Cheapside, Cleckheaton
Tel: 01274 852948

THE MODEL SHOP
88 Crossgates Road, Leeds
Tel: 01132 646117

MODEL-TIME (WHOLESALE) LIMITED
64–66 Windmill Road, Croydon, Surrey CR0 2XP
Tel: 020 8689 6622
Fax: 020 8689 6623
Suppliers to the retail trade of Victoria 1/43 scale precision
die-cast military vintage and contemporary models.

*MODELKITS
4 Rue Georges Clemenceau, 10000 Troyes, France

MODELLBAUSTUBE
Doeblinger Hpstr. 87, A-1190 Wien, Austria
Tel: 1369 1768
Fax: 1369 2955
Email: info@modellbaustube.com
Website: www.modellbaustube.com
Specialise in imported AFV and aircraft kits, conversions
and accessories. Shop and international mail order. Open
Mon-Fri 10am-6pm, Sat 10am-1pm.

MODELS GALORE
56 London Road, Stone, Dartford, Kent
Tel/Fax: 01322 278984

*MODELISME 50
35bis Blvd Robert Schumann, 50100 Cherbourg, France

*MODELISME 92
1 Rue de Billancourt, 92100 Boulogne Billancourt, France

*NANTES MODELISME
3 Allee Jean Bart, 44000 Nantes, France

NATIONAL ARMY MUSEUM SHOP
National Army Museum, Royal Hospital Road, Chelsea,
London SW34HT
Contact: Tim Errock
Tel: 020 7730 0717
Fax: 020 7823 6573
Email: nam@enterprise.net
The Museum Shop sells a wide range of military books,
postcards and prints, plus videos, tapes, models and toy
soldiers. Open seven days a week, 10.00am-5.15pm.

NEW MILL HARDWARE AND MODEL SHOP
Holmfirth Road, New Mill
Tel: 01484 684695

ON LINE MODELS
111 Belvoir Road, Coalville
Tel: 01530 457117
*OLIVIER LOISIRS
4 Rue de Varennes, 77120 Coulommiers, France

*LOURS MARTIN
107 Rue du Point du Jour, 92100 Boulogne, Billancourt,
France

*PALAIS DE LA MAQUETTE
19 Rue du Mont Desert, 54000 Nancy, France

*PAQUEBOT NORMANDIE
247 Rue de Tolbiac, 75013 Paris, France

PAUL GANDY
Email: Paul.gandy@btinternet.com
S. Wales MAFA.

PAUL DOBSON WHOLESALE
23 Leeswood, Skelmersdale, Lancashire WN8 6TH
Contact: Paul Dobson
Distributor to trade, and retail by mail order (ring/fax 9am
–9pm) The widest choice of fine scale metal military
miniatures from a single source; our illustrated lists of over
2000 figures are available for only £7.50–over 120 new
items will be added over the next year.

*PELTA
16 Swietokrzyska Street, 00 Warsaw 050, Poland
Contact: Mark Machala

PATRICKS TOYS AND MODELS
107–111 Lillie Road, Fulham, London
Tel: 020 7385 9864
Fax: 020 7385 2187

PAST-LINCS HISTORICAL CARPENTRY
75 Lincoln Road, Ruskington, Sleaford, Lincolnshire NG34 9AR
Tel: 01526 833737
Contact: Emma Cooper
Woodwork for all periods of history.

PENNINE MODELS
33–35 Mill Hey Haworth
Tel: 01535 642367

*LE PETIT DIABLE
584 Boulevard Poincare, 62400 Bethune, France

*PHILIBERT SA
12 Rue de la Grange, 67000 Strasbourg, France

*PRINCE AUGUST
BP 29, 78770 Thoiry, France

PINTUS
10 Rue de Paturages, 7390 Quaregnon, Begium
Tel: 65672557
Fax: 65661845
Website: www.militaria-pintus.com
Superb military models: all nations and races.

PUNCTILIO MODEL SPOT
Waterloo Road, Ruby Road (corner, Hinckley, Leicestershire
LE10 0QJ
Tel/Fax: 01455 230952
Email: modelspot@dial.pipex.com

THE RED LANCERS
14 Braodway, Milton, PA 17847, USA
Tel: 717 742 8118
Fax: 717 742 4814
Military miniatures for the collector. Phone orders
welcome—Mastercard or Visa.

REPLICA & MODELS WWW
Email: replicamdl@aol.com

RICHARD KOHNSTAM
13–15 High Street, Hemel Hempstead, Hertfordshire
Tel: 01442 261721
Fax: 01442 240 647

ROYAL AIR FORCE MUSEUM
Grahame Park Way, Hendon, London NW9 5LL
Tel: 020 8205 2266
Tax: 020 8200 1751
Website: www.rafmuseum.org.uk
Britain's National Museum of Aviation', displays 70 full size
aircraft. Open daily. Extensive library research facilities (week-
days only). Large free car park. Licensed restaurant. Souvenir
shop with extensive range of specialist books and model kits.

SENTINEL MINIATURES
4 Broadway, no 102, Valhalla, New York 10595, USA
Tel/Fax: 914 682 3932
Military miniatures—figure kits, resin armour, accessories, publications. Painted figures on display. Mail order catalogue
@8.50. Visa/MC/Acccss. Also 1/43 die cast vehicles.

SHQ MINIATURES
34 Copland Close, Basingstoke, Hants RG22 4JX
Range of 1/76 scale WWII figures and vehicles covering
British, German, Polish, French, Dutch, Belgian and Russian,
plus the Vietnam and Gulf War conflicts.

*SUD MODELES DIFFUSION
290 Chemin de Bertoire, BP 22, 83910 Pourrieres, France

*LE ROYAUME DE LA FIGURINE
BP 3004, 24000 Perigeux, France

*S A LE CERCLE
Art de Vivre, 78630 Orgeval, France

*S N C BONNEFOY
8 Avenue Emile Bouyssou, 46100 Figeac, France

*LA SABRETACHE
1 Rue Pargaminieres, 31000 Toulouse, France

*LE SANTA FE
49 Rue Bersot, 25000 Besancon 25000, France

SARATOGA SOLDIER SHOP
831 Route 67, Building #5, Ballston Spa, New York 12020,
USA
Contact: William F Imrie
Tel: 518 885 1497
Fax: 518 885 0100
We stock the complete line of I/R Miniatures—54mm metal
soldier kits with historical texts and colouring guides. illus-
trated catalogue US$ 11.00 by airmail.

STEVE'S MODELS
Bullens Courtyard, Mill End Mews, Ashby de la Zouch
Tel: 0800 5423071

SOMETHING WICKED
1 Wood Street, Huddersfield
Tel: 01484 537191

*TEMPS LIBRE
22 Rue de Sevigne, 75004 Paris, France

THE AIRBRUSH & SPRAY CENTRE LTD
39 Littlehampton Road, Worthing, W. Sussex BN13 1QJ
Contact: Kenneth Medwell
Tel: 01903 266991
Fax: 01903 830045
Email: airbrush@lineone.net
Airbrush and compressor equipment and materials
suppliers. Main agents for Aerograph, Badger, Iwata and
Paasche. Servicing, repairs, spares and technical advice
from factory trained staff.

THE GAMES ROOM
29A Elm Hill, Norwich, Norfolk
Tel/Fax: 01603 628140
Email: mike@thegamesroom.fsnet.co.uk

THE TURNTABLE
11/12 Belle Vue Terrace, Luddendenfoot, Halifax HX2 6HG
Contact: Howard Hookham
Tel/Fax: 01422 883489
Email: turntable@calderfind.co.uk
Aviation, Military and railway modelling specialist. Importers of Czech and Polish resin and plastic kits. Send SAE for our lists.

TORBAY MODEL SUPPLIES LIMITED
59 Victoria Road, Ellacombe, Torquay, Devon
Tel/Fax: 01803 297764

TRADITION OF LONDON LTD
33 Curzon Street, Mayfair, London W1V 7AE
Contact: Steve Hare
Tel: 020 7493 7452
Fax: 020 7355 1224
Largest range of painted and unpainted figures in 54mm, 90mm, 110mm; plus over 300 different 'Toy Soldier' style sets, including 'Sharpe' range. Full mail order, credit cards. Mon–Fri 9.00am–5.30pm, Sat 9.30am–3.00pm.

THE TUTBERRY JINNY
19a Lower High Street, Tutbury, Burton-on-Trent
Tel: 01283 814777

UNDER TWO FLAGS
4 St Christophers Place, London W1V 1LZ
Tel/Fax: 020 7935 6934
Website: www.undertwoflags.com
Toy/model soldier specialists in the centre of the West End of London. Nearest Tube: Bond Street. Open 10.30am–5pm, Tuesday–Saturday.

V C MINIATURES
16 Dunraven Street, Aberkenfig, Bridgend, Glamorgan, Mid-Wales. CF32 9AS
Contact: Lyn Thorne
Tel/Fax: 01656 725006
Established 1987, manufacturer of hand painted 54mm toy soldiers, sculpted by Lyn Thorne and specialising in the Victorian period In addition to sets of traditional toy soldiers, military and civilian vignettes and individual figures are also produced. Recently acquired Burlington Models range of racehorses, jockeys and showjump figures.

*VAN NIEUWENHUIJZEN MODELSHOP
Oude Binnenweg 91, 3012 JA Rotterdam, Netherlands
Contact: Mike Lettinga
Tel: 10 4135923
Fax: 10 4141-324

*WATERLOO 1815
Mail Box 231, Borgo dei Cappuccini 29, Livorno 57100, Italy
Contact: Andrew
Tel/Fax: (0039) 586 864596
Specialists in distribution and sales of 1/72 and 1/32 plastic figures. We sell Hat 1/72–1/32; Iniex 1/72–1/32; Call to Arms 1/32; Old Atlantic 1/72 and the new Atlantic Reissue in 1/72: trade enquiries welcome. Private collectors–if you wish to sell your personal collection of plastic figures please contact us: we are interested in buying the lot.

WONDERLAND MODELS
97–101 Lothian Road, Edinburgh, Scotland EH3 9AN
Tel: 0131 229 6428
Fax: 0131 229 7625
Leading supplier of all main kit manufacturers including paints, books and decals. Special offers on many items.

WAKEFIELD MODEL AND CRAFT CENTRE
260 Dewsbury Road Wakefield
Tel: 01924 374097

WAYLANDS MODELS
39 Derby Road, Heanor
Tel: 01773 712131

W B H LORD AND SONS
78 Commercial Street, Brighouse
Tel: 01274 713869

*ZINNFIGUREN HOFMANN
Rathausplatz 7, D-90403 Nürnberg, Germany
Contact: Claudia Hofmann
Tel/Fax: 911 204848
Tin figures, mainly 30mm flats by Heinrichsen/Scheibert, period 1618-48 and 1805-15. Mailing only within the EC.

MUSEUMS

ABINGDON MUSEUM
Abingdon Volunteer Infantry, 1st Berkshire Yeomanry
County Hall Market Place, Abingdon, Oxfordshire
Tel: 0235 223703

AIRBORNE FORCES MUSEUM
Browning Barracks, Allisons Road, Aldershot, Hampshire
GU11 1XX
Tel: 01252 349619

AIRBORNE MUSEUM HARTENSTEIN
Utrechtseweg 232, 6862 AZ Oosterbeek, Netherlands
Contact: W Boersma
Tel: 263337710
Fax: 263391785
Email: hartenstein@wxs.nl
The Airborne Museum commemorates the Battle of
Arnhem, September 1944–A Bridge Too Far. Open daily
11.00–17.00; Sunday 12.00–17.00.

ALDERSHOT MILITARY MUSEUM
Queen's Avenue, Aldershot, Hampshire GU11 2LG
Contact: Ian Maine
Tel/Fax: 01252 314598
Email: musmim@hants.gov.uk
Depicts military life over 150 years Aldershot grew up
around the cam Victorian barrack room, tailor's shop,
vehicle gallery. Open daily 10.00am 5.00pm.

AMERICAN ARMOURED FOUNDATION, INC.
3401 US Hwy 29, Danville, VA 24540, USA
Contact: William Gasser
Tel: 434 836 5323
Fax: 434 836 2532
Email: aaftank@gamewood.net
Website: www.aaftankmuseum.com
A non-profit museum exhibiting the finest collection of
tanks, artillery, weapons, headgear, uniforms, and military
memorabilia from 1509 to present with all nations repre-
sented. A living war memorial dedicated to honoring the
men and women of the tank and cavalry.

APSLEY HOUSE–THE WELLINGTON MUSEUM
149 Piccadilly, Hyde Park Corner, London W1V 9FA
Contact: Leah Tobin
Tel: 020 7499 5676
Fax: 020 7493 6576
Apsley House, 'No. 1, London', described as 'The most
renowned mansion in the capital', houses the Duke's
collection of paintings, silver porcelain, sculpture and
furniture.

ARGYLL & SUTHERLAND HIGHLANDERS REGIMENTAL MUSEUM
The Castle, Stirling, Stirlingshire
Tel: 01786 75165

ARMY MEDICAL SERVICES MUSEUM
Keogh Barracks, Ash Vale, Aldershot, Hampshire GU12 5RQ
Contact: Capt P H Starling
Tel: 01252 340212
Fax: 01252 340332
Email: Museum@keogh72.freeserve.co.uk
Caring for all aspects of the history of the Army Medical
Services and its predecessors, including uniforms, insignia,
medals and medical equipment. Open Mon–Fri 10am-3.30pm.

ARMY PHYSICAL TRAINING CORPS MUSEUM
Queens Avenue, Aldershot, Hampshire Tel. (01252) 347168

ARTEMIS ARCHERY
29 Bately Court, Oldland, S. Glos BS30 8Y2
Contact: Veronica Soar
Tel/Fax: 0117 932 3276
Email: vee_artemis@yahoo.co.uk
Longbow/archery specific: books by post; historical
research, lectures, consultancy, coaching. Also longbow
presentations, static exhibitions and longbow and arrow
manufacture. SAE for booklist or other details. Archery collection viewing strictly;y by appointment only.

ARTILLERY COMPANY OF NEWPORT
PO Box 14, Newport, RI 02840-0001, USA
Contact: Capt. Joyce Gardner
Tel: 401 821 1689
Email: RISANCOMM@aol.com
Website: www.newportartillery.org
The Artillery Company of Newport, oldest and continuous.
Chartered during reign of King George II of Great Britian in
1741. Since then we have served the state and nation in con-
tinuous service. Today, the company serves as a ceremonial
unit of the Rhode Island Militia, Council of Historic Commands.
Military Museum open every Saturday, May–Oct, 10am–4pm.

ATLANTIC WALL MUSEUM/THE TODT BATTERY
Audinghen, Cap Gris-Nez, 62179 France
Tel: 03 21329733 or 03 21826201
Fax: 03 21320067

AUTO + TECHNIK MUSEUM
D-74889 Sinsheim, Germany
Contact: Herr Boeckle
Tel: 7261 92990
Fax: 7261 13916

AVONCRAFT MUSEUM OF HISTORIC BUILDINGS
Stoke Heath, Bromsgrove, Worcs B60 4JR
Tel: 01527 831363 or 831886
Fax: 01527 876934
Email: avoncraft1@compuserve.com
Website: www.avoncraft.org.uk
Avoncraft is a fascinating world of historic buildings cover-
ing seven centuries, rescued and rebuilt on a beautiful
open-air site in the heart of the Worcersershire country-
side.

AYRSHIRE YEOMANRY MUSEUM
Rozelle House, Monument Road, Alloway by Ayr, Ayrshire,
Scotland KA9 4NQ
Contact: G A Hay
Tel: 01292 264091
Fax: 01292 289856
Email: ayrlawhay@btinternet.com
Ayrshire (ECO) Yeomanry was raised in 1798 and after 200
years' existence, now serves as a squadron in The Queens
Own Yeomanry, which Regiment has, in addition to the
Squadron in Ayr, Squadrons in Cupar, Belfast, York and
Newcastle.

*BASTOGNE HISTORICAL CENTER
B-6600 Bastogne, Belgium
Amphitheatre: the account of the Battle of Bastogne in
Multivision. Collections: the authentic uniforms, weapons
and material of the conflict. Cinema: films of the battle.

BATTERIE DE MERVILLE
Musée de la Batterie, Hotel de Ville, 14810 Merville-
Franceville, Normandy, France
Tel/Fax: 02 31914753
The Melville battery was part of the Atlantic Wall built to
repel any attack from the sea and guard the beach at
Ouistreham.

BATTLE OF BRITAIN MEMORIAL FLIGHT VISITORS CENTRE
RAF Coningsby, Lincolnshire LN4 4SY
Tel: 01526 344041
Aircraft on display feature 5 Spitfires, 2 Hurricanes, 2
Chipmunks, 1 Lancaster, 1 Dakota.

BATTLE HISTORICAL MUSEUM
Langton House, Abbey Green, Battle, E. Sussex TN33 0AQ
Linked to the site of the Battle of Hastings and Battle
Abbey, featuring various diorama, video and talked-through
displays. Open April-Sept Mon-Sat 10.00am-13.00pm and
14.00pm-17.00pm.

BAYERISCHES ARMEEMUSEUM
Parideplatz 4, 85049 Ingolstadt, Germany
Tel: 841 93770
Fax: 841 9377200
In the medieval castle: military history ranging from the
Middle Ages to the 19th century. In Reduit Tilly (a 19th
century fortification): World War I museum.

BEDFORDSHIRE & HERTFORDSHIRE REGIMENT COLLECTION
c/o Luton Museum Service, Wardown Park, Luton,
Bedfordshire LU2 7HA
Contact: Robin Holgate
Tel: 01582 546723
Fax: 01582 546703
Email: robinH2@luton.gov.uk
Display of medals, weapons, equipment and memorabilia of
the Bedfordshire and Hertfordshire Regiment, from the
Marlborough campaigns to the end of World War II.

*BEVRIJINGSMUSEUM 1944
Wylerbaan 4, 6561 KR Groesbeck, Netherlands

BLACKBURN MUSEUM & ART GALLERY
Museum Street, Blackburn, Lancashire BB1 7AJ
Tel: 01254 667130
History of the East Lancashire Regiment and its
development.

BLACK WATCH MUSEUM
Balhousie Castle, Hay Street, Perth, Perthshire PH1 5HR,
Scotland
Contact: S J Lindsay
Tel: 0131 310 8530
Email: ew.rhq@btclick.com
250 years of military history of Scotland's oldest Highland
regiment. Open May-Sept: Mon-Sat. Oct-Apr: Mon-Fri.
Entry free.

BORDER REGT & K O R BORDER REGT MUSEUM
Queen Mary's Tower, The Castle, Carlisle, Cumbria CA3 8LTR
Contact: S A Eastwood
Tel: 01228 521275
Email: rhq@kingsownborder.demon.co.uk
The museum relates the story of (Cumbria's County Infantry
Regiment, The Border Regiment and its successor The King's
Own Royal Border Regiment from 1702 to date. Located in
Carlisle (castle, the Regiment's home since 1873, the displays
on two floors include uniforms, weapons, equipment, medals,
silver, pictures, memorabilia, dioramas, video presentations,
armoured car, field and anti-tank guns. Museum shop; archives
by appointment; enquiries welcome. Admission by paid entry
to Carlisle Castle; open April-Sept, Mon-Sun 9.30am-6pm,
Oct 9.30am-dusk, Nov-March Mon-Sun 10am-4pm. (Closed
24-26 December.)

BOMBER COMMAND ASSOCIATION
Royal Air Force Museum, Grahame Park Way, Hendon,
London NW9 5LL
Contact: Douglas Radcliffe
Tel: 020 8205 2083

*BRABANTS AIRBORNE MUSEUM
Spoorstraat 1, Best, Netherlands

BRITISH IN INDIA MUSEUM
Newtown Street, Colne, Lancashire BB8 0JJ
Tel/Fax: 01282 870215 or 613129
Uniforms, medals, models, photographs and paintings covering
all aspects, 17thC-1947. Open Mon, Wed-Sat 10am-4pm.
Closed: during Christmas holidays. Admission charge.

BUCKINGHAMSHIRE MILITARY MUSEUM TRUST
c/o Dept of History, University of Luton, 75 Castle St, Luton,
Bedfordshire LU1 3AJ
Contact: Ian Beckett
Tel: 01582 489043
Fax: 01582 489014
Email: ian.beckett@luton.ac.uk
Museum collections displayed at the Old Gaol, Buckingham
and Claydon House, Middle Claydon (National Trust Property).

THE BUFFS REGIMENTAL MUSEUM
18 High Street, Cantebury
Tel: 01227 452747

BURRELL COLLECTION
Pollok Country Farm, 2060 Pollokshaws Road, Glasgow,
Strathclyde, Scotland G43 1AT
Tel: 0141 287 2550
Fax: 0141 287 2597

CABINET WAR ROOMS
Clive Steps, King Charles Street, London SW1A 2AQ
Tel: 020 7930 6961
Website: www.iwm.org.uk
Churchill's secret underground wartime headquarters.

CAEN MEMORIAL MUSEUM
Esplanade Eisenhower, BP 6261, 14066 Caen, Cedex 4,
France
Tel: 02 31060644
Fax: 02 31060670
Website: www.memorial.fr
Multimedia library, archives and photograph library, teach-
ing activities, publishing, syposiums and conferences.

CAMERONIANS (SCOTTISH RIFLES) COLLECTION
Low Parks Museum, 129 Muir Street, Hamilton, Lanarkshire,
Scotland ML3 6BJ
Contact: Liz Hancock
Tel: 01698 428688
Temporarily closed for redevelopment until early 2000.

CANNON HALL MUSEUM (see 13th/18th Hussars)
Cannon Hall, Cawthorne, Barnsley, S. Yorkshire S75 4AT
Contact: Jane Whittaker
Tel: 01226 790270
Fax: 01226 792117
'CHARGE!' The Museum of the 13th/18th Royal Hussars
(QMO) and The Light Dragoons. Housed within Cannon Hall
Museum and Country Park, Cawthorne, near Barnsley,
South Yorkshire. New galleries tell the story of the
Regiment's history from 1715-1992, which includes The
Charge of the Light Brigade (Audio/Visual). Opening Hours
Tuesday-Saturday 10.30am-5pm, Sunday 12-5pm. Closed
Mondays but open Bank Holidays. Closed Good Friday and
Christmas period.

CARMARTHEN MUSEUM
Abergwili, Carmarthen, Dyfed, Wales SA31 2JG
Tel: 01267 231691
Fax: 01267 223830
Email: cdelaney@camarthenshire.gov.uk
Regional museum with collection related to local militia
and volunteer units: Carmarthenshire Militia, Carmarthen
Yeomanry, Cavalry.

CHESHIRE MILITARY MUSEUM
The Castle, Chester, Cheshire CH1 2DN
Tel/Fax: 01244 327617
Email: r.montgomery@chester.ac.uk
Two regiments of Dragoon Guards, Cheshire Yeomanry and
Cheshire Regiment combine displays, medals, uniforms.
Small charge, open daily 10am-5pm except Christmas.

CHESTERHOLM MUSEUM
Bardon Mill, Hexham, Northumberland
Displays relating to this important Roman fort site, where
e.g. the unique Vindolanda tablets were recovered.

THE CHILTERN OPEN AIR MUSEUM
Newland Park, Gorelands Lane, Chalfont St Giles,
Buckinghamshire HP8 4AD
Email: coamuseum@netscapeonline.co.uk
Website: www.coam.org.uk
Walk into history at the Chiltern Open Air Museum which
is open daily from April to October. The Museum consists
of more that 30 historic buildings, all rescued from demoli-
tion and representative of the built heritage of the
Chilterns. Visitors are able to roam the 45-acre woodland
and parkland site at their leisure and explore the buildings.
Brick Making, Straw Plaiting, Rag Rug Making and Candle
Making are just some of the hands on activities that take
place during the course of the season that all the family
can enjoy.

**CHOLMONDELEY MODEL SOLDIER COLLECTION &
MILITARIA**
Houghton Hall, Kings Lynn, Norfolk
Tel: 01485 528569
Fax: 01485 528167

CLAYTON MUSEUM / CHESTERS ROMAN FORT
Chollerford, Hexham, Northumberland

COMBINED OPERATIONS MUSEUM
Argyll Estates Office, Cherry Park, Inverary, Argyll, Scotland
PA32 8XE
Contact: James Jepson
Tel: 01499 500218
Fax: 01499 302421
The story of 250,000 Allied troops who trained in Inveraray
for the early commando raids and major landings of WWII.
Open first Saturday in April to second Sunday in October.

COBBATON COMBAT COLLECTION
Chittlehampton, Umberleigh, Devon EX37 9RZ
Contact: Isaac: Preston
Tel: 01769 540 740
Fax: 01769 540 141
Email: info@cobbatoncombat@co.uk
Private collection of about 50 vehicles, tanks and artillery,
WWII British, Canadian, some Warsaw Pact, fully equipped.
Home Front section. Militaria shop. Open daily
April-November: Winter Mon-Fri.

COLCHESTER MUSEUMS
Museum Resource Centre, 14 Ryegate Road, Colchester,
Essex CO1 1YG
Contact: Tom Hodgson
Tel: 01206 284931/2
Fax: 07206 282925
Email: tomhodgson@colchester.gov.uk
1648 Siege of Colchester display at Castle Museum.
Collections of local militia/volunteer militaria and Civil War
armour, viewing by prior appointment only.

CORNWALL AIRCRAFT PARK (HELSTON) LTD
Flambards, Culdrose Manor, Helston, Cornwall TR13 0GA
Contact: James Kingsford Hale
Tel: 01326 573404
Fax: 01326 573344
Email: flambards@connexions.co.uk
Website: www.flambards.co.uk
Classic military aircraft, renowned war galleries; WW II, Falklands, Gulf memorabilia- acclaimed recreation of wartime street in 'Britain in the Blitz'. Many other collections and exhibitions.

CRANWELL AVIATION HERITAGE CENTRE
The Mill, Money's Yard, Sleaford, Lincs NG34 7TW
With views over RAF Cranwell and the Tucano trainers that inhabit the circuit, the Heritage Centre covers the history of this famous airfield. Free.

CRESSING TEMPLE
Witham Road, Braintree, Essex CM7 8PD
Tel: 01376 584903
Cressing Temple was bestowed upon the Knights Templar in 1137 and became the largest and most important estate in Essex. The result was two of the most spectacular medieval timber barns in Europe. Phone for details

D-DAY MUSEUM & OVERLORD EMBROIDERY
Clarence Esplanade, Southsea, Hampshire PO5 3NT
Contact: David Evans
Tel: 01705 827261
Fax: 01705 875270
Email: Pzlei130@hants.gov.uk
Tells the story of the Normandy landings, 6th June 1944. Open daily except 24-26 December, 10.00am-5.30pm, last admission 4.30pm.

D-DAY LANDING MUSEUM
Place du 6 Juin, 14117 Arromanches, Normandy, France
Tel: 02 31223431
Fax: 02 31926883
Museum tracing the development, construction and deployment of the massive portable Mulberry artificial harbours, which enabled the 1944 Invasion of Normandy to be continously supplied.

DERBYSHIRE INFANTRY MUSEUM
City Museum & Art Gallery, The Strand, Derby, Derbyshire DE1 1BS
Contact: Angela Kelsall
Tel: 01332 710656
Fax: 01332 716670
Email: akelsall@derbymuseum.freeserve.co.uk
Displays relating to Derbyshire's regular and irregular infantry since 1689, including militia, volunteer, 95th (Derbyshire) Regiment and Sherwood Foresters items. Enquiry service.

DERBYSHIRE YEOMANRY MUSEUM
City Museum & Art Gallery, The Strand, Derby, Derbyshire DE1 1BS
Contact: Angela Kelsall
Tel: 01332 716656
Fax: 01332 716070
Email: akelsall@derbymuseum.freeserve.co.uk
Display illustrating the history of the Derbyshire Yeomanry & Mounted Volunteers since 1794. Some regimental records. Enquiry service.

DOMAIN RAVERSIJDE ATLANTIC WALL MUSEUM
Diunenstraat 147, b-8400 Ostend, West-Vlaanderen, Belgium
Tel: 059 70 22 85
Fax: 059 51 45 03
The former Royal Domain of Leopold II forms the core of this museum, which during both WWI and II was used by the Germans for coastal defence. Over 60 emplacements connected by trenches and galleries survive almost completely intact.

DONCASTER MUSEUM & ART GALLERY
Chequer Road, Doncaster, S. Yorkshire DN1 2AE
Contact: G Preece
Tel: 01302 734293
Fax: 01302 735409
Email: museum@doncaster.gov.uk
Small displays relating to local Yeomanry, Hussars and Militia, and the KOYLI museum collection. Open Mon-Sat, 10am-5pm; Sun 2pm-5pm. Admission free.

DUKE OF CORNWALL'S LIGHT INFANTRY MUSEUM
The Keep, Bodmin, Cornwall PL31 1EG
Contact: Hugo White
Tel: 01208 72810
History of the Duke of Cornwall's Light Infantry, and the local Cornish forces. Excellent display of uniforms, medals and weapons. Very comprehensive reference library.

DUKE OF EDINBURGH'S ROYAL REGIMENT MUSEUM
58 The Close, Salisbury, Wiltshire SP1 2EX
Tel: 01722 414536

DUKE OF LANCASTER'S OWN YEOMANRY MUSEUM
Museum of Lancashire, Stanley Street, Preston, Lancashire PR1 4YP
Contact: Stephen Bull
Tel/Fax: 01772 264075
Email: museum@lancs.co.uk
The museum of the Duke of Lancaster's Own tells the story of the regiment from the eighteenth century to the present.

DUKE OF WELLINGTON'S REGT MUSEUM
Bankfield Museum, Akroyd Park, Halifax, W. Yorkshire HX3 6IG
Contact: J D Spencer
Tel: 01422 354823
The museum displays the history of the 33rd and 76th Foot from 1702 to the present, including material relating to the 'Iron Duke'. Admission free.

DURHAM LIGHT INFANTRY MUSEUM
Aykley Heads, Durham, Co. Durham DH1 5TU
Tel: 0191 384 2214
Fax: 0191 386 1770
Email: dli@durham.gov.uk
History of The Durham Light Infantry 1758–1968–medals, uniforms, weapons, photographs, Regimental treasures. Open Tuesday-Saturday 10am-5pm. Shop. Refreshments. Disabled access.

DUXFORD IMPERIAL WAR MUSEUM
Duxford
Tel: 01223 835000

EAST ENGLAND TANK MUSEUM
Oak Business Park, Wix Road, Beaumont, Essex CO16 0AT
Contact: Iain Greenwood
Tel: 01255 871 119
Fax: 01255 871 109
Email: iain@tankmuseum.com
Website: www.tankmuseum.com
With our linked organisation, The Battle Field Museum, we are one of the Largest collections of vehicles in the UK. We specialise in NATO and ex-Warsaw pact vehicles from WWII to the present day, together with their logistical support vehicles and communications equipment We can supply specialist information for visitors (by appointment) and can rent our vehicles out for film and business if required.We also supply excess vehicles from our collection, manuals, spares and workshop support.

ELIZABETH CASTLE
St.Aubin's Bay, Jersey, Channel Islands
Tel: 01534 723971
Fax: 01534 610338

ESSEX REGIMENT MUSEUM
Oaklands Park, Moulsham Street, Chelmsford, Essex CM2 9AQ
Contact: Ian Hook
Tel: 01245 353066
Email: chelmsfordbc@dial.pipex.com
Displays of weapons, uniforms, medals, silver and relics of The Essex Regiment (now Royal Anglian) and its forebears, the 44th and 56th Foot, including the Eagle captured at Salamanca, 1812. Biographical index for family history research. Open Mon-Sat 10am-5pm, Sun 2pm-5pm; admission free.

ESSEX YEOMANRY MUSEUM COLLECTION
TA Centre, Springfield Lyons, Colchester Road, Chelmsford, Essex CM2 5TA
Tel: 01245 361258
Fax: 01245 360662
Email: casstles@globalnet.co.uk

FALLINGBOSTEL WWII & 2RTR REGT.MUSEUM
MBB3 Lumsden Barracks, Fallingbostel BFPO 38, Germany
Contact: Kevin Greenhalgh
Museum of WWII relics/items recovered from the actions around Fallingbostel, including the POW camps 11B and 326. 2RTR Regimental Museum covers regimental history 1916 to the Gulf War; uniforms, large collection of WWII RTR items, photos, books, etc.

FIFE AND FORFAR YEOMANRY MUSEUM
Yeomanry House, Castlebank Road, Cupar, Fife, Scotland KY14 4BL

FIRE SERVICES NATIONAL MUSEUM TRUST
9 Moriand Way, Manton Heights, Bedford, Bedfordshire MK41 7NP
Contact: The Curator
A project to create a National Museum of Firefighting devoted to the exciting story of the fire services and fire prevention in this country.

FLAG INSTITUTE
44 Middleton Road, Acomb, N. Yorkshire YO2 3AS
Contact: Michael Faul

FLAGSHIP PORTSMOUTH TRUST
Poerter's Lodge, College Road, HM Naval Base, Portsmouth, Hants PO1 3LR
Tel: 01705 839766
Fax: 01705 295252
Email: signals@flagship.compulink.co.uk
HMS Victory, Mary Rose, HMS Warrior 1860, Royal Naval Museum. The world's greatest historic ships.

FLEET AIR ARM MUSEUM
RNAS Yeovilton, Ilchester, Yeovilton, Somerset BA22 8HT
Contact: Carol Rendell
Tel: 01935 840565
Fax: 01935 840181
Email: info@fleetairarm.com
World's leading naval aviation museum. History since 1908, exhibitions on World Wars, Kamikaze, WRNS, recent conflicts. New Carrier Experience–a flight deck on land–plus 11 aircraft.

FORT AUSTRATT
Lundahaugen-Orland, Norway
Three turret systems including the stern turret of the battleship Gneisenau–the shafts and tunnels for which were blasted out of the rock at Lundahaugen.

*FORT DE DOUAUMONT
55100 Verdun, France
Tel/Fax: 29841885

*FORT DE VAUX
55100 Verdun, France
Tel/Fax: 49841885

FORT DOUGLAS MILITARY MUSEUM
32 Potter St, Ft Douglas, UT 84113, USA
Tel: 801 581 1710
Fax: 801 581 9846
Email: fdouglas@webguyinternet.com
Website: www.fortdouglas.org

FORT MACARTHUR MUSEUM
3601 S. Gaffey St, San Pedro, CA 90731, USA
Contact: Stephen R Nelson
Tel: 310 548 2631
Fax: 310 241 0847
Email: director@ftmac.org
Website: www.ftmac.org
The Fort MacArthur Museum exists to educate the public about Fort MacArthur and 20th Century southern California military history. We utilize historic Battery Osgood-Farley for exhibits and living history activities. Subjects include WWI, WWII, and Cold War national defense, Coast Artillery NIKE Missles, African American servicemen, K-9 Corps, military vehicles and equipment and personal histories.

FORT SAM HOUSTON MUSEUM
1750 Greeley Road, Suite 2, Fort Sam Houston, TX 88234-5002, USA
Contact: Museum Director
Tel: 210 221 0019
Fax: 210 221 1311
Email: ftsammuseum@amedd.army.mil
Website: www.cs.amedd.army.mil/dptmsec/muse.htm
Museum depicts the history of Fort Sam Houston and of the US Army in the region. Collections include uniforms, arms, equipment, vehicles, images. Areas of interest include units stationed at Fort Sam Houston, Army operations in Texas Philippine Scouts. 2nd Infantry Division, 5th, 6th, 7th 9th, 10th, and 15th Armies; 88th, 90th, 95th, 18th Divisions.

FORT POLK MILITARY MUSEUM
PO Box 3916, 917 South Carolina Ave, Fort Polk, IA 71459-0916, USA
Contact: Dr. David S. Bingham
Tel: 337 531 7905
Fax: 337 531 4202
Email: Bingham@polk.Army.mil
Artifacts on display depict the history of Fort Polk and for the six Army Corps. Twelve Divisions and two training centers that have served at Fort Polk since it opened in June 1941. Exhibit also includes the Louisiana Maneovers held here between 1940 and 1944, and of famous servicemen who served at this installation.

FORT MUSEUM AND FRONTIER VILLAGE
PO Box 1798, Business Hwy 20 & Museum Road, Fort Dodge, IA 50501
Contact: David E. Parker
Tel: 515 573 4231
Fax: 515 573 3665
Email: thefort@frontiernet.net
Website: www.dodgenet.com/~mayorofdodge/fort
Fort Museum and Frontier Village features military history ranging from the early 1800's to Confederate General Lewis A. Armistead to Operation Desert Storm. Other collections include pioneer and Native American artifacts and horse drawn Transportation—the museum is housed in a replica Civil War era militia fort and a frontier main street.

FORT SNELLING
Ft Snelling History Center, Hwys 5 & 55, St Paul, MN 55111, USA
Contact: Site Manager
Tel: 612 726 1171
Email: fortsnelling@mnhs.org
Website: www.mnhs.org/fortsnelling
Fully restored 1820 stone fortress at the junction of the Mississippi and Minnesota Rivers Features an extensive living history program, military paegentry and exhibits.

FUSILIERS MUSEUM OF NORTHUMBERLAND
Abbot's Tower, Alnwick Castle, Alnwick, Northumberland NE66 1NG
Tel/Fax: 01665 602152 or 510211
Email: fusnorthld@aol.com

FUSILIERS VOLUNTEER & TERRITORIAL MUSEUM
213 Balham High Road, London SW17 7BQ
Tel: 020 8672 1168
Fax: 020 8071414 5594

FUSILIERS MUSEUM, LANCASHIRE
Wellington Barracks, Bolton Road, Bury, Lancashire BL8 2PL
Contact: J Hallam
Tel/Fax: 0161 764 2208
Email: rrflhq@aol.com
The Fusiliers Museum, Lancashire at Wellington Barracks is open Mon, Tues, Fri, Sat 9.30am–4.30pm. Admission £2, OAPs and Children £1.

GENIE MUSEUM
Brederodekazerne, Lunettenlaan 102, 5263 NT Vught, Netherlands
Tel/Fax: (0031) 881867

GERMAN UNDERGROUND HOSPITAL
St Lawrence, Jersey, Channel Islands JE3 1FLJ
Contact: McScowen
Tel: 01534 863442
Fax: 01534 865970
Large displays connected with German wartime occupation of Channel Islands, housed in underground complex.

GLAMORGAN ARTILLERY VOLUNTEERS MUSEUM
104 Air Defence Regt RA (V), Raglan Barracks, Newport, Gwent, Wales NP9 5XE

GLASGOW ART GALLERY & MUSEUM
Kelvingrove, Glasgow, Strathclyde, Scotland G3 8AG
Contact: Robert Woosnam Savage
European arms & armour (1000 AD–present); includes 'Avant' armour, c. 1445 (part of the R.L. Scott Collection); Whitelaw Collection (Scottish arms); Martin Collection (firearms); Scottish W Coast Volunteer Units (18th–19thC). Library closed Dec 25–Jan 1.

GORDON HIGHLANDERS MUSEUM

St Lukes, Viewfield Road, Aberdeen, Grampian, Scotland
AB15 7XH
Contact: M J Brooker
Tel: 01224 311200
Fax: 01224 319323
Email: museum@gordonhighlanders.com
The history of the Gordon Highlanders, including new
exhibitions, audio-visual theatre and interactive displays.
Tearoom and gardens. Open April–October. Closed
Mondays.

THE GREEN HOWARDS MUSEUM

Trinity Church Square, Richmond, N. Yorkshire DL10 4QN
Contact: N D McIntosh, MBE
Tel: 01748 822111 873778
Fax: 10748 826561
Email: greenhowards@virgin.net
Over 300 years of history is displayed in three galleries in
the medieval church in Richmond's historic market square.
Includes important Crimean War items and the finest
regimental uniform, medal and badge collection.

GUARDS MUSEUM

Wellington Barracks, Birdcage Walk, London SW1E 6HQ
Tel: 020 7414 3271.
Open daily 10am–4pm, except Friday and some ceremonial
days. History of the Foot Guards, the museum is located
so you can combine a visit with watching the Horse
Guards at Buckingham Palace.

GUERNSEY MILITIA MUSEUM

Candle Gardens, St Peter Port, Guernsey GY1 1UG
Contact: Brian Owen
Tel/Fax: 01481 720513
Email: brian@museum.guernsey.net
Uniforms, equipment and ephemera of the Guernsey Militia
and Royal Guernsey Light Infantry.

GURKHA MUSEUM

Peninsular Barracks, Romsey Road, Winchester SO23 8TS
Contact: Brig (Retd) C J D Bullock OBE, MC
Tel: 01962 842832
Fax: 01962 877597
Email: curator@thegurkhamuseum.co.uk
Website: www.thegurkhamuseum.co.uk
The Gurkha Museum commemorates the services of the
Gurkhas to the British since 1815. Open 10am–5pm,
Monday-Saturday. Sunday 12am–4pm. Closed Xmas, New
Year and Bank Holidays. Admission: Adults £1.50; OAPs
75p; accompanied children free. We are 10 minutes walk
from a Rail Station. Shop and Mail Order service available.

HANSTHOLM MUSEUM

Tarnvej 23, Postbox 102, 7730 Hanstholm, Denmark
Tel: 45 9796 1736
Fax: 45 9796 0595
Email: MCHkanon@Post8.tele.dk
Northen Europe's largest fortifications from WWII. Open
March to October.

HELICOPTER MUSEUM

Weston-super-Mare
Tel: 01934 635227
Easy to find, with brown road signs to direct you in the
town.

HERTFORDSHIRE REGIMENTAL COLLECTION

c/o Hertford Museum, 18 Bull Plain, Hertford, Hertfordshire
SG14 1DT
Tel: 01992 582686
Fax: 01992 534797
Open Tuesday–Saturday, 10am–5pm, admission free.

HERTFORDSHIRE YEOMANRY & ARTILLERY MUSEUM

Hitchin Museum & Art Gallery, Paynes Park, Hitchin,
Hertfordshire SG5 1EQ
Tel: 01462 43447
Fax: 01462 431316
Email: gill.riding@nhdc.gov.uk
A small display of medals and uniforms of the
Hertfordshire Yeomanry.

HMS BELFAST

Morgan's lane, Tooley Street, London SE1 2JH
Tel: 020 7490 6300
Website: www.iwm.org.uk
or: www.hmsbelfast.org.uk
The cruiser HMS Belfast, the last of her kind, served in
both WWII & the Korean War. She is now moored on the
Thames in central London as a unique historic reminder of
Britain's naval heritage and a premier floating museum.

HMS VICTORY

HM Naval Base, Portsmouth, Hampshire PO1 3LJ
Contact: Rob Griffiths
Tel: 01705 861533
Fax: 01705 295252
Email: enquiries@flagship.org.uk
Website: www.flagship.org.uk
HMS Victory–the greatest of all sailing warships. See
where Lord Nelson planned the Battle of Trafalgar, and the
tragic spot where he died.

HMS WARRIOR 1860

Victory Gate, HM Naval Base, Portsmouth, Hampshire PO1 3QX
Contact: Rob Griffiths
Tel: 01705 861533
Fax: 01705 295252
Email: enquiries@falgship.org.uk
Website: www.flagship.org.uk
HMS Warrior 1860–the world's first iron battleship. So
powerful that all other warships were made obsolete. A
mighty symbol of Queen Victoria's Empire.

HOME FRONT/DANELAW VILLAGE

Murton Park, York, N. Yorkshire YO1 3UF
Contact: Angela Hardman
Tel: 01904 489966
Fax: 01904 489159
Educational 'living history' site covering 10th-20th
centuries for schools. School visits, lectures, demonstra-
tions all periods, nationwide. Site open all year.

HOUSEHOLD CAVALRY MUSEUM
Combermere Barracks, St Leonards Road, Windsor,
Berkshire SL4 3DN
Collection contains uniforms, weapons, horse furniture, standards
and curios of the Regiment of Household Cavalry. Over 300 years
of the history of The Sovereign's Mounted Bodyguard. Open
Mon–Fri, 9.30am–12.30pm & 2.00pm-4.30pm. Free admission.

HONOURABLE ARTILLERY COMPANY MUSEUM
Armoury House, City Road
Tel: 0171 6064644

HULL CITY MUSEUMS
Wilberforce House, 23–25 High Street, Kingston-upon-Hull HU1 1NQ
Tel: 01482 613902
Fax: 01482 613710
Wilberforce House Museum is a historic house with reserve
military collections relating to the East Yorkshire Regiment
and World War I and II.

HUNTERIAN MUSEUM
Glasgow University, Glasgow, Strathclyde, Scotland G12 8QQ
Tel/Fax: 0141 339 8855
Email: e.smith@museums.gla.ac.uk

HUNTLY HOUSE MUSEUM
142 Canongate, Edinburgh, Lothian, Scotland EH8 8DD
Edinburgh's main museum of local history. Displays include
collections relating to the life of Field-Marshal Earl Haig
(1861–1928), with a reconstruction of his WWI HQ. Open
Mon–Sat 10.00am–5.00pm, Sunday 2.00pm–5.00pm
(during Edinburgh Festival). Admission free.

IMPERIAL PRESS MUSEUM GUIDE
Pantiles, Garth Lane, Knighton, Powys, Wales LD7 1HH
Contact: Shirley Wise
Tel/Fax: 015475 49160
Guide to Military Museums in the UK: full details of over
200 regimental and other military museums listed.

IMPERIAL WAR MUSEUM
Lambeth Road, London SE1 6HZ
Tel: 020 7416 5000
Fax: 020 7416 5374
Email: mail@iwm.org.uk
Unique institution telling the story of 20th century warfare.
Exhibitions on the world wars, a 'large exhibits' hall, art
galleries, library and photo archives, cafe and shop. Open
Mon–Sun 10.00am–6.00pm. Adults £4.10, concessions
£3.10. Tube Lambeth North, Elephant & Castle; British Rail
Waterloo, Elephant & Castle.

IMPERIAL WAR MUSEUM DUXFORD
Duxford Airfield, Cambridge, Cambridgeshire CB2 4QR
Contact: Frank Crosby
Tel: 01223 835000
Fax: 01223 837267
Email: mail@iwm.org.uk
Website: www.iwm.org.uk
Houses the largest collection of military and civil aircraft in
the country, totalling over 140. Also exhibiting over 100
military vehicles, artillery, and much more.

INNS OF COURT & CITY YEOMANRY MUSEUM
10 Stone Buildings, Lincoln's Inn, London WC2A 3TG
Tel: 020 7405 8112
Fax: 020 7414 3496

INTELLIGENCE CORPS MUSEUM
Templer Barracks, Ashford, Kent TN23 3HH
The history of military intelligence from Elizabethan times
to the present times. Open Tues and Thurs
9.00am–12.00am, 14.00pm–16.00pm.

JOHN GEORGE JOICEY MUSEUM
1 City Road, Newcastle upon Tyne, Tyne & Wear NE1 2AS
Tel/Fax: 0191 232 4562
Museum dedicated to The 15th and 19th King's Royal
Hussars and Northumberland Hussars.

THE KEEP MILITARY MUSEUM
The Keep, Bridport Road, Dorchester, Dorset DT1 1RN
Contact: Len Brown
Tel: 01305 264066
Fax: 01305 250373
Email: keep.musem@talk21.com
Covers Devonshire Regiment, Dorset Regiment, The
Devonshire and Dorset Regiment, Queens Own Dorset
Yeomanry, The Royal Devonshire Yeomanry, Royal North
Devonshire Hussars, Dorset Yeomanry and 94th Field
Regiment, RA.

KENT BATTLE OF BRITAIN MUSEUM
Aerodrome Road, Hawkinge Airfield, Folkestone, Kent
CT18 7AG
Tel/Fax: 01303 893140
Most important collection of Battle of Britain artefacts on
show in the country. Aircraft, vehicles, weapons, flying
equipment, prints, relics from nearly 600 crashed aircraft.

KENT AND SHARPSHOOTERS YEOMANRY MUSEUM
Hever Castle, Edenbridge, Kent TN8 7NG
Contact: Boris Mollo
Tel: 01732 865224
Email: mail@hevercastle.co.uk
Displays relating to the Kent Yeomanry and the 3rd/4th
County of London Yeomanry (Sharpshooters), including
uniforms, pictures, badges, medals, standards, weapons
and documents.

KENTWELL HALL
Kentwell Hall, Long Melford, Sudbury, Suffolk CO10 9BA
Contact: Alex Scott
Tel: 01787 310207
Fax: 01787 379318
Email: info@kentwel.co.uk
Website: www.kentwell.co.uk
Mellow redbrick Tudor manor famed for award-winning
recreations. Volunteer groups and individuals always wel-
come to apply to take part in WWII and Home Front
events. Must have own uniform/costume and be prepared
to assume 'first person' role and authenticity. Phone (in
office hours) for form. Public and groups welcome to visit.

KING'S OWN ROYAL REGIMENT MUSEUM
City Museum, Market Square, Lancaster, Lancashire LA1 1HT
Contact: Peter Donnelly
Tel: 01 524 6463 7
Fax: 01524 841692
Website: awhite@lancaster.gov.uk
Museum of the King's Own Royal Regiment (Lancaster)
and its constituent militias, 1680–1959. Displays and
regimental archives.

KING'S OWN SCOTTISH BORDERERS
Berwick Borough Museum, The Barracks,The Parade
(off Church St.), Berwick
Tel: 01289 304493

KING'S OWN YORKSHIRE LIGHT INFANTRY MUSEUM
Doncaster Museum & Art Gallery, Chequer Road, Doncaster,
S. Yorkshire DN1 2AE
Contact: G Preece
Tel: 01302 734293
Fax: 01302 735409
Email: musem@doncaster.gov.uk
History of the K.O.Y.L.I. and 51st and 105th regiments.
Open Mon-Sat, 10am–5pm; Sun 2pm-5pm. Admission
free.

KING'S REGIMENT COLLECTION
Museum of Liverpool Life, Pier Head, Liverpool L3 1PZ
Contact: Simon Jones
Tel: 0151 478 4062
Fax: 0151 478 4090
Email: sjones@nmgmmoll.demon.co.uk
Currently closed to public, reopens in 2000. The
Regimental collection of the King's Liverpool Regiment up
to 1958, and the King's Regiment from 1958.

THE KING'S ROYAL HUSSARS MUSEUM IN WINCHESTER
Peninsula Barracks, Romsey Road, Winchester, Hampshire
SO23 8TS
Tel: 01962 828539
Fax: 01962 828538
The history of three famous cavalry regiments from 1715
to the present, including the Charge of The Light Brigade,
World War I and II.

LANCASTER CITY MUSEUM
Market Square, Lancaster, Lancashire LAI 111T
Contact: Peter Donelly
Tel: 01524 64637
Fax: 01524 841692
Website: awhite@lancaster.gov.uk
History of Lancaster. Including King's Own Royal Regiment
Museum.

LANCASHIRE FUSILIER MUSEUM
Wellington Barracks, Bury
Tel: 0161 7642208

LEEDS CITY MUSEUM
Municipal Buildings, Leeds, W. Yorkshire LS I 3AA
Contact: Adrian Norris
Tel: 0113 247 8275
Fax: 0113 234 2300
Website: www.leeds.gov.uk/
At the present time the Militaria Collection is not on
display, other than a small display of medals.

LEEDS RIFLES MUSEUM TRUST
1 Ledgate Lane, Burton Salmon, Leeds, W. Yorkshire
LS25 5JY
Contact: R Addyman
Tel/Fax: 01977 676835
Items of regimental silver, pictures, scrolls, medals and
other effects accomodated exclusively in TA barracks.
Access by prior arrangement only but enquiries welcome.

LEGIO SECUNDA AUGUSTA
61 Totland Road, Cosham, Hanys PO6 3HS
Contact: David Richardson
Tel/Fax: 02392 369970
Email: legiiauy@cwcom.net
Website: www.legiiaug.org.uk
Roman living history society, depicting the life and times of
mid 1st and 2nd Century Roman Britain. Military and
civilian aspects covered. We now present gladiators—as
they should be shown!

LEICESTERSHIRE & DERBYSHIRE ARMY MUSEUM
Derby Museum & Art Gallery, The Strand, Derby, Derbyshire
DB1 1BS

LEICESTER REGIMENTAL MUSEUM
New Walk Museum, New Walk LE1 7EA
Tel: 0116 255 4100
Fax: 0116 247 3057
Website: ww.leicestermuseums.ac.uk
See how the Regiment was formed, its connections with
Leicester and Leicestershire and its role in the trenches of
WWI and the battlefields of WWII. Gallery of the
Leicestershire Regiment 1688-1964.

LIGHT DRAGOONS (15TH/19TH THE KING'S ROYAL HUSSARS) MUSEUM
Soldier's Life, Newcastle Discovery Museum, Blandford
Square, Newcastle upon Tyne NE1 4JA
Contact: Mr R Thompson
Tel: 0191 232 679
Fax: 0191 230 2614
Email: r.thompson@tyne-wear-museums.org.uk
Museum of the 15th/19th The King's Royal Hussars.

LIVERPOOL SCOTTISH REGIMENT MUSEUM
1A Centre, Forbes House, Score Lane, Childwall, Liverpool,
Merseyside L16 2NG

LONDON IRISH RIFLES MUSEUM
Duke of York's HQ, Kings Road, Chelsea, London SW3 4RX
Museum for present and past soldiers of Regiment. Being
on Ministry of Defence ground not open to general public.
Correspondence regarding archives to above address.

LIGHT INFANTRY MUSEUM
Peninsula Barracks, Romsey Road, Winchester
Tel: 01962 828530

LONDON SCOTTISH REGIMENTAL MUSEUM
95 Horseferry Road, Westminster, London SW1P 2DX
Contact: Leslie McDonnell
Tel: 020 7630 1630
Fax: 020 7233 7909
Email: leslie.mcdonnell@btinternet.com
Private museum viewed by appointment only.

LONGUES SUR MER BATTERIE
14400 Longues-sur-Mer, Normandy, France
Tel: 02 31060605
German bunker artillery battery of the WWII Atlantic Wall,
which gave the Allied ships a pounding on 6th June. It is
the only coastal battery to have kept its guns.

LOUGHBOROUGH WAR MEMORIAL MUSEUM
Leicestershire Yeomanry, Leicestershire Tigers
Tel: 0509 26637

LUNT ROMAN FORT
Coventry Road, Baginton, Coventry, W. Midlands
Partially reconstructed fort including gateway, ramparts, granary
and unique gyrus. Interpretive exhibition and tape-tour guide.
Good access for disabled. Address for correspondence: Herbert
Art Gallery & Museum, Jordan Well, Coventry CV32 6DY, Tel:
04203 832381, fax: 01203 832410.

MAIDSTONE MUSEUM
St Faith's Road, Maidstone, Kent ME14 1LH
The Queen's Own Royal West Kent Regimental Museum.

MARITIME MUSEUM
Albert Dock, Liverpool, Merseyside L3 4AA
Contact: Lorraine Knowles
Tel: 0151 207 0001
Fax: 0151 478 4590
Email: lknowles@nmgmlmk.demon.co.uk

MARY ROSE SHIP HALL & MUSEUM
HM Naval Base, Portsmouth, Hampshire PO1 3LX
Contact: Andy Newman
Tel: 01705 750521
Fax: 01705 8 70588
Email: maryrose@cix.compulink.co.uk
Website: www.maryrose.org
Experience the breathtaking hull and museum of unique
artefacts from King Henry VIII's favourite warship. Open all
year, it is a moment captured in time.

MARY ROSE TRADING COMPANY
No 5 Boathouse, HM Naval Base, Portsmouth, Hampshire PO1 3PX
Contact: Sally Charleton
Tel: 01705 839938
Fax: 01705 870588
Email: maryrose@cix.compulink.co.uk
From replica artefacts to clothing and confectionery, the
Mary Rose Gift Shop has something for everyone interest-
ed in Tudor life and times. Mail order available.

MEMORIAL DAY MUSEUM
31 East Williams St, Waterloo, NY 13165, USA
Contact: James T Hughes
Tel: 315-539-3674
Fax: 315-529-7798
The museum is dedicated to commemorating the founding
of Memorial Day in Waterloo, and to the sacrifice of our
veterans in all our wars. Exhibits include period rooms
(1866) and military uniforms and equipment.

MEMORIAL PEGASUS
Avenue du Major Howard, 14860 Ranville, Normandy, France
Tel: 02 31781944
Fax: 02 31781942
This memorial museum is dedicated to the men of the 6th
British Airbourne Division who were the first liberators to
arrive in Normandy on the night of 5/6 June 1944.

MIDLAND AIR MUSEUM
Coventry Airport, Baginton, Warwickshire CV8 3AZ
Tel/Fax: 01230 301033
Email: midlandairmuseum@aol.com

MILITARY HERITAGE MUSEUM
West Street Auction Galleries, Lewes, E. Sussex
BN7 2NJ
Contact: Roy Butler
Tel/Fax: 01273 480208
Email: auctions@wallaceandwallace.co.uk
Collection of Military History, 1660–1914, including
Uniforms, headdresses, weapons and equipment. Admission
by prior appointment only.

MILITÄRHISTORISCHES MUSEUM DRESDEN
Olbrichtplatz 3, 01099 Dresden, Germany

MILITARY TRANSPORT MUSEUM
Stiftefelsen Militarfordonmuseum, Bergsgatan 12, S-640 32
Malmkoping, Sweden
Tel: 46 157 20452
Fax: 46 157 21240
Mainly military vehicles used by the Swedish forces since
1920 to the present, both WWII surplus and vehicles pro-
duced by Volvo, Scania and others.

MILITARY VEHICLE MUSEUM
Exhibition Park Pavilion, Newcastle
Tel: 0191 2817222

MONTROSE AIR STATION MUSEUM
104F Castle Street, Montrose, Angus, Scotland DDIO 8AX
Contact: G McIntosh
Tel/Fax: 01674 673107
Email: 106212.152@compuserve.com
Website:
http://ourworld.compuserve.com/homepages/airspeednews
Montrose Air Station Museum. Open Sundays, 12am–5pm.
Outside usual hours Tel: 01674 672035/675401/674210 or
673107 for info. RFC/RAF and wartime artefacts etc.

MUSÉE 39/45 DE LA POCHE DE ST NAZAIRE
44740 Batz-sur-Mer, Bretagne, France
Tel/Fax: 02 40 23 88 29
The museum has been created in an authentic command
post/bunker system of the WWII German Atlantic Wall. On
five levels, this bunker held out along with fortress
St Nazaire until 11 May 1945.

MUSÉE AMERICA/GOLD BEACH
2 Place Amiral Byrd, F14114 Ver-sur-Mer, Normandy, France
Tel/Fax: 02 31 22 58 58
Museum commemorating both the 1927 first airmail link
between France and the USA, and the Gold Beach British
bridgehead of the 1944 Allied Invasion of WWII.

*MUSÉE D'ART ET D'HISTOIRE
Chateau de Belfort, 90000 Belfort, France

*MUSÉE D'ART MILITAIRE
1 Rue Jeanne-d'Arc, 88440 Nomexyu, France

*MUSÉE DE L'ARMÉE
Hotel National des Invalides, 75007 Paris, France
The French national museum of military history; not to he
missed by any Paris visitor.

*MUSÉE DE L'ARMISTICE
Carrefour de l'Armistice, 60200 Compiègne, France
Displays connected with WWI Armistice railway carriage;
photo-library.

*MUSÉE DE LA BATAILLE DES ARDENNES
08270 Novion-Porcien, France
1870, WWI, but particularly important WWII vehicle,
uniform, and weapon collection.

*MUSÉE DE LA CAVALERIE
Ecole d'AABC, 49409 Saumur, France
Open by appointment, afternoons except Fridays; closed
August. All periods, but important WWII AFV collection,
housed at French Army Armoured Cavalry School.

*MUSÉE DE LA CAVERNE DU DRAGON
Chemin des Dames, 02160 Oulche la Vallee Foulon, France

*MUSÉE DES CHASSEURS A PIED
Chateau de Vincennes, 94300 Vincennes, France

*MUSÉE DE LA COOPERATION FRANCO-AMERICAINE
Blerancourt, 02300 Chauny, France
Open 15 Apri-15 October (except Tuesdays),
10am-12.30am and 2pm-5pm; 16 October-14 April,
2pm-5pm weekdays, also 10am-12.30 Saturdays and
Sundays.

MUSÉE D-DAY OMAHA
Rte de Grandcamp—14710, Vierville-sur-mer, Normandy,
France
Tel/Fax: 02 31217180
Website: www.vierville-sur-mer.htm
This special new museum is dedicated to the memory of
the WWII soldiers who landed and fought at Omaha Beach.
Vierville-sur-mer is where freedom exacted the highest
price. Equipment and displays feature American, English,
French and German material. Open April-May:
10am-12.20pm/2pm-6pm. June-September:
9.30am-7.30pm. October-November: 10am-12.30pm/2pm-6pm.

MUSÉE DU DEBARQUEMENT UTAH BEACH
50480 Sainte Marie du Mont, Normandy, France
Tel: 02 33715335
Fax: 02 33715800

*MUSÉE DE L'EMPERI
Chateau de l'Emperi, 13300 Salon de Provence,France
The former Brunon Collections, now owned by the Musée
de l'Armée—large, superbly presented, and of internatinnal
importance, particularly Napoleonic and Second Empire
exhibits.

MUSÉE DES EPAVES SOUS-MARINS DU DEBARQUEMENT
Route de Bayeux, Commes, 14520 Port-en-Bessin,
Normandy, France
Tel: 02 31 21 17 41
Fax: 02 31 21 85 11
25 years of underwater operations have brought up some
impressive remains and personal items from the sea bed,
found in the great warships sunk on or around 6 June 1944.

*MUSÉE DES EQUIPAGES & DU TRAIN
Quartier de Beaumont, Rue du Plat-d'Etain, 37034 Tours,
France

*MUSÉE DE GUERRE
Citadelle souterraine, 55100 Verdun, France

*MUSÉE DE L'INFANTERIE
Quartier Guillaut, Avenue Lepic, 34057 Montpellier, France
Closed weekends.

*MUSÉE DE LA FIGURINE HISTORIQUE
28 Place de l'Hotel de Ville, 60200 Compiègne, France
Closed Mondays. Large displays and dioramas. 100,000
civil and military figurines, individual or in settings.

*MUSÉE DE LA LEGION ETRANGERE
Quartier Vienot, 13400 Aubagne, France
Major official museum of the Foreign region, all periods,
housed at the Legion's depot. Closed Mon, and Sat
mornings, June-Sept; open Wed, Sat and Sun Oct-May.

MUSÉE DE LA LIBÉRATION
Fort du Roule, 50100 Cherbourg, Normandy, France
Tel: 02 33201412

*MUSÉE DE LA LIBERATION DE NORMANDIE
Route Nationale 13, Surrain, 14710 Trevieres, France

MUSÉE DE LA LIBERTÉ
50310 Quinéville, Normandy, France
Tel: 02 33214044
Fax: 02 33215220

MUSÉE LECLERC
31/33 Rue du Pont Neuf, 61000 Alencon, Normandy, France
Tel: 02 33262726

MUSÉE MEMORIAL DE LA BATAILLE DE NORMANDIE
Boulevard Fabian Ware, 1400 Bayeux, Normandie, France
Tel: 02 31929341
Fax: 02 31218511
Located in the first French town to be liberated, the museum covers the Allied invasion of 1944.

MUSÉE DU MUR ATLANTIQUE
Batterie Todt, 62179 Audinghen, Normandy, France
Tel: 03 21329733 or 03 21826201

MUSÉE DU MUR DE L'ATLANTIQUE
Le Grand Bunker, Avenue du 6 Juin, 14150 Ouistreham, Riva Bella, Normandy, France
Tel: 02 31972869
Fax: 02 31966605
This museum is situated inside the old German HQ which was in charge of the batteries covering the River Orne and the Canal—a 52ft high concrete tower restored to its original apperance.

*MUSÉE DE LA POCHE DE ROYAN
BP15, 17600 Le Gua, France

*MUSÉE DES PARACHUTISTES
Camp d'Astra, Route de Bordeaux, 64023 Pau, France
Tel/Fax: 59320597

MUSÉE DE LA SECONDE GUERRE MONDIALE AVRANCHES
Le Val St Pere, 50300 Avranches, Normandy, France
Tel: 02 33683583
Museum on the site of the great breakout of the Allied Forces during the 1944 invasion of WWII.

MUSÉE DE LA SECONDE GUERRE MONDIALE CALAIS
Parc St Pierre, 62100 Calais, France
Tel: 03 21342157
Email: ot@calais.fr

*MUSÉE DE LA SECONDE GUERRE MONDIALE MESSAGE 'VERLAINE'
4 bis Avenue de la Marne, 59200 Tourcoing, France
The XVth German Army headquarters, where the D-Day message was decoded. Located in Generaloberst von Salmuth's bunker.

*MUSÉE DES SPAHIS
Musée du Haubergier, 2 Place Notre Dame, 60300 Senlis, France

MUSÉE DES TROUPES AEROPORTÉES
Place du 6 Juin, 50480 Sainte Mere Èglise
Tel: 02 33414135
Fax: 02 33417887
Museum of the American 82nd and 101st Airborne Divisions.

*MUSÉE DES TROUPES DE MARINE
Quartier Colonel Lecocq, Route de Bagnols en Fôret, 83608 Fréjus, France
French Colonial and Marine Infantry collection. Open June–Sept 10am–12am, 2pm-5.30pm; Oct–May, pm only; closed Tuesday.

*MUSÉE DU FORT DE LA POMPELLE
Route de Chalons-sur-Marne, 51100 Reims, France

*MUSÉE DU PARA
27 Rue de la Bienvenue, 45000 Orleans, France

*MUSÉE DU SOUVENIR GENERAL ESTIENNE
Route Nationale 44, Berry-au-Bac, 02190 Guignicourt, France
Tel/Fax: 23799525
Displays connected with WWI founder of French tank arm. By appointment only.

*MUSÉE FRANCO-AUSTRALIEN
1, Route de Corbie, 80380 Villers-Bretonneux, France

*MUSÉE LUCIEN-ROY
Chemin de Maillot, 25720 Beure, France
French army, 20th century; closed Saturdays.

*MUSÉE MASSEY
Jardin Massey, 65000 Tarbes, France
Major international collection of Hussar uniforms.

*MUSÉE MILITAIRE DE BORDEAUX
Caserne Boudet, 192 Rue de Pessac, 33000 Bordeaux, France

*MUSÉE MILITAIRE DU HACKENBERG
Veckring, 57920 Kedange-sur-Canner, France
Important Maginot Line museum; open to large groups daily by arrangement; individuals, Sat and Sun afternoons.

*MUSÉE MILITAIRE DU PERIGORD
32 Rue des Farges, 24000 Perigueux, France

*MUSÉE PIERRE NOEL/ MUSÉE DE LA VIE DANS LES HAUTES-VOSGES
Place Georges Trimouille, 88107 St Die-des-Vosges, France
Important military collection, France/Germany 1800-1960. Open 10am-noon, 2pm-7pm Tues-Sat; 2pm-7pm Sun (May–Sept). 2pm-6pm Tues-Sun during Winter.

*MUSÉE REGIONAL D'ARGONNE
Chateau de Braux-Ste Cohiere, 51800 Sainte Menehould, France

*MUSÉE SERRET
3 Rue Clemenceau, 68550 Saint-Amarin, France
Open afternoons, May to September.

MUSEUM OF ARMY FLYING
Army Air Corps Centre, Middle Wallop, Hampshire SO20 8DY

MUSEUM OF ARMY TRANSPORT
Flemingate, Beverley, N. Humberside HU17 ONG
Tel: 01482 860445
History of Army transport from the Boer War to the present
day. Over 110 vehicles; extensive archives, workshops,
restoration, Sir Patrick Wall model collection, Blackburn
Beverley aircraft, book/gift shop. Open daily 10am–5pm;
free parking; cafeteria.

MUSEUM OF ARTILLERY
The Rotunda, Woolwich, London SE18 4BQ
Comprehensive museum of artillery weapons spanning
nearly 500 years. Free admission, open Monday to Friday
afternoons. Closed weekends and public holidays.

MUSEUM OF BADGES & BATTLEDRESS
The Green, Crakehall Nr. Bedale, N. Yorkshire DL10 1KJ
Tel: 01677 424444

MUSEUM OF LANCASHIRE
Stanley Street, Preston, Lancashire PR1 4YP
Contact: Stephen Bull
Tel: 01772 264075
Fax: 01772 264079
Email: museum@lancs.co.uk
The museum covers the local regiments, especially the
14/20th King's Hussars, Queen's Lancashire Regiment,
Duke of Lancaster's Own Yeomanry Volunteers. Open
Mon-Sat except Thurs, 10.30am–5pm.

MUSEUM OF LEATHERCRAFT
Central Museum, Guildhall Road, Northampton
Tel: 01604 238548

MUSEUM OF LINCOLNSHIRE LIFE
Old Barracks, Burton Road, Lincoln, Lincolnshire LN1 3LY
Tel/Fax: 01522 528448
Features displays relating to The Lincolnshire Yeomanry, a
WWI tank developed in Lincoln, and an entire gallery
devoted to the 300 year history of The Lincolnshire
Regiment. Open May-Sept everyday, 10.00am-5.30pm, Oct-
April Mon-Sat 10.00am-5.30pm, Sun 2.00pm-5.30pm.

MUSEUM OF THE MANCHESTERS
Ashton Town Hall, Market Place, Ashton-under-Lyne,
Manchester, Gt. OL6 6DL
A social & military history of The Manchester Regiment
from 1758 to 1958. Open Mon-Sat, 10am–4pm. Admission
free. Park on town centre car parks.

MUSEUM OF NORTH DEVON
The Square, Barnstaple, Devon EX32 8LN
Permanent display of the history of the Royal Devon
Yeomanry. Open Tues-Sat 10.00-16.30.

MUSEUM OF THE ORDER OF ST. JOHN
St. John's Gate, St. John's Lane, London EC1M 4DA
Contact: Pierre de Salis
Tel: 020 7253 6644   7 3 2 4 4 0 0 0
Fax: 020 7336 0587
Sixteenth century gatehouse containing armour, silver,
coins, medals and other objects of the Knights of St. John.
Also uniforms, equipment, memorabilia and records of St.
John Ambulance and wartime medical services. Mon-Fri
10.00am-5.00pm, Sat 10.00am-4.00pm. Tours of Gate-
house and Norman Crypt Tues, Fri & Sat I 1.00am-2.30pm.

MUSEUM OF THE SCOTTISH HORSE
The Cross, Dunkeld, Perthshire PH8 OAA, Scotland
This museum holds a unique collection of uniforms, arms,
trophies, maps, photographs, and regimental records of this
famous regiment, The Scottish Horse.

MUSEUM OF THE ROYAL ARMY CHAPLAINS
Bagshot Park, Surrey GU19 5PL
History of the ministry to the Army, including four VCs won
by chaplains. Open Mon–Fri 10.00-12.00 & 14.00 16.00,
by appointment.

*MEMORIAL DE VERDUN
Fleury-devant-Douaumont, 55100 Verdun, France
Important collection including uniforms, equipment,
artillery, dioramas, etc.

*MEMORIAL SUD-AFRICAIN DU BOIS DELVILLE
Longueval, 80360 Somme, France
Museum and memorial to South African troops in France,
First World War. Open, free of charge, April-October
10am-5.45pm; November-March 10am-3.45pm; closed
January, every Monday, and local holidays.

*NATIONAAL OORLOGS-EN VERZETSMUSEUM
Museumpark 1, 5825 AM Overloon, Netherlands

9TH/12TH ROYAL LANCERS MUSEUM
See Derbyshire Museum Art Gallery, The Strand, Derby,
Derbyshire DE1 IBS
Contact: Angela Kelsall
Tel: 01332 716656
Fax: 01332 716670
Email: akelsall@derbymuseum.freeserve.co.uk
Information panels, audio system, and displays relating the
history of the Regiment and its predecessors from 1715 to
the present. Enquiry service.

NATIONAL ARMY MUSEUM
Royal Hospital Road, Chelsea, London SW3 4HT
Contact: Julian Humphrys
Tel: 020 7730 0717
Fax: 020 7823 6573
Email: nam@enterprise.net
The story of the British soldier from Agincourt to the pres-
ent. Videos, models, and reconstructions bring the soldier's
story to life. Treasures on display include medals, paintings,
weapons, silver and uniforms. Regular special exhibitions
(see press for details). Normally open daily 10am-5.30pm.
Admission free.

NATIONAL MARITIME MUSEUM
Park Row, Greenwich, London SE10 9NF
Tel: 020 8858 4422
Fax: 020 8312 6632
Britain's national museum of naval and maritime history,
set in magnificent surroundings by the Thames at
Greenwich. Historic exhibits, models, art collection, docu-
mentary and pictorial archives. Open September-April,
Mon-Sat 10am-5pm, Sun 12am-5pm; May-October,
closes 6pm.

NATIONAL MUSEUM OF MILITARY HISTORY
10 Bamertal, PO Box 104, L-9209 Diekirch, Luxembourg
Contact: Roland Gaul
Tel: 808908
Fax: 804719
Email: mnhmdiek@pt.lu
Important collections from Battle of the Bulge 1944-45,
life-size dioramas, uniforms, vehicles, weapons, equipment.
Open from January 1-March 31: daily 14.00hrs-18.00hrs;
April 1-November 1: daily 10.00hrs-18.00hrs; November
2-December 31: daily 14.00hrs-18.00hrs; last ticket sold
17.15hrs.

NATIONAL MUSEUMS OF SCOTLAND
Chambers Street, Edinburgh, Lothian, Scotland EH1 1JF
Contact: Dr David H Caldwell
Tel: 0131 225 7534
Fax: 0131 247 4070
Email: dhc@nms.ac.uk
Website: http://www.nms.ac.uk
Collection of arms and armour, particularly Scottish
weaponry of the 17th-18th centuries.

NEDERLANDS KUSTVERDEDIGINGSMUSEUM
Postbus 9, 3150 AA, Fort an den Hoek van Holland,
Netherlands
Tel: 0174 382898
Fax: 0174 310128
Bunker system museum of the German WWII Atlantic Wall.

NEWARK AIR MUSEUM
The Airfield, Winthorpe, Newark, Nottinghamshire NG24 2NY
Contact: Howard Heeley
Tel/Fax: 01636 707170
Email: newarkair@lineout.net
Based on an original World War II bomber dispersal, nearly
half of our 40 aircraft are displayed under cover; artefacts
and engine display-, book and souvenir shop.

NEWARK MUSEUM
Appleton Gate, Newark, Nottinghamshire NG24 1JY
Small collection relating to the 8th Battalion, Sherwood
Foresters. Admission free. Open: Mon-Sat (closed Thurs),
10am-1pm and 2pm-5pm; Sun (April to September)
2pm-5pm.

NORFOLK & SUFFOLK AVIATION MUSEUM
The Street, Flixton, Bungay, Suffolk NR35 1NZ
Contact: H J Fairhead
Tel/Fax: 01986 896644 Sun/Tue
Email: nasamflixton@vergin.net

Over 20 historic aircraft. Unique indoor exhibitions. 446th
BG museum, RAF Bomber Command Museum and ROC
museum. Admission free. Open Sun & Bank Holidays,
Easter-October, 10am-5pm.

NORTHAMPTONSHIRE REGT & YEOMANRY MUSEUM
Abington Museum, Abington Park, Northampton,
Northamptonshire NN1 5LW
Contact: Judith Hodgkinson
Tel: 01604 631454
Fax: 01604 238720
Military exhibits form part of social history displays within
historic house set in park. Tuesday-Saturday and Bank
Holiday Mondays: 13.00hrs-17.00hrs. Admission free.

NORTH EAST AIRCRAFT MUSEUM
Washington Road, Sunderland, Tyne & Wear
Tel: 0191 5190662

OXFORDSHIRE REGIMENTAL MUSEUM
TA Centre, Slade Park, Headington, Oxfordshire OX3 7JL
Regimental museum of the Oxfordshire and
Buckinghamshire Light Infantry.

PWRR & QUEEN'S REGIMENT MUSEUM
Dover Castle, Dover, Kent CT16 1HU
Contact: Alan Lee
Tel/Fax: 01304 240121
Email: pwrrqueensmuseum@tinyworld.co.uk
Forbear regimental history with life-like displays, scenes
and sounds. Has longest sample of World War I trench.
Interactive video with complete World War II menu.

*PANZERMUSEUM MÜNSTER
Hans Kruger Strasse 33, 29633 Munster, Germany

PASSMORE EDWARDS MUSEUM
Romford Road, Stratford, London E15 4LZ

PEMBROKE YEOMANRY TRUST
Scolton Manor Museum, Spittal, Haverfordwest,
Pembrokeshire SA62 5QL, Wales
Contact: Mark Thomas
Tel: 01437 731328
Military displays: Pembroke Yeomanry, Pembrokeshire
Militia, WWII gallery. Study facilities: Pembroke Yeomanry
archive available for research at study centre by appoint-
ment.

POLISH INSTITUTE & SIKORSKI MUSEUM
20 Princes Gate, London SW7 1PT
Tel: 020 7589 924
Access by arrangement.

PRESTON HALL MUSEUM
Yarm Road, Stockton, Cleveland
Tel: 01642 781184
Fax: 01642 788907

Q A R A N C MUSEUM

Keogh Barracks, Ash Vale, Aldershot, Hampshire GU12 5RQ
Tel: 01252 340212
Fax: 01252 340224
Email: museum@keogh72.freeserve.co.uk
The QARANC Museum relates the history of military nursing, Crimea to date, providing fascinating displays including uniforms, medals, memorabilia and photographs. Open Mon–Fri 0900-1530 hours.

QUEBEC HOUSE (NATIONAL TRUST)

Quebec Square, Westerham, Kent TN16 1TD
National Trust's boyhood home of General James Wolfe. Open April to October, 2pm-6pm on Tuesday and Sunday. Exhibition, memorabilia, publications; Quebec campaign miniatures sold.

QUEEN ALEXANDRA'S ROYAL ARMY NURSING CORPS MUSEUM

RHQ, Royal Pavillion, Farnborough Road, Aldershot, Hants GU11 1PZ
The history of the Army Nursing Service from 1854 to the present day.

QUEENS LANCASHIRE REGIMENT MUSEUM

Fulwood Barracks, Preston, Lancashire PR2 8AA
Contact: Lt Col Mike Glover MA AMA
Tel: 01772 260362
Fax: 01772 260 583
Housed in one of Preston's finest listed buildings are the Regimental Museum, Archive and Library. The unique regimental heritage collection incoporates historic material relating to the East Lancashire, South Lancashire (PWV), Loyal (North Lancashire) and Lancashire (PWV) Regiments and associated Rifle Volunteers, Militia and Territorials.

QUEENS ROYAL LANCERS REGIMENTAL MUSEUM

Belvoir Castle, Grantham
Tel: 0115 9573295

QUEEN'S OWN HIGHLANDERS REGIMENTAL MUSEUM

Fort George, Ardersier, Inverness, Scotland. IV2 7TD
Tel: 01463 224 380
Magnificent display of uniforms, medals, pictures etc of Seaforth, Camerons, Queen's Own Highlanders, Lovat Scouts. Comprehensive library and archives. Museum shop. Housed in Lieutenant Governor's house at 18th century Fort George. Open April–September 10am–6pm daily. October–March 10am–4pm Monday–Friday.

QUEEN'S OWN HUSSARS MUSEUM

Lord Leycester Hospital, High Street, Warwick, Warwickshire CV34 4BH
The regimental museum of The Queen's Own Hussars, the senior light cavalry regiment of the British Army. Open Tues-Sun incl. 10.00am–5.00pm. Museum shop and restaurant.

QUEEN'S OWN ROYAL WEST KENT REGIMENT MUSEUM

Maidstone Museum & Art Gallery St Faith's Street, Maidstone, Kent ME14 1LH
Contact: The Curator
Tel: 01622 754497
Fax: 01622 602193
Email: dred@mbcmusi.demon.uk
Uniforms, medals, weapons and general militaria of the regiment from 1756. Admission free. Museum shop and coffee shop. Open 10am-5.15pm. Sundays 11am–4pm.

QUEEN'S ROYAL IRISH HUSSARS MUSEUM

The Redoubt Fortress, Royal Parade, Eastbourne, E. Sussex BN22 7AQ
Contact: Richard Callaghan
Tel: 01323 410300
Fax: 01323 732240
Email: redoubt@breathemail.net
History of the 4th and 8th Hussars, including Charge of the Light Brigade and Gulf War exhibits and a Centurion tank from the Korean War.

QUEEN'S ROYAL LANCERS MUSEUM

c/o Hume HQ, Prince William of Glos Bks, Grantham, Lincolnshire NG31 7TJ
Contact: Capt I M Holtby
Tel: 0115 9573295
Fax: 0115 9573195
Website: www.os-net.de/~ironside3/
Traces the history of the 5th, 16th, 17th, 21st, 16th/5th and 17th/21st Lancers and The Queen's Royal Lancers. Displays include uniforms, weapons, medals, and relics from 1759 to present day. Museum open April–September 11am-5pm except Fri & Mon.

QUEEN'S ROYAL SURREY REGIMENT MUSEUM

Clandon Park, Guildford, Surrey GU4 7RQ
Contact: The Curator
Tel: 01483 223419
Fax: 01483 224636
Email: queenssurreys@care4free.net
This museum tells the story of the infantry regiments of Surrey. It is housed in the magnificent setting of the National Trust mansion at Clandon Park. Research facilities by appointment. Open April-October. Admission Free.

RAF REGIMENT MUSEUM

RAF Regiment Depot, RAF Honington, Bury St Edmunds, Suffolk IP31 1EE
Museum not open to the general public. Visitors by appointment only. Apply to: The RAF Regiment Secretary/Museum Manager, RAF Honington, Ext. 7824/7755.

REME MUSEUM OF TECHNOLOGY
Isaac Newton Road, Arborfield, Berkshire RG2 9NJ
Contact: Lt Col (Retd) I W Cleasby, MBE
Tel: 0118 976 3227
Fax: 0118 976 3575
Email: reme-museum@gtnet.gov.uk
Website: www.rememuseum.org.uk
The REME Museum of Technology collection is composed of a vehicle fleet; a small Arms collection; an electronic and aeronautic collection and the Corps of REME history, memorabilia, medals and uniform. There are also the Corps Archives, Documentary, Technical and Pictorial, a place of deposit for the PRO.

THE ROYAL FUSILIERS MUSEUM
Sovereigns House, The Mall, Armagh, Co Armagh, Northern Ireland. BT61 9DL
Contact: Amanda Moreno
Tel/Fax: 02837522911
Email: rylirfusiliermus@cs.com
Website: www.rirfus-museum.freeserve.co.uk
This unique collection is housed in a listed building. This museum relates the history and traditions of the Regiment from 1793 to 1968. This regiment took the first Napoleonic Eagle at the Battle of Barrosa in 1811. Open daily all year. Research facilities. Shop. Wheelchair access.

ROYAL GUNPOWDER MILLS
Beaulieu Drive, Waltham Abbey, Essex EN9 1JY
Tel: 01992 767 022
Website: www.royalpowdermills.com
Set in 175 acres of natural parkland and boasting 21 buildings of historical importance, the site mixes fascinating history, the evolution of Gunpowder technology and beautiful surroundings to produce a magical trip for both old and young.

ROYAL MARINES MUSEUM
Southsea, Hants PO4 9PX
Contact: Jorj Jarvie
Tel: 023 9281 9385
Fax: 023 9283 8420
Email: info@royalmarinesmuseum.co.uk
Website: www.royalmarinesmuseum.co.uk
The 330-year story of Britain's Sea Soldiers is told through dramatic displays, exciting films and videos, state-of-the-art interactives and even a live snake and scorpion! But the museum is not just about war stories. Sumptuous rooms filled with priceless silver, sweeping stairways with splendid portraits and halls adorned with a world famous medal collection ensure there's something of interest to everyone.

REGIMENTS OF GLOUCESTERSHIRE MUSEUM
Custom House, Gloucester Docks, Gloucester, Glos GL1 2HE
Tel/Fax: 01452 522682
Fax: 01452 311116
Award-winning museum tells story of Glorious Glosters and Gloucestershire Yeomanry. Open all year, closed Mondays. Admission charge. Shop. Send SAE for mail order list.

ROCK ISLAND ARSENAL MUSEUM
SOSRI-CFS, 1 Rock Island Arsenal, Rock Island, IL 61299-5000, USA
Contact: Kris Leinicke or William Johnson
Tel: 309 782 5021
Fax: 309 782 3598
Email: leinckek@ria.army.mil
Website: www.ria.army.mil
Second oldest US Army Museum opened on 4 July 1905. Primary mission is history of Rock Island Arsenal, currently the largest US government owned and operated arsenal. The museum is nationally recognized for its impressive small arms collection. Over a thousand US foreign, civilian, and military weapons are exhibited.

ROMAN ARMY MUSEUM
Carvoran, Greenhead, Carlisle, Cumbria
Tel/Fax: 0169 72485

ROYAL AIR FORCE MUSEUM
Grahame Park Way, Hendon, London NW9 5LL
Tel: 020 8205 2266
Fax: 020 8200 1751
Website: www.rafmseum.org.uk
Britain's National Museum of Aviation, displays 70 full size aircraft. Open daily. Extensive library research facilities (weekdays only). Large free car park. Licensed restaurant. Souvenir shop with extensive range of specialist books and model kits.

ROYAL ARMOURIES—FORT NELSON
Down End Road, Fareham, Hampshire PO17 6AN
Contact: David Goodwin
Tel: 01329 33734
Fax: 01329 822692
Email: dgoodwin@armouries.org.uk
Website: armouries.org.uk
The Royal Armouries is home to one of the best collections of artillery in Europe, housed in a superbly restored Victorian Fort. Imaginative scenes, daily gun firings and guided tours tell the story of artillery from its early beginnings to present day. Varied events programme.

ROYAL ARMOURIES—LEEDS
Armouries Drive, Leeds LS10 1CT
Contact: Nicholas Boole
Tel: 0115 220 1948
Fax: 0113 220 1955
Website: http://www.armouries.org.uk
The Royal Armouries is the national museum of arms and armour and museum of the Tower of London. It has three sites each dealing with a different aspect of its subject.Royal Armouries HM Tower of London (Tower history), is scheduled to re-open fully to the public in summer 1998, Tel: 020 7480 6358, Royal Armouries at Fort Nelson near Portsmouth (artillery collection), Tel: 01329 233734, and Royal Armouries Museum in Leeds (arms and armour) 0990 106666.

Bridgette d. frond library.

ROYAL ARMOURIES—LONDON
Tower of London, London EC3N 4AB
Tel: 020 7480 6358
Open March–October, Monday–Saturday 9.30am–5.45pm, Sunday 2–5.30pm. November–February closes at 4.30pm daily. The personal weapons and armour of British rulers and notable figures, and a superb collection from the Civil War period 1642–1651.

ROYAL ARMY CHAPLAINS' DEPARTMENT MUSEUM
Netheravon House, Salisbury Road, Netheravon, Wiltshire SP4 9SY
Contact: M A Easey
The museum's exhibits include photographs, POW items, church silver and memorabilia, uniforms and medals.

ROYAL ARMY DENTAL CORPS MUSEUM
HQ & Central Group RADC, Evelyn Woods, Aldershot, Hants GU11 2LS
Displaying a collection including uniforms, medals and early dental instruments. Open Mon–Fri 10.00am–12.00am and 14.00pm–16.00pm.

ROYAL ARMY EDUCATION CORPS MUSEUM
Wilton Park, Beaconsfield, Buckinghamshire HP9 2RP
Tel: 01494 683232
Fax: 01494 683291
The museum of education in the British Army. Exhibits including uniforms, weapons & photographs. Extensive archives.

ROYAL ARMY MEDICAL CORPS MUSEUM
Keogh Barracks, Ash Vale, Nr Aldershot, Hants GU12 5RQ
History of the Army Medical Service since Tudor times. Exhibits include personal belongings of Napoleon and Wellington, items from the Crimean War up and over 2,000 medals.
Open Mon–Fri 8.30am–4.00pm.

ROYAL ARMY VETERINARY CORPS MUSEUM
RAVC Support Group, Gallwey Road, Aldershot, Hampshire GU11 2DQ
Tel: 01252 348534
Fax: 01252 348535
Email: ravrs@ukonline.co.uk

ROYAL ARSENAL WOOLWICH
Tel: 020 8855 7755
Website: www.firepower.org.uk
Discover the science of artillery and tales of human endeavour from Crécy to Bosnia, including the dramatic 'field of fire' and many other interactive displays.

ROYAL CORPS OF MILITARY POLICE MUSEUM
Rouisillon Barracks, Broyle Road, Chichester
Tel: 01243 534225

ROYAL DEVON YEOMANRY MUSEUM
40 Oakleigh Road, Barnstaple, Devon EX32 8JT
Contact: Al Hoddinott

ROYAL ENGINEERS MUSEUM
Prince Arthur Road, Gillingham, Kent ME4 4UG
Contact: J E Nowers
Tel: 01634 406397
Fax: 01634 822371
Email: remuseum.shgre@gtnet.gov.uk
Website: http://www.yell.co.uk/sites/remuseum/
See 24 Victoria Crosses, Wellington's Waterloo battlemap, mementoes of Gordon of Khartoum and Field Marshal Lord Kitchener, Engineer tanks, Harrier aircraft and much more.

ROYAL FUSILIERS MUSEUM
HM Tower of London, Tower Hill, London EC3N 4AB
Tel/Fax: 020 7488 5612
Email: rhq@thefusiliers.org.uk

ROYAL GLOS, BERKS & WILTS REGT MUSEUM
The Wardrobe, 58 The Close, The Castle, Enniskillen, Salisbury, Wiltshire SP1 2EX
Contact: Major H Peters
Tel: 01722 414536
Fax: 01722 421626
The Royal Gloucestershire, Berkshire and Wiltshire Regiment (Salisbury) Museum offers excellent collections, a fine medieval house, riverside garden and renowned tea-room, all in Salisbury Cathedral Close. Open daily April–October. 10am–4.30pm.

ROYAL GREEN JACKETS MUSEUM
Peninsula Barracks, Romsey Road, Winchester, Hampshire SO23 8TS
Tel: 01962 828541
Regimental museum for the Oxfordshire and Buckinghamshire Light Infantry, The King's Royal Rifle Corps and The Rifle Brigade. The Waterloo Diorama has twenty thousand model figures and a sound and light commentary. For further details contact the museum.

ROYAL HAMPSHIRE REGT MUSEUM
Serle's House, Southgate St, Winchester, Hampshire SO23 9E
Tel: 01962 863658
Fax: 01962 888302
Museum of the Royal Hampshire Regiment 1702–1992.

ROYAL HIGHLAND FUSILIERS MUSEUM
518 Sauchiehall Street, Glasgow, Strathclyde, Scotland G2 3LW
Tel/Fax: 0141 3322 0961
Email: assregsec@rhf.org.uk

ROYAL HOSPITAL MUSEUM
The Royal Hospital, Royal Hospital Road, Chelsea, London SW3 4SR
Contact: Major R A G Courage
Tel/Fax: 020 7730 0161
Email: roylhospch@aol.com
Open: 10am–12am, 2pm–4pm Mon–Sat daily; April–Sept only, Sun 2pm–4pm. Pictures, medals, uniforms connected with the Royal Hospital. Admission free; no parking.

ROYAL HUSSARS MUSEUM
Peninsula Barracks, Romsey Road, Winchester
Tel: 01962 828541

ROYAL INNISKILLING FUSILIERS MUSEUM
The Castle, Enniskillen, Co Fermanagh, N. Ireland BT74 7BBI
Contact: Hugh Forrester
Tel: 02866 32142
Fax: 02866 320359
Regimental museum of the Inniskillings, telling the story of
the famous regiment from 1689 to 1968. Open all year,
half day Mondays.

ROYAL IRISH FUSILIERS MUSEUM
Sovereign's House, The Mall, Armagh, Co Armagh, N. Ireland
BT61 9DL
Contact: Amanda Moreno
Tel/Fax: 01861 522911
Housed in a fine Georgian residence this refurbished
museum relates the history of this Regiment from 1793 to
1968. Open daily, Monday to Friday.

ROYAL IRISH REGIMENT MUSEUM
c/o RHQ Royal Irish Regiment, Ballymena, Co Antrim BFPO
808, N. Ireland
Tel: 01200 01355
Fax: 01266 66778
The museum, through commentary, audio-visuals and exhibits
traces the history of our antecedent regiments, commencing
with the Inniskillings in 1689 to the present regiment.

THE ROYAL REGIMENT OF WALES MUSEUM CARDIFF OF THE WELCH REGIMENT
The Black and Barbican Towers, The Castle, Cardiff, South
Glamorgan, Wales CF10 2RB
Contact: John Dart
Tel: 029 20 229367
Website: www.rrw.org.uk
The museum commemorates the service of the 41st and
69th Regiments of foot, later the 1st and 2nd Battalions of
the Welch Regiment, and also the service of the associated
Militia, Volunteer Territorial forces, the Territorial Army and
the Royal Regiment of Wales—1969 to the present day.

ROYAL LEICESTERSHIRE REGT MUSEUM
The Newarke, Oxford Street, Leicester, Leicestershire
Tel: 0116 255 4100
Fax: 0116 247 0403

ROYAL LINCOLNSHIRE REGIMENTAL MUSEUM
Museum of Lincolnshire Life, Burton Road, Lincoln,
Lincolnshire LN1 3LY
Tel: 01522 528448
Fax: 01522 521264
Royal Lincolnshire Regiment gallery and collection; Lincolnshire
Yeomanry display; WWI tank. Open May–Sept daily 10am–
5.30pm; Oct–April Mon–Sat 10am–5.30pm, Sun 2pm–5.30pm.

ROYAL LOGISTIC CORPS MUSEUM
Princess Royal Barracks, Deepcut, Nr Camberley, Surrey
GU16 6RW
Contact: Frank O'Connell
Tel: 01252 340871
Fax: 01252 340875
Email: frank.oconnell@btinternet.com
Open Mon–Fri 10.00–16.00hrs; Sat 10.00–15.00hrs.
Admission free. Guided tours, lectures, access to archives
available by prior arrangement with Curator.

ROYAL MARINES MUSEUM
Southsea, Portsmouth, Hampshire PO4 9PX
Contact: Jorj Jarvie
Tel: 01705 819385
Fax: 01705 838420
The history of the Royal Marines from 1664 to the present.
Open 7 days a week. Library and archives by arrangement.

ROYAL MILITARY POLICE MUSEUM
Roussillon Barracks, Chichester, W. Sussex PO19 4BL

ROYAL NAVAL MUSEUM
HM Naval Base, Portsmouth, Hampshire PO1 3NU
Contact: Rob Griffiths
Tel: 01705 861533
Fax: 01705 295252
Email: enquiries@flagship.org.uk
Website: www.flagship.org.uk
Magnificent galleries telling the story of the navy which
ruled the waves.

ROYAL NAVY SUBMARINE MUSEUM
Haslar jetty Road, Gosport, Hampshire PO12 2AS
Tel: 01705 529217
Email: rsnubbs@submarine-museum.demon.co.uk
Enjoy a guided tour of HMS Alliance, a postwar submarine
and discover the stories of lives dedicated to service under
the seas, through fascinating exhibits and crew members
personal effect.

ROYAL NETHERLANDS ARMY AND ARMS MUSEUM
Armamentarium, Korte Geer 1, 2611 CA Delft, Netherlands
Contact: Jan A Buyse
Tel: 152 150500
Fax: 152 150544
Depicts military life from the Roman period onwards until
recent army actions, worldwide (NATO, LJN). Weapons,
armour, uniforms, flags, models, transport, communications,
paintings, photographs, books. Open all week, except
Mondays. Admission charge. Tours on request.

ROYAL NORFOLK REGIMENT MUSEUM
Shirehall, Market Avenue, Norwich, Norfolk NR1 3JQ
Contact: Miss K Thaxton
Tel: 01603 493649
Fax: 01603 493623
Social and military history of the county regiment from
1685 to 1959. Open Mon–Sat 10am–5pm. Sun 2pm–5pm.

MUSEUM OF THE ROYAL SCOTS
The Castle, Edinburgh, Lothian, Scotland EH1 2YT
Interesting and colourful story of The Royal Scots covering
over 350 years service of the oldest Regiment of Infantry
in the British Army. Excellent shop.

ROYAL SIGNALS MUSEUM
Blandford Camp, Blandford Forum, Dorset DT11 8RH
Tel: 01258 482267
Fax: 01258 482084
Email: royalsignalsmuseum@army.mod.uk
Website: www.royalsignals.army.org.uk/museum/
Displays items relating to the history of army signalling
since the Crimean War and the history of Royal Signals.
Open Mon–Fri 10.00am–5.00pm, Sat/Sun May–Sept only,
10.00am–4.00pm.

ROYAL SUSSEX REGIMENT MUSEUM (see Queens Own
Royal Irish)
The Redoubt Fortress, Royal Parade, Eastbourne, E. Sussex
BN22 7AQ
Contact: Richard Callaghan
Tel: 01323 410300
Fax: 01323 732240
Email: redoubt@breathemail.net
History of the Royal Sussex Regiment from its formation in
1701. Exhibits include Afrika Korps General Von Arnim's
staff car, and rare Napoleonic Volunteer uniforms.

ROYAL ULSTER RIFLES MUSEUM
RHQ The Royal Irish Regt, 5 Waring Street, Belfast,
Co Antrim, N. Ireland BT1 2LW
Tel/Fax: 01232 232086
Email: rurmuseum@yahoo.co.uk

ROYALWARWICKSHIRE REGT MUSEUM
St John's House, Warwick, Warwickshire
Tel: 01926 491653
Fax: 01869 257633

ROYAL WELCH FUSILIERS MUSEUM
Queen's Tower, Caernarfon Castle, Caernarfon, Gwynedd,
Wales LL55 2AY
Contact: Peter Crocker
Tel: 01286 673362
Fax: 01286 677042
Email: wfusiliers@uk.com
History of Wales's oldest line regiment since 1689.
Marvellous collection of uniforms, weapons, medals, pic-
tures, etc. The Regiment of Sassoon, Graves, David Jones,
Frank Richard, 'Hedd Wyn", Thomas Atkins, and the 'Black
Flash'. New and enlarged museum open from Easter 1999.

RUTLAND COUNTY MUSEM
Catmose Street, Oakham, Rutland LE15 6HW
Contact: T Clough
Tel: 01572 758440
In a splendid late 18th century military riding school near Oakham
town centre, Rutland County Museum has extensive rural life collections. These include farming equipment, rural tradesmen's tools
and domestic displays, but there is also special emphasis on the
history of the Volunteer Soldiers in Leicestershire and Rutland.

SCOTTISH UNITED SERVICE MUSEUM
The Castle, Edinburgh, Lothian, Scotland EH1 2NG
Contact: Stephen Wood
Tel: 0131 225 7534
Fax: 0131 225 3848
Email: scw@nms.ac.uk
All museum galleries closed to visitors for major redevelop-
ment until Easter 2000. Library and archive still available
for use by appointment (tel. ext. 204).

SHERWOOD RANGERS YEOMANRY MUSEUM
TA Centre, Carlton, Nottingham, Nottinghamshire NG4 3DX
Contact: The Adjutant
Tel: 0115 9618722
The museum contains documents and artefacts tracing the
military and social history of the Regiment since its raising
in 1794.

SHRAPNEL'S BATTERY
9 Firgrove Hill, Farnham, Surrey GU9 8LH
Contact: Brian Miller
Tel: 01252 721332
1770s British Royal Artillery. Fully uniformed demonstrations of flintlock pistol, musket, mortar and field guns,
along with explanations of technical details and the
lifestyle of the men who served with the guns. Also tactics
used by infantry, cavalry and artillery explained–ammunition used–its range and effects. Demonstrations of casting,
linstock, quill making and flint knapping.

SHROPSHIRE REGIMENTAL MUSEUM
The Castle, Shrewsbury SY1 2AT
Contact: P Duckers
Tel: 01743 262292
Fax: 01743 270023
Email: shropsrm@zoom.co.uk
Website: www.shropshireregimental.co.uk
The museum houses the collection of the military units of
Shropshire–the 53rd & 85th Rgts the KSCI, the Shropshire
Yeomanry, the Shropshire RHA and the county Militia,
Volunteers and Territorials.

SHUTTLEWORTH COLLECTION
Old Warden Aerodrome, Biggleswade, Bedfordshire
SG18 9EP
Tel: 01767 627288
Fax: 01767 626229
Large collection of historic aeroplanes and vehicles on stat-
ic display–open daily; flying displays each month. Adults
£6.00, children £3.00; group and school party rates.

SILENT WINGS MUSEUM
Route 3, Box 393, Lubbock, TX 79403, USA
Tel: 806 775 2047
Museum dedicated to telling the story of the military glider
pilots of World War II. Exhibits include restored combat
gliders. Collection includes uniforms, archives and
weapons.

SOMERSET MILITARY MUSEUM
County Museum, The Castle, Taunton, Somerset TA1 4AA
Contact: Brig A I H Fyfe
Tel: 01823 333434
Fax: 01823 351639
Correspondence address: c/o Light Infantry Office, 14
Mount Street, Taunton TA1 3QE.

SOUTH WALES BORDERERS & MONMOUTHSHIRE MUSEUM OF THE ROYAL REGIMENT OF WALES
The Barracks, Brecon, Powys, Wales LD3 7EB
Contact: Martin Everett
Tel: 01874 613 310
Fax: 01874 613 275
Email: rrw@ukonline.co.uk
Website: http://www.ukonline.co.uk/rrw/index.htm
The museum contains interesting artefacts and archives
relating to the history of the South Wales Borderers (24th
Foot) from 1689 to the present day as the Royal Regiment
of Wales. The collection contains 16 Victoria Crosses and
many items relating to the battles of Saratoga,
Chillianwallah, Isandhlwana and Rorke's Drift and both
world wars.

ST PETER'S BUNKER MUSEUM
St Peter's Village, Jersey, Channel Islands JE3 7AF
Contact: Anita Mayne
Tel: 01481 2481048
Fax: 01481 2481630
The largest collection of genuine German militaria, occupa-
tion relics and photographs, housed in an actual German
bunker. Open daily, March to October.

STAFF COLLEGE MUSEUM
Camberley, Surrey GU15 4NP
Contact: Cot PS Newton
Tel/Fax: 01276 412602
Deals with the history and dress of the staff of the British
Army since the formation of the Staff College in 1799. By
appointment only.

STAFFORDSHIRE REGIMENT MUSEUM
Whittington Barracks, Lichfield, Staffordshire WS14 9PY
Contact: Major E Green
Tel: 0121 311 3229
Fax: 0121 311 3205
Email: museum@rhqstaffords.fsnet.co.uk
Open weekdays 9am–4pm, admission free. Military muse-
um telling the story of the Staffords and their predecessor
regiments since 1705. Outside exhibits include armoured
vehicles, a WWI trench and WWII Anderson Shelters.
Displays of the Regiment's history, uniforms, medals,
badges, weapons, vehicles, memorabilia. Car park; shop;
picnic area; school parties welcome.

STIRLING REGIMENTAL MUSEUM
Stirling Castle, Stirling, Grampian, Scotland FK8 IEJ

STOKE MUSEUM & ART GALLERY
Bethesda Street, Hanley, Stoke-on-Trent, Staffordshire
ST1 3DW
Tel/Fax: 01782 202173

SUFFOLK REGIMENT MUSEUM
The Keep, Gibraltar Barracks, Bury St Edmunds
Tel: 01284 752394

SUSSEX COMBINED SERVICES MUSEUM
The Redoubt Fortress, Royal Parade, Eastbourne, E. Sussex
BN22 7AQ
Contact: Richard Callaghan
Tel: 01323 416300
Fax: 01323 72240
Email: redoubt@breathemail.net
A restored Napoleonic fortress, the museum illustrates the
history of three services in Sussex. Over 5,000 exhibits
including uniforms, medals and weapons. Re-enactment
weekend in July.

SUSSEX YEOMANRY MUSEUM
198 Dyke Road, Brighton, E. Sussex BN1 5AS
Tel/Fax: 01273 556041

SUTTON HOO
Tranmer House, Sutton Hoo, Woodbridge, Suffolk IP2 3DJ
Tel: 01394 689700
Fax: 01394 389702
Email: asoksx@smtp.ntrust.org.uk
Museum based around the extraordinary Anglo-Saxon ship
burial warrior finds

TANK MUSEUM
Bovington Camp, Wareham, Dorset BH20 6JG
Tel: 01929 405096
Fax: 01929 405360
The world's most comprehensive collection of AFVS. Free
'Firepower & Mobility' displays Thursdays 12 noon, July,
August, September. Open daily 10am–5pm.

TANGMERE MILITARY AVIATION MUSEUM
Tangmere Airfield, Nr Chichester
Tel: 01243 775223

TENBY MUSEUM
Castle Hill, Tenby, Pembrokeshire SA70 7BP, Wales
Tel/Fax: 01834 842809
Email: tenbymusem@aol.com

TOWNELEY HALL ART GALLERY
Towneley Hall, Burnley, Lancashire BB11 3RQ
Contact: Miss J S Bourne
Tel: 01282 424213
Fax: 01282 36138
Email: towneleyhall@burnley.gov.uk
Exhibits relating to the East Lancashire Regiment.

13TH/18TH ROYAL HUSSARS MUSEUM
Cannon Hall, Cawthorne, Barnsley, S. Yorkshire
Tel: 01226 790270
Fax: 01226 792117
Set within the beautiful country park and gardens, with shop, tea rooms etc. Open Tues–Sun inclusive; closed Mondays, but open on Bank Holidays.

TEXAS MILITARY FORCES MUSEUM
2200 W. 35th Street, Camp Mabry Bldg. #6 Austin TX 78703, USA
Contact: John C.L. Scribner
Tel: 512 782 5659
Fax: 512 782 6750
Email: museum@pgd.state.tx.us
Website: www.kwanah.com/txmilus
Depicts the history of the military forces of Texas from the Texas Revolution (1835) to the present. Special exhibits include the 36th Division Gallery, Texas Air National Guard, Lost Battalion-Construction of the 'Death Railway' in WWII, WWII home front, history of the development of military aviation, and numerous armored vehicles, aircraft and artillery pieces. (WWII to the present, American and German.)

THE TIRPITZ BATTERY
Tirpitz-Stillingen, Tane Hedevej, DK-6857 Blavand, Denmark
Part of the German WWII Atlantic Wall defences.

US ARMY TRANSPORTATION MUSEUM
300 Washington Blvd, Besson Hall, Fort Eustis, VA 23604-5260, USA
Contact: David Hanselman
Tel: 757 878 1115
Email: bowerb@eustis.army.mil
Website: www.eustis.army.mil/DPTMSEC/museum.html
Where you will find a truck that walks and a ship that flies? The history of Army transportation from colonial days to present, including dioramas, uniforms, equipment, and videos inside and almost five acres of full-size aircraft, amphibians, trucks and rail rolling stock.

WALLACE COLLECTION
Hertford House, Manchester Square, London W1M 6BN
Tel: 020 7935 0687
Fax: 020 7224 2155
Email: admin@the-wallace-collection.org.uk
This museum contains a magnificent collection of Medieval and Renaissance arms and armour, and also a superb array of Oriental weaponry, predominantly Indian and Persian. Admission free. Location: North from Oxford Street, behind Selfridges. Opening Hours: 10am–5pm, Mon–Sat; 2pm–5pm, Sun. Nearest tube stations: Bond Street or Baker Street.

WARSHIP PRESERVATION TRUST
HMS Plymouth, Dock Road, Birkenhead, Merseyside PL41 1DJ
Tel: 0151 650 1573
Fax: 0151 650 1473
Email: manager@warships.freeserve.co.uk
Historic warships at Birkenhead–Falklands War veterans, the former Royal Navy frigate 'Plymouth' and submarine 'Onyx' are open to the public daily from 10am. New - German U Boat 534 now open.

WARWICKSHIRE YEOMANRY MUSEUM
The Court House, Jury Street, Warwick, Warwickshire CV34 4EW
Tel: 01926 492212
Fax: 01926 494837
Open Good Friday to end September, Fridays to Sundays and Bank Holidays, 10am–4pm. Uniforms, medals and militaria of the regiment since 1794. Entrance fee.

WEST HIGHLAND MUSEUM
Cameron Square, Fort William, Invernessshire, Scotland PH33 6AL
Contact: Fiona C Marwick
Tel: 01397 702169
Fax: 01397 701927
Small collection of 18th and 19th century weapons used in the Highlands, some uniforms, medals etc.

WELLINGTON MUSEUM
Apsley House, 149 Piccadilly, Hyde Park Corner, London W1V 9FA.
Tel: 020 7499 5676.
Open Tuesday-Sunday, 11am–5pm, closed Monday Also known as Number 1, London, the Apsley House exhibits include paintings, decorations and relics of the Duke of Wellington, victor of Waterloo.

PAINTINGS, PRINTS & POSTCARDS

ALIX BAKER, FRSA
The Orchards, Forton, Andover, Hampshire SP11 6NN
Contact: Alix Baker
Tel/Fax: 01264 720715
Email: alix.baker@talk21.com
Internationally collected artist working full time for British regiments and museums. Paintings, prints, postcards, greeting cards. Illustrated catalogue £1 + SAE or 5 IRC.

ANGLO LONGBOWS
No 101 Wooth Farm, Pymore, Bridport, Dorset DT6 5LE
Contact: M and J Foote
Tel: 01308 458137
Website: www.anglolongbows.co.uk
Native American, Viking and Celtic artwork—originals and prints.

BATTLE SCENE PICTURES
Sherwood House, 14 Norwood Drive, Brierley, Barnsley, S. Yorkshire S72 9EG
Contact: Andy Taylor
Tel/Fax: 01226 717195
Email: battlescene@tinyworld
Specialists in military pictures and prints, including Napoleonic, Victorian conflicts, Zulu wars, WWI and II, Falklands, Gulf War. Send £1 & large SAE for listings and brochure.

CRANSTON FINE ARTS
Torwood House, Torwoodhill Road, Helensburgh, Dunbartonshire, Scotland G84 8LE
Contact: David Higgins
Tel: 01436 820269
Fax: 01436 82047
Email: originals@cranston-military-prints.co.uk
Leading publishers of military prints, over 800 images, from Ancient period to IFOR Bosnia. 5 catalogues available, £7 each.

DAVID CARTWRIGHT
Studio Cae Coch Bach, Rhosgoch, Anglesey, Gwynedd, Wales LL66 0AE
Contact: David Cartwright
Tel: 01407 710801
Military artist specializing in Napoleonic and Crimean scenes on canvas. Commissions undertaken. Contact for further details of originals and limited edition prints.

DAVID ROWLANDS
6 Saville Place, Clifton, Bristol, Avon BS8 4LJ
Contact: David Roulands
Tel/Fax: 0117 9731722
Email: djrowlands@supanet.com
Military artist. Military prints. War artist in the Gulf War and Bosnia. Many paintings commissioned by the Army. Historical and modern subjects.

E G FRAMES MILITARIA UK
7 Saffron, Amington, Tamworth, Staffordshire B77 4EP
Contact: Tony Cooper
Tel/Fax: 01827 63900
Email: tony@egframes.co.uk
Website:http://www.egframes.co.uk
We specialise in military framing, in addition we sell British Army badge, museum qulity reproduction medals, Third Reich Insignia and MOD issue pace sticks and canes.

FLINTLOCK PUBLISHING
10 Westbourne Road, Walsall, W. Midlands WS4 2JA
Contact: Rob or Angela Chapman
Tel/Fax: 01922 644078
Email: Achapman10@aol.com
Website: www.flintlockpublishing.co.uk
Publishers of postcards, prints and exhibition materials from original artwork by leading artists in military and costume history. Commissions/collaborations undertaken.

FRONTISPIECE
Concourse Level, Cabot Place East, Canary Wharf, London E14 4QS
Contact: Reginald Beer
Tel: 020 7363 6336
Fax: 020 7515 1424
Email: frontispiece@canarywharfconcourse.freeserve.co.uk
Website: www.frontispiece.co.uk
Half a million anitique prints. British Army campaigns; American Civil War; Napoleonic uniforms. Thousands of naval prints (and some airforce). 24 hour answerphone.

GALLERY MILITAIRE
1 Holstock Road, Ilford, Essex IG1 1LG
Fine and investment art dealers and publishers, supplying original paintings, limited edition prints, reproductions, plates and postcards. All types of framing and art commission, undertaken. European dealers and distributors for major military artists. Gallery viewing by appointment. Mail Order. Large A4 illustrated catalogue £3.00 UK, £4.00 Europe $10.00 USA Airmail.

GEOFF WHITE
19 Rushmoor Lane, Backwell, Bristol BS48 3BN
Contact: Geoff White
Tel/Fax: 01275 462346
Publishers of military postcards. All items are designed to supply reference material for collectors, modellers and other enthusiasts. Send SAE for illustrated catalogue.

HISTOREX AGENTS
Wellington House, 157 Snargate Street, Dover, Kent CT17 9BZ
Contact: Lynn Sangster
Tel: 01304 206720
Fax: 01304 204528
Email: sales@historex-agents.demon.co.uk
Website: www.historex-agents.demon.co.uk
UK distributors of uniform plates and prints by Rousselot, Le Cimier, Le Hussard du Marais and R.J.Marrion. Napoleonic, Ancien Regime, and American War of Independence and Civil War.

HISTORIC ART COMPANY
Ashleigh House, 236 Wokingham Road, Reading, Berkshire
RG6 1JS
Contact: H G Crabtree
Tel: 0118 926 1236
Fax: 0118 931 4432
Email: hugh@farmex.co.uk
Website: www.chriscollingwood.com
Limited and open edition prints, cards and notelets
exclusively featuring the work of Christopher Collingwood.
Trade and private commission enquiries welcome. Please
call for details.

I K WREN (POSTCARD PUBLISHER)
14 Elmbridge Road, Cranleigh, Surrey GU68NH
Tel/Fax: 01483 272551
Email: Ian.Wren@tesco.net
Modern artist-painted postcards; prints produced by other
publishers and regiments are also sold. A finders service
for pre WWI postcards also operates.

*LIBRAIRIE UNIFORMOLOGIQUE INTERNATIONALE
111 Avenue Victor Hugo, Galerie Argentine, 75116 Paris,
France

J C MUMMERY MILITARY ART
65 Riverside Gardens, Romsey, Hampshire SO51 8HN
Contact: JackMummery
Tel/Fax: 01794 512177
Publisher and dealer in military prints, bronzes, hand
coloured engravings, varnish texturing and custom framing.
Mail order facility, SAE for lists on request. Personal visi-
tors by arrangement.

MILITARY FINE ARTS
5 Feversham Road, Salisbury, Wilts SP1 3PP
Contact: Guy Jennings-Bramly
Tel: 01722 328523
Fax: 01722 329765
Website: www.militaryfinearts.com
Military Fine Arts is Britain's leading British fine arts dealer.
Established 12 years ago, the company has access to all
UK publishers, artists and dealers. A catalogue listing of
over 2,500 items at £4 (US $8) is available. Cheques
made payable to G Jennings-Bramly. Picture framing and
engraving service including medal/presentation cases also
available.

OSSIE JONES TECHNICAL ORIGINATION
135 Ashbourne Road, Liverpool, Merseyside L17 9QQ
Tel: 0151 727 3661
Superb maritime, aviation and military transport drawings
and paintings to commission from this up-and-coming
artist. Research undertaken. Contact for details and
samples.

PATRICE COURCELLE
38 Avenue Des Vallons, B-1410 Waterloo B-1410, Belgium
Contact: Patrice Courcelle
Email: courcelle@linkline.be
Illustrator and painter. Main periods: American Revolution,
French Revolution & Napoleonic wars. Publisher of the
plate series 'Ceux Qui Bravaient l'Aigle' and of the
'Waterloo' prints.

PLANCHES PRO-PATRIA
16 Rue Beaurepaire, 75010 Paris, France

*R I G O / LE PLUMET
Louannec, 22700 Perros-Guirrec, France

R M K FINE PRINTS
13 Keere Street, Lewes, E. Sussex BN7 1TY
Tel/Fax: 01273 477959
Carefully researched fine limited edition prints: Japanese
Samurai (54 diferent titles), European Medieval, Civil War
and Military: colour and line. SAE for catalogue.

STUART CATHRO
19 Johnstone Street, Menstrie, Clackmannanshire, Scotland
FK11 7DB
Tel: 01259 761665
Full calligraphy & heraldry service.

THE POMPADOUR GALLERY
PO Box 11, Romford, Essex RM7 7HY
Contact: George Newark
Tel/Fax: 01375 384020
Email: christopher.newark@virgin.net
Publishers and distributors of military books, postcards and
reproduction cigarette cards. Books: 'Kipling's Soldiers',
'Uniforms of the Foot Guards' and our latest book
'Uniforms of the Royal Marines 1664 to the Present Day'.
Send SAE for full details of all our publications.

TONY JACKSON & ASSOCIATES
Forge View, Lindsey Tye, Suffolk IP7 6PP
Contact: Tony Jackson
Tel: 01449 741609
Fax: 01449 741805
Email: tja@lindseytye.freeserve.co.uk
Publishers of 'Insignia Cards', a classic series of collector's
cards featuring elite military and aviation units of WWII,
together with their insignia, awards and decorations.

YOSHIKO
78 Whitley Wood Lane, Reading, Berkshire RG2 8PP
Contact: Mike Brown
Tel/Fax: 0118 987 4946
Email: steve@lav-tech.com
Importer of Japanese woodblock prints offers for sale a
range of classical plus limited edition prints. For copy cata-
logue send four 1st class stamps.

PHOTOGRAPHIC & VIDEO

CANTIACI
24 Johnson Avenue, Gillingham, Kent ME7 1FD
Contact: Christine Toomey
Tel: 01634 58170
Email: cantiaci.livinghistory@virgin.net
Cantiaci Iron Age living history group offer a range of fully researched craft displays that we can tailor to the requirements of the client. We have extensive experience of reconstruction acting, for film and television, research and consultation services, school visits and festival organisation. Versatile, professional and archeologically correct.

CAPTURED IMAGES
Contact: Sean Vatcher
Tel/Fax: 01342 836749
Mobile: 0772 0618301
Email: capturedimages@talk21.com
Military photography.

CHRIS HONEYWELL
c/o Collections Picture Library, 13 Woodberry Crescent, London N10 1P
Contact: Brian Shuel
Tel: 0181 883 0083
Fax: 0181 883 9215
Email: collections@btinternet.com
This library holds a large selection of photographer Chris Honeywell's colour photographs of English Civil War re-enactments and reconstruction subjects, as published in his 'The English Civil War Recreated in Colour Photographs' (Windrow & Greene, 1993).

DUKE MARKETING LTD
PO Box 46, Milbourn House, St Georges Street, Isle of Man IM99 1DD
Tel: 01624 623634
Fax: 01624 629745
Email: duke.video@enterprise.net

THE DEFENCE PICTURE LIBRARY
Sherwell House, 54 Staddiscombe Road, Plymouth PL9 9NB
Tel: 01752 401800
Specialists in military stock photography.

HISTORYMAN UK
2 Coburn Drive, Four Oaks, Sutton Coldfield B75 5NT
Contact: John White
Tel: 0121 308 4103
Email: jwhite02@globalnet.co.uk
Website: historyman.uk.net
Considerable experience with film and TV companies in the area of costume and historical productions. Specialising in late Georgian/Regency/Napoleunic period. Shows, talks and displays at various locations. Credits include work for the BBC. Contact for more details.

INTERNATIONAL HISTORIC FILMS, INC.
Box 29035, Chicago, Illinois 60629, USA
Contact: Peter Bernotas
Tel: 773 927 9091
Fax: 775 927 9211
Email: intrvdeo@2x.netcom.com
Website: www.ihffilm.com
Military, political and social history on videocassette. Over 600 original newsreels, documentaries and feature films including Nazi and Soviet propaganda films. All titles on VHS and all worldly standards; write or fax for free catalogue.

MAYHEM PHOTOGRAPHICS
Contact: Dick Clark
Tel: 0771 843 3054
History in camera.

MILITARY FEATURES & PHOTO AGENCY
Hollyville, Maesycrugiau, Pencader, Carmarthen, Wales SA39 9DL
Contact: John Norris
Tel: 01559 395301
Email: john.norris3@btinternet.com
Re-enactment photographer and columnist and battlefied tour guide for WWII sites. Travels extensively to cover re-enactor special events. Commissions undertaken.

THE MILITARY PICTURE LIBRARY INTERNATIONAL LTD
Eureka House, 28a Station Road, Aldershot, Hants. GU11 1HT UK
Tel: 01252 350547
Fax: 01252 350546
ISDN: 01252 408305
E-mail: info@mpli.co.uk
Website: www.mpli.co.uk
Digital/hard copy military picture library.

RUNNING WOLF PRODUCTIONS (VIDEO ETC)
Crogo Mains, Corsock, Castle Douglas, Kirkcudbrightshire, Scotland DG7 3DR
Contact: M Loades
EmaiL: rwprods@aol.com
Video production company—suppliers of 'Archery—Its History and Forms' and 'The Blow by Blow Guide to Swordfighting'. Mike Loades also available for lectures, workshops and fight arranging assignments.

V S-BOOKS
PO Box 20 05 40, D-44635 Herne, Germany
Contact: Torsten Verhülsdonk
Tel: 2325 73818
Fax: 2325 792311
Email: vs.books@cityweb.de
Transparencies and prints of modern military and police subjects for illustration and advertising; also re-enactments of various periods; some historical material; commissions undertaken.

TOMAHAWK
Tomahawk Films
Email: stan.googe@virgin.net

VIDEOLINES
32 Mount Pleasant, Paddock Wood, Kent TN12 6AG
Tel: 01982 833368
Fax: 01892 838059
Email: videolines@btinternet.com
Website: www.railwayvideos.fsnet.co.uk

WARRIOR VIDEOS
38 Southdown Avenue, Brighton, E. Sussex BN1 6EH

RE-ENACTMENT GROUPS & SOCIETIES

AASVOGELI
ANMOD DRACAN
ARMSTRONG HOUSEHOLD
Imladris, 224 Coatham Road, Redcar, Cleveland TS10 1RA
Contact: John Watson
Tel: 01642 489227
Mobile: 0468 527795
Societies dedicated to accurate depiction of everyday life throughout the ages using a highly skilled group of demonstrators and TV/film extras.

AD HISTORICAL INTERPRETATION
165 The Chantrys, Farnham, Surrey GU9 7AH
Contact: David Cadle
Tel: 01252 711047

AGE OF CHIVALRY
59 Kirkwall Road, Crown Hill, Plymouth, Devon PL5 3TL
Contact: Richard Babbage
Tel: 01752 705 878

AGE OF PENDA
25 Richmond Street, Halesowen, W. Midlands B63 4BB
Contact: Andy Colley
Tel: 0121 602 8079

AIRBORNE ALLIANCE
The Willows, Benover Road, Collier Street, Marden, Kent TN12 9RD
Contact: Gary Howard
Tel: 01892 730229

*AIRLANDING BATTALION (WWII)
18 Rue Clovis Cappon, 76190 Yvetot 76190, France
Contact: Bruno Bourgine

ALBA RE-ENACTMENT & CLAN HERITAGE TRUST
34 St Serf's Road, Tulibody, Clackmannanshire, Scotland
Contact: Kenneth or Margaret MacSorley
Tel: 01259 217287
Breathtaking full contact weapon displays by a highly trained display team.

AMERICAN CIVIL WAR SOCIETY
PO Box 54, Brighouse, W. Yorkshire HD6 1JQ
Contact: Phillip Clark or Pat Cooney
Tel: 01625 431500 or 01254 775964

AMERICAN INFANTRY PRESERVATION SOCIETY
Contact: Stuart
Tel: 01323 843456
Email: www.vietnam.fsnet.co.uk/index.htm
Busy schedule throughout the year taking part shows and private events. The aim of the society is to serve as a living memorial to the day to day events of American and Vietnamese infantryman.

THE ANGEVIN KNIGHTS OF ENGLAND
58 Redworth Road, Billingham, Durham TS2 3JF
Contact: Shaun Douglas-Henderson
Tel: 01642 806413
Email: chairmouse@hotmail.com

AN DAL CUINN CLAN
Clan Resource Centre, B4D, Balbutcher Lane, Dublin 11, Co Dublin, Ireland

ANTONINE GUARD
29 Letham Rise, St David's Bay, Fife, Kinrosshire, Scotland KY11 5FW
Tel: 01383 825149
Email: r.i.richardson@tesco.net
Website: www.theantonineguard.org.uk
The Antonine Guard is a Living History society portraying the Romans in Scotland during 1st/2nd centuries AD. We do public displays, television and schools. Demonstrations of Roman military drills. We also have a ladies section.

ARCHERS OF THE BLACK PRINCE
Gittdom, 3 Bryn Castell, Caergwrle, Wrexham, N. Wales LL2 9HB
Contact: Paul Harston
Tel: 01978 762313

ARMS & ARCHERY
The Coach House, London Road, Ware, Herts SG12 9QU
Tel: 01920 460335
Fax: 01920 461044
Email: tgou104885@aol.com
Website: armaand archery.co.uk
Film and TV props and costumes. Makers of plate armour, chainmail and fighting swords (titanium) for stunt work only.

ARMS OF THE WHITE ROSE
46 Wandsworth, Kingstanding, Birmingham, W. Midlands B44 9LU
Contact: Paul Ward
Tel: 0121 360 7014

ARRIERE BANS
Lilliput Cottage, 23 Hight Street, Old Oxted, RH8 9LN
Contact: Mark Bourne
Tel: 01883 716197
Email: markbourne@talk21
Medieval mercenaries for hire. Authentic 15th century with our own wooden stockade and siege weapon, available for corporate events, film/TV work. We run the Fryland medieval experience for schools and clubs and of course attend re-enactments.

ARTILLERY COMPANY OF NEWPORT
PO Box 14, Newport, RI 02840-0001
Contact: Capt. Joyce Gardner
Tel: 401 821 1689
Email: RISANCOMM@aol.com
Website: www.newportartillery.org
The Artillery Company of Newport, oldest and continuous. Chartered during reign of King George II of Great Britian in 1741. Since then we have served the state and nation in continuous service. Today, the company serves as a ceremonial unit of the Rhode Island Militia, Council of Historic Commands. Military Museum open every Saturday, May–Oct, 10am–4pm.

*ARTILLEURS DE MARINE (NAP)
19 Rue Toncrre-Bailly, 62470 Calonne-Ricouart, France
Contact: Frederic Gilliot

ASSOCIATION BRITANNIC DE LA GARDE IMPERIALE ARTILLERIE À PIED / GRENADIERS À PIED / POLISH GUARD LANCERS
10 Skipton Road, Silsden, W. Yorkshire
Contact: George Lumbonski
Tel: 01585 654118

*ASSOC NAPOLEONIENNE DU BOULONNAIS
97 Rue Louis Duflos, 62200 Boulogne sur Mer, France
Contact: Michel Lamesh
Tel: 2180496

*ASSOCIATION 1944
35 Avenue Paul Deroulede, 94300 Vincennes, France
Tel/Fax: 1436508

*ASSOCIATION BIG RED ONE (WWII)
44 Rue de Bretagne, 76600 Le Havre, France
Tel/Fax (0033) 35430374

*ASSOCIATION CORBINEAU (NAP)
2 Rue du 8 Mai 1945, 59215 Abscon, France
Contact: Regis Surmont

THE ASSOCIATION OF CROWN FORCES 1776
13 Greenland Road, Weston-Super-Mare, Somerset BS22 8JP
Contact: Colin Adams
Tel: 01934 642441

*ASSOCIATION D-DAY
52 Avenue du General Leclerc, 77320 La Ferte Gaucher, France
Contact: Gerard Signac

THE AUDLEY HOUSEHOLD
3 Mervyn Road, Winshall, Burton-on-Trent, Staffs DB15 0LW
Contact: Jan Stanbridge
Tel: 01283 568580

*AUSTRIAN NAPOLEONIC RE-ENACTMENT GROUP
Brugger Strasse 71, 6973 Hochst Norarlberg, Austria
Contact: Helmut Huber

AXHOLMR & THE DANNAE
15 Mond Avenue, Goole, East Yorkshire DN14 6LQ
Contact: Matt Jones
Tel: 01405 763550
Email: axholmruik@aol.com
Website: www.axholmr.co.uk
Historical re-enactment society covering 3rd–11th centuries. Anglian, Saxon, Viking and Norman periods covered. Also 3rd century BC–3rd century AD Celtic. Combat, living history, research, family friendly, archery, crafts, TV/film and photographic.

*BALDEN VILLINGEN GARDE (NAP)
Rietstrasse 38, 7730 VS Villingen, Germany
Contact: Wolfgang Kunle

BALHAG WARRIORS
6 Wilton Street, Redcar, Cleveland TS10 3EU
Contact: Dave Ayton
Tel: 01642 476216
Fax: 01642 444351

*BATAILLON DES MARINS DE LA GARDE (NAP)
19 Rue de la Gilette, B-5646 Stave, Belgium
Contact: Jean Gerard
Group recreating sailors of the French Imperial Guard of the Napoleonic period, including officers, drum major, standard bearer, petty officers, sailors, and a Cantiniere; campaign dress and parade uniforms represented.

THE BEAUFO HOUSEHOLD
65 Spencer Avenue, Yarnton, Kidlington, Oxfordshire OX5 1NQ
Contact: Penny Roberts or Kevin Broughton
Tel: 01865 378140
Fax: 01865 272821
Email: pmr@bodley.ox.ac.uk
A small local group representing the household and combatants of an Oxfordshire family—mainly 15th century but also some earlier events.

BILLS AND BOWS
248 Wetmore Road, Buton-on-Trent, Staffs DE14 1RB
Contact: Graham Smith
Tel/Fax: 01283 517871

BLACK LEGION
8 Melrose Place, Cove, Farnborough, Hants
Contact: Mark Copley
Tel: 01252 652988

BLACK FLAG
50 Cardign Crescent, Winchwen, Swansea, S Wales SA1 7DY
Contact: David O'Neill
Tel: 01792 797094
Email: darthon9@netscape.net

THE BLACK PRINCE'S ARCHER GUARD
Plas Adda, Bach Tre'rddol, Corwen, Denbighshire LL21 OEL
Contact: Alison Jones
Tel/Fax: 01490 413148

BLAZON KNIGHTS
1 Manor Rise, Chasetown, Burntwood, Staffs WS7 8TR
Contact: Daave Gibbons
Tel: 01543 675042

BLODD PAR RYGGEN (BLOOD EAGLES)
12 Stanway Close, Middleton, Manchester M24 1HE
Contact: Andy Howard
Tel: 0161 643 496

BODMIN RE-ENACTMENT ASSOCIATION (DARK AGE) TUDOR
SOCIETY (BRATS)
51 Northey Road, Bodmin, Cornwall PL31 1 JF
Contact: J Valencia de Valencia
Iel: 01208 7399

BOTELER HOUSEHOLD
9 Miller Street,Warrington,Cheshire WA4 1BD
Contact: Tony Whittaker
Tel: 01925 659756
Medieval and Tudor living history, 1150-1586, portraying
the former Lords of Warrington, who were originally butlers
to the notorious Earls of Chester. Asvailable for all kinds of
events—TV/film, video work etc. Emphasis on domestic and
social life. New members welcome.

BOWMEN OF THE ROSE
17 Cairbryn Terrace, Cairbryn, Ammanford, Carmarthemshire
SA18 3DX
Contact: Ray Rees
Tel: 01269-85071

BRAN GWYN (WHITE CROW)
203 Bicester Road, Aylesbury, Buckinghamshire HP19 3BD
Contact: Tom Green
Tel: 01296 487518

*BRACTWO RYCERSKIE ZAMKU GNIEWSKIEGO
Muzeumkrcheologiezne, Ul. Mriacka 25/26, 80-958 Gdan'sk,
Poland
Contact: Barbara Gostyn'ska

*BRAUNSCHWFIGISCHES FELDCORPS (NAP)
Freiherr vom Stein 22, 55774 Baumholder 55774, Germany
Contact: Daniel S Peterson

BRIGANTIA
67 Paulsgrove Road, North End, Portsmouth, Hants PO2 7HP
Contact: Karl Gallagher
Tel: 023 9269 6897
Email: karl@lugodoc.demon.co.u

BRITANNIA THE ARTHURIAN RE-ENACTMENT SOCIETY
13 Ardleigh, Basildon, Essex SS16 5RA
Contact: Dan or Susanna Shadrake
Tel: 01268-544511

BRITISH FEDERATION FOR HISTORICAL SWORDPLAY
15 Halmyre Street, Edinburgh, Scotland EH6 8QA
Contact: Paul Macdonald
Tel: 0131 538 0745
Email: macdonaldacademy@aol.com
Website: www.bfhs.co.uk
The British Federation for historical swordplay is a national
umbrella organisation for UK societies practicing historical
fencing workshops as well as offering an extensive library
of facsimile historical treatises.

BRITISH PLATE ARMOUR SOCIETY
82 Skinner Street, Poole, Dorset BH15 1RJ
Contact: Dave Barnes,
Tel/Fax: 01202 683519
Mobile: 0797 979 429

BROTHERHOOD OF THE BLACK KNIGHT
14 Morden Close, Tadworth, Surrey KT20 5LF
Contact: P Rotherham
Tel: 01737 277063

BUCKINGHAMS RETINUE
Meadow View, 64–65 Main Road, Pyebridge, Derbyshire DB55 4NY
Contact: Chris Howell
Tel: 101773 528804
Email: darren@buckingham-retinue.freeserve.co.uk

BUCKS HOUSEHOLD 1460
14 Keep Hill Drive, High Wycombe, Bucks HP11 1DU
Tel: 01494-440277

BURGUNDIAN MERCENARIES
68 Minerva Street, Bulwell, Nottingham NG6 8GR
Contact: Adrian Elliston,
Tel: 0115 916 0726

CALEDONIAN HISTORICAL RE-ENACTMENT SOCIETY
22 Drummie Road, Devonside Tillicoultry, Clackmannanshire,
Scotland FKI3 6HT
Contact: Bobby Redmond
Tel: 01259-75293

CAMBRIDGE ARMY CADET FORCE
ACF Centre, Denny End Road, Waterbeach, Cambridge
CB5 9QU
Tel: 01223 862949
Fax: 01223 441830
Email: Cambsacf@fsnet.co.uk
Website: www.cambsarmy.cadets
Rock climbing, canoeing & cross country expeditions and
supporting activities, annual weekend camps, military skills.
We attend major festivals and displays.

CAMELOT MEDIEVAL SOCIETY
1 Fromond Close, Lymington, Hants
Contact: Stephen Hoey

Tel: 01590 67846
CAMPFOLLOWERS
26 Rotherham Avenue, Luton, Beds LU1 5NP
Contact: Heidi Finnerty
Tel: 01582 653401
Email: campfollowers@hotmail.com

CANTIACI
24 Johnson Avenue, Gillingham, Kent ME7 1FD
Contact: Christine Toomey
Tel: 01634 58170
Email: cantiaci.livinghistory@virgin.net
Cantiaci Iron Age living history group offer a range of fully
researched craft displays that we can tailor to the requirements of the client. We have extensive experience of
reconstruction acting, for film and television, research and
consultation services, school visits and festival organisation.
Versatile, professional and archeologically correct.

THE CAPTAIN GENERALL'S MUSICKE
150 St. Pancras, Chichester, W Sussex PO1 91SH
Contact: Ralph Willatt
Tel: 01243 78764

CARADOG'S TEULU
19 Down Terrace, Brighton, E. Sussex BN2 2ZJ
Contact: Pat Harrill-Morris
Tel: 01273 70002

CATUVELLAUNI
27 Swains Lane, Flackwell Heath, Buckinghamshire
HP10 9BN
Contact: Teri Fredicksen
Tel: 01628 521 675
Email: tfrede01@bucksco.ac.uk

CELTIC WARRIOR ARTS
404 Goresbrook Road, Dagenham, Essex RM9 4UX
Contact: Barry Simmans
Mobile: 07713 752945

*CENTRE EQUESTRE D'ATTELAGE (NAP)
Domaine de la Roussie, 33140 Cadaujac, France
Contact: M Castelot

CHAPTER OF SAINT BARTHOLOMEW
68 Minerva Street, Bulwell, Nottingham NG6 8GR
Contact: Adrian Elliston
Tel: 0115 916 072

*CHASSEURS ALPINS (WWII)
Mandrion, 73100 Trevighin, France
Contact: Laurent Demouzon

*CHASSEURS À CHEVAL DE LA GARDE (NAP)
10 Escadron, 48 Rue Chapon, 75003 Paris, France
Contact: Michel Fourrey

*CHASSEURS A PIED DE LA GARDE (NAP)
8 Rue de l'ancien hopital, Le Sans Souci, 21200 Gevrey-
Chambertin, France
Contact: Vincent Bourgeot

CHEPSTOWE GARRISON
CarrCarters Coftage, Hitchen, Blakeney, Glos GL15 4BJ
Contact: Nadine Carr
Tel: 01594-51607
Musters held at Chepstow Castle.

*LES CHEVALIERS D'ÎLE DE FRANCE (MED)
25 Rue Roland Garros, 78140 Velizy Villacoublay, France
Contact: Daniel Georges

*LES CHEVALIERS DE FRANCHE-COMTÉ (MED)
4 Chemin des Chalettes, 39150 Morez, France
Contact: Jean-Claude Crotti

CHEVALIERS DE GUISE
46 St John's Court, Princess Crescent, Finsbury Park,
London N4 2HL
Contact: Philip Burthem

CHIVALRY IN ACTION
104 Clark Road, Wolverhampton, W. Midlands WV3 9PB
Contact: Tony Westmancoat
Tel: 01902 426879

CHURCH, STATE & HOUSEHOLD
51 Cobden Street, Gosport, Hants PO12 4QH
Contact: Steve Brittain
Tel: 02392426254
Email: cshlivinghistory@hotpop.com

CIRCLE OF ARMS
27 Hunters,Road, Broomfield, Herne Bay, Kent CT6 7BD
Contact: Samantha Gilbey
Tel: 01227 366612
Email: sam@danddinteriors.co.uk

CIVIL DEFENDERS
Leigh Cottage, Bakers Road, Belchamp St.Paul, Sudbury,
Suffolk CO10 7DG
Contact: Nick or Dawn Champion
Tel: 01787 277748
Email: champions@ostlers.demon.co.uk

CLAN MACKENNA (CLAN MACCIONNAITH)
Ennismor, 12 Marske Road, Saltburn-by-the-Sea, N. Yorkshire
TS12 1PZ
Contact: Lanette Dineley
Tel: 01287 625744
Email: secretary@reivers.demon.co.uk

CLAN WALLACE
Seoras Wallace, 68 Darnley Street, Pollockshields, Scotland
G41 2SE
Tel: 0141 429 6968 or 0141 429 6915

CLARENCE HOUSEHOLD
32 Norman Road, Birkby, Huddersfield, W. Yorkshire
HD2 2UB
Contact: William Butcher
Tel: 01484 429447
Email: kpaskin@-aol.com

CLIFFORD HOUSEHOLD
New House, Murton Appleby in Westmoreland, Cumbria
CA16 9ND
Contact: Adrian or Elaine Waite
Tel/Fax: 01768 351498
Mobile: 07971 321863

CO B 9TH KENTUCKY VOLUNTEER INFANTRY
83 Albury Drive, Pinner, Middlesex HA5 3RL
Contact: Chris O'Brien
Tel: 020 8866 9870
Mobile: 0958 928975
Email: cob9ky@aol.com

COHORS QUINTA GALLORUM
Arbeia Roman Fort, Baring Street, South Shields, Tyne &
Wear NE33 2BB
Contact: Alex Croom
Tel: 0191 454 4093
Research and re-enactment group representing third
century Roman auxiliary soldiers and civilians.

COLCHESTER HISTORICAL ENACTMENT SOCIETY
80 Greenstead Road, Colchester, Essex
Contact: Paul Adams
Tel: 01206 866166
Fax: 01206 764732
Email: ches@aspects.net

COLCHESTER ROMAN SOCIETY
2 Cooper Beeches, Colchester, Essex CO3 5YB
Contact: Zane Green
Tel: 01206 502247

THE COLDSTREAM REGIMENT OF FOOT GUARDS
50 Church Street, Donisthorpe, Derbyshire DE12 7PY
Contact: John Litchfield or Debbie Goldsmith
Tel: 01530-273638
Email: john@civilwardrobe.demon.co.uk

COMBROGI
60 Calton Road, Gloucester GL1 5DY
Contact: Gary Waidson
Tel: 01452 304442 or 01452 730630 (work)
Fax: 01452 731888

COMMISSION OF ARRAY
Post Office Cottage, Main Street, Aslockton, Notts NG13 9AL
Contact: Bruce Maclellan
Tel: 01949 857252
Living History and combat group specialising in 13th-14th
century. We host events throughout England and Scotland.

COMPANIE OF CANTERBURY, KENT SOCIETY
92 Albion Road, Broadstairs, Kent CT10 2UT
Contact: Bob Burton
Tel: 01843 869480
Mobile: 0793 167 6191

COMPANIE DAGHES (MAGPIES)
25 Egleston Road, Morden, Surrey SM4 6PN
Contact: Diana & Colin Lempriere-Knight
Tel: 020 8395 3729
Fax: 020 8286 6039

*COMPAGNIE DE LA ROSE
5 rue des Granges, Estavayer le Lac CH 1470, Switzerland
Contact: Katia Laurent

*COMPAGNIE MEDIEVALE MAC'HTIERN
Ancienne Ecole, 35190 St Thual, France
Contact: Eric Magnini

THE COMPANIONS OF THE BLACK BEAR
c/o 5 Kings Lane, Norton, Evesham, Worcs WR11 11TJ
Contact: Jane Baalam
Tel: 01386 871908
Email: battle.tewkesbury@bigfoot.com
Living history encampment depicting aspects of Medieval
life. Displays include: archery, woodcarving, pewter casting,
limining, candlemaking, cookery. Hosts of Tewkesbury
Medieval Festival.

COMPANIONS OF THE BLACK PRINCE
Tutbury Castle, Tutbury, Staffs DE13 9JF
Contact: Barrie Vallans
Tel: 01283 812129

COMPANIONS OF THE CROW
22 Halliday Hill, Oxford, Oxfordshire OX3 9PU
Contact: Carl Sprake
Tel: 07929 160389
Email: carl@cas-net.co.uk
Website: www.companions ofthecrow.co.uk
A medieval combat re-enactment group covering the period
1066-1485. Based in Oxfordshire but will travel widely.
Families welcome. Shows, education and film work under-
taken.

COMPANY ECORCHEUR
5 Ollison Drive, Streetly, Sutton Coldfield, W. Midlands B74 3DZ
Contact: Nigel Wheeler
Tel: 0121 353 6673

COMPANY OF THE GOLDEN PHOENIX
73 Kinson Park Road, Kinson, Bournemouth, Dorset
BH10 7HG
Contact: Baron Andre De'Flaville
Tel: 01202 575521

COMPANY OF MERCENARY ARCHERS (HERBERT
HOUSEHOLD)
133 Tiverton Road, Winklebury, Basingstoke, Hants RG23 8EH
Contact: Peter Hibbett
Tel: 01256 811571
Fax: 01256 850600
Email: peter.hibbett@ecophon.co.uk
Re-enactment society concentrating on the time between
the Hundred Years War and the Wars of the Roses. The
main focus of the group is archery, but hand weapons are
also taught and used.

COMPANY OF ORDINANCE
20 Deerhurst Way, Toothill, Swindon, Wilts SN5 8AF
Contact: Colin Armstrong
Tel: 01793 487253
Email: company_of_ordinance@blgfoot.com

COMPANY OF THE RED CROW
159 Rayne Road, Braintree, Essex CM7 2QD
Contact: Zarah Nicholls
Tel: 01376343235
A group of 15, consisting of sword, axe, bill men (and women), we wear Black and Green emblazoned with a Red Crow and have been re-enacting for 10 years. We re-enact three periods: Dark Ages/15th Century Medieval/Pirates and are always looking for new events and members.

*COMPANY OF ST GEORGE
4 Rue Coulon, CH-2000 Neuchatel, Switzerland
Contact: John Howe
Tel/Fax: 24711775
Late 15th century artillery company, also halberdiers, archers, general 'living history' activities. High standard of authenticity and discipline; multi-national membership; events in Europe. British contact: Victor Shreeve, Vern Path, Melplash, Bridport, Dorset, DI6 3UD.

COMPANY OF THE SILVER GRIFFIN
Hilltop Mink Farm, Swanwick, Derbyshire DE55 1AT
Contact: Mark Dakin
Tel: 01773 602014
Fax: 01773 540116
Email: mdakin@yahoo.com

A COMPANY OF THIEVES
39 Deanston Drive, Glasgow G41 3AG
Contact: Jennie Hood
Tel: 0141 632 1608
Email: kelot@hotmail.com

COMPANY OF THE WHITE BOAR
48 Noel Street, Hyson Green, Nottingham, Notts NG7 6AW
Contact: Tony Rotheram
Tel: 0115 847 8735
Mobile: 0790 902 4019

COMPANY OF THE WHITE LION
63 Hutland Road, Ipswich, Suffolk IP4 4HQ
Contact: Simon de Montfort
Tel: 01473 273207

COMPANY OF 1415
42 Churchill Road, Gravesend, Kent DA11 7AQ
Contact: George Beeching
Tel: 01474 362490

CONFEDERATE STATES NAVY
7 Markstakes Corner, South Chailey, E. Sussex BN8 4BP
Contact: Commander Fry
Tel: 01273 400037

CONFEDERATE UNION RE-ENACTMENT SOCIETY (CURS)
13 Amythyst Road, Fairwater, Cardiff, South Wales CF5 3MS
Contact: Phil Buck Day
Tel: 02920 317980
Email: p.day@ntlworld.com
Website: www.homestead.com/curs1/index.html
We recreate American Civil War infantry units 23rd VA, 97th NY, Medical Corps and Artillery, and participate in battle re-enactments and living history displays 1860-1865. Soldier and civilian impressions at their best. New members welcome. Also postal members. The Society was founded in 1997.

CONQUEST
66 Roseberry Park, Redfield, Bristol BS5 9ES
Contact: John Phillips or Dave Page
Tel: 0117 941 222

CONTACT!
4 Yarmouth Road, Stevenage, Herts SG1 2LW
Contact: Dean Wayland
Tel: 01438 368177
Fax: 01438 22933

CONTINENTAL MARINES
7 Arcadia Way, Trevethin, Pontypool, Gwent NP4 8UX
Contact: Allan Jones
Tel: 01495 750479
Email: continentalmarine@hotmail.com
Website: www.marine76.8m.com
We are a re-enactment group set in the period of the American War of Independence 1775-83. The continental marines are seen as the forerunners of the United Stes Marine Corps, and our group has earned praise from both serving marines and USMC veterans.

THE COURTENEYE HOUSEHOLD & COMPANIE
Kingsford Bottom, 52 The Heathers, Okehampton, Devon
Contact: Ross Kingsford
Tel: 01837 528830

CROWN IMPERIAL
37 Wolsey Close, Southall, Middlesex UB2 4NQ
Contact: Lt Cdr W Thornton, MBE
Tel: 020 8574 4425

CRUCESIGNATI—KNIGHTS OF JERUSALEM
35 Barbury Crescent, Widewell, Plymouth, Devon PL6 7EL
Contact: Darren Macdonald
Tel: 01752 216080
Email: sirmac@sirmac.eurobell.co.uk

CYLCH IDDUR—A MEDIEVAL EXPERIENCE
2 Rock Villa, Criccieth, Gwyne LL52 0ED
Contact: Roger Clark
Tel: 01766 5220

DANELAW MERCENARIES
15 Elmore Road, Luton, Bedfordshire LU2 0QB
Contact: Jim Sizer
Tel: 01582 757466
Email: jim.sizer@currantbun.com

THE DARK AGES CHARITABLE TRUST
Rosemary Cottage, Camp Road, Canwell, Sutton Coldfield
B75 5RA
Contact: Paul Craddock
Tel: 0121-323-4309
Fax: 0121-323-4309
Email: MerciaS@hotmail.com
Website: DarkAgesTrust.org.uk
An historical and nature conservation charity, near
Birmingham, specialising in the period 500-1500 AD. We
have our own seven-acre site with a reconstructed ringfort
and lake. We have planted about 200 rare fruit trees and
are looking for more volunteers. We run groups for The
Vikings and Regia Anglorum.

THE DARK AGES SOCIETY
32 Framfield Road, Uckfield, E. Sussex TN22 5AH
Contact: Neil Bell
Tel: 01825 76955

DAWN DUELLISTS SOCIETY
15 Halmyre Street, Edinburgh, Scotland EH6 8QA
Contact: Paul Macdonald
Tel: 0131 538 0745
Email: macadonaldacademy@aol.com
The Dawn Duellists Society practices fencing and duelling styles
from the 13th-19th centuries. Training is held weekly and open to
all. Demonstrations of historical fencing offered, outlining the development of European swords and swordmanship.

DE MONTFORT HOUSEHOLD
147 Main Road, Kesgrave, Ipswich, Suffolk IP5 2NP
Contact: Guy Lown
Tel: 01473 622209

DE SUTTON HOUSEHOLD
Haughton Cottage, Neen Sollars, Worcestershire DY14 0AH
Contact: Martin de Sutton
Tel: 01299 270938

DESTRIER
43 Vera Crescent, Rainworth, Lincolnshire NG21 0EH
Contact: D Sewell
Tel: 01623 797485
Email: destrierriders@hotmail

THE DEVIL'S HORSEMEN
Wychwood Stud, Salden Mursley, Milton Keynes, Bucks
MK17 0HX
Contact: Gerard Naprous
Tel: 01296 720854
Mobile: 0860 321284
Fax: 01926 720855

THE DIEHARD COMPANY–VICTORIAN MILITARY SOCIETY
21 Addison Way, North Bersted, Bognor Regis, W. Sussex
PO22 9HY
Contact: Tim Rose
Tel: 01243 860036
Email: tl.rose@virgin.net
Website: www.diehards.org.uk
This award winning group represents soldiers of the 1st
Battalion of The Middlesex Regiment on home service in
the 1880s. We also recreate the 24th Foot, British Infantry
of the Zulu War and Boer Commandos of 1899-1901.
Ancillary units include Army Medical Corps and Naval
Landing Party.

DIABOLUS IN MUSICA
Contact: Paul: 01384 295210 or Pam: 01527 875033
Email: paul@diabolus-in-musica.freeserve.co.uk
Website: www.diabolus-in-musica.freeserve.co.uk
Authentic music of merriment. 16th and 17th century spe-
cialists. Everything from lutes to bagpipes. We also make
and supply authentic replica instruments.

THE DORSET LEVY
28 Hopsfield, Milborne St Andrew, Dorset DT11 0LD
Contact: Adrienne Shipsey
Tel: 01258 837525
Email: dorset@levies.freeserve.co.uk

DOUBLE TIME
1 Golden Noble Hill, Colchester, Essex CO1 2AG
Contact: Alison or Dave Roberts-Roddham
Tel: 01206 768517
Email: roddau@essex.ac.uk

DRAGON SVIETER
127 Fitzworthy Avenue, Poole, Dorset BH16 5BA
Contact: Peter Power

DRAGONLORDS
32 Forest Grove, Tonbridge, Kent TN10 3ES
Contact: Animal
Tel: 01732 259945
Email: animule@hotmail.com

DUN BRIGHANTE CELTIC HERITAGE SOCIETY
85 Healey Road, Ossett, W. Yorkshire WF5 8LT
Contact: Sarah Mawson
Tel: 01924 306641(work)

THE EARLS OF CHESTER
9 Miller Street, Warrington, Cheshire WA4 1BD
Contact: Tony Whitaker
Tel: 01925 659756
Medieval living history, 1071-1237, depicting the life and
times of medieval England's most powerful earls. Available
for tourism promotion, commemorative events, TV/film,
video and documentary work–anything connected to
Cheshire history of this period. New members welcome.
Particularly families.

EARL OF OXFORD'S HOUSEHOLD
The Paddock, Manor Road, Pitsford, Northamptonshire
NN6 9AR
Contact: Brian Lymn
Tel: 01604 88066

EARLY MEDIEVAL ALLIANCE
2 Rock Villa, Criccieth, Gwyned, Wales LL52 OED
Contact: Roger Clark
Tel: 01766 52208

EAST GERMAN BORDER ARMY GROUP
18 Northumberland Avenue, Reading, Berks RG2 7PW
Contact: Michael Passmore
Tel: 01189 8638

ELY FEUDAL LEVY
2 Downham Road, Ely, Cambridgeshire CB6 1AH
Contact: Adrian Hudson
Tel: 01353 662536

ENGLISH CIVIL WAR SOCIETY
70 Hailgate, Howden, North Humberside DN14 7ST
Tel/Fax: 01430 430695
Contact: Jonathan Taylor
Email: j.parker@jpbooks.com

ENGLISH RENAISSANCE
248 Wetmore Road, Burton-on-Trent, Staffs DE14 1RB
Contact: Graham Smith
Tel/Fax: 01283 517871

ENGLISH SETTLEMENT SOCIETY
Stanley House, Front Street, Newcastle-upon-Tyne, Tyne &
Wear NE39 2FH
Contact: Paul Mullis
Tel: 01207 544876

THE ERMINE STREET GUARD
Oakland Farm, Dog Lane, Witcombe, Gloucester, Glos GL3 4UG
Contact: Chris Haines
Tel: 01452 862235
Fax: 01452 862235
Email: theESG@aol.com
Website: www.ESG.ndirect.co.uk
Roman re-enactment society formed in 1972. We have a
worldwide reputation for authenticity, with displays for
English Heritage and others. Film work also undertaken.

THE ERPYNGHAM RETINUE
28 Hindhead Point, Wanborough Drive, Roehampton, London
SW15 4AW
Contact: Chris Skinner
Tel/Fax: 020 8789 8483
Email: information@knights-resources.co.uk
or: erpl4l5@paladins-of-chivalry.freeserve.co.uk

ESCAFELD MEDIEVAL SOCIETY
Dale Dyke House, Bradfield Dale, Sheffield, S. Yorkshire S6 6LE
Contact: Irene Deakin
Tel/Fax: 0114 285 1233
Medieval combat. Family entertainment. Archery.

THE ESSEX MILITIA
27 Shalford Road, Billericay, Essex
Contact: Dennis Ward
Tel: 01277 655612
Email: dennis@essex1648.freeserve.co.uk
The Militia covers the period from the English Civil War
through to the restoration of Charles II (1640s–1660s). We
can people a castle, stately home or encampment, as well
as give civil or corporate presentations.

ETERNITY TO OBLIVION
9 Miller Street, Warrington, Cheshire WA4 1BD
Contact: Tony Whittaker
Tel: 01925 659756

THE EUROPEAN NAPOLEONIC SOCIETY
7 Box House, Old Lane, Luddenden, Halifax, W. Yorkshire
HX2 6QA
Contact: Richard Moon
Tel: 01422 885938
Email: firstbat@dialstart.net

EXCALIBUR MEDIEVAL SOCIETY
59 Embankment Road, St Judes, Plymouth, Devon PL4 9HX
Contact: Cliff Beaumont or Helen Harris-Beaumont
Tel: 01752 662311

THE EXILES
67 Ibscott Close, Dagenham, Essex RM10 9YT
Contact: Rob Lovett
Tel: 020 8592 1821
Email: rob_lovett@hotmail.com

*FANFARE DU 9E HUSSARDS (NAP)
L'Avenir de Ste Colombe, 4 Rue de la Baude, 77650 Sainte
Colombe, France
Contact: Olivier Rousell
Tel/Fax: 64001243

FASTOFT'S 1,000
82 Skinner Street, Poole, Dorset BH15 IRJ
Contact: Dave Barnes
Tel/Fax: 01202 683519
Mobile: 0797 979 429

FAUCONBERGS
6 Ridgeway, Aldridge, Walsall, W. Midlands WS9 OHL
Contact: MarkArnold
Tel: 01922 453166
Mobile: 0976 77094

**FEDERATION OF INDEPENDENT SOCIETIES OF AMERICAN
CIVIL WAR (FISACW)**
8 Beech Avenue, Ham Manor Park, Llantimit Major, South
Glamorgan CF61 1BL
Contact: Dick Fisher
Tel: 01446 794318

FEUDAL ARCHERS
12 Holdenby Close, Retford DN22 6UB
Contact: Mark Wilkinson
Mobile: 07939 62595 4

THE FEW
338 Holt Road, Horsford, Norwich, Norfolk NR10 3EE
Contact: Glenn Wilken
Tel: 01603 898531

THE FIRST BATTALION
7 Box House, Old Lane, Luddenden, Halifax, W. Yorkshire
HX2 6QA
Contact: Richard Moon
Tel: 01422 885938
Email: firstbat@dialstart.net

THE FIRST DRAGOONS
52 Beaumont Park Road, Huddersfield, W. Yorkshire HD4 5JP
Contact: Mike Grove
Tel: 01484 653294
Fax: 01484 657437
Email: thefirstdragoons@aol.com

FIRST IN THE FIELD
2 Coburn Drive, Four Oaks Sufton Coldfield, W. Midlands
B75 5NT
Contact: John White
Tel: 0121 308 4103
Email: jwhite02@globalnet.co.uk
Living history and re-enactment group that portrays camp
and campaign life during the Peninsular War of
1808–1814. We have achieved a high standard of authenticity our displays complement a range of historic buildings
and settings. We offer specialised presentations, talks and
displays music, food/cooking, social history.

*LA FLAMME IMPERIALE (NAP)
BP 80, 83602 Frejus Cedex, France
Contact: Roger Romero

FLANDERS WORLD WAR ONE RE-ENACTMENT SOCIETY
331 High Barns, Ely, Cambridgeshire CB7 4RW
Contact: Richard Mathews
Tel: 01353 667593
Email: richard.matthews@dtn.ntl.com

FLASHMAN SOCIETY
Bron Berllan, St Asaph Road, Trefnant, Denbighshire
LL16 5UD
Contact: David Tibbetts
Tel: 01745 730373
Fax: 01745 73059
Email: dtibbe2926@aol.com

*FRANCE 1940
72C Rue de Coulommes, 77860 Quincy Voisins, France
Contact: Didier Coste

FRASER'S HIGHLANDERS
33 Frank Street, Stoke-on-Trent, Staffordshire ST4 2JP
Contact: John Chisholm
Tel: 01782 862308

*FREIE GILDEN
Alte Schmelzl, Aumenau 65606, Germany
Contact: Manfred Struben

THE FRONTLINE ASSOCIATION
3 Plym Grove, Longhill, Hull, E. Yorkshire HU8
Contact: Andy Marsh
Tel: 01482 811569
A growing re-enactment/living history society in the North
re-enacting 1914 to 1945–German, Russian, British–military and civilian. Can convert uniforms and provide tailor-
ing/helmet conversion as well as static displays and pyro-
filled battles and most things in between. Looking for
recruits–especially British infantry.

GADDGEDLAR
39 Deanston Drive, Glasgow G41 3AG
Contact: Jennie Hood
Tel: 0141 632 1608
Email: kelot@hotmail.com

*LE GARDE CHAUVIN (NAP)
44 Rue des Ouches, Echillais, 17620
Echillais, France
Contact: Daniel Dieu

*GARDE IMPERIALE
Brandenburger Strasse 53, 07980 Finsterwalde, Germany
Contact: Hans-Michael Hillebrand

THE GARRISON
11e The Square, Wingham, Canterbury, Kent CT31AW
Contact: Gary Hughes
Tel: 0976 661275

THE GENERALL'S MUSICK AND PLAYERS
150 St Pancras, Chichester, W. Sussex PO19 7SH
Contact: Alison Wiley
Tel: 01858 565537
Fax: 01858 565392
Email: alisowiley@compuserve.com
The group encompasses the years 1590–1660, the period
of Netherland Independence, Huguenot-Catholic, Thirty
Years War and English Civil War, reflecting the period's
musical experience. Using early violins, 'cello, lute, harpsichord, recorders, shawms, crumhorns, racket and sordunes, the group perform the songs, dances and instrumental music of the european capitals.

GLOUCESTER HOUSEHOLD
5 Ollison Drive, Streetly, Sutton Coldfield, W. Midlands B74 3DZ
Contact: Nigel Wheeler
Tel: 0121 353667
GNOMES LOT
Flat 6, 113 Hampton Road, London E4 8NP
Contact: Mike Lang
Tel: 020 8524 7344
Email: mike.lang@arup.com

GOBBI THEATRE COMPANY
47 Baxter Close, Runcorn, Cheshire WA7 6HU
Contact: John Glennard
Tel: 01928 713341
Fax: 0161 228 0670
Email: aangieson@aol.com

THE GOLDEN EAGLE ARCHERS & KNIGHTS OF ENGLAND
7 Huddleston Road, Tufnell Park, London N7 ORE
Contact: Roger Summers
Tel: 020 7609 8552

GOLDEN LIONS OF ENGLAND
Wincott, Kings Street, Sancton, York YO4 3QP
Contact: Khrys Yuen
Tel: 01430 827185

GOSPORT LIVING HISTORY SOCIETY
18 New Road, Lovedean, Waterlooville, Hants PO8 9RU
Contact: R Towner
Tel: 023 9259 8423

*LA GRANDE ARMÉE
2 rue de Mai 1945, 59215 Abscon, France
Contact: Regis Surmont
Admin body for Napoleonic re-enactment in France.

THE GREAT WAR SOCIETY
22 Alwyne Drive, Shipton Road, York, N. Yorkshire YO3 6RS
Contact: Pamela Squires
Tel: 01904 639760

*GRENADIERKORPS VILLINGEN 1810 E.V.
Hochstrasse 44, 78048 Villingen, Germany
Contact: Wolfgang Kunle

THE GREY GOOSE WING TRUST—HISTORIC ARCHERY
46 Commonwealth Way, Abbeywood, Greenwich, London
SE2 OLB
Contact: Phil Wyborn
Tel: 020 8312 2708

GRIMWOOD
15 St Catherines Cross, Bletchingley, Surrey RH1 4PX
Contact: Miki Dennis
Tel: 01883 742143
Email: mikidennis@aol.com

THE GUILD
118 High Street, Winslow Buckinghamshire MK18 3DQ
Contact: Daphne Hilsdon
Tel: 01296 713643
575 Norwich Road, Ipswich, Suffolk IP1 6JU
Contact: Kay Forsdyke
Tel: 01473 425274
Email: kayseamstress@aol.com

THE GUN COMPANY
152 Borrowfield Road Spondon, Derbyshire E21 7HG
Contact: Lyn or Jon Allen
Tel: 01332 669049
Mobile: 0411 298354

GYLDA CINQUE PORTUUM
7 Grant Street, Brighton, E. Sussex BN2 2UN
Contact: Geoff Turner
Tel: 01273 699789

HAMPSHIRE RIFLE & RE-ENACTMENT SOCIETY
c/o 49 Vellum Drive, Carshalton, Surrey SM5 2TP
Contact: Byron Lazarus
Tel: 020 8241 1065
Email: byronlazarus@lycos.co.uk
Website: hampshireregiment.co.uk
We portray a WWII British infantry unit from 1939–45,
from Dunkirk, North Africa, Italy and NW Europe. We are
available for public shows, both static and battle displays.
Also film and TV work.

HANDOWN FREE BOWMEN
105 Pempath Place; Strathcona Road, Wembley, Middlesex
HA9 8QR
Contact: Ron Fraser
Tel: 020 8908 3326

HANS REITERS FAN REGIMENT DES CUNRAD PFENING
1549
26 Jib Close, Littlehampton, W. Sussex BN17 6TD
Contact: Sandra Goodwin
Tel/Fax: 01903 731804
Email: sandra_goodwin@yahoo.com

HARLECH MEDIEVAL COMBAT SOCIETY
2 Rock Villa, Criccieth, Gwynedd, Wales LL52 OED
Contact: Roger Clark
Tel: 01766 522089

THE HARRINGTON HOUSEHOLD
49 Washington Grove, Bentley, Doncaster, S. Yorkshire DN5 9RJ
Contact: Sally Ann Chandler
Tel: 01302 876343
Mobile: 0498 883379
Email: s.a.chandler@shu.ac.uk

HAUPTQUARTIER KOMPANIE
8 St Davids Close. Beverley, E. Yorkshire HU17 OUA
Contact: A Marsh
Pager: 0336 726839

HERBERT HOUSEHOLD
133 Tiverton Road, Basingstoke, Hants RG23 8EH
Contact: Jaki Lake
Tel: 0125 811571
Email: simon.dickinson@zurich.com

THE HERITAGE CENTRE
32 Lloyd, Road, Northampton
Contact: Andy Nettleship
Tel: 01604 638695
*HESSISCHE ARTILLERIE DG/FLG
Alt Griesheim 34, 65933 Frankfurt, Germany
Contact: Dieter Schule

*HESSISCHE JAEGER DG/FLG
Ringstrasse 3, 56739 Bermel, Germany
Contact: Klaus Westphale

*HIGHLAND BRIGADE (42ND & 79TH REGTs)
Postfach 1450, 65795 Hattersheim, Germany
Contact: Jurgen Weber

HELLEQUIN
133 Tiverton Road, Winklebury, Basingstoke RG23 8EH
Contact: Jaki Lake
Tel: 01256 811571
Email: captainbob@coma.freeserve.co.uk
Horse group for owner-riders and riders—male and female
welcome. Dfisplays for the public at historic sites or fayres.
Periods covered range from Norman to Medieval. Displays
of the skills and training of horsemen from history.

HEURISTICS
PO 5514, Matlock, Derbyshire DE4 5ZP
Contact: Don Holton
Mobile: 0860 966251
Email: don@heuristics.demon.co.uk
Website: www.heuristics.org.uk or www.thetudors.org.uk or
www.medievalrealms.org.uk
Specialist presentations on Medieval and Tudor history.
Education and entertainment. Subjects include: medicines,
herbs and spices, tile making, history of woolspinning and
weaving, history of the Hour (time), monasticism and the
monastic orders' history of games. A five hour show.

HISTORIC HAUTE CUISINE
105 Sandpit Lane, St.Albans, Hertf.ordshire AL4 0BW
Contact: Annie Thompson
Tel: 01727 857444

THE HISTORICAL NOVEL SOCIETY
Marine Cottage, The Strand, Starcross, Devon EX6 8NY
Contact: Richard Lee
Tel: 01626 891962

HISTORICAL PROMOTIONS
Bulstone Business Centre, Petrockstowe, Okehampton, Devon
EX20 3ET
Contact: Rob Butler
Tel/Fax: 01837 811243
Website: www.historicalpromotions@aol.com
Planning, management, promotion and delivery of
historical re-enactments and events for councils, historic
properties, museums, show organisers and heritage bodies.
We undertake costumed interpretation, living history and
multi-period spectaculars throughout the UK and abroad.
We provide service to film and television production com-
panies including historical extras, location services and
vehicles.

HISTRIONIX
Bromley Cottage, Overthorpe, Banbury, Oxfordshire OX17
Contact: David or Shona Rutherford-Edge
Tel: 01295 712677

HOI POLLOI
Ourse Cottage, Lingfield Common Road, Lingfield, Surrey RH7 6BZ
Contact: Andy Robertshaw
Tel: 01342 832167

HOLY ORDERS
17 Bramley Rise, Beccles, Suffolk
Contact: Dan Bolane
Tel: 01502 715005

THE HORDE (LOWESTOFT DARK AGE SOCIETY)
9 Crowhurst Close, Carton Coalvill Lowestoft, Suffolk
NR33 8SB
Contact: Jim Ward

HORRARIUM
176 Tom Lane, Sheffield, S. Yorkshire S10 3PG
Contact: Bill Greaves
Tel: 0114 2307051

HORSES HISTORICA
12 Ampthill Road, Shirley, Southampton, Hants SO15 8LP
Contact: Sue Grove
Tel: 02380 786849
Fax: 01296 630326
Mounted falconry & swordsmanship.

HOUNDS OF THE MORRIGAN
20 Myland Close, Oakridge Basingstoke, Hants RG21 5RB
Contact: Phil Roberts
Tel: 01256 353997

HOUSE OF BAYARD
2 Cottington Road, Hanworth Feltham, Middlesex TW13 6AJ
Contact: Richard Spicer
Tel: 020 8707 4566
Mobile: 0403 775 424

HOUSE OF GLAMORGAN
17 Hilltop Avenue, Cilfynydd, South Wales CF37 4HZ
Contact: Val Strange
Tel: 01443 493058

HOWARD'S RETINUE
25 Haldane Road, Rotherham, S. Yorkshire S65 1LR
Contact: Kerry Mullins
Tel: 01709 305421

HOWARD'S HOUSEHOLD
96 Walkley Road, Sheffield, South Yorkshire S6 2XP
Contact: John Ansari
Tel: 0114 233 8062

HUNGERFORD HOUSEHOLD
c/o 5 Camerton Close, Saltford, Bristol BS31 3BT
Contact: June Simpson
Tel: 01225 872586
Re-enactment of Tudor Domestic life. (Occasional late
medieval events). Available to houses, castles, museums
and private functions, mainly in Southwest England.

*LES HUSSARDS DE LASALLE (NAP)
7 Impasse des Balmes, F-78540 Villepreux, France
Contact: Jean-Pierre Mir
Re-enactment 7th and 5th Hussars Regiment, 2nd Horse
Artillery with one Gribauval four-pound gun.

*I G LUTZOWER FREICORPS 1813
Wilhelm-Michel-Strasse 13, 04249 Leipzig, Germany
Contact: Frank Zetzsche

INTER-MEDIEVAL
INTERNATIONAL MEDIEVAL ALLIANCE
c/o 18 Asgate Valley Road, Ashgate, Chesterfield, Derbyshire
S40 4AX
Contact: Roger Lankford
Tel: 01246 270090
Email: roger@lancaster-armry.demon.co.uk
Website: england@intermedieval.org
International Medieval Alliance is a dream—a new born
babe weened to bring together all the true knights and
merry medieval re-enactors from all over the world. A
brotherhood bound by honour and commitment to promote
our heritages for all.

*IZUM HUSSAR REGIMENT (NAP)
Flat 7, Leninst 132, Tulchin, Vinitza Region 288300raine
Contact: Vladimir Beltser

*JACOBITE REGIMENT (17TH/18TH centuries)
67 Avondale, Sligo, Co Sligo, Ireland
Contact: Noel Connolly

JACK TAR
52 St.Johns Road, Swalecliffe, Whitstable, Kent CT5 2RJ
Contact: Lynne Breft
Tel/Fax: 01227 792609

THE JACOBITES
32 Sandhill, Farnborough, Hampshire GU14 8EW
Contact: John Whalen
Mobile: 0410 761890
Fax: 01252 403701

JESSANT DE LIS
17 Manby Road, Immingham, Lincolnshire DN40 2LF
Contact: Romney
Tel: 01469 518888

JOMSVIKINGS
11a Waddicor Avenue, Ashton under-Lyne, Lancashire OL6 9HE
Contact: Mark Harrison
Tel: 0161 344 1324

KENTWELL HALL
Kentwell Hall, Long Melford, Sudbury, Suffolk CO10 9BA
Contact: Alex Scott
Tel: 01787 310207
Fax: 01787 379318
Email: info@kentwel.co.uk
Website: www.kentwell.co.uk
Mellow redbrick Tudor manor famed for award-winning
recreations. Volunteer groups and individuals always wel-
come to apply to take part in WWII and Home Front
events. Must have own uniform/costume and be prepared
to assume 'first person' role and authenticity. Phone (in
office hours) for form. Public and groups welcome to visit.

THE KINGMAKERS
1 Lyng Lane, North Lopham, Norfolk IP22 2HR
Contact: Duke Henry Plantagenet
Tel: 01953 681676
Email: kingmakers@calltoarms.com

KING'S COMMISSION OF ARRAY
6 Ivanhoe Villas, Escourt Street, Kingston-upon-Hull,
Humberside HU9 2SN
Contact: Tim Brown
Tel: 01482 588324
Email: tim.brown@kca2000.demon.co.uk

KING'S GERMAN LEGION
Flat 11, Marlborough Court, Marlborough Hill, Harrow
HA1 1UF
Contact: Dennis Wraight
Tel: 020 8861 0830
Website: www.kingsgermanlegion.org.uk
Re-enactment group comprising one light infantry battalion
and an artillery section. Members of the Napoleonic
Association. Battle re-enactment and living history displays.

THE KINGS PAGEANT
9 Savage Road, Plymouth, Devon PL5 1BP
Contact: Fleur West
Tel: 01752 367743

THE KNIGHTS OF ARKLEY
Glen Sylen Farm, Five Roads, Llanelli, Carmarthenshire,
Wales SAI5 5BJ
Contact: Penny Hard
Tel: 01269 861001
Email: knights@arkley.totalserve.co.uk
Website: www.knightsofarkley.com
Medieval jousting tournaments, corporate days, film, TV
and promotions. Vast selection of horse costumes, banners,
tents and props for hire. Medieval knights costumes made
to order. Consultancy service for all Medieval events.

KNIGHTS OF ASHBOURNE
19 Victoria Terrace, North Allerton, North Yorkshire
DL7 8TW
Contact: Trica Lovell,
Tel: 01609 778009
Email: t.lovell@pulse.york.ac.uk

KNIGHTS OF AVALON
9 Westcliff Road, Dawlish, Devon EX7 9EB
Contact: Michael Savva
Tel: 01626 888943

KNIGHTS IN BATTLE
96 Walkley Road, Sheffield, South Yorkshire S6 2XP
Contact: John Ansari
Tel: 0114 233 8062

KNIGHTS OF THE CRUSADES
Camelot, 14 Berkeley Wave, Heston, Hounslow, Middlesex
TW5 9HC
Contact: Michael Ellis
Tel: 020 8570 9073

THE KNIGHTS OF DEVONIA & THE KNIGHTS OF LEGEND
8 Mill Street, Crediton, Devon EX17 3AA
Contact: Andrew Turner
Tel: 01363 774502

KNIGHTS OF HERSTMONCEUX
Ground Floor, Three Brunswick Place, Hove, E. Sussex BN3 1EA
Contact: Clive Geisler
Tel: 01273 723249
Email: geisler@mgel.com
Website: www.mgel.com
We organise the Herstmonceux Castle Medieval Festival—
Britain's largest, held annually on the 500 acre castle sit
each August Bank Holiday Weekend. 10th anniversary year.
Re-enacting events covering the period 1379–1485—the
Wars of the Roses—based at Herstmonceux Castle.

KNIGHTS OF HONOUR
The Old Dairy Ground, Duns, Tew, Oxfordshire OX6 4JS
Contact: Andy Speicher
Tel: 01869 349000

KNIGHTS OF LONGSHANK
22 Clay Street, Bromley Cross, Bolton, Lancashire BL7 9BU
Contact: Paul Adamson
Tel: 01204 480022
Email: paul@longshank.co.uk

KNIGHTS OF ROYAL ENGLAND
Stocks Farm, Crowhurst, Lingfield, Surrey RH7 6LP
Contact: Jeremy Richardson
Tel: 01342 892811

KNIGHTS OF THE WHITE ROSE
18 Clover Road, Highfields, Sheffield, S. Yorkshire S2 4UP
Contact: Martin Bellamy
Tel: 0114 255 4059

THE KYNGS FEUDAL LEVY
Olwen Farm, Tregaron Road, Lampeter, Ceredigion, S. Wales
SA48 8LT
Adam Murray
Tel: 01570 423948
Email: The_english_lord@hotmall.com

L.A.M.B.S.(Landsknecht and Mercenary Battle Society)
29 Caledonian Road, Brighton, E. Sussex
Contact: Shane Tomkinson
Tel: 01273 231603

LACE WARS
26 Charter House Drive, Frome, Somerset BA11 2XT
Contact: Geoff King
Tel: 01373 452817

LANCASTER'S ARMOURIE
18 Ashgate Road, Ashgate, Chesterfield S40 4AX
Contact: Roger Lankford
Tel: 01246 270090
Email: roger@lancasters-armry.demon.co.uk
Website: lancasters-armry.demon.co.uk
Manufacturer's of medieval weapons and armour for full
contact medieval combat and martial arts specialists.

LEGACY
105 Vicarage Road, Mickleover, Derby DE3 5ED
Contact: Lee Carnwell
Mobile: 07971 584827
Email: thelegacygroup@hotmail.com

LEGIO 11 ADIUTRIX
32 St.Andrews Road, South, St.Annes, Lancashire FY8 1PS
Contact: Adrian Warrell
Tel: 01253 780401

LEGIO IX HISPANA
87 Langland Drive, Burton, Stoke-on-Trent, Staffs ST3 2ET
Contact: Mark Shore
Website: megamoose@cwctv.net
Academic research into the history of the 9th Legion
Hispana.

LEGIO SECUNDA AUGUSTA
61 Totland Road, Cosham, Hants PO6 3HS
Contact: David Richardson
Tel/Fax: 02392 369970
Email: legioaug@cwcom.net
Website: www.legiiaug.org.uk
Roman living history society, depicting the life and times
of mid 1st and 2nd Century Roman Britain. Military and
civilian aspects covered. We now present gladiators—as
they should be shown!

LEGIO VIII AUGUSTA MGV
2a Scaurbank Road, Carlisle, Cumbria CA3 9PH
Contact: Robin Brown or Cathryn Banks
Tel: 01228 593500
Email: robin.brown5@virgin.net

*LEGIO XIIII GEMINA MARTIA VICTRIX
Freiherr vom Stein 22, 55774 Baumholder, Germany
Contact: Daniel S Peterson

*LEIB-INFANTERIE-REGIMENT
Salierring 9, D-50677 K61n, Germany
Contact: Andreas Hetzert
Royal Prussian Line infantry.

*LEIBGARDE-GRENADIER REGIMENT 1813
Heinrichsruher Weg 3, 03238 Finsterwalde, Germany
Contact: Uwe Bergmann

LINCOLN CASTLE GARRISON
75 Lincoln Road, Ruskington, Sleaford, Lincolnshire
NG34 9AR
Contact: Emma Cooper
Tel: 01526 833737

THE LION RAMPANT MEDIEVAL RE-ENACTMENT SOCIETY
2 Hillside, Totteridge, High Wycombe, Buckinghamshire
HP13 7LG
Contact: Izzy Legg
Tel: 01494 473129

LIONHEART COMPANY OF BOWMEN
209 Thorpe Road, Melton Mombray, Leicestershire LE13 1SH
Contact: Richard Drewe
Tel: 01664 852837 or 01664 564079
Email: drewe@supanet.com

LIVERY & MAINTENANCE
12 Shakespeare Street, Long Eaton, Nottinghamshire
NG10 4L
Contact: Neil McGurk
Tel: 0115 972 1009

LONGSHIP TRADING COMPANY
342 Albion Street, Wall Heath, Kingswinford, W. Midlands
DY6 0JR
Contact: Ivor Wilcox
Tel: 01384 292237
Email: info@longship.org.uk
Website: www.longship.org.uk
Viking & Saxon Education Days in schools and museums, corporate entertainment, displays, banquets, craft displays, costume hire, film, TV and theatre work. Prop weapon and armour hire.

LORD SCROPE HYS BATTERY
93 Cross Lane, Scarborough, North Yorkshire YO12 6DL
Contact: W Black
Tel: 01723 366214

LORDS OF THE RINGS
55 Marsden Road, Eastbourne, E. Sussex BN23 7EE
Contact: Angela Jupp
Tel: 01323 461925

LOTHENE EXPERIMENTAL ARCHAEOLOGY
127 Bruntsfield Place, Edinburgh, Lothian, Scotland
EH10 4EQ
Contact: Alastair Saunders
Tel: 0131 229 9466
Email: nicky@lothene.demon.co.uk
Website: www.lothene.demon.co.uk
Lothene researches and recreates aspects of life in South East Scotland, particularly in the 11th, 13th, 14th and 15th centuries.

*LUTZOW'S FREICORPS (NAP)
Sander Strasse 3a, 21029 Hamburg, Germany
Contact: Ulf Kretschmann

*LYS ET LION
7 Allie des Troenes, 59650 Villeneuve d'Ascq, France
Contact: Dom Delgrange

LYGTUM RAIDERS
76 Trident Drive, Houghton Regis, Dunstable, Bedfordshire LU5 5QG
Contact: Sally or Andy Chillmaid
Tel: 01582 882272

MACSWEENY GALLOGLASS
Mariebank House, Longdon, Tewkesbury, Glos GL20 6AR
Contact: Chris or Hannah While
Tel: 01684 295598

MADDOGS HISTORICAL RE-ENACTMENT GROUP
10 Bowhays Walk, Eggbuckland, Plymouth, Devon PL6 5SH
Contact: Wayne Pearce
Tel: 01752 786839

MAHAREN
180 The Mallards, Leominster, Herefordshire HR6 8UN
Contact: Liz Dolloway
Tel: 01568 613938

MAISNIE NICOLAS
44 Poppyfields, Welwyn Garden City, Hertfordshire AL7 2HJ
Contact: Colin Kendal
Tel/Fax: 01707 339258 or 01707 895428

THE MARCHER KNIGHTS
490 Bryn Road, Aston in Makerfield, Lancashire WN4 8AN
Contact: Anna Louise Calder
Tel: 01942 274655

THE MEDICOS
Ourse Cottage, Lingfield Common Road, Lingfield, Surrey RH7 6B2
Contact: Andy Roberdhaw
Tel: 01342 832167
Fax: 01342 836860
The Medicos was formed to recreate the Royal Army Medical Corps 1914–1918. Projects so far have included film and television work, museum based events and an annual recreation of a dressing station on the Somme.

MEDIEVAL COMBAT SOCIETY
Flat 2, Clyde House, 93 Surbiton Road, Kingston, Surrey KT1 2HW
Contact: David Debono
Tel: 020 8541 0146
Email: david@novarltd.demon.co.uk

THE MEDIEVAL FREE COMPANY
8 Back Lane, Marshfield, Chippenham, Wiltshire
SN14 8NQ
Contact: Helen Ruddell
Tel: 01225 891832
Email: userstumpy@aol.com

MEDIEVAL HERITAGE SOCIETY
18 Corfe Crescent, Wiltshire SN11 9EB
Contact: Tina Stokes
Tel: 01249 812946
Fax: 01249 811359
Email: medievalheritagesociety@calne9l.freeserve.co.uk

MEDIEVAL SIEGE SOCIETY
57 Church Road, Bexley Heath, Kent DA7 4DL
Contact: Sheila Naylor
Tel: 020 8303 5640

MEDIEVAL SOCIETY
Newlands, Orpington Road, Badgers Mount, Sevenoaks, Kent
TN14 7AQ
Contact: John Asmus
Tel: 01959 534256
Mobile: 0374 458438
Fax: 01689 850917

MEDIEVAL SUPPLIES
20 Weaver Drive, Western Downs, Stafford, Staffs ST17 9DD
Contact: Neil Butler
Tel/Fax: 01785 243637
Email: butlerneil@aol.com
Hand made padded jacks, gambasons, akatons, coates of plates, and brigandines for full contact fighting, from the 5th to the 15th century. We also make clothing for the same period.

MELFORD HYS COMPANIE
c/o Wotwayin, The Street, Great Barton, Bury St Edmunds, Suffolk IP31 2NP
Contact: Hal Wagstaff
Tel: 01284 788128
Email: tudorhal@tesco.net
Melford Hys Companie are a group of re-enactors who recreate the lives of travelling players between the late Medieval through Tudor periods. We also specialise in domestic re-enactment, we maintain first person—staying in role while open to the public. Many and varied plays, dances, sports and cartts. We interact with the visitors not demonstrate to them.

MERCIA SVEITER
Rosemary Cottage, Camp Road, Canwell, Sutton Coldfield B75 5RA
Contact: Paul Craddock
Tel/Fax: 0121 323 4309
Email: MerciaS@hotmail.com
Website: MerciaS.co.uk
We specialise in equipment for re-enactors between 500-1500 AD. We do cauldrons, chain mail (links & ready-made), horns, swords, helmets, pressed shield bosses and loads of jewellery! We are based near Birmingham and have our own historical site See Dark Ages Charitable.

MERCENARIE GILD
Ffos Yr Ewig, Llanfynydd, Carmarthen, Wales IA32 7DD
Contact: Michael Hickling
Tel/Fax: 01558 668771
Email: michael@ab-figures.demon.co.uk

MILITARY HERALDRY SOCIETY
37 Wolsey Close, Southall, Middlesex UB2 4NQ
Contact: Lt Cdr W Thornton MBE
Tel: 020 8574 4425

MILITARY MUSIC RE-ENACTORS SOCIETY
17 Booth Street, Handsworth Birmingham, W. Midlands B21 0NG
Contact: Trevor Horne
Tel: 0121 554 8170

MILITARY ODYSSEY
PO Box 254, Marden, Tonbridge, Kent TN12 9ZQ
Contact: Gary Howard
Tel/Fax: 01892 730233
Email: militaryodyssey@aol.com
Website: www.military-odyssey.com
The country's largesr multi-period historical living history extravaganza. Over 400+ trade stalls, over 400 military vehicles. Displays and dioramas; battle re-creations; children's sactivities. A packed weekend for all—too much to be seen in one day. Historical 'In Camp' Talks—from the Romans through to the Gulf War.

MILWRMORGANWG
66 Caefelinparc, Hirwaun, Mid Glamorgan, Wales CF44 9QQ
Contact: Eric Bool
Tel: 01685 811747
Email: admin@milwr.freeserve.co.uk

*MUSIQUE DE LA GARDE (NAP)
Avenue Prince Charles 18, B-1410 Waterloo, Belgium
Contact: Pierre Grapin

NAPOLEONIC ASSOCIATION
16 Manor Park, Maids Moreton, Bucks MK18 1QY
Contact: Ed Parker
Tel: 01280 815844
Email: edwin_parker@hotmail.com
More than just a re-enactment society, the Napoleonic Association represents the interests of everyone with an interest in this period of history, whether re-enactors, wargamers or researchers. Members regularly participate in a variety of events and activities throughout the UK and in Europe. Over 25 affiliated organisations.

*NAPOLEONISCHE GESELLSCHAFT (ADMIN BODY)
Zum Rott 19, D-49078 Osnabruck, Germany
Contact: Karl-Heinz Lange
Tel: 54148850
Fax: 54148070
Admin body for Napoleonic re-enactment in Germany; some 20 affiliated regiments include Prussian Line and Landwehr, KGL, Brunswickers, French, and Confederation of the Rhine units.

THE NATIONAL ASSOCIATION OF RE-ENACTMENT SOCIETIES
9 Durleigh Close, Headley Park, Bristol BS13 7NQ
Contact: J Kim Sidhorn
NARES acts as a professional association for re-enactment societies. Representing over 80% of British re-enactors, applications are welcome from independent societies re-creating any period of history. However, membership is not available to individuals.

NEW FRANCE & OLD ENGLAND
54 Lower Whitelands, Radstock, Bath BA3 3JP
Contact: Ralph Mitchard
Tel: 01761 437543
Email: ralph@rmitchard.freeserve.co.uk

NEW JERSEY PROVINCIAL REGIMENT (JERSEY BLUES)
7 Arcadia Way, Trevethin, Pontypool, South Wales
NP4 8DX
Contact: Allan Jones
Tel: 01495 750479
Email: 23@lightbob.freeserve.co.uk

NOBLE ALLIANCE
Contact: Martin de Sutton
Hauyhton Cottage, Neen Sollars, Worcestershire DY14 0AH
Tel: 01299 270938

NORFOLK'S LONGBOWMEN
1 Trunel Road, Swafield, Norfolk NR28 6PF
Contact: Rachel Everett
Tel: 01692 406661

NORTH DEVON JOUSTING ASSOCIATION
8 Mill Street, Crediton, Devon EX17 3AA
Contact: Andrew Turner
Tel: 01363 77450

NORTH GUARD
8 Leechmere Way, Ryhope, Sunderland, Tyne & Wear
SR2 0DH
Contact: Eddie Barrass
Tel/Fax: 0191 523 6377
Email: eddie-roman@ic24.net
Website: http://www.northguard.freeservers.com

*NORTH HISTORICAL (ACW)
41 Avenue Gabriel Peri, 91550, Paray-Vielle-Poste, France
Contact: Jean-Claude Renaudi

NORTHAMPTON MEDIAEVAL SOCIETY—KNIGHTS OF THE ROSE
6 Simons Walk, Spring Borough, Northampton NN1 2SR
Contact: Joe Joyce
Tel: 01604 631 442
Mobile: 07768 982637
Fax: 01604 238338
Email: joe.a.joyce@royalmail.co.uk
Website: www.kotrnet.co.uk
Medieval campaign camp set up and craft demonstrationc
circa 1300-1450.

NORTHAMPTONSHIRE YEOMANRY CAVALRY
120 Penrhyn Road, Northampton NN4 8ED
Contact: Rachel Watts
Tel: 01604 706501

NORTHLAND MERCENARIES—CORNISH SVIETER
Merton Cottage, Tregatta, Tintagel, Cornwall PL34 0DY
Contact: Raven
Tel: 01840 770381

NORTHLAND MERCENARIES—DERBY SVIETER
152 Borrowfield Road; Spondon, Derbyshire DE21 7HG
Contact: Lyn or Jon Allen
Tel: 01332 669049
Mobile: 0411 298354

NORWICH & NORFOLK MEDIEVAL ASSOCIATION
60 Holworthy Road, Bowthorpe, Norwich, Norfolk
Contact: Simon Ireson
Tel: 01603 748890

ORDER OF THE GOLDEN TREE
21 Harebill Way, Rugby, Warwickshire CV23 0TT
Contact: Nick Musson
Tel: 01788 560345
Mobile: 0802 403970

ORDER OF THE POOR KNIGHTS OF CHRIST & THE TEMPLE OF SOLOMAN—KNIGHTS TEMPLAR
39 Penistone Road, Middlesbrough. North Yorkshire TS3 0DJ
Contact: Jonathan Ealsby

ORDRE OF THE BLAK PRYNS
52 St Johns Road, Swalecliffe, Whitstable, Kent CT5 2RJ
Contact: Lynne Brett
Tel/Fax: 01227 792609
or
The Thatch Cottage, 140 Canterbury Road, Lydden, Kent CT15 7ET
Contact: John or Carol
Tel: 01304 830535

OVERLORD LIVING HISTORY ASSOCIATION
Trustee Farm, Old Fen Bank, Wainfleet, Skegness,
Lincolnshire PE24 4LA
Contact: John Wheatley
Tel: 01754 882764

OXFORD OUTLAWS
22 Halliday Hill, Headington, Oxford OX3 9PU
Contact: Carl Sprake
Tel: 01665 451904
Fax: 0870 125 4797
Email: outlaws@casnet.co.uk

PALADINS OF CHIVALRY
28 Hindhead Point, Wanborough Drive, Roehampton, London
SW15 4AW
Contact: Chris Skinner
Tel/Fax: 020 8789 848
Email: information@knights-resources.co.uk or
erpl4l5@paladins-of-chivalry.freeserve.co.uk

PERCY HOUSEHOLD
176 Tom Lane, Fuliwood, Sheffield, South Yorkshire S10 3PG
Contact: Darren Greaves
Tel: 0114 230 7051

PERIOD FENCERS GUILD
18 Broad Meadow Lane, Kings Norton, Birmingham,
W. Midlands B30 3NS
Contact: Mark Vance
Tel: 0121 628 3127
Email: mark@sword-dance.co.uk
Website: www.sword-dance.co.uk
Dedicated to the study and demonstration of western
martial arts from the 12th century through to the 19th
century, based upon the surviving texts of Talhoffer,
Marozzo, DiGrassi, Fiore, Capo Aerro, Angels etc.

PERSHING'S DOUGHBOYS
46 Simons Walk, Pattishall, Northamptonshire NN12 8NK
Contact: Howard. Aran
Tel: 01327 830812
Email: 106402.713@compuserve.com

PLANTAGENET MEDIEVAL SOCIETY
37 Willowslea Road, Worcester WR3 7QP
Contact: J Kerslake,
Tel: 01905 455192
Email: 106671.1672@compuserve.com

THE PLYMOUTH LEVY MEDIEVAL SOCIETY
59 Embankment Road, St.Judes, Plymouth, Devon PL4 9HX
Contact: Helen Harris-Beaumont
Tel: 01752 662311
Medieval society trhat re-enacts the period 1350–1450.
We bring history to life through tournament combat
displays between armoured knights, squires and men at
arms. We also portray lords and ladies at court through
Medieval dancing.

*LE POILU DE LA MARNE (WWI)
10 Rue Bourg de Vesles, 51480 Fleury la Riviere, France
Contact: Didier Blanchard

POOR KNIGHTS OF ST DYSMAS
27 Winchester Avenue, Chadderton, Oldham, Lancshire
L9 0RH
Contact: Paul Turner
Tel: 0161 628 8368
Email: poor_knights@hotmail.com,

PORTSDOWN ARTILLERY VOLUNTEERS
2 Chapel Lane, Blackwater, Surrey GU17 9ET
Contact: Ian Main
Tel: 01276 32011

*PREUSSISCHE FELDDRUCKEREI 1813
Davidstrasse 3, Leipzig 04109, Germany
Contact: Peter Mechler

RAGGED STAFF MEDIEVAL SOCIETY
14 Dingle Dell, Leighton Buzzard, Bedfordshire
LU7 7JL
Contact: Michael Oates
Tel: 01525 853257
Mobile:0913 279668
Email: karenoates@virgin.net

*RATATOSKA HEIM & WARAGER (DARK AGES)
Uhlandstrasse 3, 30851 Langenhagen, Niedersachsen,
Germany
Contact: Michael Stadtler

THE RAVEN
35 Carnarvon Rd, Leyton, London E10 6DW
Contact: Jeanette Ellis
Tel: 0208539 3569
Email: caduceuspaganfestivals.com
The Raven, with a few other groups in this country are trying to revive the Celtic/Medieval art of Gianting. Our
Giantess is 15 1/2 foot tall, THE MORRIGAN is carried by
only one person (handmade by Paul and Jeanette). She
like all Goddesses, has a retinue of devoted followers,
drummers, sword bearers, and other motley crew, all in
costume making a rather grand site and a loud noise!!

RAVEN TOR
32 St Clares Gardens, North Bersted, Bognor Regis,
W. Sussex PO21 5UD
Contact: Anna Frances
Tel: 01243 829897

THE REAVERS DARK AGE COMBAT SOCIETY
14 Wren Close, Heathfield E. Sussex TN21 8HG
Contact: E T or K M Bradfield
Tel: 01435 863993
Mobile: 0410 86179

THE RED GAUNTLET MEDIEVAL SOCIETY
11e The Square, Wingham
Contact: Gary Hughes
Tel: 0976 661275

THE RED WYVERN SOCIETY
New House, Murton, Appleby in Westmoreland, Cumbria
CA16 6N
Contact: Adrian & Elaine Waite
Tel/Fax: 01768 351498
Mobile: 07971 321863

REGIA ANGLORUM
9 Durleigh Close, Headley Park, Bristol BS13 7NQ
Contact: J K Siddorn
Tel: 0117 964 6818
Email: 101364.35@compuserve.com

RENT A PEASANT
104 Dan's Castle, Tow Law, Bishop Auckland, Durham
DL13 4BB
Contact: Louisa Gidney
Tel/Fax: 01388 731848
Email: ljgidney@durham.ac.uk

RING OF STEEL
2 Rock Villa, Criccieth, Gwynedd, Wales LL52 0ED
Contact: Roger Clark
Tel: 01766 522089

THE RINGWOODS OF HISTORY
34 Sandford Road, Mapperley, Nottingham NG3 6AL
Contact: Ralph Needham
Tel: 0115 9692922
Accurately costumed historical presentations from Viking to WWII Home Guard. Specialist subject 17th Century military surgery. We provide lectures for schools, historic sites and history groups anywhere in the UK. For further details please contact us at the above.

ROMAN MILITARY RESEARCH SOCIETY
23 Gilbert Scott Court, Towcester, Northamptonshire
NN12 6DX
Contact: Mark Olejnik
Tel: 01327 353370
Email: suavis@nationwideisp.net

ROSA MUNDI
53 Dene Street, Silksworth, Sunderland, Tyne & Wear
SR3 1DA
Tel: 0191 522 0903
Email: scroopisec@hotmail.com
Rosa Mundi work to the highest standards of research and practical skills to present all aspects of military and domestic life of the late 15th century (1475-1500). Our hierarchical military structure demonstrates the skills and technologies of late Medieval warfare using authentic period fighting techniques.

ROUGH DIAMONDS
Bwlch, Beguildy, Powys ILD7 IUG
Contact: Barry Carter
Tel: 01547 510289

R S A M—BOARD OF ORDNANCE ROYAL SAPPERS & MINERS
26 Jib Close, Littlehampton, W. Sussex BN17 6TD
Contact: Sandra Goodwin
Tel/Fax: 01903 731804
Email: sandra_goodwin@yahoo.com

RUADAIN REIVERS GAELIC WARBAND
85 Healey Road, Ossett, West Yorkshire WF5 8LT
Contact: Sarah Mawson
Tel: 01924 306641 (work)

*RUSSISCH-DEUTSCHE LEGION (IR NR 31)
Prager Strasse 345, 04289 Leipzig, Germany
Contact: Uwe Meyer

RYE MEDIEVAL SOCIETY
Half House, Military Road, Rye, E. Sussex TN31 7NY
Contact: Norman Bennett
Tel: 01797 223404

*SACHSICHE FELDPOST
Blumenstrasse 12, 04445 Liebertwolkwitz, Germany
Contact: Peter Hainke

*SACHSISCHES I R PRINZ CLEMENTZ
Rathausstrasse 40,04416, Markkleeberg, Germany
Contact: Otto Schaubs

SAMHAIN WELSH MEDIEVAI SOCIETY
Bag End, 13 Castle Street, Caergwrle, Flintshire
LL12 9DW
Contact: Michael Roberts
Tel: 01978 762845
Email: studio@chronicle.u-net.com

*SCHINDERHANNES-BANDE
Lucas-Cranach-Strasse 2, 65527, Niedernhausen, Germany
Contact: Jutta Seliger

*SCHLESISCHE LANDWEHR 1813 E.V.
Mijhlstrasse 50 (Im Museum), 04435 Schkeuditz, Germany
Contact: Joerg Rojahn

SCROPE'S HOUSEHOLD
Pebble Forge, North Cawton, North Allerton, North Yorkshire
DL7 OHG
Contact: John or Lesley Thurston
Tel: 01325 37869

S.C.U.M. (SOUTH COAST UNAFFILIATED MERCENARIES)
115A Preston Road, Brighton, E. Sussex BN1 6AF
Contact: Dawn Rowatt
Tel: 01273 505741
or
46 Buckingham Road, Brighton, E. Sussex BNI 3RQ
Contact: Shaun Benjamin
Tel: 01273 770060

SEALED KNOT
PO Box 2000, Nottingham, Notts NG2 5LH
Contact: Ian Allen
Tel: 01384 295939
Email:info@sealedknot.org

*SECHSPFUNDIGE FUGBATTERIE No. 3
Im Rottfeld la, D-40239 Dusseldorf, Germany
Contact: Dr. Martin Kloffler
Royal Prussian Artillery 1813–1815. Special fields of interest: reconstruction of historical artillery equipment of the Napoleonic era.

SHIRE OF INSULA DRACONIS (SCA)
31 Green Road, Didcot, Oxfordshire OX11 8SY
Contact: Hywel Phillips
Tel: 01235 211283

SHIRE OF NEW EGAILL
Top Right, 15 Forest Park Road, Dundee, Scotland
DDI 5NZ
Contact: Douglas Clark
Tel: 01382 200431
Mobile: 0468 765734
Email: idakin@hotmail.com

SHOGUN
4 Yarmouth Road, Stevenage Hertfordshire SG1 2LW
Contact: Dean Wayland
Tel: 01438 368177
Fax: 01438 229337

SHRAPNEL'S BATTERY
9 Firgrove Hill, Farnham, Surrey GU9 8LH
Contact: Brian Miller
Tel: 01252 721332
1770s British Royal Artillery. Fully uniformed demonstrations of flintlock pistol, musket, mortar and field guns, along with explanations of technical details and the lifestyle of the men who served with the guns. Also tactics used by infantry, cavalry and artillery explained—ammunition used—its range and effects. Demonstrations of casting, linstock, quill making and flint knapping.

SIEGE GROUP
Flat 11, Marlborough Court, Marlborough Hill, Harrow, Middlesex HA1 1UF
Contact: Dennis Wraight
Tel: 020 8861 0830

SILURES IRON AGE CELTIC SOCIETY
25 High Beech Road, Bream, Lydney, Forest of Dean
Contact: Elaine Connelly
Tel: 01594 563278

SIR JOHN PASTON'S HOUSEHOLD
14 Hillside Road, Teg Down, Winchester, Hants SO22 5NW
Contact: Ian Lawson
Tel: 01962 853188
This high quality living history group mainly covering the period 1469-1471 is based on the employees of John Paston III. Although most demonstrations are of a military nature, general crafts are also covered. Source material is taken from the Paston Letters.

SIR THOMAS BURGH, HYS HOUSEHOLD & RETINUE
1 Marsh Lane, Carlton Colville, Lowestoft, Suffolk NR33 8BW
Contact: Ian Pycroft

SIR WILLIAM,GASCOIGNEL'S FELLOWSHIP OF SIR HENRY PERCY, EARL OF NORTHUMBERLAND ARRAY
12 Shakespeare Street, Long Eaton, Nottinghamshire NG10 4LW
Contact: Vicky Shearman
Tel: 0115 972 1009
Email: saxvjs@nottingham.ac.uk

THE SMOKEY DRAGON ARTILLERY COMPANY
12 Ribble Way, Riverdene, Basingstoke, Hants RG21 4DL
Contact: G Steele
Tel: 01256 414615
Mobile: 0441 097931 or 0777 1558862

SOCIETY OF ARCHER-ANTIQUARIES
61 Lambert Road, Bridlington, East Yorkshire YO16 5RD
Contact: Douglas Elm
Tel: 01262 601604

SOMERSET'S HOUSEHOLD
9 Westland Grove, Westland, Sheffield, South Yorkshire S20 8BU
Contact: John Naylor
Tel: 01793 524465
Email: tinker@uk-99.yahoo.com

SOUTHERN SKIRMISH ASSOCIATION
318 Cricklade Road, Swindon, Wiltshire SN2 6AY
Contact: May Griffiths
Tel: 01793 524465
American Civil War battle re-enactment and living history.

*SPECTACLE ET CHEVALERIE (MED)
La Ferte-Clairbois, 53270 Chammes, Maine 53270, France
Contact: Gilles Raab
Promotion and demonstration of the XIIIth Knightly ideal and associated virtues, by means of historical reconstruction and artistic celebration.

SPIRIT OF ENGLAND MEDIEVAL THEATRE COMPANY
48 Noel Street, Hyson Green, Nottingham NG7 6AW
Contact: Tony Rotherham
Tel: 0115 847 8735
Mobile: 0790 902 4019

ST BARBARA'S CLUB WITH SHRAPNEL'S BATTERY, ROYAL ARTILLERY
9 Firgrove Hill, Tolworth, Surrey GU9 8LH
Contact: Brian Miller
Tel: 01252 721332

STAFFORD HOUSEHOLD
248 Wetmore Road, Burton-on-Trent, Staffs DE14 1RB
Contact: Graham Smith Tel/Fax: 01283 517871

THE STAFFORDSHIRE LEVY
87 Langland Drive, Blurton, Stoke-on-Trent, Staffs ST3 2ET
Contact: Mark Shore
Email: megamoose.com@cwctu.net
Large scale battle re-enactments and film work only.

THE STEEL BONNETS (BORDER REIVERS)
Ennismor, 12 Marske Road, Saltburn-by-the-Sea, N. Yorkshire; TS12 1PZ
Contact: Lanette Dineley
Tel: 01287-625744
Email: secretary@reivers.demon.co.uk

STEPHEN & MATILDA GROUP
16 Monks Way, Eastleigh, Hants SO50 5BD
Contact: Mike Betteridge
Tel: 023 8034 3290
Email: spanner60@telinco.co.uk

SUSSEX GODINS
56 Finiahs Field Barns Green, Horsham, W. Sussex RH13 7NQ
Contact: Richard M Hobbs
Tel: 01403 732171

SUSSEX HISTORICAL NAVAL UNIT
Redoubt Fortress, Royal Parade, Eastbourne, E. Sussex BN22 7AQ
Tel: 01323 410300
Email: redoubt@breathmail.net
The history of the Royal Navy in Sussex. Our section is part of the military living history at the fortress. We also research all maritime subjects that relate to Sussex.

SUSSEX LEVY
54 Willow Way, Hurstpierpoint, W. Sussex BN6 9TJ
Contact: Richard Fitch
Tel/Fax: 01273 834822
Email: richardj.fitch@virgin.net

SWORDS OF PENDRAGON
34 Walpole Road, Great Yarmouth, Norfolk NR30 4NF
Contact: Henry King
Tel: 07010 709330 or 07010 709331
Mobile: 07010 709332
Email: swords@macula-arma.co.uk

TALBOT HOUSEHOLD
10 St.Wilfred's, Road, Worthing, W. Sussex BN14 8BA
Contact: John or Coral Beer
Tel: 01903 523459

TALBOT RETINUE
40 Rugeley Road, Armitage, Rugeley WS15 4BD
Contact: Steve Carthy
Tel: 01543 492687

THOMAS LEWIS OF ST. PIERRE HERBERT'S RETINUE
18 Sandy Lane, Caldicot, Monmouthshire NP6 4NA
Contact: Mike or Angie Day
Tel: 01291 422146

*TÊTE DE COLONNE, GARDE GRENADIERS (NAP)
BP 1510, Hotel de Ville, 21033 Dijon Cedex, France

THOMAS, LORD BURGH KG's RETINUE 1460–1496
54 Grantham Road, Waddington, Lincoln, Lincolnshire
LN5 9LS
Contact: Paul Mason
Tel: 07762 300656
Fax: 01522 875763
Email: lordburgh@aol.com
Website: www.lord-burgh.com
Social and military re-enactment and living history from
the Wars of the Roses, based within a knight's household.
Featuring cookery, religion, arms & armour, clothes, hands-
on archery, talks & demonstrations. Available for film & TV
work. Period covered 1460–1496.

THREE SHIRES MEDIEVAL SOCIETY
65 Friar Gate Court, Friar Gate, Derby DE1 1HF
Contact: Betty Taylor
Tel: 01332 29996

*TIRAILLEURS CORSES (NAP)
Villa Erbajola, Chemin du Finosello, 20090 Ajaccio, Corsica
Contact: Rene Chazivin

*TRADITIONSCORPS 1813 FINSTERWALDE
Brandenburger Strasse 53, 03238 Finsterwalde, Germany
Contact: Hans Michael Hillebrandt

TRAILBLAZERS WESTERN RE-ENACTORS ASSOCIATION
38 Harewood Road, Harrogate, North Yorkshire HG3 2TW
Contact: Tony Rollins
Tel: 01423 502442
Website: www.4thcavalry.co.uk
We are a Western re-enactment and living history association who enjoy researching and recreating all aspects of
19th century American life. Based in Yorkshire we can
often be seen at the Yorkshire Farming Museum, York, as
4th Cavalry. Available for shows as a means of raising
funds for charity.

TROOP OF SHEW–KING'S LIFEGUARD HORSE
120 Penrhyn Road, Northampton NN4 9ED
Contact: Stanley Wafts
Tel: 01604 706501

TUATH DEORAD
41 Clifford Avenue, Portobello Wakefield, W. Yorkshire
WF2 7LF
Contact: Linda Rigby
Tel: 01924 210851

THE TUDOR GROUP
16 Lower Street, Quainton, Buckinghamshire HP22 4BJ
Contact: Ruth Goodman
Tel: 01296 655309

TUDOR HOUSEHOLD
19 Down Terrace Brighton, E. Sussex BN2 2ZJ
Contact: Paul Hull
Tel: 01273 700025

*U S ARMY RECONSTITUTION GROUP (WWII)
9 Rue Desmazieres, 59110 La Madeleine, France
US Navy 'Seabees'; GIs of the 29th Infantry Division; 1st
Bn. Gordon Highlanders of 51st HD; or French Fusiliers-
Marins, all with correct drill.

*USMC (WWII)
89 Les Fontinettes, 59620 Leval, France
Contact: Bertrande Dejonghe

*UNION OF EUROPEAN MILITARY-HISTORICAL CLUBS
Schonburgstrasse 50/17, A-1040 Wien, Austria
Contact: Friedrich Nachazel
The Union embraces all respective groups in Europe for
common fostering of military traditions in Europe, currently
in 16 countries.

VALE OF THE RED HORSE BOWMEN
School House, Queensway School, Brentwood Rise, Banbury,
Oxon OX16 9NF
Contact: Colin Hewitt
Tel: 01295 251631

THE VAUGHAN HOUSEHOLD OF TRETOWER
20 Weaver Drive, Western Downs, Staffordshire ST17 9DD
Contact: Neil Butler or Richard Illman
Tel: 01785-243637
Email: butlerneil@aol.com

VENTA SILURUM 456
18 Sandy Lane, Caldicot, Monmouthshire, Scotland NP6 4NA
Contact: Mike & Angie Day
Tel: 01291 422146

VEXILLATIO LEGIONIS GEMINAE
23 Gilbert Scott Court, Towcester, Northamptonshire
NN12 6DX
Contact: Mark Olejnik
Tel: 01327 7353370
Email: suavis@nationwideisp.net

VI VICTRICS PIA FIDELI
8 Leechmere. Way, Ryhope, Sunderland, Tyne & Wear
SR2 0DH
Contact: Eddie Barrass
Tel: 0191 523 6377

*VICTORY ASSOCIATION (WWII)
BP 36, 01480 Jassans-Riottier, France
Contact: Pascal Raymond
The Victory Association specialises in films, re-enactments, etc. in France and abroad. We are also looking for new members in Europe, the USA and the Commmonwealth.

VICTORIAN MEDICAL SOCIETY
17 Park Road, Southville Road, Bristol BS3 1PU
Contact: Chris Jordan
Tel: 0117-953-8710
Vicmed@hotmail.com
We are a small group of enthusiasts who portray in costume (English Navy and Confederate), a smal Victorian Field Hospital. Most of our medical and pharmaceutical equipment is original from the period. We give talks to the public on conditions of the period and the use of the equipment.

VICTORIAN PRISON RE-ENACTMENT
Friends of Lincoln Castle, 7 Chestnut Close, Ludbrooke, Lincolnshire LN2 2RD
Contact: Jane Briggs
Tel: 01522 752955

VICTORY IN EUROPE RE-ENACTMENT ASSOCIATION (V.E.R.A.)
PO Box 64, Pontefract, West Yorkshire
Tel: 01642 619081
Fax: 01642 624337

VIETNAM HLZ
Contact: Ken or Tracy Sturgeon
Tel: 01892 667795
The living museum, in respect and recognition of American military commitment in Vietnam.

THE VIKING EXPERIENCE
12 Cefnfaes Street, Bethesda, Gwynedd, Wales LL57 3BW
Contact: R Scott
Tel: 01248 600605

THE VIKINGS
2 Stanford Road, Shefford, Bedfordshire SG17
Contact: Sandra Orchard
Tel: 01462 812208
Email: sandra.orchard@roche.com
Many affiliated local/provincial organisations and warbands.

*VOLKERSCHLACHT LEIPZIG 1813
Im Alten Rathaus, Markt 1, 04109 Leipzig, Germany
Contact: Stefan Poser

THE VOLUNTEER CORPS OF FRONTIERSMEN
57 Bush Hill, Weston Favell, Northampton NN3 2PD
Tel: 01604 408942

WARRIORS OF THE SKULL
4a High Street, Great Dunmow, Essex CM6 IAG
Contact: Jahni Fitzsamuel-Nicholls
Tel: 01371 875838

WAR MACHINE
BCM Box 220, London WC1N 3XX
Contact: Stuart Andrews
Tel: 020 8809 6119

THE WARLORDS DISPLAY TEAM
14 Wren Close, Heathfield, E. Sussex TN21 8HG
Contact: E T or K M Bradfield
Tel: 0145 863993
Mobile: 0410 861796

WARS OF THE ROSES FEDERATION
43 Vera Crescent, Rainworth, Muhsfield, Nottinghamshire NG21 0EU
Contact: Dominic Sewell
Tel: 01623 797485

WARSAW PACT FORCES GROUP
Contact: David Brennan
Email: dave@iconism.net
We are a group of collectors who respectfully and correctly depict the forces of the Eastern Bloc during the Cold War period of the last century. The WPFG is a non-political organisation which wishes to advance living history through the enthusiasm and enjoyment of its members.

WARWICK CASTLE GARRISON
18 Broad Meadow Lane, Kings Norton, Birmingham, W. Midlands
Contact: Mark Vance
Tel: 0121 628 3127
Email: mark@sword-dance.co.uk

WESSEX DARK AGES SOCIETY
23 Eddison Avenue, Fordington, Dorchester, Dorset DT1 1NX
Contact: Stacie Shane
Tel: 01305 266315

THE WESTMORELAND YEOMEN
48 Macadam Way, Penrith, Cumbria CA11 9HF
Contact: Joseph Jackson
Tel: 01768 868436
Email: longswordl461@yah6o.com

WHITE BOAR FIGHT CREW
48 Noel Street, Hyson Green Nottingham NG7 6AW
Contact: Tony Rotherham
Tel: 0115 847 8735
Mobile 0790 902 4019

THE WHITE COMPANY
1 Upgate, Poringland, Norwich, Norfolk NR14 7S
Contact: Catherine Tranter
Tel: 01508 492158

THE WHITE DRAGON MERCENARIES
140 Elphinstone Road, Hastings, E. Sussex TN34 2BN
Contact: Patrick Cooper
Tel: 01424-430935
Email: pcooper@cwcom.net

WHITEROSE
Unit 59 Clock Tower Business Centre, Works Road,
Hollingwood, Chesterfield S43 2PE
Tel: 01246 475 782
Fax: 01246 471 123
Website: www.white-rose-armourys.co.uk
or
www.white-rose-castings.com
Arms and armour from Ancient Greek to Civil War. Brass
and bronze castings.

WOGAN HOUSEHOLD
25 Rowan Close, Scarborough, N. Yorkshire YO12 6NJ
Contact: Gary Hughs
Tel: 01723 367746

WOLFBANE HISTORICAL SOCIETY
4 Heath Villa, Colwell Lane, Freshwater, Isle of Wight
Contact: Dork Normanson

WOLFSHEAD BOWMEN
Guestlings, Hastings, E. Sussex TN35 4HJ
Contact: John Watts
Tel: 01424 813114
Email: john.watts@virgin.net
Website: www.wolfshead-bowmen.com
We are a Medieval archery group who perform at castles
or private functions. We can provide all types of craft
demonstration, a one hour archery show aimed at being
historically correct as well as entertaining and educational.
We are available for film and TV work.

WOLF GUARD
57 Clarence Road, Newport, Isle of Wight
Contact: Julie Goulder
7th–14th centuries–battles and living history. Schools and
educational events undertaken. We specialise particularly in
10th century Viking life.

THE WOODVILLE HOUSEHOLD
30 Culver Road Basingstoke, Hants RG21 3LS
Contact: Mark Brookshaw
Tel: 01256 354660

THE WORCESTER MILITIA
16 Hazledan Road, Arle Farm, Cheltenham, Glos GL5 0QF
Contact: Chris Jackson

WORLD OF FANTASY
2 Windmill Road, Hampton Hill, Middlesex TW12 1RH
Contact: Terry Denton de Gray
Tel: 020 8941 1595
Fax: 020 8783 1366

WWII DISPLAY TEAM
97 Lime Walk, Chelmsford, Essex UK CM2 9NJ
Contact: Davan Winch,
Tel: 01245 490659
Mobile: 0956 507210
Email: davan@ww2.org.uk

WW 2 DISPLAY TEAM
Tel: 01245 355703 or 0961 750442
Website: www.users.zetnet.co.uk/ww2
'Living History'.

WORLD WAR TWO LIVING HISTORY ASSOCIATION
Home Farm Cottage, Mill Lane, Wigsley, Newark,
Nottinghamshire NG23 7ES
Contact: Clinton Knight
Tel: 01522 703362

WULFINGAS AD450 SOCIETY
9 Crick's Retreat, London Road, Great Glen, Leicestershire LE8 9FF
Contact: Richard Knox
Tel: 0116 259 3067

WYCHWOOD WARRIORS
Keble College, Parks Road, Oxford OX1 3PG
Contact: Bruno Goh Luse
Tel: 01865 272727
Email: bruno.luse@keb.ox.ac.uk

YE COMPANYE OF CHIVALRYE
14 Larch Close, Melksham, Wiltshire SN12 6UD
Contact: Arron Nuttall
Tel: 01225 90384

YORK CITY LEVY
54 Broadwell Road, Easterside, Middlesbrough, N. Yorkshire
TS4 3NP
Contact: Paul Morris
Tel: 01642 273624
Email: vikly@freenet.co.uk

YORKS HORSES
6 Stafford Leys, Leicester Forest, Leicestershire LE3 3LH
Contact: Neil Elverson
Tel: 0116 239 0050
Mobile: 07977 628886

THE YORKSHIRE YEOMEN (SIR JOHN SAVILE'S HOUSEHOLD)
7 Kingwell Road, Ward Green, Barnsley, S. Yorkshire S70 4AG
Contact: Peter Rice
Tel: 01226 206856
Email: yeomen0001@aol.com

*1ERE TIRAILLEURS-GRENADIERS (NAP)
9 Rue du Chemin Vert, 91360 Epinay sur Orge, France
Contact: Christian Scoupe
Tel/Fax: 169090735
The society re-enacts a section of this Young Guard regiment. Members participate in all European events of quality, on Napoleonic themes.

1st ARKANSAS VOLUNTEER INFANTRY
136 Snakes Lane, Woodford Green, Essex IG8 7HZ
Contact: Michael Freeman
Tel/Fax: 020 8585 0662

1st FOOT GUARDS
6 Arden Avenue, Brounstone, Leicestershire

1st LIGHT BATTALION KING'S GERMAN LEGION
Flat 11, Marlborough Court, Marlborough Hill, Harrow, Middlesex HA1 1UF
Contact: Dennis Wraight
Tel: 020 8861 0830

THE 1914-21 SOCIETY
(Formerly The Eastern Front Association)
165 Marlborough Avenue, Kingston-upon-Hull, Humberside HU5 3LG
Tel: 01482 447188
Contact: Marlyn Clarke
Email: martyn@pixelcreations.co.uk
The Society recreates the Eastern Front 1914-17 and Russian/Finnish civil wars. It has its own site and use of a period style village, with training and practical help supplied. Loan of kit also available. Four events a year. TV work undertaken. Museum quality turnout. First ever all-female re-enactment combat formation.

20e BCA (WWII)
15 Impasse Remi Cocheme, 51100 Reims, France
Contact: Jean Paul Lebailly
Tel/Fax: 26361672

*2e HUSSARDS (NAP)
Route de Paris, 77171 Sourdun, France

2nd GUARDS RIFLE DIVISION—RED ARMY
21 Elsing Close, Meadow Rise, Newcastle-upon-Tyne, Tyne & Wear NE5 4SW
Email: MTA4145@aol.com

2nd (QUEENS) REGIMENT OF FOOT
18 Lilac Close, Bellfields, Guilford, Surrey GU1 1PB
Contact: George Brown
Tel: 01483 574455

2nd US ARTILLERY
Thickets, Odstock, Salisbury, Wiltshire SP5 4JE
Contact: Mike Boyd-Camps
Tel: 01722 329712

2nd US CAVALRY
6 Avenue, Bournemouth, Dorset BH10 4HE
Contact: Richard Beardall
13 Kinsbourne
Tel: 01202 537110
Fax: 01 202 462090
Email: rbz@globalnet.co.uk

3rd BTN, 1ST FOOT GUARDS (NAP)
Waterloo Museum, Crow Hill, Broadstairs, Kent CT10 1HN
Foot Guards re-enactment unit (1812–1816).

*4e REGIMENTO DEL REAL CUERO DE ARTIMERIA
(1802–1809)
Canton Pepuento 25-Bajo, Corunna 15003, Spain
Spanish artillery group of the Peninsular War, Napoleonisc Spanish association (1802–1814) Mounted Artillery and foot artillery.

*5. WESTFALISCHES LANDWEHR-REGT (NAP)
Am Wiesgraben 2, D-69190 Walldorf, Germany
Contact: Dietrich Pott
Tel/Fax: 62274859
'Living history' group depicting German militia of the Napoleonic period. High standards required.

5. WESTFALISCHES LANDWEHR-REGT (NAP)
98 Winstanley Road, Wellingborough, Northamptonshire NN8 1JF
English contingent of a German based re-enactment unit of the highest quality. We operate in Europe, at least once per year.

9me LÈGERE, L'AVANT-GARDE DE LA 27e DIVISION MILITAIRE
82 Finchley Park, London N12 9JL
Contact: Martin Lancaster
Mobile: 0378 307883
Email: 101332.567@compuserve.com

9th NEW YORK CAVALRY
The Willows, Benover Road, Collier Street, Marden, Kent TN12 9RD
Contact: Garry Howard
Tel: 01892 730229

12th LIGHT DRAGOONS (NAP)
Shepherds Cottage, Fernhill, Glemsford, Suffolk CO10 7PR
Contact: Martin Render
Tel/Fax: 01787 280077
Email: mjrender@cullen38.freeserve.co.uk
British cavalry regiment of the Napoleonic Association. A mounted battle re-enactment and 'living history' unit, emphasising high standards of authenticity and horsemanship.

17th CENTURY LIFE & TIMES
Flat 11, Marlborough Court, Marlborough Hill, Harrow,
London HA1 1UF
Contact: Dennis Wraight
Tel: 020 8861 0830
Email: lifextimes@livinghistory.co.uk
Website: www.livinghistory.co.uk/homepages/life&times
17th century re-enactment society and a nationwide group
dning a mixture of battle re-enactment, living history and
role playing.

17th CENTURY LIVING HISTORY HERITAGE CENTRE
25 Connaught Street, Northampton, Northamptonshire NN1 3BP
Contact: Mrs J H Thompson

17 LANCERS DISPLAY TEAM
429 Oxford Street, London W1R 2HD
Contact: Mark Selwood
Tel: 020 7973 3678
Fax: 020 7973 3430

*18e INFANTERIE DE LIGNE (NAP)
Dobereiner Strasse 12, 07745 Jena, Germany
Contact: Rolf Peter Graf

18th MISSOURI INFANTRY
98 Winstanley Road, Wellingborough, Northamptonshire
NN8 1JF
Contact: John Hopper
Tel: 01933 442213
Fax: 01933 273318
Email: ksbelt@globalnet.co.uk
The 18th Missouri Infantry re-enactment group portray
soldiers of the Union Army of Tennessee 1864. Part of the
Southern Skirmish Association. Family oriented group.

21e INFANTERIE DE LIGNE (NAP)
22 Swallow Street, Oldham, Lancashire OL8 41D
Contact: Christopher Durkin
Tel/Fax: 0161 652 1647
A regiment of the Napoleonic Association, recruiting
nationwide, dedicated to the study and recreation of this
French unit during the Napoleonic era.

*22e DEMI-BRIGADE DE LIGNE
Memmelsdorfer Str 102, 96052 Bamberg, Germany
Contact: Hans-Karl Weiss
The group portrays French line infantry 200 years ago and
has a special interest in bicentennials. Approximately 50
members in Belgium, England, Germany and Italy.

*23e CHASSEURS (NAP)
15 Sentier Desire, 94350 Visire sur Marne, France
Contact: Daniel Hubert

*23e DRAGONS (NAP)
53his Rue Claude Terrasse, 75016 Paris, France
Contact: Joel Levleux

23rd REGIMENT OF FOOT
7 Arcadia Way, Trevethin, Pontypool, Gwent, Wales NP4 8DX
Contact: Allan Jones
Tel/Fax: 01495 750479
Email: light.bob@virgin.net
Website: http://freespace.virgin.net/ligbt.bob/23
Recreates the Royal Welch Fusiliers 1689–1815, including
the Battle of the Boyne, American War of Independence
and Napoleonic Wars.

23rd FOOT, ROYAL WELCH FUSILIERS RE-ENACTMENT SOCIETY
c/o 15 Llancaiach View, Nelson, Treharris CF46 6EW
Contact: Colin Rogers
Tel: 01443 451 754
Email: colrogers@lineone.net
Website: www.kingsgrenadiers.co.uk
The Kings Grenadiers (23rd Foot) RWF re-enact the
Regiment's history during the Peninsular War against
Napoleon from 1809-1814., and the Waterloo Campaign of
1815. Members reside anywhere in the UK and families are
most welcome as part of our large living history campsite.
The Unit has appeared on television and videos, including
the BBC's Vanity Fair and the Cromwell video series.

24th MICHIGAN INFANTRY COMPANY K
26 Burlington Avenue, Formby, Merseyside L37 8D?
Contact: Keith Lomax
American Civil War 'living history' unit, north England
based, portraying all aspects of Union infantry, particularly
mid-war campaign impression. Substantial free info pack
on request. Member of ACWS.

29th DIVISION FRENCH HISTORICAL ASSOCIATION
9 Clos des Saules, 77860 Roissy en Brie, France
Promotion and preservation of the 29th US Infantry
Division's history during WWI; ceremonies at memorials,
re-enactments.

33rd WEST YORKSHIRE REGIMENT OF FOOT
42 Woodside Road, Halifax, West Yorkshire HX3 6EL
Contact: J Eeles
Email: tapper@tiscali.co.uk
The 33rd Foot are a re-enactment/living history group of
British Redcoats and their families circa1812-1816. We
portray a battalion company of a line regiment, the empha-
sis being on the life of a private soldier. Based in
Yorkshire, we attend events across the UK and in Europe.

36th REGIMENT OF FOOTE
Rydal House, Old Pitch, Tirley, Gloucestershire GL19 4ET

36th (TEXAS) INFANTRY DIVISION
24 Marlfield Close, Ingol, Preston Lancashire PR2 7AL
Contact: Tim Dean
Tel/Fax: 01772 768272

37th REGIMENT OF FOOT
44 Chapel Street, Bishop's Itchington, Leamington Spa, Warwickshire CV33 0RB
'Living history' unit representing the British redcoat of the 1770s and 1790s, esp. American War of Independence. Recruits nationally. Events throughout the UK and some abroad.

40th REGIMENT OF FOOT
37 Lee Avenue, North Springvale, Melbourne, Victoria 3171, Australia

42nd ROYAL HIGHLAND REGIMENT OF FOOTE—THE WATCH
26 Brighton Road, Horley, Surrey RH6 7HD
Contact: Keith Jepson
Tel: 0797 971 8367
A military and civilian re-enactment group covering mid to late 18th Century life in Europe and North America. We cover the War of the Austrian Succession, the French and Indian Wars and the American Revolution.

45e INFANTERIE DE LIGNE (NAP)
29 Bayley Court, Winnersh, Wokingham, Berkshire RG11 5HT
Napoleonic French Fusiliers group portraying c 1808-09 troops and their ladies 'living history' camps and battle re-enactments; recruiting nationally.

45th (1st NOTTS) REGIMENT OF FOOT
62 Fairway, Keyworth, Nottingham, Nottinghamshire NG12 5DU
Based on a Grenadier flank company, we put together living history displays and cameos using period tents and equipment.

46e INFANTERIE DE LIGNE (NAP)
Bower House, Park Lane, Sulgrave, Oxfordshire OX17 2RX
Contact: Mike Crawshaw
Represents the Grenadier Company, 1st Battalion, and attached Regimental Artillery; uniformed according to 1793 regulations.

47th REGIMENT OF FOOT
c/o 60 Oakcroft, Woodend, Clayton-le-Woods, Chorley, Lancashire PR6 7UJ
Contact: Nigel Hardacre
Tel/Fax: 01772 315192
Email: nhardacre47@hotmail.com
The 47th is a small but dedicated group who portray the life of the British soldier in camp and on campaign during the time of the American War of Independence (1775-1783). In addition to the living history displays we take part in skirmishes organised by 'New France Old England' in the UK.

50th (WEST KENT) REGIMENT OF FOOT
116 Nelson Road, Gillingham, Kent ME7
Contact: John Edmead

68th (DLI) SOCIETY & DISPLAY TEAM
40 The Rowans, Orgill, Egremont, Cumbria CA22 2HW
Contact: Philip Mackie
Tel: 01946 820 110
Email: carol@peakpartnership.demon.co.uk
Website: www.68dli.com
The 68th Society exists to research and perpetuate the history of the 68th Durham Light Infantry Regiment, from 1758 to its demise in 1968. The 68th (DLI) Display Team is equipped and uniformed for the year 1814, when the Regiment completed its service in Wellington's 'Peninsular Army'. Any public event can be undertaken by the team.

71st HIGHLAND LIGHT INFANTRY
24 Highcroft Green, Parkwood, Maidstune, Kent ME 1 5 9PN
Contact: M. Foreman
Recreates the regiment in the period 1810-1815.

85th FOOT (BUCKS VOLUNTEERS) INFANTRY
26 Bencombe Road, Marlow Bottom, Buckinghamshire

88th REGIMENT OF FOOT CONNAUGHT RANGERS
12 Hale Road, Farnham, Surrey GU9 9QH
Contact: Robert Anderson
Tel: 01252 726258
Email: robanderson@ukonline.co.uk
Website: www.88thfoot.co.uk
Our club based in Farnham, Surrey, depicts the 88th Foot on campaign in the Peninsular War in 1812. We participate in Napoleonic battle re-enactments in the UK and Europe, and organise our own battle display annually at Farnham Castle Park. We plan to organise another battalion in the west of Ireland.

93rd SUTHERLAND HIGHLAND REGIMENT OF FOOT LIVING HISTORY UNIT
PO Box 100011, Fort Worth, Texas 76185, USA
A leading Napoleonic re-enactment group in the USA, recruiting nationally. Some recreation of Crimean and Mutiny periods. Member, Napoleonic Association, VMS, North America British Brigade.

95th RIFLES, 2ND BATTALION
51 Armitage Road, Birkby, Huddersfield, West Yorkshire HD2 2UB
Contact: Steve Barker
Tel: 1484 534219

1471
The Gardeners Cottage, Mansel Lacy, Hertfordshire EN5 2LE
Contact: John Bowden
Tel: 01432 342440

RE-ENACTMENT SERVICES & SUPPLIES

ABBEYHORN OF LAKELAND
Holme Mills Industrial Estate, Holme, Carnforth, Lancashire
LA6 1RD
Contact: Dawn Pinson
Tel: 01524 782387
Fax: 01 524 782099
Email: info@abbeyhorn.co.uk
Website: www.abbeyhorn.co.uk
We specialise in making goods from ox horn, stag antler and bone; our range includes kitchenware, shoehorns, walking sticks, soldiers' mugs, and much more.

ALWYN'S ARROWS
Contact: Paul
Tel: 01273 307109
Email: paul.sue@btinternet.com
Medieval arrows—self nocked, whipped and with bodkin heads. Also longbows and metalwork.

ANCESTRAL INSTRUMENTS
Tudor Lodge, Pymoor Lane, Pymoor, Ely, Cambridgeshire
CB6 2EE
Contact: David Marshall
Tel: 01353 698084
Email: pipesandfiddles@ancestral.co.uk
Website: www.ancestral.co.uk
Ancient musical instruments (Reeds). Roman/Greek Aulos. Phrygian Tibia. Roman Bagpipe—Hellenistic bagpipe. Medieval/ Renaissances bagpipes, shawms and hornpipes. Musical horns from ox/antelope. Special commissions.

ANDREW BUTLER MILITARIA & INSIGNIA
10 Avebury Avenue, Ramsgate, Kent CT11 8BB
Contact: Andrew Butler
Tel/Fax: 01843 582216
Email: sales@abinsignia.com
Website: www.abinsignia.com
US and UK military insignia. Re-enactment insignia also made and supplied. Wholesale available. Museums supplied.

ANGLO LONGBOWS
1 Old Worth Farm, Pymore, Bridport, Dorset DT16 5LE
Contact: Mike & Judy Foote
Hand crafted Saxon/Viking bows.

ANNE LAVERICK
Vale Head Farm, 52 Pontefract Road, Knottingley,
W. Yorkshire WF11 8RN
Contact: Anne Laverick
Tel: 01977 677390
Historical costumier, and supplier of specialised fabrics for all periods. Cottons £1.75 yd, linen. £3.75 yd, wool from £4.75 yd. Postal service available.

ARCHERY CENTRE
Highgate Hill, Hawkhurst, Kent TN18 4LG
Contact: Tom Foy
Tel/Fax: 01424 777183
Email: sales@archery-centre.co.uk
Website: www.archery-centre.co.uk

ARMS & ARCHERY
The Coach House, London Road, Ware, Herts
SG12 9QU
Tel: 01920 460335/6
Fax: 01920 461044

ARRIERE BANS
Lilliput Cottage, 23 Hight Street, Old Oxted, RH8 9LN
Contact: Mark Bourne
Tel: 01883 716197
Email: markbourne@talk21
Medieval mercenaries for hire. Authentic 15th century with our own wooden stockade and siege weapon, available for corporate events, film/TV work. We run the Fryland medieval experience for schools and clubs and of course attend re-enactments.

ARROWS FOR RE-ENACTORS
Craft Cottage, Bookham Lodge Stud, Cobham Road, Stoke
d'Abernon, Surrey KT11 3QG
Tel/Fax: 01932 865181
Medieval arrows, Longbow kits, archery videoss, magazines, quivers, armguards belt pouches etc. Longbow Classes. SAE for price list and location map.

ARTEMIS ARCHERY/LONGBOW PRESENTATIONS
29 Batley Court, Old Land, S. Glos BS30 8YZ
Contact: Hugh or Veronica Soar
Tel/Fax: 0117 932 3276
Research consultancy, talks, lectures, artefact-based exhibitions, traditional English Longbow. Television consultancy a speciality. Thesis advice by arrangement. Equipment sought and purchased.

ARTISAN ARMOURS
Hope Farm, Halegate Road, Eidnes, Cheshire WA8 8LZ
Contact: Simon Brindle
Tel/Fax: 0151 425 2500
Hardened leather plate armours, leather jacks. Historical and fantasy. Design and production.

A S BOTTOMLEY

The Coach House, Huddersfield Road, Holmfirth, W. Yorkshire HD7 2TT
Contact: Andrew Bottomley
Tel: 01484 685234
Fax: 01484 681551
Email: andrewbottomley@compuserve.com
Established 30 years with clients overseas and in the UK. A fully illustrated mail order catalogue containing a large range of antique weapons and military items despatched world wide. Every item is guaranteed original. Full money back if not satisfied. Deactivated weapons available. Valuations for insurance and probate. Interested in buying weapons or taking items in part exchange. Business hours Mon–Fri 9am–5pm. Mail order only. All major credit cards welcome. Catalogue UK £5, Europe £7, rest of world £10.

ATTLEBOROUGH ACCESSORIES

White House, Morley St Peter, Wymondham, Norfolk NR18 9TZ
Contact: C E Pearce
Tel: 01953 454932
Fax: 01953 456744
Email: sales@attacc.com
Website: www.attacc.com
Militaria and memorabilia, including: Sheffield-made Fairbern Sykes 3rd pattern and commemorative knives; K-Bar USMC knives; knife-making supplies, etc. Large SAE for full lists.

AWICS

New House, Murton, Appleby in Westmoreland, Cumbria CA16 6ND
Contact: Adrian Waite
Tel: 017683 52165
Email: awaite@ukonline.co.uk
Website: www.awics.co.uk
Working in schools and museums. Presenting and planning events, presentations, demonstrations and lectures. Publications and historical research. Supply of reproduction costume, weapons, tents and artifacts.

AXHOLMR & THE DANNAE

15 Mond Avenue, Goole, East Yorkshire DN14 6LQ
Contact: Matt Jones
Tel: 01405 763550
Email: axholmruik@aol.com
Website: www.axholmr.co.uk
Historical re-enactment society covering 3rd–11th centuries. Anglian, Saxon, Viking and Norman periods covered. Also 3rd century BC–3rd century AD Celtic. Combat, living history, research, family friendly, archery, crafts, TV/film & photographic.

BAINBRIDGE TRADITIONAL BOOTMAKERS

The Square, Timsbury, Bath BA3 1HY
Contact: David McCabe
Tel/Fax: 01761 471430
Makers of high quality reproduction and traditional footwear for museums and 'living historians' worldwide. Clients include: Museum of London, National Army Museum, Tower Armouries.

BILBO THE TRADER

52 Barnards Yard, Norwich, Norfolk NR3 3DS
Contact: B Dunion
Tel/Fax: 0163 766959
Email: b.dunion@netcom.co.uk
Specialist in Dark Age jewellery; show attendance sales only—will also attend Medieval shows. No stock list as stock changes constantly.

BIRKFIELD (HERALDIC FLAGS)

Birkfield, Rumbling Bridge, Kinrossshire KY13 7PT, Scotland
Contact: Dr Patrick Barden
Tel/Fax: 01577 840598
Heraldic banners, standards, gonfannons, pipe-banners etc. No bogus heraldry. Hand-painted on polyester, bunting, satin etc. Commissions only—no stock kept.

BODGERARMOUR

129 Kent Road, Mapperley, Nottinghamshire NG3 6BS
Contact: Dave Hodgson
Tel/Fax: 0115 9525711

DOLTON TARPAULIN COMPANY

Unit 1, Orchard Trading Estate, Langley Road South, Salford M6 6SD
Tel: 0161 745 8717 or 01204 306484
Tent makers and suppliers.

BROADSWORDS

4 High Street, Rochester, Kent ME1 1PT
Contact: Tara Keating
Tel: 01634 827027
Mobile: 07980 404487
Everything you need for authentic living history.

BUTTON LADY

16 Hollyfield Road South, Sutton Coldfield, W. Midlands B76 1X
Contact: Pauline Walker
Tel/Fax: 0121 329 3234
Buttons and clasps made from natural materials—pewter, china, shell, wood, horn etc. Spinning wheels, books, fibres and supplies.

CADUCEUS

35 Carnarvon Road, Leyton, London E10 6DW
Contact: Morgana
Tel/Fax: 020 85393569
Email: Caduceus@talk21.com
We make an extensive range of pagan and historical jewellery in gold and silver; hand-crafted swords and knives. Mail order catalogue kl.45- shop open 9.30am–5.30pm, close Thursdays.

CALL TO ARMS
1 Lyng Lane, North Lopham, Norfolk IP22 2HR
Contact: Duke Henry Plantagenet
Tel/Fax: 01953 681670
Email: duke@calltoarms.com
The Worldwide Directory of Historical Re-enactment Societies and Traders. Published once a year with continuous updating service—fax and email supported—entry in our listings is free. Listings are uniquely annotated with society size / activity data. Also contains high quality articles of news, research and development. To find out anything about Historical Re-enactment and Living History, first you buy 'Call to Arms'. Get your copy now.

CAROL ARCHERY
Craft Cottage, Bookham Lodge Stud, Cobham Road, Stke d'Abernon, Surrey KTH 3QG
Contact: Carol
Tel/Fax: 01932 865181
Email: carolarchery@faxvia.net
Website: www.carolarchery.com
Medieval and competition arrows and most leather goods associated with archery. I also do corporate, group and individual longbow tuition.

CHAPMANS PAD
Bwlch House, Beguildy, Radnoreshire Wales LD7 1UG
Contact: Barry Carter
Tel/Fax: 01547 510289
Historical costume accessories moulded from original antiquities—Roman-Celtic, Anglo-Saxon, Viking, Medieval, Tudor, Stuart, Georgian—badges, brooches, buckles, buttons, strap ends, pendants, pins etc. Also replica Georgian, Napoleonic and ACW coinage and commemorative medals—Charles I, Cromwell, napoleon, Nelson, Wellington, Culloden, Minden, Marengo, Albueria, Corunna, Waterloo, etc.

CHARISMA COSTUMES
7 Milton House, Severn Road, Halesowen, W. Midlands B63 2LS
Contact: Paul Finn or Charis Jones
Tel: 01384 833642
Email: charis@charisma9.freeserve.co.uk

CHILTERN OPEN AIR MUSEUM (COSTUME)
Gorelands Lane, Chalfont St Giles, Buckinghamshire HP8 4AD
Tel: 01494 871117
Fax: 01494 872163
Email: coam@tessco.net
Website: www.coam.org.uk
Museum of historic buildings, including a 1940s prefab, Toll House and working Victorian farm. 'Living History' displays and demonstrations. 24 hour Info Line: 01494 872163

CLINK ARMOURY
1 Clink Street, London SE1 9DG
Tel: 020 74083 6515
Fax: 020 7403 5813

CML
5 Heol Fach, Llangyfelach, Swansea, Wales SA5 7JH
Tel: 01792 790293 or 07788 921315
Contact: Chris Evans

COPPICE TRADING POST
Beck Farm Buildings, Rosier Farm, RH14 9DF
Contact: R M Hobbs
Tel: 01403 732171
Wattle hurdles, gabbions, rustic poles, charcoal, ethnic structures.

CORRIDORS OF TIME (HISTORICAL PRESENTATIONS) LTD
22 Palace Street, Canterbury, Kent CT1 2DZ
Contact: Alan Jeffery
Tel: 01227 478990
Fax: 01227 478991
Email: corridors@argonet.co.uk
Website: www. corridors-of-time.co.uk
Retail outlet to provide genuine, antique, military, museum quality and legendary artefacts, from swords to armour, buttons to badges. Gifts, souvenirs, momento's all linked to British history, including organisers of major centenial and comemorative events. 35 years exeperience and still enthisiastic.

COTSWOLD FORGE
2 Exmouth Street, Leckhampton, Cheltenham, Glos GL53 7NS
Contact: Terry Andrews
Tel/Fax: 01242 242754

CREATE THE MOOD
Redcote, 228 Sydenham Road, Croydon, Surrey CR0 2EB
Contact: Frances E Tucker
Tel/Fax: 020 8684 1095
Email: thegarter@createthemood.fsnet.co.uk
Historic haberdashery. Frances' stall, crammed with unusual things old and new, creates a bustling atmosphere at costume and heritage events, 1066-1930. Invitations accepted.

DAPHNE HILSDON
118 High Street, Winslow, Buckinghamshire MK18 3DQ
Contact: Daphne Hilsdon
Tel: 01296 713643
Email: daphnehilsdon@theguild.fsnet.co.uk
Hand finished reproduction clothing and uniforms from iron age to WWI. Supplier to museums, film and re-enactors. Catalogues on request. Period dress Roman to 1920s made, both civilian and military. Also demonstrations and displays of dress, cookery and social history.

THE DARK AGES CHARITABLE TRUST
Rosemary Cottage, Camp Road, Canwell, Sutton Coldfield B75 5RA
Contact: Paul Craddock
Tel: 0121-323-4309
Fax: 0121-323-4309
Email: MerciaS@hotmail.com
Website: DarkAgesTrust.org.uk
An historical and nature conservation charity, near Birmingham, specialising in the period 500-1500 AD. We have our own seven-acre site with a reconstructed ringfort and lake. We have planted about 200 rare fruit trees and are looking for more volunteers. We run groups for The Vikings and Regia Anglorum.

DARR PUBLICATIONS
Thorshof, 106 Oakridge Road, High Wycombe, Buckinghamshire HP11 2PL
Contact: Thorskegga Thorn
Tel: 01494 451814
Fax: 01494 784271
Email: thorskegga@calltoarms.com
Large number of historical booklets, both theoretical studies and 'how-to-do-it' manuals. Heavily researched but inexpensive, practical and easy to read. SAE for details.

EAGLE CLASSIC ARCHERY
41, Spring Walk, Worksop, Notts S80 1XQ
Contact: H Abbott
Tel: 01909 478935
Fax: 01909 488115
Email: sales@eagleclassicarchery.co.uk
Website: eagleclassicarchery.co.uk
An Aladdin's Cave for the traditional archer and re-enactor. Please phone for free colour brochure.

ENGLISH ARMOURIE
Department 10, 1 Walsall Street, Willenhall, W. Midlands NW13 2EX
Contact: Alan Jones
Tel/Fax: 01902 870579
Website: www.englisharmourie.fsnet.co.uk
Armour manufacturers from Roman to English Civil War. Also makers of muzzle loading muskets. De-activated guns. General militaria dealers covering all periods.

ENGLISH HERITAGE SPECIAL EVENTS UNIT
Portland House, Stag Place, London SW1E 5EE
Contact: Howard Giles
Tel: 020 7973 3457
Fax: 020 79733430
Website: http://www.englishheritage.org.uk
Creation and direction of outdoor events, specialising in authentic historical re-enactments and living histories. English Heritage sites only. Also contact Thomas Cardwell or Natasha Lees.

ENSIGN EMBROIDERY
Kilcreggan, Dunbartonshire, Scotland
Tel/Fax: 01436 842581 or 842716
Email: sales@ensignmotifs.co.uk

'1st CLASS MARINE' MILITARIA
1 Mansfield Road, Chessington, Surrey KT9 2PJ
Contact: Richard Heath
Tel: 07974 400206
Email: marine@blueyonder.co.uk
Website: www.marine.pwp.blueyonder.co.uk
WWII to the present day, British and Commonwealth clothing and equipment, webbing etc. Suitable for the re-enactor.

FIRST CLASS MAIL
9 Miller Street, Warrington, Cheshire WA4 1BD
Contact: Tony Whittaker
Tel: 01925 659756
Riveted mail, wirework, hand-sewn turnshoes. Demonstrations of riveted mail-making for museums, events etc. Also for TV/film, video and documentary work. Riveted mail of the highest quality made to order, sample pieces, loose rings etc for schools, museum displays etc.

FREDERICK & KNIGHTS
Owenshaw Mill, The Wharf, Sowerby Bridge, W. Yorkshire HX6 2AF
Contact: Jill Knights
Tel: 01422 316438
Email: f-and-k@lineone.net
Costumiers and clothing.

THE FRONTLINE ASSOCIATION
3 Plym Grove, Longhill, Hull, E. Yorkshire HU8
Contact: Andy Marsh
Tel: 01482 811569
A growing re-enactment/living history society in the north re-enacting 1914 to 1945—German, Russian, British—military and civilian. Can convert uniforms and provide tailoring/helmet conversion as well as static displays and pyro-filled battles and most things in between. Looking for recruits—especially British infantry.

FUNN STOCKINGS TRADITIONAL HOSIERY
PO Box 102, Steyning, W. Sussex BN44 3DS
Contact: Graham Huntley
Tel/Fax: 01903 892841
Email: funnltd@mailcity.com
Traditional silk, cotton, wool stockings; also cotton Fustian, and over-the-knee opaque cotton stay-ups, as used in over 1000 plays, films, musicals etc.

GALLERY MILITAIRE
2 Weald Hall Cottages, Weald Hall Lane, Thornwood, Epping, Essex CM16 6NB
Contact: Rod Gander
Mobile: 07759 616860
Military consultant for film/TV companies and actors, providing all aspects of military information: uniform, drill, protocol, traditions. All periods.

GAUNT D'OR (WEAPONSMITH)
58 Springfield Road, Wolverhampton, W. Midlands
WV10 0LJ
Contact: Brian Gunter
Tel/Fax: 01902 683875
Email: gauntdor@compuserve.com
For authentic reproduction swords, daggers and other
weapons from the Dark Ages through to Renaissance.
Suitable for re-enactment, display or wall hangings.

GUILD OF MASTER CRAFTSMEN
166 High Street, Lewes, E. Sussex BN7 1XU
Contact: Information Officer
Tel: 01273 478449
Fax: 01273 478606
Email: fionag@gmcgroup.com
The Guild is a trade association for skilled crafts-people
and companies. It covers over 400 different trades—the
helpline can provide selective lists of members.

GUILDHOUSE & APPLEBY DESIGNS (COSTUME)
16 Treesdale Road, Harrogate, N. Yorkshire HE2 0LX
Contact: Jon Beavis-Harrison
Tel/Fax: 01423 560585

HANDWEAVERS STUDIO & GALLERY
29 Haroldstone Road, London E17 7AN
Tel/Fax: 020 8521 2281
Email: handweaversstudio@man.com
Spinning/weaving supplies: books, tuition, fibres, fleece,
spinning wheels, spindles, carders, yarns, looms, shuttles,
rigid heddles, etc.

HARRIET WATERHOUSE
8 Southern Road, Southbourne, Bournemouth, Dorset BH6 3SR
Tel/Fax: 01202 434057
Mobile: 07931 568467
Hand stitched flax linen jacks, arming doublets, coifs,
partlets etc. Hair and wool fleece padding.

RICHARD HEAD LONGBOWS
Address 405 The Spa, Melksham, Wilts SN12 6QL
Contact: Richard Head
Tel/Fax: 01225 790452
Email: headbow@hotmail.com
Website: www.english-longbow.co.uk
Makers of fine english longbows and arrows, we sell
materials for the budding fletcher and bowyer, bracers,
tabs, quivers, all the accessories you could possibly want
for traditional archery.

HECTOR COLE IRONWORK
The Mead, Great Somerford, Chippenham, Wiltshire
SN15 5JB
Contact: Hector Cole
Tel: 01666 825794
Fax: 01249 720485
Email: hectorcole@lineone.net
Specialist in medieval ironwork techniques with particular
reference to arrow and blade smithing. All London Museum
type arrowheads forged to order. SAE for details.

HERITAGE ARMS
Units 58/59 Clocktower Centre, Hollingwood, Chesterfield,
Derbyshire S43 2PE
Contact: J & P Chester
Tel/Fax: 01246 475782

HILLTOP SPINNING & WEAVING SUPPLIES
Windmill Cross, Canterbury Road, Lyminge, Nr. Folkestone,
Kent CT18 8HD
Contact: Sue Chitty
Tel/Fax: 01303 862617
Email: info@handspin.co.uk
Website: www.handspin.co.uk
Spinning, weaving, dyeing, feltmaking, braid equipment and
accessories. One to one tuition or group courses made to
measure to your requirements, here at Lyminge or at your
venue. Re-enactment clothes for children made in
conjunction with noble textiles.

HISTORICAL PROMOTIONS
Bulstone Business Centre, Petrockstowe, Okehampton, Devon
EX20 3ET
Contact: Rob Butler
Tel/Fax: 01837 811243
Website: www.historicalpromotions@aol.com
Planning, management, promotion and delivery of historical
re-enactments and events for councils, historic properties,
museums, show organisers and heritage bodies. We undertake costumed interpretation, living history and multi-period
spectaculars throughout the UK and abroad. We provide
service to film and television production companies
including historical extras, location services and vehicles.

HISTORYMAN UK
2 Coburn Drive, Four Oaks, Sutton Coldfield B75 5NT
Contact: John White
Tel: 0121 308 4103
Email: jwhite02@globalnet.co.uk
Website: historyman.uk.net
Considerable experience with film and TV companies in the
area of costume and historical productions. Specialising in
late Georgian/Regency/Napoleonic period. Shows, talks
and displays at various locations. Credits include work for
the BBC. Contact for more details.

THE KING'S LIVERY COMPANY
63 Hutland Road, Ipswich, Suffolk IP4 4HQ
Tel: 01473 273207 or 01473 446550
All types of shields made to your requirements.

INTERKNIFE
PO Box 107, Wymondham NR18 9EQ
Tel: 01953 606457
Fax: 01603 748570
Email: See Website
Website: www.interknife.co.uk
Authentic knives and daggers—Dark Age to Tudor—made by
Rod Matless. Also Musem quality copies as supplied to the
Mary Rose Trust and other organisations. See out travelling
stall at major Battles and re-enactment markets.

THE IRISH HISTORY COMPANY
Northside Resource Centre, Forthill, Sligo, Ireland
Contact: Kay Erb
Tel: 7147616
Email: info@irishhistoryco.com
Website: www.irishhistoryco.com
Providers of quality historical garments at reasonable prices. 18th and 19th centuries are a specialty as are 17th century Irish garments. Research services are also offered.

INTER-MEDIEVAL INTERNATIONAL MEDIEVAL ALLIANCE
c/o 18 Asgate Valley Road, Ashgate, Chesterfield, Derbyshire S40 4AX
Contact: Roger Lankford
Tel: 01246 270090
Email: roger@lancaster-armry.demon.co.uk
Website: england@intermedieval.org
International Medieval Alliance is a dream—a new born babe weened to bring together all the true knights and merry medieval re-enactors from all over the world. A brotherhood bound by honour and commitment to promote our heritages for all.

JAMES HOLYWOOD WOODEN BOWS
37 Dale Close, South Ockendon, Essex RM15 5DR
Tel/Fax: 01708 670661
Roman to Victorian bows at sensible prices. Repairs also undertaken.

THE JELLING DRAGON
Flat 4, The George Centre, 30 North Parade, Matlock Bath, Derbyshire DE4 3NS
Contact: RobertTaylor.
Tel: 01629 760120 or 07714 088132
Email: admin@jelldragon.com..
Website: www.jelldragon.com.
Manufacturer and supplier of weapons, armour & crafts from Roman, Viking & Medieval times. Battle ready and museum replica swords, leather craft, horn craft, iron work and Viking jewellery.

JEREMY TENNISWOOD
PO Box 73, Aldershot, Hampshire GU11 1UJ
Contact: Jeremy Tenniswood
Tel: 01252 319791
Fax: 01252 344339
Email: 100307.1735@compuserve.com
Established 1966, dealing in collectable firearms civil and military, de-activated and for shooters; also swords, bayonets, medals, badges, insignia, buttons, headdress, ethnographica; and books. Regular lists of firearms and accessories; nedals; edged weapons; headdress, headdress badges and insignia; comprehensive lists specialist and technical books. Office open 9am–5pm, closed all day Sunday. Medal mounting service.

KAY HOUSE
4 Sandringham Drive, Welling, Kent DA16 3QU
Tel: 020 8856 8297
Email: kay.kit@talk.21.com
15th century bespoke dress and accessories. Craft demonstrations and educational displays.

KEVIN GARLICK (FOOTWEAR)
21 South Street, Ventnor, Isle of Wight PO38 1NG
Tel/Fax: 01983 854753

KING & COUNTRY
1510 North Hollowood Way, Burbank, CA 91505, USA
Contact: Harlan Glenn
Tel: 818 566 1660
Fax: 818 566 188 7
Email: kngcntry@westworld.com
Website: http://www.westworld.com/-kngcntry/index.html
Reproduction WWII Denison smocks, collarless shirts, khaki drills and maroon para berets (WWII specifics). Also orginal WWII British collectables.

KIT & KABOODLE
38 Lockwood Road, Wheatley, Doncaster, S. Yorkshire DN1 2TT
Contact: Gini Newton
Tel/Fax: 01302 562875
Email: kaboodle@mcmail.com
Website: www.kaboodle.mcmail.com
Hand made, high quality 12th-19th centuries museum exhibit replica buff coats and padded arming jocks.

THE KNIGHTS OF ARKLEY
Glen Sylen Farm, Five Roads, Llanelli, Carmarthenshire SAI5 5BJ
Contact: Penny Hard
Tel: 01269 861001
Email: knights@arkley.totalserve.co.uk
Website: www.knightsofarkley.com
Medieval jousting tournaments, corporate days, film, TV and promotions. Vast selection of horse costumes, banners, tents and props for hire. Medieval knights costumes made to order. Consultancy service for all Medieval events.

LANCASTER'S ARMOURIE
18 Ashgate Valley Road, Ashgate, Chesterfield, Derbyshire S40 4AX
Contact: Roger
Tel: 01246 270090
Email: roger@lancasters-armry.demon.co.uk
Website: www.lancasters-armry.demon.co.uk
Medieval arms and armour for the re-enactor, including our own best selling self-assembly 'flat pack' armour.

LIONHEART REPLICAS
1 Westhill Cottages, Seaford Road, Alfriston, E. Sussex BN26 5TT
Contact: Colin Torode
Tel: 01323 870803
Replica Medieval Pilgrim and secular badges.

LINNET THE SEAMSTRESS
19 Cowper Close, Mundesley, Norfolk NR11 8JS
Tel/Fax: 01263 721574
Authentic hand-finished 12th-15th centuries' costume. Shirts, braies, hose, doublets, kirtles, gowns etc. Other periods considered. Price lists on request, also talks and 'living history'.

LIVING HISTORY RESOURCES (COSTUME, ETC)
43 Croft Road, Yardley, Birmingham, W. Midlands
BS26 1SQ
Contact: R & J Sheard
Tel/Fax: 0121 784 6408

LONGSHIP TRADING COMPANY
342 Albion Street, Wall Heath, Kingswinford, W. Midlands
DY6 0JR
Contact: Ivor Wilcox
Tel: 01384 292237
Email: info@longship.org.uk
Website: www.longship.org.uk
Viking and Saxon education days in schools and museums, corporate entertainment, displays, banquets, craft displays, costume hire, film, TV and theatre work. Prop weapon and armour hire.

M J HINCHCLIFFE (BLADESMITH)
73 Minterne Waye, Hayes, Middlesex UB4 0PE
Contact: Martin Hinchcliffe
Tel/Fax: 0181 561 5996

MACDONALD ARMOURIES
At the Sign of the Cross and Sword, Brunswick St Lane, Edinburgh
Contact: Paul Macdonald
Email: macarmouries@aol.com
Website: http://users.ox.ac.uk/~zoo10328/macdonald.html
Macdonald Armouries manufactures functional reproduction historical edged weaponry, specialising in accurate weight/balance swords and daggers for the historical fencing market. Weapons are made individually to order, recreating original examples or catering to customer specifications. All styles of European weaponry from Celtic to 19th century can be created.

MACDONALD ACADEMY OF ARTS
15 Halmyre Street, Edinburgh, Scotland EH6 8QA
Contact: Paul Macdonald
Tel: 0131 538 0745
Email: macdonaldacademy@aol.com
The Macdonald academy of arts is a historical fencing academy offering professional tuition in historical swordsmanship and European martial arts from the 13th to 19th centuries, presently offering open classes twice weekly. The academy also offers weapons workshops, bespoke private tuition and informative talks and demonstrations on the history of European swordsmanship.

MACULA ARMA
34 Walpole Road, Great Yarmouth, Norfolk NR 30 4NF
Contact: Henry King
Tel: 07010 717199
Fax: 07010 717198
Email: macula@macula-arma.co.uk
Website: www.macula-arma.co.uk
All periods and styles of mail.

MADREGAL DESIGNS
Unit 9, Suprema Estate, Edington, Bridgewater, Somerset TA7 9LF
Tel: 01278 723483
Fax: 01278 723497
Email: MADREGAL723483@aol.com
Manufacturers of replica arms and armour of all periods. SAE for brochure. Quality reproductions hand forged to excellent standards.

THE MAILMAN
Plague Pit Cottage, 71 Church Street, Chesham, Buckinghamshire HP5 1HY
Contact: Ken Polton
Tel/Fax: 01494 776320
Email: lys@globalnet.co.uk
Round wire rings in steel or brass, two sizes. Advice on construction and sympathy. I may be able to supply finished articles, but no promises.

MARCUS MUSIC
Tredegar House, Newport, Gwent, Wales NP10 8YW
Contact: Marcus
Tel: 01633 815612
Fax: 01633 816979
Email: mail@marcusmusic.co.uk
Website: www.marcusmusic.co.uk
Manufacturers of all kinds of drums for re-enactment. Also small Celtic harps and psalteres.

MEDIEVAL CLOTHING COMPANY
49 Washington Grove, Bentley, Doncaster, S. Yorkshire DN5 9RJ
Contact: Sally Ann Chandler
Tel/Fax: 01302 876343
Email: medcc@medcc.3-online.co.uk
Authentic reproduction clothing and uniforms for re-enactment, schools and museums from the Conquest to early 20th century hand-made to order.

MEDIEVAL SUPPLIES
20 Weaver Drive, Western Downs, Stafford, Staffs ST17 9DD
Contact: Neil Butler
Tel/Fax: 01785 243637
Email: butlerneil@aol.com
Hand-made padded jacks, gambasons, akatons, coates of plates, and brigandines for full contact fighting, from the 5th to the 15th centuries. We also make clothing for the same period.

MERCIA SVEITER
Rosemary Cottage, Camp Road, Canwell, Sutton Coldfield B75 5RA
Contact: Paul Craddock
Tel/Fax: 0121 323 4309
Email: MerciaS@hotmail.com
Website: MerciaS.co.uk
We specialise in equipment for re-enactors between 500 and 1500 AD. We do cauldrons, chain mail (links & ready-made), horns, swords, helmets, pressed shield bosses and loads of jewellery! We are based near Birmingham and have our own historical site—see Dark Ages Charitable Trust on page 28.

MERLIN ENTERPRISES
30 Westminster Road, York, N. Yorkshire YO30 6LY
Tel/Fax: 01904 611537
Email: merlin.enterprise@bigfoot.com
Website: www.konect.mcmail.com/merlin
Import-export and supply of re-enactment weapons, period arms and armour—fencing equipment from A to Z. PX upgrades, secondhand kit and theatrical props.

MICHAEL REAPE—HISTORIC ARCHERY
Fortshaus Strasse 4, 65606 Langhecke, Germany
Contact: Michael Reape
Tel/Fax: 6474881962
Authentic medieval archery equipment for the re-enactor historian. Warbows or longbows of self yew or elm. High quality arrows made to order. Hand forged war points. Free catalogue.

MILITARY COLLECTABLES
93 Lynwood Crescent, Pontefract, W. Yorkshire NW8 3QX
Contact: PA Hampton
Tel/Fax: 01977 792084
World War 11 British, US and Allied uniforms, webbing equipment, personal kit etc. Mail order, telephone enquiries; personal callers by appointment.

MILITARIA ETZEL ANTIQUITÄTEN
Friedhofstrasse 2, 73630 Remshalden-Grunbach, Germany
Tel: 07151 72121
Fax: 07151 72949
Historical props for film and theatre.

MILITARY FEATURES & PHOTO AGENCY
Hollyville, Maesycrugiau, Pencader, Carmarthen, Wales SA39 9DL
Contact: John Norris
Tel: 01559 395301
Email: john.norris3@btinternet.com
Re-enactment photographer and columnist and battlefied tour guide for WWII sites. Travels extensively to cover re-enactor special events. Commissions undertaken.

MILITARY ODYSSEY
PO Box 254, Marden, Tonbridge, Kent TN12 9ZQ
Contact: Gary Howard
Tel/Fax: 01892 730233
Email: militaryodyssey@aol.com
Website: www.military-odyssey.com
The country's largesr multi-period historical living history extravaganza. Over 400+ trade stalls, over 400 military vehicles. Displays and dioramas; battle re-creations; children's sactivities. A packed weekend for all—too much to be seen in one day. Historical 'In Camp' Talks—from the Romans through to the Gulf War.

MOUNTAINSTONE FORGE & ARMOURY
8 Fairfield Road, Morecambe, Lancashire LA3 1ER
Contact: Peter Constantine
Tel/Fax: 01524 401292
Viking, Norman, Medieval and fantasy swords, daggers, scrams, axes, helmets, shields, polearms, hearth furniture and fittings. All weapons made to order. Blacksmith products, ironwork etc. Museums etc supplied.

THE NEW POSTMASTER
Bwlch House, Beguildy, Radnorshire LD7 1U9
Contact: B Carter
Tel: 01547 510 289
Original 19th century newspapers, containing despatches and reports from the Napoleonic Wars, the Crimea, American Civil War, European and Colonial conflicts, the Anglo-Boer War, etc. Also available: titles for WWI and II.

NICHOLAS MORIGI—THE REGALIA SPECIALIST
PO Box 103, Newmarket, Suffolk CB8 8WY
Contact: Nicholas Morigi
Fax: 01440 821246
Specialist in cloth and metal insignia of all countries from to present day. Specialising in WWI, Vietnam and current. Countries represented include Great Britain, United States, Third Reich Germany, Soviet Union and France. Mail order only. Full colour catalogue £3 (£5 overseas).

PAESCOD
38 Cowleigh Road, Malvern, Hereford &Worcester WR14 1QD
Contact: Phil Howard
Tel/Fax: 01684 292940
Email: paescod@malverns.demon.co.uk
Website: www.malverns.demon.co.uk/paescod
A troupe of raggle-taggle musicians (12th to 17th centuries). Parades, marches, victory banquets and open-air performances.

PAST TENTS
New Farm, Main Street, Clarborough, Walesby, Newark, Northamptonshire NG22 9NU
Tel/Fax: 01623 862480
Website: www.past-tents.demon.co.uk
The world's leading supplier of historical tents covering all periods. Individual commissions and designs welcomed.. Hire and repair services also available.

PAST UNLIMITED
111 Stamford Street, Ratby, Leicester, Leics LE6 0JU
Contact: Cormac O'Neill
Tel: 0116 239 5788
800-1250AD period leatherwork, footwear, costume, armour, weapons and props.

PERIOD CROSSBOWS
7 Alexandra Close, Milton Regis, Sittingbourne, Kent ME10 2JP
Contact: Robin Knight
Tel: 01795 427461
Manufacturers of crossbows and bows of all periods. Repair services offered to museums and collectors of original pieces. Seminars and lectures offered.

PETTY CHAPMAN
20 Macaulay Road, Birkby, Huddersfield, W. Yorkshire HD2 2US
Contact: David Rushworth
Tel/Fax: 01484 512968
Suppliers of natural fibre textiles for all periods of re-enactment, full-sized patterns, costume handbooks, buttons and accessories. Mail order friendly.

PLANTAGENET SHOES
82 Cozens Hardy Road, Sprowston, Norwich, Norfolk
NR7 8QG
Contact: Morgan Hubbard
Tel: 01603 414045
Email: morgan@plantagenetshoes.freeserve.co.uk

PLESSIS ARMOURIES
Contact: Kevin Legg
Tel: 01494 473129 or 0370 584830
Bespoke armour made to order.

THE PLUMERY
16 Deans Close, Chiswick, London W4 3LX
Tel/Fax: 020 8995 7099
Email: theplumery@amserve.net
The only manufacturers of horse hair, feather and wool
military plumes in the world. Ceremonial headdress, elec-
tro-forming, badges, shakos. Contractors to the MOD, the
Palace, Household Cavalry, the Foot Guards, British and
Foreign armies, TV, film, theatre, living history and haute
couture.

REDCOAT
37 Lee Avenue, North Springvale, Melbourne, Victoria 3171,
Australia
Contact: Terence Young
18th and 19th century military reproductions.

RELICS
20 St Wilfrid's Green, Hailsham, E. Sussex
BN27 1DR
Contact: Colin Hodgson
Tel: 01323 846 007
Fax: 01323 842 234
Email: relicsarms@hotmail.com
Website: www.relics.org.uk
Replica weaponry from WW I and II to the present day war
theatres—and into the future! Hand built, full size accurate
copies of guns, grenades, mines and missiles. Illustrated
catalogue available £4. 'Auld Arms' catalogue £5—includes
Wild West guns, flintlock pistols and muskets, crossbows,
swords and daggers. We supply worldwide maiol order
only.

REDHEADS
PO Box 107, Wymondham NR18 9EQ
Tel: 01953 606457
Fax: 01603 748570
Email: See Website
Website: www.interknife.co.uk
Protective arrowheads designed especially for re-enactors.
Safety rubber arrowheads especially designed to shoot
further and more accurately. With extra rubber to deter
shaft penetration. All at a bargain price!

RICHARD J UNDERWOOD
77 Stanton Road, Raynes Park, London SW20 8RW
Tel: 020 8879 0874
Mobile: 07958 449161
German Militaria. Repro kit catering for re-enactors.

THE RINGWOODS OF HISTORY
34 Sandford Road, Mapperley, Nottingham NG3 6AL
Contact: Ralph Needham
Tel: 0115 9692922
Expert historical presentations by husband and wife duo.
Fourteen characters portrayed from Medieval physician to
WWII Home Guard. Specialists in 17th century military surgery costume and artefacts of the highest possible standard. Presentations lasting from 30 minutes to 1 1/2 hours
for themed events, historical buildings, museums and history groups.

ROBES D'ÉPOQUE
12 Amphill Road, Shirley, Southampton, Hants
SO15 8LP
Tel: 01703 786849
12th-19th centuries bespoke banqueting and special
occasion wear.

ROSA MUNDI
53 Dene Street, Silksworth, Sunderland, Tyne & Wear SR3 1DA
Tel: 0191 522 0903
Email: scroopisec@hotmail.com
Rosa Mundi work to the highest standards of research and
practical skills to present all aspects of military and
domestic life of the late fifteenth century (1475-1500).
Our hierarchical military structure demonstrates the skills
and technologies of late Medieval warfare using authentic
period fighting techniques.

ROY KING
Sussex Farm Museum, Horam, Nr Hathfield, E Sussex TN21 0JB
Tel: 01435 813733
All types of European arms and armour, from Roman to
English Civil War. Available for lecture/demonstrations and
film/television work. 30 years experience. Trade stand
available for large events. UK supplier for 'Deltin' swords.

RUNNING WOLF PRODUCTIONS (VIDEO ETC)
Crogo Mains, Corsock, Castle Douglas, Kirkcudbrightshire
DG7 3DR, Scotland
Contact: M Loades
Video production company—suppliers of 'Archery—Its
History and Forms' and 'The Blow by Blow Guide to
Swordfighting'. Mike Loades also available for lectures,
workshops and fight arranging assignments.

ST GEORGE ARMOURY
10 Beech Drive, Braunstone Town, Leicester LE3 3DA
Tel: 0116 2246202
Living history quality armour, swords and daggers, all hand
crafted for re-enactors, museums, the film industry and
collectors.

SAEMARR (ARMOUR ETC)
73 Howdale Road, Downham Market, Norfolk PE38 9AH
Contact: Peter Seymour
Tel: 01366 384316
Dark Ages, Medieval clothing, weapons, armour, leather-
ware, domestic and military artwork and utensils.
Specialists in heathen Germanic jewellery, regalia; free
runelore tuition and divination service.

SALLY GREEN HISTORICAL COSTUME
1 Lyng Lane, North Lopham, Diss, Norfolk IP22 2HR
Contact: Sally Green
Tel/Fax: 01953 681676
Email: sally.green@calltoarms.com
Website: www.calltoarms.com/sallygreen.htm
12th to 19th century accurate, quality costume at reasonable prices. 17th and 15th century clothing for re-enactors a speciality. Other periods and requirements to order.

SARAH JUNIPER
109 Woodmancote, Dursley, Gloucestershire GL11 4AH
Tel: 01453 545675
Footwear—Roamn, Tudor, 17th 18th, early 19th centuries. Not Medieval.

SARAH THURSFIELD HISTORICAL COSTUMES
Ashgrove, Overton Road, St Martins, Oswestry, Shropshire SY11 3DG
Tel/Fax: 01691 778019
Email: sarah.thursfield@btinternet.com
Patterns, demonstrations and technical advice—museum quality clothing and sewn accessories especially pre-1650. Capacity limited, only one pair of hands.

SENTIMENTAL JOURNEY
35-37 Chapelgate, Sutton St James, Spalding, Lincolnshire PE12 0EF
Contact: Ian Durrant
Tel/Fax: 01945 440289
Email: mail@sentimentaljourney.co.uk
Website: www.sentimentaljourney.co.uk
Specialists in items relating to Britain's conflicts between 1914 and 1965: uniforms, webbing, personal kit, signals equipment, manuals, newspapers, magazines, books and ephemera relating to the armed and civilian forces. Mail order only, catalogue published quarterly. Importers for Service Publications titles. Online shop available at website.

SHIELDS UP!
Imladris, 224 Coatham Road, Redcar, Cleveland TS10 1RA
Contact: John Watson
Tel: 01642 489227
Mobile: 0468 527795
Curved shields a speciality, Norman teardrop and flat top kites, short medieval heaters.

SOLDIERS III
Brent
Tel: 01342 835669 0860 236291
Blank firing. De-Act. Air Soft. Replica weapons.

SPOILS OF WAR
Plas Adda Bach Tre'rddol, Corwen, Denbighshire, Wales
Contact: Brett or Alison Jones
Tel/Fax: 01490 413148
All kinds of equipment covering all periods.

STEVE RALPHS
Street Farm Barn, Market Place, Kenninghall, Norfolk NR16 2AH
Tel: 01953 887669
Mobile: 07788 487423
Email: steve.ralphs@virgin.net

TARPAULIN & TENT COMPANY
101–103 Brixton Hill, London SW21 AA
Tel: 020 8674 0121
Fax: 020 8674 0124

THE TIME LORDS (MED) BCM
Box 220, London WC1N 3XX
Contact: Stuart Andrews
Tel/Fax: 020 8809 6119
Email: trustu@flexnet.co.uk
Specialists in presenting and producing your re-enactment event. Pyrotechnics and stunts arranged; PA systems and sound production; video and theatrical events catered for; 15 years experience.

THOMAS, LORD BURGH KG's RETINUE 1460–1496
54 Grantham Road, Waddington, Lincoln, Lincolnshire LN5 9LS
Contact: Paul Mason
Tel: 07762 300656
Fax: 01522 875763
Email: lordburgh@aol.com
Website: www.lord-burgh.com
Social and military re-enactment and living history from the Wars of the Roses, based within a knight's household. Featuring cookery, religion, arms & armour, clothes, hands-on archery, talks & demonstrations. Available for film & TV work. Period covered 1460–1496.

TRAILBLAZERS WESTERN RE-ENACTORS ASSOCIATION
38 Harewood Road, Harrogate, North Yorkshire HG3 2TW
Contact: Tony Rollins
Tel: 01423 502442
Website: www.4thcavalry.co.uk
We are a Western re-enactment and living history association who enjoy researching and recreating all aspects of 19th century American life. Based in Yorkshire we can often be seen at the Yorkshire Farming Museum, York, as 4th Cavalry. Available for shows as a means of raising funds for charity.

VICTOR JAMES (TENT MAKER)
427 Anglesey Road, Burton-on-Trent, Staffordshire DE14 3NE
Contact: Victor James
Tel/Fax: 0128310285
Email: vicstents@mariee.new.labour.org.uk
Victor James makes historical tents for the re-enactor from the best quality 12oz duck cotton rot and water retardant, from Roman to ACW. Send SAE for catalogue.

VIKING CRAFTS
20 Snowbell Square, Ecton Brook, Northampton
NN3 5HH
Contact: Mike Haywood
Tel/Fax: 01604 412672
Email: mike@vikingcrafts.co.uk
Website: www.vikingcrafts.co.uk
We supply replicas, 'in the style', and copies of historical artefacts and games from the Dark and Viking ages. These include: pewter, bronze and silver, pendants, mythological figures and belt fittings, leatherwork, weapons, helmets, shields, woodwork and horn and games such as: Hnefatafl, Nine Mans Morris, chess, Runes etc.

WW 2 GERMAN RE-ENACTMENT
Brian 01553 774543
Clothing, equipment, medals, awards etc bought, sold, exchanged. Genuine Third Reich items also bought and sold.

WHITEROSE
Unit 59 Clock Tower Business Centre, Works Road, Hollingwood, Chesterfield S43 2PE
Tel: 01246 475 782
Fax: 01246 471 123
Website: www.white-rose-armourys.co.uk or www.white-rose-castings.com
Arms and armour from Ancient Greek to Civil War. Brass and bronze castings.

TOY SOLDIER MANUFACTURERS & SUPPLIES

ALL THE QUEEN'S MEN
The Old Cottage, Gilmorton, Lutterworth, Leicestershire
LE17 5PN
Contact: D Cross
Tel: 01455 552653
Fax: 01455 557787
Email: derek@allthequeen'smen.com
Website: www.allthequeen'smen.com
Designers & producers of military miniatures (toy soldiers). 490 sets available. Full colour catalogue with descriptive lists. Plus unique exquisite interlocking base vignettes. Visits to our showroom/museum by appointment.

ARKOVA
29 Taw View, Fremington, Barnstaple, Devon EX31 2NJ
Contact: Allan R Over

ARMOURY OF ST JAMES
17 Piccadilly Arcade, Piccadilly, London SWIY 6NH
Contact: Richard Kirch
Tel: 020 7493 5082
Fax: 020 7499 4422
Specialists in Orders of Chivalry of the world and hand painted military and historical model figures.

ARMY SUPPLY COMPANY
6 Old Bank, Ripponden, Halifax, W. Yorkshire HX6 4DG
Contact: Michael Carter

*AU PLAT D'ETAIN
16 Rue Guisarde, 75006 Paris, France

AVANT GARDE MODELS
22 Barcaldine Avenue, Chryston, Glasgow, Strathclyde, Scotland G69 9NT
Contact: Derek McCarron
Manufacturers of quality toy soldiers; mail order only. Ranges include ACW, WWII, Scottish and Montenegrin figures. Commissions undertaken. Send SAE or IRC for list.

B F M COLLECTABLES
Nuthatches, Crown Gardens, Fleet, Hampshire GU13 9PD
Contact: B Ford
Producers of superb historical figure sets realistically sculpted and painted in traditional style. SAE for leaflet; trade enquiries welcome.

BASTION MODELS
36 St. Mary's Road, Liss, Hampshire GU33 7AH
Contact: Andre,w Rose
Tel/Fax: 01730 893478
54mm quality toy soldiers, covering American Civil War, British colonial wars, European armies, Boxer Rebellion, world wars and more.

CAMPAIGN MINIATURES
5 Barrowgate Road, Chiswick, London W4 4QX
Contact: Peter Johnstone

*CEARD-STAOINE
Liebigstr 8, D-91052 Erlangen, Germany
Contact: Friedrich Frenzel
Tel/Fax: 9131 34973
Producer of flats: 30mm Celtic and British history, 30mm English literature, 10mm doll's house tin figures, 20mm dioramas in matchboxes.

CHARLES HALL PRODUCTIONS
Paisley Terrace, Edinburgh, Lothian EH8 7JW, Scotland
Contact: Charles Hall

DEREK CROSS (A Q M) LTD
The Old Cottage, Gilmorton, Lutterworth, Leicestershire LE17 5PN
Contact: Derek Cross
Tel: 01455 552653
Fax: 01455 557787
Email: derek@allthequeensmen.com
We are designers & producers of military miniatures (toy soldiers); over 373 sets available. Full colour catalogue with descriptive lists. Visits to our showroom/museum by appointment.

DRUMBEAT MINIATURES
4 Approach Road, Ramsey, Isle of Man IM8 1EB
Contact: Peter Rogerson
Tel/Fax: 01624 816667
Email: dbeatmin@aol.com
A large and rapidly expanding range of toy soldiers covering many periods and unusual subjects. Sets can be varied on request and a sculpting service is offered.

DUCAL MODELS
5 Weavilis Road, Eastleigh, Hampshire SO50 8HQ
Contact: Thelma Duke
Tel: 01703 692119
Fax: 01703 602456
Email: jackandthelma@fort-ducal.co.uk
Website: www.fort-ducal.co.uk
Makers and distributors of an international range of hand crafted and painted 54mm metal ceremonial figures, mounted and on foot. World wide mail order; colour illustrated catalogue £3.95 (overseas postage extra) includes badges and postcards. Visitors welcome to see our extensive display weekdays 9am–4.30pm; also some Saturdays, by appointment. Phone for directions.

ENSIGN HISTORICAL MINIATURES
32 Scaitcliffe View, Todmorden, Lancashire OL14 8EL
Contact: Paul Wood
Tel/Fax: 01706 818203
Manufacturers of white metal 54mm traditional toy soldiers. Ranges include: English Civil War, Colonial, Indian Army and Vikings. Available painted or as castings.

F & S SCALE MODELS
227 Droylsden Road, Audenshaw, Greater Manchester, M34 5RT
Tel/Fax: 01613703235
Email: frank/sue@fsmodels.fsnet.co.uk

FORBES & THOMSON
Burgate Antiques Centre, 10c Burgate, Canterbury, Kent
Contact: Rowena Forbes
Specialist dealers in old toy soldiers by Britain's, Johillco etc. and related lead and tinplate toys. Model soldiers & kits by Rose Models and Chota Sahib. Painted military miniature figures. Mail order and office address, PO Box 375, South Croydon, CR2 6ZG. Open Mon–Sat 10.00am–5.00pm.

FUSILIER MINIATURES (MAIL ORDER)
The Command Post, 23 Ashcott Close, Burnham-on-Sea, Somerset TA8 1HW
Contact: Tony Moore
Tel/Fax: 01278 786858
A wide range of hand-painted, well-detailed figures and guns in 1:32 scale. Sets and single figures available. SAE and £1.50 for current catalogue.

GEORGE OPPERMAN
Flat 12, 110/112 Bath Road, Cheltenham, Gloucestershire GL35 7JX
Contact: George Opperman
Private collector with large collection to sell. 50,000 lead soldiers, military books and magazines, post and cigarette cards. Send SAE and three 1st class stamps for lists. Mail order only.

GLEBE MINIATURES
Retreat House, Dorchester Road, Broadwey, Weymouth, Dorset DT3 5LN
Contact: Peter Turner
Tel/Fax: 01305 815300
Glebe Miniatures, in addition to their original range, now offer marching sets to complement action sets, and action sets to complement marching sets—all in the original Britain's' style. The first sets represent the Balkan Wars and the Russian/Japanese conflicts. There are new mounted officers and action artillery sets. Other period sets will follow.

GOOD SOLDIERS
246 Broadwater Crescent, Stevenage, Hertfordshire SG2 8HL
Contact: Alan Goodwin
Tel/Fax: 01438 354362 (pm)
Producers of 'toy style' soldiers and figures, also cartoon characters and personalities. These are available painted and unpainted. SAE for lists. Trade enquiries welcomed.

H ZWICKY AU VIEUX PARIS
1 Rue de la Servette, CH-1201 Geneva, Switzerland
Tel: 227342576
Fax: 227347709
Shop open in 1964: everything for the military modeller.

HENLEY MODEL MINIATURES
24 Reading Road', Henley-on-Thames, Oxfordshire RG9 1AB
Contact: David Hazell
Tel/Fax:01491572684
Email: enquiries@toysoldier.co.uk
We stock the widest range of painted toy soldiers available
in the UK, together with castings, paints and modelling
materials. Mail order a pleasure.

J S DIETZ TOY SOLDIERS
2726 Shelter Island Drive, San Diego, CA 92106, USA
Tel/Fax: 619 223 1503
Website: http://home.earthlink.net/-jsdietz/
Manufacturer of new 54mm toy soldiers. Napoleonic
specialists. Also Jacobite rebellion, French and Indian wars,
WW I artillery and machine gun sets. Trade enquiries
welcome.

*JEAN-PIERRE FEIGLY
BP 66, 93162 Noisy le Grand, France

KING & COUNTRY
20 Rockingham Way, Portchester, Fareham, Hampshire PO16
8QS
Contact: Mike Neville
Tel/Fax: 01329 233141
Email: mike@kingandcountry.co.uk
Suppliers of fine quality, all-metal, handpainted 54mm
military and civilian figures, plus handcarved 1:32 scale
desk top display. Aircraft and vehicles. Mail order our
speciality.

LONE WARRIOR
PO Box 16171, Glasgow, Scotland G13 1YJ
Contact: Les White
Manufacturer of quality metal 54mm toy soldiers, specialist
in unusual military periods. Commissions undertaken.
Supplier of new, reissue and original plastic figures. List
available.

*M D M LES GRANDES COLLECTIONS
9 Rue Villedo, 75001 Paris, France
Manufacturer of tin soldiers, miniatures for collectors;
Napoleonics; French Regimental standards of US War of
Independence; mail order service.

MARKSMEN MODELS
(Dept MDS), 7 Goldsmith Avenue, London W3 6HR
Contact: Michael Ellis
Tel: 020 8992 0132
Fax: 020 8992 5980
High quality, low cost plastic figures from 25mm to
120mm, most periods from ancient to Korean War. Mostly
cast from original Marx and Ideal moulds. Also sculpting
and visualising for many leading manufacturers.

MILITIA MODELS
Rosedean, Gorsty Knoll, Coleford, Gloucestershire GL16 7LR
Contact: Esme Walker
Cottage industry still producing—after sudden death of
founder Ken Walker—small number of new 54mm figures
in limited edition action sets, 1870-1902 period.

NAEGEL
Stand B23, Grays Antique Market, 1–7 Davies Mews, Davies
Street, London W1
Contact: Stephen Naegel
Tel: 020 7491 3066
Fax: 020 7784 514 7
Email: toysoldiers.naegel@btinternet.com
Website: http://www.btinternet.com/-naegel
Largest display of lead toy soldiers in Europe. Books; list
available; mail order welcome. Open 10am–4pm, Mon–Fri.

NEW CAVENDISH BOOKS
3 Denbigh Road, London W11 2SJ
Tel: 020 7229 6765
Fax: 020 7792 0027
Email: narisa@new-cav.demon.co.uk
Specialist publishers of quality illustrated books on toys
and other collectables.

PATRICKS TOYS AND MODELS
107–111 Lillie Road, Fulham, London
Tel: 020 7385 9864
Fax: 020 7385 2187
Website: www.patrickstoys.co.uk

PAX BRITANNICA
Tharn Cottage, 67 Malcolm Road, Peterculter, Aberdeen,
Scotland AB14 0XB
Contact: T Brown
Manufacturer of hand painted toy figures in traditional
style, specialising in Scottish civilians. Range includes
Highland games, personality, sporting and clan figures.

PIPER CRAFT
4 Hillside Cottages, Glenboig, Lanarkshire, Scotland ML5 2QY
Contact: Thomas Moles
Tel: 01236 873801
Fax: 01236 873044
Manufacturer of white metal military and non-military
figures designed to a general scale of 75mm. Suppliers to
museums, places of historic interest, shops and collectors.
Established 1985. Send SAE or two IRCs for a complete
illustrated list.

*PIXI
25 Ruc Amelot, 75011 Paris, France

PRIDE OF EUROPE
Shamrock Villa, Southernhay, Clifton Wood, Bristol, Avon
BS8 4TL
Contact: R J Dew
Pride of Europe produce an economically priced range of
new, old style toy soldiers made of metal alloy and hand
painted to a high standard.

QUALITY MODEL SOLDIERS
Hippins Farm, Blackshawshead, Hebden Bridge, W. Yorkshire HX7 7JG
Contact: G M Haley
Tel/Fax: 01422 842484
Quality Model Soldiers is pleased to announce the re-launch of toy soldiers from the Franco-Prussian War. These finely cast colourfully painted and realistically animated models were first issued in the late 1970s and early 1980s and soon gained a devoted following. The new range with entirely new figures will be produced on a thematic basis representing regiments that figured prominently in actions from the campaign. Foot, cavalry, artillery and equipment will be made, production ,being limited to 150 sets, obtain-able from the manufacturer only. There will be the option of obtaining limited edition single figures. In addition, a special display set will be available of 50 sets only for each action, featuring scenery or buildings. For further details on the first sets 'Action at Schirlendorf' please contact us at the above address.

RANK & FILE
16 Oxburton, Stoke Gifford, Bristol, Avon BS12 6RP
Contact: P Tarrant
Produce toy soldiers for the connoisseur from the late 1800s. Also high detail model waterline ships of the Merchant and Royal Navy. Bands of the county regiments, rifle brigades and fusiliers are available to order. Send SAE for price list.

REPLICA MODELS
40 Durbar Avenue, Foleshill, Coventry, W. Midlands CV6 5LU
Tel: 01203 684338

SAC LTD
Studio Anne Carlton, Flinton Street, Hull, N. Humberside HU3 4NB
Contact: M A Schofield
Tel: 01482 327019
Fax: 01482 210490
Email: info@sac-games.com
Website: www.sac-gaities.com
Manufacturers of the finest hand made and hand decorated chess sets in the world, many of them featuring military campaigns and battles.

SARUM SOLDIERS LTD
2A Upper Tooting Park, London SW17 7SW
Contact: Patrick Willis
Tel: 020 8767 1525
Fax: 020 8677 5503
Manufacturer and retailer of Sarum Studio Figurines and Sarum Traditional Soldiers in 54mm scale. Studio Figurines include the 'History of the Regiments' series designed by Andrew C Stadden, and the 'Chota Sahib' range by Sid Horton. Toy soldiers include 'Armies of the Great Powers 1870-1914', and modern British army in ceremonial uniforms.

SOLDIER PAC
2 Holland Drive, Muxton, Telford, Shropshire TF2 8RA
Contact: Mr Chris Bartlett
Tel/Fax: 01952 676822
Producers of re-cast W.Britain figures (1893-1969): horses, vehicles, guns and wagons. Hundreds of spare parts. Send A5 SAE for listing.

TOY ARMY WORKSHOP
The Hollies, Roe Downs Road, Medstead, Alton, Hampshire GU34 5LG
Contact: Grabani Pettitt
Specialist in WWI vehicles, equipment and soldiers in 54mm scale in toy style. Send SAE for list.

TOYWAY
Unit 20 Jubilee Trade Centre, Jubilee Road, Letchworth, Hertfordshire SG6 1SG
Contact: Richard Morriss
Tel: 01462 672509
Fax: 01462 672132
Email: toys@toyway.co.uk
Toyway manufacture and distribute Timpo 54mm figures and accessories.

TRADITION OF LONDON LTD
33 Curzon Street, Mayfair, London W1V 7AL
Contact: Steve Hare
Tel: 020 7493 7452
Fax: 020 7355 1224
Largest range of painted and unpainted figures in 54mm, 90nim, 110mm plus over 300 different 'Toy Soldier' style sets, including 'Sharpe' range. Full mail order, credit cards. Shop open Mon-Fri 9.00am-5.30pm, Sat 9.30am-3.00pm.

TROPHY MINIATURES WALES LTD
Unit 4, Vale Enterprise Centre, Sully, Penarth, S. Glamorgan CF64 5SY, Wales
Tel: 01446 721011
Fax: 01446 732483
Email: sales@trophyminiatures.co.uk
Toy soldier manufacturer—catalogue, mail order. Factory open for visitors—phone for directions and appointment.

V C MINIATURES
16 Dunraven Street, Aberkenfig, Bridgend, Glamorgan, Mid-Wales, CF32 9AS
Contact: Lyn Thorne
Tel/Fax: 01056 725006
Established 1987, manufacturer of hand painted 54mm toy soldiers, sculpted by Lyn Thorne and specialising in the Victorian period. In addition to sets of traditional toy soldiers, military and civilian vignettes and individual figures are also produced. Recently acquired are Burlington Models range of racehorses, jockeys and showjumping figures.

VENTURA CASTINGS
119 Farnham Road, Guildford, Surrey GU2 5QE
Contact: Tony Pope
Tel: 01483 300574
Fax: 01483 452374
Email: tonypope@ukonline.co.uk
Manufacturers of Elite Forces, P & B and A.R.T.S. Trade
and retail sales. Casting and mould making service
available.

W D MODEL FAIRS
c/o Garden Flat, 75 Bouverie Street West, Folkestone, Kent
CT20 2RL
Contact: Richard Windrow
Tel/Fax: 01303 240006
Organisers of International Toy Soldier Fair held annually on
a Saturday in March at a venue on The Lees, Folkestone.
All trade stands (from @30), toy soldier manufacturers
and dealers; open to public. Enquire for up-to-date details.

WHITTLESEY MINIATURES
75 Mayfield Road, Eastrea, Whittlesey, Peterborough,
Cambridgeshire PE7 2AY
Contact: Keith Over
Tel/Fax: 01733 205131
Manufacturers and suppliers of high quality, painted 'toy'
soldiers. Currently specialising in Medieval and Ancient
subjects in 54mm. Master and mould making services are
available.

WOLFE TOY SOLDIERS
445 Wisden Road, Stevenage, Hertfordshire SG1 5JS
Contact: Ken George
British Army and colonial figures c. 1900. Sets of six
painted, single figures painted and castings. All compatible
with early Britain's figure 54mm.

YEOMANRY MINIATURES
10 Dolphin Lodge, Grand Avenue, Worthing, W. Sussex BN11 5AL
Contact: Brian Harrison
Manufacturers of finely sculpted cavalry figures for the
connoisseur. Available hand-painted in the modern toy
style to the highest standards or as castings.

TRAVEL

ACCRINGTON PALS
Email: andrew.jackson@btinternet.com_

ANGLO ZULU TOURS
18 Beaconsfield Road, Canterbury, Kent
Contact: Ian Knight
Tel: 01227 455148
Fax: 01227 766422
Email: mahaweni@compuserve.com
Specialising in tours to the Anglo-Zulu war battlefields in
Natal.

BARTLETTS BATTLEFIELD JOURNEYS
Chart House, 9 Tudor Park, Horncastle, Lincolnshire LN9 5EZ
Contact: David or Jean Bartlett
Tel: 01507 523128
Fax: 01507 523128
Email: enquiries@battlefields.co.uk
Western Front battlefield tours.

BIRMINGHAM WAR RESEARCH SOCIETY
43 Norfolk Place, King Norton, Birmingham B30 3LB
Contact: Alex Bulloch
Tel: 0121 459 9008
Fax: 0121 459 8128
Battlefield tours, cemetery visits Northern Europe.

BURMAH TRAVEL SERVICE
36c Sisters Avenue, London SW11 5SQ
Contact: Nicholas Greenwood
Tel/Fax: 020 7223 8987
Email: travel@burmah.co.uk
Burma: war tours to all areas, including Arakan, Chindwin,
Myitkyina, Mandalay, Meiktila, Maymyo, Lashio, Pegu,
Moulmein, Htaukkyant and Thanbyuzayat cemeteries.

FRONT LINE BATTLEFIELD TOURS
10 Ashburton Avenue, Birkenhead, Merseyside L43 8TJ
Contact: Graham Maddocks
Tel/Fax: 0151 653 7108
Author of 'Liverpool Pals' and 'Battleground Europe–
Montauban' specialising in tours of the Somme and
Montauban battlefields.

GALINA INTERNATIONAL BATTLEFIELD TOURS
1 Tokenspire Business Park, Woodmansey, Beverley,
N. Humberside HU17 0TB
Contact: Barry Matthews
Tel: 01482 880602
Fax: 01482 880603
Email: info@schooltours.co.uk
Official tour operators Normandy Veterans' Association.
Group, school, coach tours, self-drive tours. Programme
includes Western Front, Dunkirk, Normandy, Arnhem, Italy,
Gallipoli. Escrow Bonded Trustee Account.

GRAPESHOT TOURS
Bristow House, Castle Street, Mere, Wiltshire BA12 6JF
Contact: Ann & Michael Hannon
Tel/Fax: 01747 800149
Email: grapeshot@talk21.com
In the footsteps of the Emperor–tours which bring the whole
exciting story of the Napoleonic age to life, with lectures, visits,
superb hotels and transport. Write or ring for colour brochure.

HISTORIC TOURS
Email: ww2tour@aol.com

HISTORICAL TOURS
PO Box 3241, Parklands, Gauteng 2121 South Africa
Contact: Mike Hardisty
Tel: 27114478574
Fax: 27114423479
Email: marleneh@medscheme.co.za

HOLTS, TOURS (BATTLEFIELDS & HISTORY)
15 Market Street, Sandwich, Kent CT13 9DA
Contact: John Hughes-Wilson
Tel: 01304 612248
Fax: 01304 614930
Email: www.battletours.co.uk
Europe's leading military historical tour operator, offering annual worldwide programme spanning history from the Romans to the Falklands War. Holts provides tours for both the Royal Armouries Leeds and the fWM. Every tour accompanied by specialist guide-lecturer. Send for free brochure.

HOVERLAND EUROPEAN HOLIDAYS
61 Bradford Street, Walsall, W. Midlands WS1 3QD
Contact: Steve Gouldby
Tel: 01922 614444
Fax: 01922 720728
Email: sales@hoverland.co.uk
Website: www.hoverland.co.uk
European battlefield tours.

IAN FLETCHER BATTLEFIELD TOURS
PO Box 112, Rochester, Kent ME1 2EX
Contact: Ian Fletcher
Tel: 01634 319973
Fax: 01634 324263
Email: fletchertour@aol.com
Website: www.members.aol.com/fetchertour
Specialising in the Napoleonic Peninsular war tours.

LEGER HOLIDAYS
Canklow Meadows, Rotherham S60 2XR
Contact: Ralph Bennett
Tel: 01709 839839
Fax: 01709 833826
Email: reservations@leger.co.uk
Website: www.leger.co.uk
Battlefield tours specialists.

MIDAS HISTORIC TOURS LIMITED
Grosvenor Cottage, Barleyfields, Gillingham, Dorset SP8 4EU
Contact: Alan Rooney
Tel: 01747 826520
Fax: 01932 405000
Email: info@midastours.co.uk
Escorted tours to the battlefields of the world, including Ancient, Medieval, Napoleonic, ACW, South Africa, India, Crimea, WWI, WWII. Specialised group tours organised. ATOL 3716.

MIDDLEBROOK-HODGSON BATTLEFIELD TOURS
48 Linden Way, Boston, Lincolnshire PE21 9DS
Contact: Martin Middlebrook
Tel: 01205 364555
Specialist battlefield tours by WWI expert author.

MILITARY HISTORICAL TOURS
Email: mht@miltours.com

REGEL COACH HOLIDAYS
60 King Street, Drighlington, W. Yorkshire BD11 1EL
Contact: Bryn Slack
Tel: 0113 287 9191
Fax: 0113 287 9110
Email: regel @holiday50.freeserve.co.uk
WWI and II European battlefield tours.

ROYAL BRITISH LEGION PILGRIMAGES DEPARTMENT
Royal British legion Village, Aylesford, Kent ME20 7NX
Contact: Piers Storie-Pugh
Tel: 01622 716729
Fax: 01622 715768
Email: info@britishlegion.org.uk
Worldwide battlefield tours department specialising in sub-sidised tours for widows and families to visit the graves of their loved ones.

SOCIETY OF FRIENDS OF THE NATIONAL MUSEUM
c/o National Army Museum, Royal Hospital Road, London SW3 4HT
Contact: Derek A Mumford
Tel/Fax: 020 7730 0717
The Society of Friends of the National Army Museum assists the museum in the acquisition of significant militaria; and members enjoy lectures, private views, battlefield and army establishment excursions, and newsletters. annual subscription £8.00; contact Secretary/Treasurer above.

SOMME BATTLEFIELD TOURS
19 Old Road, Wimborne, Dorset BH21 1EJ
Contact: James Power
Tel: 01202 840520
Fax: 01202 840520
Email: jamespower@btinternet.com
Non-profit making tours of the Somme battlefields.

TOURS INTERNATIONAL
1 Sheffield Road, Tunbridge Wells, Kent TN4 0PD
Contact: Ralph Bennett
Tel: 01892 515825
Fax: 01892 515815
Email: res@tours-international.co.uk
Website: ww.tours-with-experts.com
Battlefield tours with historical experts covering all periods.

TOURS WITH THE EXPERTS
Red Lion Building, 1 Liverpool Road North, Maghull L31 2HB
Tel: 0151 526 0075
Fax: 0151 531 0052
Email: info@twel.fsnet.co.uk

TRANS EUROPE TOURS
Email: alan@destinationseurope.com

TRAVELLING TOGETHER
44 High Street, Meldreth, Near Royston, Herts SG8 6JU
Contact: Geoff Robinson
Tel: 01763 262190
Fax: 01763 262356
Mobile: 0802 767643
Email: travellingtogether@ukbusiness.com
Tailor-made tours for private groups.

WAR RESEARCH SOCIETY
27 Courtway Avenue, Maypole, Birmingham B14 4PP
Contact: Ian or Jean Alexander
Tel: 0121 430 5348
Fax: 0121 436 7401
Email: battletour@aol.com
Battlefield tours.

WHITEGROUNDS WORLDWIDE
Thornthorpe, Malton, North Yorkshire YO17 9LX
Contact: Roger Preston
Tel: 01653 658305
Fax: 01653 658598
Email: whiteground@aol.com
Website: www.whitegrounds.ndirect.co.uk
Specialising in British South African battlefield tours.

UNIFORMS, INSIGNIA, ARMOUR & GENERAL MILITARIA DEALERS

*A & V A HOFFMANN
Kolonnenstrasse 46, 10829 Berlin, Germany

ABA
Stand 54, Marché Jules Vallés, Puces se St Ouen, France
Tel: 06 07851919
For corrrespondence and orders: 750 Avenue de la Gare, 77310 St Fargeau-Ponthierry, France
Tel: 01 60657833
Fax: 01 60657834
Email: ste.aba@libertysurf.fr
Militaria covering all wars and countries 1870–1960.

A B I
118 Chapelon, Clascote Heath, Tamworth, Staffs B77 2EW
Contact: D Preece
Tel: 01827 62055
Mobile: 07774 447965
Fax: 01827 284217
Email: info@abimilitaria.co.uk
Website: www.abimilitaria.co.uk
British and foreign militaria.

AIR DEFENSE ARTILLERY ASSOCIATION
PO Box 6101, Bldg 1735 Pleasanton Rd, Fort Bliss, TX 79906, USA
Contact: Max Winegar
Tel: 915 564 4331
Fax: 915 568 9407
Email: adaagifts@aol.com
Website: www.firsttofire.com
We sell a variety of Air Defense memorabilia for soldiers and civilians.

A J W MILITARIA
PO Box HP96, Leeds, Yorkshire LS6 3XU
Contact: J Anderson
Tel/Fax: 011327 58060
Email: militaria@ajwmil.freeserve.co.uk
Organiser of Berwick, Chester, Richmond, Beverley and Morecambe Militaria Fairs. All fairs run three to four times a year and have up to forty tables at each event.

ALADDINS SURPLUS
38 Comberton Hill, Kidderminster, Worcestershire DY10 1QN
Contact: Steve Langer
Tel/Fax: 0152 863464
Ex Government surplus stockists, also general militaria, cap badges, uniforms. From wartime to modern day. A real Aladdin's cave.

ALDA MILITARIA
Email: alda@tpg.com.au

ALL OUR YESTERDAYS
56 Fort Cumberland Road, Southsea, Portsmouth PO4 9LQ
Contact: Margaret Toft
Tel/Fax: 023 9286 3248
Vintage clothes, accessories and other items.

AMAC (UK) LTD
Unit 41, Crossley Park, Crossley Road, Greater Manchester M19 2SH
Contact: David Sykes
Tel: 0161 442 7224
Fax: 0161 442 4140
Email: sales1@amacuk.co.uk
Sells all clothing, textiles and tentage which was previously sold by auction or tender by the Ministry of Defence. House of business 8.30am-5pm Mon-Fri.

AMERICAN BADGE COMPANY
PO Box 29, Morley, Leeds LS27 7UD
Contact: Gynn Roberts
Tel?fax: 01923 226508
Email: sales@americanbadge.co.uk
Website: www.american.co.uk

AMES SWORD COMPANY
Email: sales@amessword.com

A M S MILITARIA
25 Rue Sans Souci, B-1050 Brussels, Belgium
Tel: 00 32 25 11 53 25
Fax: 0032 25 11 19 45
Website: www.amsmilitaria.com
General militaria covering all countries.

ANCHOR SUPPLIES LTD
Peasehill Road, Ripley, Derbyshire DE5 3JG
Contact: Barbara Merrett
Tel: 01773 570139
Fax: 01773 570537
Email: sales@govvsurplus.co.uk
Anchor Supplies, one of Europe s largest genuine government surplus dealers. Specialising in clothing, tools, electronics, domestic ware, furniture, watches, military vehicles, you name it! Goods are available mail order, or visit our Derbyshire or Nottingham depots. Please ring for directions.

ANDERSON'S
B12, Grays Antique Market, 1-7 Davies Mews, London W1
Tel/Fax: 020 7491 3066
Email: info@btinternet.com/-maegel
Full Dress British uniforms and headdress- postcards and other small ceremonial items. Open Mon-Fri 10am-4pm.

ANDREW BUTLER MILITARIA & INSIGNIA
10 Avebury Avenue, Ramsgate, Kent CT11 8BB
Contact: Andrew Butler
Tel/Fax: 01843 582216
Email: sales@abinsignia.com
Website: www.abinsignia.com
US and UK military insignia. Re-enactment insignia also made and supplied. Wholesale available. Museums supplied.

ANDY'S ARMOURY
Beacon Hill Road, Beacon Hill, Hindhead, Surrey
Tel: 01428 609356
Mobile: 0385 542475
Militaria and Army Surplus. Old and new goods bought and sold. Open six days a week. Mon-Wed 1pm-5pm. Thurs-Sat 1pm-6pm.

ANTIQUE AND COLLECTABLE FIREARMS AND MILITARIA HQ
Email: hq@oldguns.net

ANTHONY D GOODLAD
26 Fairfield Road, Brockwell, Chesterfield, Derbyshire
S40 4TP
Tel/Fax: 01246 204004
General militaria, with emphasis on German World War I and II items. Exhibitor at many UK arms and militatria fairs. Personal callers by appointment only.

ANTIQUE AMERICAN FIREARMS
The Meadows, Guildford Road, Cranleigh, Surrey GU6 8PF
Contact: Pete Holder
Tel: 01483 277788
Fax: 01483 277784
Email: pete.holder@cableol.co.uk
Antique American firearms; specialist dealer in Colt percussion, early cartridge and single-action weapons; also Remington, Winchester, Smith & Wesson. I buy, sell and exchange.

ANTIQUE ARMOURY
Moorside Farm, Cauldon Lowe, Stoke-on-Trent, Staffordshire
ST10 3ET
Contact: D R Cooper
Tel: 01538 702 738
Fax: 01538 702 662
Email: davercooper@talk21.com
Bought/,sold: antique arms/armour, British military medals, headgear, badges, uniforms etc. Specialising in pre-1920, and militaria to Staffs Regiments.

ANTIQUES
Main Street, Durham-on-Trent, Nottinghamshire NG22 0TY
Contact: R G Barnett
Tel/Fax: 01777 228312
Antique flintlock and percussion pistols and long arms, swords, daggers and armour our speciality. Also buy and sell general antiques, furniture, etc.

ARMS FAIRS LTD (PM)
PO Box 2654, Lewes, E. Sussex BN71BF
Tel/Fax: 01273 475959
Organisers of London Antique Arms & Military Fairs held in April and September each year. Both fairs open for two days—140 tables.

ARMES. ACCESSOIRES. SURPLUS
BP15 78470 Saint-Remy-les-Chevreuses, France
Tel/Fax: 01 30467006
Email: jean-claude.laurent@wanadoo.fr
Import and Export. General Militaria of all countries.

ARMS AND ARMOUR UK
Email: enquiries@arms-and-armour.co.uk

ARMS TO ARMOR
Email: carussell@arms2armor.com

ARMY RADIO SALES COMPANY
109 Booth Road, Colindale, London NW9 5JU
Email: sales@armyradio.com
Website: www.armyradio.com

ARMY SURPLUS
60 Tib Street, Greater Manchester M4 1LG
Contact: Vince Spencer
Tel: 0161 834 6118
Fax: 0161 834 7483
Email: lode@stone.u-net.com
Website: www.stone.u-net.com
Supply of Swedish/British ex-government surplus, textiles, vehicles and goods plus fold-a-cup and messkit from Sweden plus footwear, boots and shoes.

ARMY SURPLUS STORE
(Props) BYC Summerscales, 1063 Thornton Road, Bradford,
W. Yorkshire BD8 0PA
Contact: Charles Summerscales
Tel/Fax: 01274 816945
A full range of military and outdoor clothing, footwear, hats, caps, knitwear, equipment, camping, flags, insignia, medals, ribbons, decorations, badges, etc., low prices. Sorry—no lists.

ASS. CULT. MILITARIA RESEARCH WW1 & 2
Via E Q Visconti, 12/14-00193, Rome, Italy
Email: info@militaria-research.it
Website: www.militaria-research.it
Militaria including: uniforms, helmets, decorations, accessories and old photos. Research undertaken.

ATTLEBOROUGH ACCESSORIES
White House, Morley St Peter, Wymondham, Norfolk NR18 9TZ
Contact: C E Pearce
Tel: 01953 454932
Fax: 01953 456744
Email: sales@attacc.com
Militaria and memorabilia, including: Sheffield-made Fairbarin Sykes 3rd pattern and commemorative knives; K-Bar USMC knives; knife-making supplies, etc. Large SAE for full lists.

AU PETIT CAPORAL
Le Croissen 56880 Ploeren, France
Contact: Laurent Rouanne
Tel/Fax: 02 97 44 82 04
Email: petitcaporal@infonie.fr
Antique and old militaria–historical souvenirs–insignia–decorations.

AVIS ARMY SUPPLIES
98 Wheetshaw Lane, Shafton, Barnsley S72 8PZ
Contact: Mrs A Barraclough
Tel: 01226 710824
All types of government clothing and miscellaneous.

AVIATION ANTIQUES
Rivendell, Kings Road, Biggin Hill, Kent TN16 3XU
Contact: Rosemary Sutton
Tel/Fax: 01959 576424
Email: sutt999@aol.com
Buy and sell aviation and military collectables; books, china, RAF and airline items, travel agent display models, Action Man dolls, all plastic kits. Collections purchased and collected.

BLACK PIG TRADING
36 Dundrine Road, Castle Weelan, Co Down, N. Ireland BT31 9EX
Contact: Mark C Myles
Tel: 073967 78678
Fax: 012385 42151
Email: max@mba.dnetco.uk
All types of military surplus and militaria from all over the world, from 1900 right up to 1999. All stock is guaranteed original. Mobile 0831 833367.

BLACK FLAG
Contact: Steve
Tel: 01702 305335
Third Reich specialists, all items bought and sold.

BLITZ MILITARIA
Via Ippocrate 45, 05100 ITALY
Contact: Corvi Andrea
Tel: 0039 0744 273105
Fax:.0039 0744 272794
Email: blitzmil@omnibus.net
Website: http://utenti.tripod.it/blitzmil
Sale and trade militaria items WWI and II steel helmets, gas masks, Italian items.

BLUNDERBUSS ANTIQUES
29 Thayer Street, London WIM 5LJ
Contact: Chris Greenaway
Tel: 020 7486 2444
Fax: 020 7935 1127
Email: c g@blunderbuss.demon.co.uk
Specialists in original antique, world wars, modern uniforms, equipment, weapons etc. World wide export via our mail order catalogue. Details on request.

BOSCOMBE MILITARIA
86, Palmerston Road, Boscombe, Bournemouth, Dorset BH1 4HU
Contact: E A Browne
Tel: 01202 304250
Fax: 01202 733696

BRANDENBURG MILITARIA
PO Box 530372, Harlingen, TX 78553-0372, USA
Contact: Howard L Kelley
Tel: 956 412 8405
Email: HKelley@compuserve.com
Website: www.historyunderglass.com
Collector and dealer of WWII German, Japanese, and US medals, badges, daggers, uniforms, helmets, flags, paper items, and cloth insignia. 100% original period items. Buy, Sell Trade. Member, NRA, OMSA, South Texas Military Collector's , MAX Certified Dealer.

BRIC-A-BRAC
16 Walsingham Lane, Truro, Cornwall TR12RP
Contact: Lynne or Richard Bonehill
Tel: 01872 225200
Email: richard@bonehill3.freeserve.co.uk
Website: www.bonehill3.freeserve.co.uk
One of the last shops in Cornwall dealing in medals, badges, helmets, swords and a range of militaria. Visit our web for on line stock lists of militaria. Visit our website for online stock lists of militaria, Royal commemoratives and Police items. Original Royal Household Division and DCLI items wanted. Established 1991. Open Mon–Sat 9.30am–5pm.

BRITISH ARMY BADGES
Email: order@egframes.powernet.co.uk

BRITISH & SCOTTISH MILITARIA
Email: rupertx@aol.com

BRITISH HERITAGE COLLECTABLES
PO Box 43, Ashford, Kent TN23 6ZZ
Tel:01233 647777
Fax: 01233 647700
Email: bhcuk@aol.com

BRITISH COLLECTIBLES (MILITARIA) LTD.
Email: Britcolmilitaria@aol.com

A BURGESS ANTIQUE ARMS
Email: abur5582@aol.com

BURGATE ANTIQUES
Email: vkreeves@burgate1.fsnet.co.uk

JOHN R BURKHART
1001 Vermont Ave/Apt4, Pittsburgh PA15234-1122, USA
Contact: John R Burkhart
Tel: 412 343 5942
Email: johnrburkhart@cs.com
Buying and selling US military shoulder patches WWI to
present—Including pocket patches, theatre made patches—
originals only—collecting and selling since 1948.

BYGONE'S
Tel: 01268 734030 (shop)
01702 526588 (home)
European, British Colonial & American militaria & Go-Withs.
All periods covered including Home Front.

C & D ENTERPRISES
PO Box 7201, Arlington, Virginia 22207-7201, USA
Email: hfp@ix.netcom.com
Military elite insignia and parachute badges, MAC-SOG and
aviation material. Publisher Elite Insignia Guides. List @
£2.00.

CAIRNCROSS AND SONS
31 Bellevue Street, Filey, N. Yorkshire YO14 9HU
Contact: George Cairncross
Tel/Fax: 01723 513287
Email: george@cairnxson.freeserve.co.uk
Website: www.cairnxson.freeserve.co.uk
Regimental ties, blazer badges, cap badges, medals, minia-
ture medals, insignia, blazer buttons, caps, helmets, tunics,
postcards, cigarette cards, wall plaques, cufflinks, books, etc.

CANNON MILITARIA
21 Bulford Road, Durrington, Salisbury, Wiltshire SP4 8DL
Tel: 01980 655099
Email: leonard.webb@tinyworld.co.uk
Website: ww.cannonmilitaria.co.uk
A traditional militaria shop dealing in everything from cap-
badges to inert artillery ammunition.

CARTRY
Eurl—BP10, 14160 Périers-en-Auge, France
Tel: 02 31 29 32 30
Fax: 02 31 91 72 36
Specialising in deacrivated weapons: Russian, German,
French, American and English.

CASQUE & GAUNTLET MILITARIA
55–59 Badshot Lea Road, Badshot Lea, Farnham, Surrey
GU9 9LP
Contact: Ray or Annie Holt
Tel/Fax: 01252 320745
Email: casqueandgauntlet@x-stream.co.uk
We have been dealing in a broad range of militaria from
this same store for 26 years and offer a complete service
to our customers. Guaranteed items. Money back if not
satisfied. Item sourcing. Restoration service.

CAVALIER SUPPLIES
PO Box 2, Gilberdyke, Brough, E. Yorkshire HU15 2YR
Tel: 01430 441315 or 01459 115560
Hand-painted regimental wall plaques.

CHRISTIAN'S BAYONETS
Email: christian.mery@wanadoo.fr

C H MUNDAY
Oxford House, 8 St Johns Road, St Johns Woking, Surrey
GU21 1SE
Tel: 01483 771588
Fax: 01483 756627
Squadron Command and Unit wall shields, crested ties, fly-
ing overall badges, blazer crests, cap badges, engraved
pewter tankards.

C L HEYS
PO Box 615 , Middleton, Tamworth, Staffs B78 2AZ
Contact: C L Heys
Tel/Fax: 01827 874856
Email: badges@cheys.fsnet.co.uk
For over 25 years specialists in the sale and purchase of
genuine world military and police badges, titles, collars and
cloth items. Sample lists free.

C & J MEDALS
Email: southern@cjmedals.co.uk
CHUTE AND DAGGER/UK
21 Old Brickfield Road, Aldershot, Hampshire GU11 3JE
Contact: Roy Turner
Tel/Fax: 01252 650833
Email: scribes@cableol.co.uk
Parachutists and special forces insignia collectors group;
by subscription.

CLASS II SUPPLIES
Contact: Mike Chapman (01227 273210) or Andy King
(01304 826822)
Email: General Militaria: class.ii.supplies@lineone.net
Email: German Helmets: stahlhelm@tinyworld.co.uk
Website: www.militariaonline.co.uk
Specialists in pre-1946 Militaria—especially WWI and II US
militaria & German helmets.

CLEMENTS TRADING
Rijksweg zuid 44, 6662 KE Elst (Gld), Netherlands.
Tel: 0031 481352460

COINCOLLECTABLES.COM
Email: collectors_choice@coincollectables.com

COLDSTREAM MILITARY ANTIQUES
55A High Street, Marlow, Buckinghamshire SL7 1BA
Contact: Steven Bosley
Tel: 01628 488188
Fax: 01628 488111
Fine 19th and 20th century head-dress and badges of the British Army. All items are original and carry a money-back guarantee. Regret no general catalogue available, but 'wants' lists most welcome. Valuations undertaken for insurance, probate or private treaty. Postal service only. Members of LAPADA, OMRS, MHS, Crown Imperial.

COLLECTORS ARMOURY & MILITARIA
Gold Coast War Museum, Springbrook Road, Mudgeeraba, Australia. 4123
Contact: Victor Coote
Tel: 55 305222
Fax: 55 305464
Email: sales@collectorsarmoury.com.au
Wesite: www.collectorsarmoury.com.au
Military museum . Also a large range of militaria of all nationalities: Aussie, German etc for sale. Free catalogue available. Mail Order service.

COLLECTORS CORNER
Email: sales@militarycollectables.co.uk

COLLECTORS MARKET
London Bridge BR Station, London Bridge, London EC4
Tel/Fax: 020 8398 8065
Over 60 stands including medal dealers,badges and militaria on the concourse of London Bridge Main Line Station every Saturday.

CORRIDORS OF TIME (HISTORICAL PRESENTATIONS) LTD
22 Palace Street, Canterbury, Kent CT1 2DZ
Contact: Alan Jeffery
Tel: 01227 478990
Fax: 01227 478991
Email: corridors@argonet.co.uk
Website: www. corridors-of-time.co.uk
Retail outlet to provide genuine, antique, military, museum quality and legendary artefacts, from swords to armour, buttons to badges. Gifts, souvenirs, momento's all linked to British history, including organisers of major centenial and comemorative events. 35 years' experience and still enthusiastic.

COMPTOIR FRANCAIS DE L'ARQUEBUSERIE
Gallerie de Mars 98, Avenue Pasteur, 93260 Les Illas, France
Tel: 01 43637317
Fax: 01 60293230
General WWI and II militaria.

COMPTON WEBB
Gosforth Road, Derby DE24 8HU
Tel: 0332 42616
Fax: 0332 372360
Leading manufacturer of combat uniforms and head-dress.

CONSTANTINE'S COLLECTION
Email: militari@hol.gr

CROWDFREE.COM
Email: sales@crowdfree.com

DESERTFOXX.NET
Email: webmaster@desertfoxx.net

DEWAR AND DEWAR MILITARIA
Angus Dewar: home/fax: 01255 435789
Arron Dewar: home: 01508 548603
Interesting military items

DIE-STRUCK MUSEUM QUALITY REPLICA MEDALS
Email: order@egframes.powernet.co.uk

D J S MILITARIA
Contact: Dave Storey
Tel: 01268 777381
Action men, toys, models.

DOUBLE D DUMP
Kerkstraat 86, 3764 CV Soest, Nederland
Contact: D J van Vugt
Tel: 6090560
Fax: 6090561
Email: Dick@dddump.nl
Militaria and outdoor surplus.

D & R MILITARIA
1700 Preston Dr., Tarboro, NC, 27886-4716, USA
Contact: Don Pixley
Tel: 252 823 1671
Email: pixddrcol1@aol.com
Website..http://hometown.aol.com/pixddrcol1/index.htm
General Militaria of WWII Germany and East Germany to include insignia, uniforms, medals, and similar items.

DROP ZONE SUPPLIES
318 Molesey Road, Walton-on-Thames, Surrey KT12 4SQ
Contact: Nick Parker
Tel: 01932 229326
Fax: 01932 227464
Mobile: 0797 969 1423
Email: nick@army-surplus.co.uk
Website: www.army-surplus.co.uk
Genuine army surplus Mail Order specialist.

DROP ZONE
99 Bognor Road, Chichester, W. Sussex PO19 2NW
Contact: P J Green
Tel/Fax: 01243 779971
Mobile: 07850 257649
Military surplus and collectables.

EDDIE PARSONS
Tel: 01883 712589
Allied/worldwide badges and militaria.

EDELWEISS MILITARIA
Email: chris@stby.com

E G FRAMES MILITARIA UK
7 Saffron, Amington, Tamworth, Staffordshire B77 4EP
Contact: Tony Cooper
Tel/Fax: 01827 63900
Email: tony@egframes.co.uk
Website.http://www.egframes.co.uk
We specialise in military framing, in addition we sell British Army badge, museum qulity reproduction medals, Third Reich Insignia and MOD issue pace sticks and canes.

ENGLISH ARMOURIE
Department 10, 1 Walsall Street, Willenhall, W. Midlands NW13 2EX
Contact: Alan Jones
Tel/Fax: 01902 870579
Website: www.englisharmourie.fsnet.co.uk
Armour manufacturers from Roman to English Civil War. Also makers of muzzle loading muskets. De-activated guns. General militaria dealers covering all periods.

EUREKA MILITARIA
Email: militaria@start.com.au

FINE ANTIQUE ARMS
Email: thporter.antiques@btinternet.com

FIRST CLASS MAIL
9 Miller Street, Warrington, Cheshire WA4 1BD
Contact: Tony Whittaker
Tel: 01925 659756
Riveted mail, wirework, hand-sewn turnshoes. Demonstrations of riveted mail-making for museums, events etc. Also for TV/film, video and documentary work. Riveted mail of the highest quality made to order, sample pieces, loose rings etc for schools, museum displays etc.

FIRST WORLD WAR MILITARIA
Email: johmil@mailexcite.com

FRENCH COLLECTORS PORTAL
Email: webmaster@cashprod.com

FSU CONNECTIONS LTD
9 Heatherlands, Sunbury-on-Thames, Middlesex TW16 7QU
Contact: Oleg Savochkin
Tel: 01932 770836
Fax: 01932 786257
Email: fsu@rusmilitary.com
Website: www.rusmilitary.com
Russian military & outdoor clothing and equipment. Plus 2WD Ural Army combinations, night vision goggles, binoculars, sights, rifle scopes, deactivated AKs, air rifles, assault vests, insignia etc. Manufacturer's catalogues available.

FUSILIER MILITARIA
9 Bolam Avenue, Blyth, Northumberland NE24 5BU
Contact: D W Fairbairn
Tel/Fax: 01670 356469
Email: derekmedals@militaria.fsnet.co.uk
Website: www.medals.freeserve.co.uk
All orders, decorations, medals, badges and militaria bought, sold and exchanged. Medals mounted full size and miniature. Replacement medals supplied. Regimental bullion wire and silk blazer badges supplied, including your own designs. Feather plumes all colours and sizes supplied and specialist plumes made to your specification. If it's military I'm interested.

GERMAN MILITARIA & COLLECTIBLE
Email: info@german-militaria.co.uk

GERSTBAU BADER
99085 Erfurt, Bebelstasse 36, Germany
Tel: 0361 540 3400
Fax: 0361 540 3401

GHOST 2 MILITARIA
Email: anne.Barratt@sympatico.ca

GOODLAD MILITARIA
26 Fairfield Road, Brockwell, Chesterfield, Derbyshire S40 4TP
Contact: Anthony D Goodlad
Tel: 01246 204004
General militaria, with an emphasis on German and French WWI items and German WWII militaria. Exhibitor at many UK fairs. Personal callers by appointment only.

GRAHAM PILGRIM
15 Ticehurst Close, Worth, Crawley RH10 7GN
Tel: 01923 885388
Automobile historian, specialising in sales brochure and catalogue dating, from the early 1900s to the present day.

GREEN ISSUES
Units G1-3, York Road Indoor Market, Southend-on-Sea, Essex
Contact: Andy
Tel/Fax: 01268 490257
Email: green-issues@gofornet.co.uk
Specialising in British and US kit and more.

GRENADIERS MILITARIA
Email: Grenadiers@btinternet.com

HARALD GRIMM
Zeppelin Strasse 40, 13583 Berlin, Germany
Tel: 303714598
German Deco-Ammo and equipment,

THE GUNNER
35-37 Chapelgate, Sutton St James, Spalding, Lincolnshire
PE12 0EF
Contact: Ian Durrant
Tel/Fax: 01945 440289
Email: thegunner@sentimentaljourney.co.uk
Website: www.sentimentaljourney.co.uk/sj/armoury1.htm
We sell deactivated weapons and accessories including a
large range of items for the Vickers MG. From the 3-inch
mortar through AK-47 to the .38 calibre pistol, our range
constantly expands. List available. Our online shop and cat-
alogue hosted at Sentimental Journey's website.

HENLEY'S MILITARIA, COINS & COLLECTABLES
Email: rhenley@netcom.ca

HISTORY, BY GEORGE!
129 W. Main Street, Mesa, AZ 85201, USA
Contact: George Notarpole
Tel: 480 898 3878
Fax: 480 668 2721
Email: gnotarpole@historybygeorge.com
Website: historybygeorge.com
Militaria, stamps, coins and general antiques. Specializing
in fine medals and orders. We buy, sell and trade. Let us
know what you have!

HISTORICALWEAPONS.COM
Markoviceva 27, Krizevci 48260, Croatia
Contact: Kruno Kovacic
Tel: 00385 91 5295040
Fax: 00385 48 712390
Email: webmaster@historicalweapons.com
Website: http://www.historicalweapons.com
Online store selling antique and replica arms and armour
dating from Roman times through the present day, swords,
military sabres, daggers, knives, guns, cannons, medieval
shields, suits of armour, books, art prints and articles
with tips for edged weapons collectors.

HOBSON & SONS
Kenneth Road, Thundersley, Essex SS7 3AF
Tel: 0268 793097
Fax: 0268 566024
Manufacturers of service uniforms, head-dress and leather
equipment and other accoutrements.

HOPE AND GLORY
6 New Road, Kelvedon, Essex CO5 9JW
And 1c Feering Hill, Feering, Essex CO5 9NH
Contact: Diana Cherry, John Knight, Steve Siviter.
Tel: 01376 570717 or 01376 573467
Military and Home Front collectables bought and sold.

HO WILDENBERG BV
Remmerden 44, 3911TZ Rhenen, Postbus 80-3910 AB
Rhenen, Holland.
Tel: 31 0317618218
Fax: 31 0317615515
Email: wildenberg@planet.nl

INSIGNIA OF THE THIRD REICH
Email: problems@egframes.powernet.co.uk

INTERNATIONAL COLLECTIBLES, BELTS AND MILITARIA
44 Bliss Mine Road #1, Middletown, RI 02842, USA
Contact: Don Palen
Tel: 401 848 7252
Fax: 401 849 7440
Email: don@icbm.com.
Website: www.icbm.com
icbm.com website has a variety of military qualification
insignias from around the world (para/pilot/submarine/
ship/special forces), watches, submarine clocks, books,
binoculars, all sorts of other related goodies and even kgb
stuff! A fun website with lots of good natured humor,
worth a stop even if you don't buy anything.

INTER MILITARIA & COLLECTIBLES NEDERLAND
Oude Molenstraat 7a, 5342 GA Oss, Nederland
Contact: Mark van Thiel
Tel/Fax: 31 0412 625042
Specialising in British, German and American uniforms and
equipment up until 1945.

ITALIAN MILITARIA COLLECTORS ASSOCIATION
Email: amiciweb@aol.com

J B MILITARY ANTIQUES
Email: jbmilitary@aol.com

J HIRST & SONS
Fragmentation Works, Hurstbourne Station, Whitchurch, Hants
RG28 7RT
Tel: 01246 738397 / 426
Fax: 01264 738747
Cash buyers of all grades of metal. Ex-government surplus.
All reuseables.

JMF COLLECTIONS INTERNATIONAL
BP 164, 73204 Albertville Cedex, France
Tel: 04 79374520
Fax: 04 79377144
Email: jmfcol@aol.com
Specialising in uniforms, headdress and insignia of all
WWII forces, with emphasis on those of France and
Germany.

JOHNSON REFERENCE BOOKS & MILITARIA
403 Chatham Square Office Park, Fredericksburg, VA 22405,
USA
Contact: LTC (Ret.) Thomas M. Johnson
Tel: 540 373 9150
Fax: 540 373 0087
Email: ww2daggers@aol.com
Website: johnsonreferencebooks.com, ww2daggers.com
Specializing in WWI and WWII German edged weapons,
uniforms, medals, decorations, insignia, accoutrements,
parts, and reference publications (new and out-of-print).
Our sales catalog includes over 2,100 original items. The
cost per catalog (airmail, overseas & Canada) is $15.00;
domestic (U.S.) is $10.00. On-line catalog is available at
JohnsonReferenceBooks.com.

JON'S SWORDS
Email: jjaj@konnections.com

J S FRANKLIN
Franklin House, 151 Strand, London WC2R 1HL
Tel: 020 7836 5746
Fax: 020 7836 2784
Manufacturers of military uniforms, footwear, webbing and personal equipment to all requirements.

JUST MILITARY
701 Abbeydale Road, Sheffield, S. Yorkshire S7 2BE
Tel/Fax: 0114 255 0536
Dealers in all types of military memorabilia and collectables. Full medal mounting and framing service including the supply of miniature and replacement medals.

KAMPFGRUPPE MEDALS
Email: contact@kampfgruppemedals.com

KATC INTERNATIONAL
Email: katc@skt.cumsats.net.pk

KENT ADVENTURE TRAINING CORPS
Contact: Major Clive Richards
Tel: 01843 290799

KING & COUNTRY
Email: qmsglenn@kingncountry.com

KING & COUNTRY
15 10 North Hollowooct Way, Burbank, CA 91505, USA
Contact: Harlan Glenn
Tel: 818 566 1660
Fax: 818 566 1887
Email: kngcntry@westworld.com
Website: http://www.westworld.com/-kngcntry/index/html
Reproduction)MII Denison smocks, collarless shirts, khaki drills and maroon para berets (WWII specifics). Also orginal WWII British collectables.

KLAUS W DRASPA
In der Welheimer Mark 55, 46238 Bottrop, Germany
Tel/Fax: 0204118189
Brtish militaria collector. Badges, uniforms, headdress, prints, books, music.

KRIEGSMARINE COLLECTABLES
210 Darlington Lane, Stockton-on-Tees TS19 8AD
Contact: R M Coverdale MBE
Tel: 01642 603627
Fax: 01642 602952
Email: jennifer.weatherall.@ntlworld.com
Specialising in WWI and WWII German original militaria. Send large SAE for free list.

LAURENCE CORNER
62–64 Hampstead Road, London NW1 2NU
Tel: 020 7813 1010
Fax: 020 7813 1413
Probably the largest selection of Government surplus clothing and equipment anywhere. Including innumerable items of militaria. Costumes and accessories dating from early 1800s onwards. These are unique one-off collectable wearables.

LANCE CORKE AERO
Email: solotk@totalise.co.uk

THE LAST POST
The Barn Collectors Mkt, Seaford
Tel: 01323 898551
Email: bob@thelastpost.cjb.net
Militaria and curios.

LANDSER MILITARIA INTERNATIONAL
Niederwernerstrasse 56, D-97421 Schweinfurt, Germany
Contact: Jim Calhoun
Tel/Fax: 49 9721 83643
Mobile: Germany: 49 0173 4830787 Belgium: 32 0477 862532
Email: aircav@hotmail.com or cavhero@yahoo.com
Military surplus. Film and theatre technical advisor. Aviation advisor.

L & E MILITARIA
Email: L_E_Militaria@hotmail.com

LE CUIRASSIER
BP 2410, 69219 Lyon Cedex 02, France
Tel: 04 78 92 81 75
Mobile: 06 13 80 75 52
Email: lecuirassier@wanadoo.fr
Website: www.lecuirassier.com
Specialising in French and German militaria, 1789–1954.

LE HUSSARD
Website: www.lehussard.fr
Original weapons, militaria, munitions, replicas, books, documents and photographs. Visit our website for our extensive collection.

L'ENTENDARD
3, Rue Porte Neuve, 62200 Boulogne-sur-mer, France
Tel: 03 21318517
Fax: 03 21318519
Specialising in deactivated weapons from all nations involved in WWII.

LE POILU
18, Rue Emile Duclaux, 75015 Paris, France
Tel: 0143067732
General militaria and books.

LEGION SUPPLY HOUSE
PO Box 656, Nutley, NJ 07110, USA
Contact: John Casino
Tel: 973 759 2520
Email: ostfront@aol.com
Dealing in quality German cloth militaria of both world wars since 1979–uniforms, caps, insignia, and personal equipment offered for sale conservation and authentication services and consultation offered. Max Show Life Member, and member in good standing of the Certified Dealer Program.

LIBERTY CRUZ AREO'S
Canvey Island, Essex SS8 0DA
Tel/Fax: 01268 683684
Email: liberty@easynet.co.uk
Sculpted mahogany fighter planes.

LION GATE ARMS & ARMOUR
Email: hussar@liongate-armsandarmour.com

LIVERPOOL MEDAL COMPANY LTD
Email: liverpoolmedals@online.rednet.co.uk

LUCKY FORWARD MILITARIA
Box 1950 (c/o Stan Wolcott), Costa Mesa, CA 92628-1950, USA
Contact: Stan Wolcott
Tel: 714 641 342
Fax: 714 559 8319
Email: luckyforward@earthlink.net
Website: home.earthlink.net/~luckyforward
Stan Wolcott's Lucky Forward Militaria is an outgrowth of Stan's own collecting of US Militaria of 1916–1945. Stan offers a wide selection of US Militaria of all branches of the Armed Services, including uniforms, equipment, paper ephemera, and some insignia items.

MAC'S MODELS
Nineveh House, Tarrant Street, Arundel, Sussex
Contact: Dave McDermott
Tel: day: 01903 884 307 evenings: 01923 546541
Police & military collectables, medals, badges, uniforms, equipment, bayonets, helmets etc bought and sold.

MACDONALD ARMOURIES
At the Sign of the Cross and Sword, Brunswick St Lane, Edinburgh
Contact: Paul Macdonald
Email: macarmouries@aol.com
Website: http://users.ox.ac.uk/-zoo10328/macdonald.html
Macdonald Armouries manufactures functional reproduction historical edged weaponry, specialising in accurate weight/balance swords and daggers for the historical fencing market. Weapons are made individually to order, recreating original examples or catering to customer specifications. All styles of European weaponry from Celtic to 19th century can be created.

MALCOM J DICKINSON
Tel: 01462 643739
General Army Surplus, also specialising in kids combat wear. Wellinbrough, Bedford, Milton Keynes, North Weald.

CHRIS MASON ANTIQUES
PO Box 6130, McLean, VA 22106, USA
Contact: Chris Mason
Tel: 703 356 8564
Email: mcmason@starpower.net
Original WWII German and US military artifacts bought and sold. 30 years in the hobby. Lifetime guarantee of originality on every piece sold. Specializing in Airborne and Luftwaffe items. Uniforms, equipment, headgear, medals, patches, insignia, badges, documents, postcards, and original photographs. Send SAE for free sales list.

MARTIN DUCHEMIN
6 Knights Close, Eaton Socon, Cambs PE19 8DP
Contact: Martin Duchemin
Tel: 01480 212843
Regimental cufflinks, tie pins, sweetheart brooches, lapel badges, medlas, mounting display cases, blazer buttons and badges.

MEMORIES
20 Market Place, Alford, Lincolnshire LN13 9EB
Contact: T Wbudworth
Tel: 01507 462541

MFC SURVIVAL
Naval Yard, Tonypandy, Mid-Glamorgan, Wales CF40 1JS
Tel: 01443 433075
Fax: 01443 437846
Email: info@mfc-survival.com
Website: www.mfc-survival.com
Rapid response shelters.

M HAND & CO LTD
25 Lexington Street, London W1R 3HQ
Contact: A M R Macleod
Tel: 020 7 437 4917
Fax: 020 7287 5742
Email: Carne@handembroidery.com
Website: www.handembroidery.com
Hand embroidery: gold and silver lace, braids, cords, military & civil accoutrements and embroidery design including standards, colours, pennants, sashes and badges.

MICHAEL McLAUGHLIN
BCM CAMPFIRE, London WC1N 3XX
Tel: 0836 384112
Third Reich audio/cassette/CD/video. Repro Third Reich, Folk heritage art posters, postcards, Military and political Books.

MILLAIS ANTIQUES
PO Box 545, Crawley, Sussex RH10 6FG
Contact: Geoffrey or Elisabeth Dexter
Tel: 01293 552655
Fax: 01293 520077
Mobile: U7710 259465
Scientific instruments, antique arms, armour and militaria. Fine quality items bought and sold.

MILLWEB
PO Box 125, Herne Bay CT6 5GH
Contact: Nigel Hay
Tel: 01304 814071
Email: nigel@millweb.net
Website: www.millweb.net
The world's biggest internet resource for military vehicle collectors, dealers and restorers. Free classified adverts updated daily. Full events listings. Special film hire section. Militaria adverts welcome. 25,000 plus pages per week!

MILITARY WAREHOUSE
Email:relics@sherbtel.net

MILITARIA ARCHIV CARSTEN BALDES
Email: office@militaria-baldes.de

MILITARIA MAD
12 Summerleaze Crescent, Bude, Cornwall EX23 8HH
Contact: Bob Bowman
Tel: 01288 356831
Email: enquiries@militariamad.co.uk
Email: info@militarymania.com

MILITARIA ONLINE COLLECTOR DATABASE
Email: info@militaria-online.com

MILITARIA ONLINE GERMANY
Email: webmaster@germanmilitaria.de
Militaria On the Web
Website: www.arbeia.demon.co.uk/mart/index4.htm
Buy, sell and exchange militaria on the web.

MIL-TECH MANUALS
Email: surplsal@tl.infi.net

MISH MASH
Wellington Street, Kettering, Northants NN16 8RQ
Tel/Fax: 01536 518030
Government surplus and militaria. WWII flying kit and other collectables.

MILITARY HERALDRY SOCIETY
27 Sandbrook, Itetley, Telford, Shropshire TF1 5BB
Contact: Hubert Long
Tel: 01952 408 830
The Military Heraldry Society was founded in 1951 to enable collectors and others interested in cloth formation signs to get together to exchange information and material. The scope of the society, which has a worldwide membership, includes formation signs (shoulder sleeve insignia), shoulder titles, regimental and unit flashes and similar cloth items. The society journal 'The Formation Sign' is published four times a year.

MONS MILITARY ANTIQUES
221 Rainham Road, Rainham, Essex RM13 7SD
Contact: Richard Archer
Tel: 01277 810558
Fax: 01277 811004
Email: mms.mil1@tesco.net
Premier buyers and sellers of WWI, interwar and WWII British and German militaria including headdress, uniforms, equipment, badges and medals. Mail order and militaria fairs only.

MORRIS MILITARIA
The Old Chapel, The Green, Crackchall, Bedale, N. Yorkshire DL8 1HP
Contact: B L Morris
Tel: 01677 423301
Email: barrie@mbattledress.freeserve.co.uk
Website: www.mbattledress.freeserve.co.uk
We buy and sell British cloth formation signs, cloth/metal titles, trade badges, buttons, uniforms and miscellaneous militaria. SAR for quarterly list. Money back guarantee on all items.

MR S KING
19 Mount Pleasant Road, Luton, Bedfordshire LU3 2RR
Tel: 01582 493747

M & T MILITARIA
Email: l3mnt@aol.com

MUCK & BULLETS
Contact: Laura Wilson
Tel: 01689 842 186

MULLER-MILITARIA
Email: t.yeomans@virgin.net

MURPHY'S MEDALS & MILITARIA
Email: murphys@netvigator.com

NICHOLAS MORIGI—THE REGALIA SPECIALIST
PO Box 103, Newmarket, Suffolk CB8 8WY
Contact: Nicholas Morigi
Fax: 01440821246
Specialist in cloth and metal insignia of all countries from VM to present day. Specialising in WWII, Vietnam and current. Countries represented include Great Britain, United States, Third Reich Germany, Soviet Union and France. Mail order only. Full colour catalogue £3 (£5 overseas).

NOLASCO
BP 1010/427 Rue Elie Gruyelle, 62257 Hénin-Beaumont cedex, France
Tel: 03 21753088
Fax: 03 21492551
Website: www.perso.wanadoo.fr/nolasco
Weapons ancient and modern, covering all countries.

THE OLD BRIGADE
10A Harborough Road, Kingsthorpe, Northampton,
Northamptonshire NN2 7A7
Contact: Stewart Wilson
Tel: 01604 719369
Fax: 01604 712489
Email: theoldbrigade@easynet.co.uk
Website: www.theoldbrigade.co.uk
Specialist dealer in Imperial German and Third Reich collectors items. Illustrated catalogue £5.00 and SAE. You will find a large selection of daggers, uniforms, medals, swords, headdress, SS items and reference books. Specialist dealer in Third Reich militaria, daggers, uniforms, medals, badges, flags, helmets, etc also a good selection of Imperial German items and militaria from other countries. Please visit our web site or visit our shop in person, visitors by appointment only please.

OVERLORD
96 Rue de la Folie Mericourt, 75011 Paris, France
Tel/Fax: 01 43552119
Specialising in US militaria.

OVERLORD MILITARIA
140 Tonge Moor Road, Bolton, Lancashire BL2 4DP
Tel: 01204 39871735
Weapons, uniforms and equipment, World War I to present day. Specialises in US uniforms and associated equipment. Open 10am-5.30pm.

P G WING
The Warehouse, Peggy's Walk, Littlebury, Saffron Walden, Essex CB11 4TG
Contact: Peter Wing
Tel: 01799 522196 or 521801
Fax: 01799 513374
Email: sales.pgwing@i12.com
We are the largest Government Surplus Wholesaler in the U.K. We stock military uniforms, boots, socks, combat and camouflage trousers, jackets and parkas; French, German, U.S.A., Spanish, British; steel helmets, gasmasks, webbing, bandoliers, leather belts and helmets, bayonets, knives, machetes, ammo boxes, jerricans, rucksacks, kitbags, flags, badges, and many unique and hard-to-find articles. We are Trade/Wholesale only—no retail. We are only five miles from Imperial War Museum, Duxford.

PASTIMES
2 Lower Park Row, Bristol, Avon S16 5BN
Contact: Andy Stevens
Tel: 0117 9299330
We buy and sell medals, badges, swords, bayonets, Nazi and Italian pre-1945 items, secondhand military books etc.

PETER GREEN
5 Old Silk Mill, Brook Street, Tring, Hertfordshire HP23 5EF
Contact: Peter Green
Tel/Fax: 01442 825722
Email: p_r_green@hotmail.com
British badges from Waterloo today's amalgamations, also commonwealth, Police, Nazi. I can also manufacture badges from any pattern supplied. SAE for extensive list.

THE PLUMERY
6 Deans Close, Whitehall Gardens, Chiswick, London W4 3LX
Tel/Fax: 020 8995 7099
Military plume makers to the household Cavalry, Foot Guards; British and foreign armies, TV, theatre, associations, collectors—all periods and nationalities. reproduction Napoleonic shakos—£85 + VAT British, £140 + VAT French. Phone enquiries preferred.

R E CORPS ENTERPRISES LIMITED
Brompton Barracks, Chatham, Kent ME4 4UG
Contact: David Moffatt
Tel/Fax: 01634 814138
Email: corpsenterprises.rhqre@gtnet.gov.uk
All goods Royal Engineer based, from glassware to uniform items, leisurewear to jewellery and figurines, and paintings both past and present.

RAVEN ARMOURY
Handleys Farm, Dunmow Road, Thaxted, Essex CM6 2NX
Contact: Simon Fearnham
Tel/Fax: 01371 831088
Handcrafted swords, chainmail and armour for collectors and re-enactors. Sword range includes historical reproductions on display at The Royal Armouries Shop in the Tower of London. Fully guaranteed.

RAMCALL
Contact: Roger Manning
Tel: 01752 403588
Email: intercom@lineone.net
Website: www.ramcall.dabsol.co.uk
Military radio spares to collectors and enthusiasts.

RELIC HUNTER
PO Box 245, Whitehall, PA18052, USA
Contact: Gerard Stezelberger
Tel: 610 760 8220
Fax: 610 760 8257
Email: idols2@fast.net
Website: www.ancientidols.com/ww2.htm
Only 100% original WWII collectables—especially German and US items. Headgear, uniforms, accoutrements, awards, Knights Cross winners signed photos, German WWII officer and general research service. All items guaranteed orginal for life. Try our website.

RELICS
20 St Wilfrid's Green, Hailsham, E. Sussex BN27 1DR
Contact: C Hodgson
Tel: 01323 846 007
Fax: 01323 842 234
Email: relicsarms@hotmail.com
Website: www.relics.org.uk
Replica weaponry from WWI and II to the present day war theatres—and into the future! Hand built, full size accurate copies of guns, grenades, mines and missiles. Illustrated catalogue available £4. 'Auld Arms' catalogue £5—includes Wild West guns, flintlock pistols and muskets, crossbows, swords and daggers. We supply worldwide maiol order only.

RICHARD GRAHAM
15 Irwin Road, Onslow Village, Guildford, Surrey GU2 5PW
Tel: 01483 565673
Fax: 01483 533009
Mobile: 0831 435174
Collector of British military equipment of the two world wars.

R J VAN IERSEL
Postbus 263, 4940 AG Raamsdonksveer, Netherlands
Tel: 01621 19659 / 0162 51659
Wings, SF badges SF berets worldwide.

ROGER G ELLIS
PO Box 570, Orpington, Kent BR6 7WZ
Tel: 01689 858284
Specialist in scientific, nautical, naval and marine instruments. Restoration undertaken.

R WILLIAMSON MILITARIA
Email: willi@blvl.igs.net

R D O MILITARIA
Corporation Farmhouse, Loymondham Road, Hethel, Norfolk, England NR14 8EU
Email: rick_overy@man.com
Mainly British militaria bought and sold. Mail Order only. SAE or e-mail for list.

ROD AKEROYD & SON
101–103 New Hall Lane, Preston, Lancashire PR1 5PB
Tel: 01772 794947
Fax: 01772 654535
Email: info@firearmscollector.com
Extensive stock of British, Continental, and Japanese guns, swords, helmets and armour. Callers welcome.

RYTON ARMS
PO Box 7, Retford, Nottinghamshire DN227XH
Tel: 01909 500222
Fax: 01909 530231
Wide range of deactivated military weapons, including machine guns etc., complete with inert ammunition, accessories, etc. for impressive displays.

SABRE SALES
85 Castle Road, Southsea, Hants PO5 3AY
Contact: Nick Hall
Tel: 023 9283 3394
Fax: 023 9283 7394
Email: baza@ampatrol.freeserve.co.uk
Website: www.milweb.net/go/sabre
Largest shop and warehouse in the south of England for collectors, re-enactors, stage and film pertaining to military matters of the 20th century. Boots, uniform,s weapons, buttons, badges, webbing etc etc.

SCE MEDALS
Email: info@scemedals.com

SCHEDULE OF EUROPEAN ARMS & MILITARIA FAIRS
Email: geschichtsverein@gmx.de

SEAMS HISTORIC
3 Birtley Avenue, Tynemouth NE30 2RR
Contact: Angela Essenhigh
Tel/Fax: 01912583472
Email: angela.essenhigh@ukgateway.net
Website: www.seams-historic.co.uk
Museum quality reproductions of costumes and uniforms. Most periods covered.

SEAN LACEY
Jacobs Antique Centre, West Canal Wharf, Cardiff, Wales
Tel: 029 20463217
Mobile: 0468 287044
Antique arms and militaria.

SENTIMENTAL JOURNEY
35–37 Chapelgate, Sutton St James, Lincolnshire PE12 0EF
Contact: Ian Durrant.
Tel/Fax: 01945 440289
Email: sales@sentimentaljourney.co.uk
Website: www.sentimentaljourney.co.uk
Specialist supplier of items relating to Britain's military and civilian services 1914–1965. We sell uniforms, maps, manuals, ephemera, 78s, books and webbing. As collectors ourselves we provide a service by collectors for collectors. Our shop should open this year.

78TH INFANTRY DIVISION
Email: 78th@angelfire.com

S G & D S MILITARIA
Email: Militaria@Gmx.De

ST PANCRAS ANTIQUES
150 St Pancras, Chichester, W. Sussex PO19 7SH
Contact: Ralph Willatt
Tel: 01243 787645
An antique business, established for 20 years, specialising in high quality arms and armour, militaria and medals, early furniture, pre-1820 fine glassware and ceramics.

S M WHOLESALE
Email: kursk43@inreach.com

SNYDER'S TREASURES
3520 Mullin Lane, Bowie, MD 20715, USA
Contact: Charles Snyder
Tel: 301 262 5735
Fax: 301 352 0314
Email: snyderstr@aol.com
Website: www.snyderstreasures.com
Militaria—ancient to modern, specializing in WWII, Japanese, German, and American.

SOLDIERS III
Armoury House, 20 Drivers Mead, Lingfield, Surrey RH7 6EU
Tel/Fax: 01342 835669
Mobile: 0860 236291

SOVEREIGN 2000
4a St Luke's Avenue, Maidstone, Kent ME14 5AL
Contact: Mark Day
Tel: 01622 209062
Mobile: 0771 8423692
Email: daym@cablenet.co.uk

SPECIAL AIR-SEA SERVICES
St George's Works, St George's Quay, Lancaster, Lancs LA1 5QJ
Tel: 01524 64204
Top of the range military clothing and equipment.

SPEEDLOADERS.COM
Email: info@speedloaders.com

SPITFIRE MILITARIA
Email: spitmil@mnsi.net

SPORTS ARMYMAN
'Woodpeckers', 102a Tower Ride, Uckfield, E. Sussex
Tel: 01825 768077
Mobile: 07957 888328
Army surplus. Sports wear. Children's armywear.

STATIC LINE
16 Rue de Général de Gaulle, BP11, 50480 Ste Mère Eglise,
Normandie, France
Tel: 02 33410242
Fax: 02 33410269
Email: staticlin@aol.com
Specialising in French militaria. Latest items relating to
Indo China and Algeria.

**STEWART'S MILITARY ANTIQUES & 19TH CENTURY
PHOTOGRAPHY**
108 W. Main St., Mesa, AZ 85201, USA
Contact: Larry & Terri Stewart
Tel: 480 834 4004
Fax: 480 834 3380
Email: Lstew14244@aol.com
Website: www.stewartsmilitaryantiques.com
We specialize in military collectables from WWII with a
heavy emphasis on American and German interests. We
feature equipment, bayonets, uniforms, headgear, and some
insignia. A specialty item are WWII German equipment
boxes. We offer a lifetime guaranty of originality for our
customers.

SULLIVAN'S CLASSIC ARMS & MILITARIA
Email: sullivan@sullivansclassicarms.com

SUNSET MILITARIA
Dingdon Cross, Herts HR2 6PF
Contact: David Seeney
Tel: 01432 870420
Fax: 01432 870309
Email: sunsetmilitaria@btinternet.com
Military research all periods. WWI medal cards and com-
puter check £5, if number and Regt known, otherwise £8
if vague. Badges, medals, ribbons and mini-medals
stocked. SAE all enquiries.

SYDNEY VERNON ORDERS, MEDALS AND DECORATIONS
Email: svernon@inland.net

SOLDIER OF FORTUNE
Unit 18, Tyn y Llidiart Ind Estate, Corwen, Clwyd, Wales LL21 9RR
Contact: Peter Kabluczenko
Tel: 01490 412225
Fax: 01490 412205
Email: sof@chesternet.co.uk
Website: www.sofmilitary.co.uk
Specialising in reproduction WWII clothing and equipment.
British, German and the USA. Catalogue available.

SQUADRON PRINTS
Terrane House, Nisby Way Ind Estate, Lincoln, Lincolnshire
LN6 3LQ
Contact: Jane Rumble
Tel: 01522 697000
Fax: 01522 697154
Email: sales@terrain.co.uk
Embroidery manufacturers and screen printers. Official
suppliers to HM Armed Forces and RAF Aerobatic Team,
Red Arrows. Please send SAE for lists of mail order goods.

STRINGTOWN SUPPLIES
29 High Street, Polegate, E. Sussex BN26 5AB
Contact: Clive Hodgson
Tel: 01323 488844
Fax: 01323 487799
Email: stringtownsupplies@talk21.com
Military, outdoor and survival clothing and equipment,
militaria, swords, antique firearms, replicas, flags etc. New
shop now open Mon–Sat 9.30am–5.30pm, Polegate High
Street.

TANKS IN WW2
Email: jaro.pitonak@post.sk

TARGET ARMS
Email: webmaster@targetarms.co.uk

T L O MILITARIA
Longclose House, Common Road, Eton Wick, nr Windsor,
Berkshire SL4 6QY
Contact: Tony Oliver
Tel: 01753 86263 7
Fax: 01753 841998
Email: tlo.militaria@virgin.net
Specialists in DDR collectables at all levels of scarcity and
price. Mail order; callers welcome seven days a week, BY
PRIOR APPOINTMENT.

TOYE, KENNING & SPENCER
Regalia House, Newton Road, Bedworth, Warwickshire
CV12 8QR
Tel: 01203 315634
Fax: 01203 643018
Manufacturers of medal ribbons, miniature and full-sized
medals, brooch bars, ribbon bars, clasps and emblems.
Medal mounting and framing service available.

20TH CENTURY COMBAT HELMETS
Email: rrynning@c2i.net

TIGER COLLECTIBLES
104 Victoria Avenue, Swanage, Dorset BH19 1AS
Contact: Mark Bentley
Tel: 01929 43411
Fax: 01929 423410
Email: tiger@bentleyccs.com
All militaria and collectable items, land, sea and air, from
both world wars, mail order catalogue available. Visitors
only by appointment. Militaria fairs attended.

THE TREASURE BUNKER
21 King Street, Glasgow, Scotland G1 5QZ
Contact: Kenny Andrew
Tel: 0141 552 8164
Fax: 0141 552 4651
Email: info@treasurebunker.com
Website: www.treasurebunker.com
We specialise British and German militaria from WWI and WWII.
We also stock items from before this period and have a stock of
most nationalities from all conflicts. We offer a mail order cata-
logue @ £4 for UK and £6 overseas. We also offer a state of
the art e commerce web site and high street retail premises.

UNI-BADGE COMPANY
Email: univer.pk@usa.net

US ADVENTURE
13, Rue de Courtonne, 1400 Caen, France
Tel: 02 31945556
Fax: 02 31931749
US surplus militaria from 1939–45. Also French militaria
covering Indochina, Algeria and Viet Nam, Liberation flags,
souvenirs of 1944, insignia, uniforms etc.

USAAF : USAF
Contact: Simon Butler
Tel: 0441 073666
Jo Chambers
Tel: 0958 563364
American militaria bought and sold.

ULRIC OF ENGLAND
6 The Glade, Stoneleigh, Epsom, Surrey KT17 211B
Tel: 01694 781 354
Fax: 01694 781 372
Ulric of England produces a fully illustrated catalogue of
Third Reich items. Send £4 (UK/Europe), £5 (Overseas).
Personal callers by appointment only.

WAR ZONE
Contact: Robert
Tel: 027 690 7628
Mobile: 0958639236
Military clothing, security products, night vision equipment,
body armour, ballistic and anti-stab vests. Combats,
trousers, jackets, belts, T-shirts, socks, smocks, dog tags,
flak jackets.

VAN DE POL
Goedentijd 2, 5131 AS Alphen (N Br)
Tel/Fax: 013 508 1307

VICTORIAN MILITARIA
Contact: Chris Berry
Tel: 020 8886 4730
Mobile: 0779 080 6364
Specialists in quality pre-1914 British and Colonial military
antiques.

VINTAGE MILITARIA INTERNATIONAL
91 Portland Road, Highlands, NJ 07732, USA
Contact: Fritz Ianni and Giovanni Carabalone
Tel: 732 8721477
Fax: 732 291 2540
Email: vintmilint@home.com
Specializing in Italian militaria from 1860 to the present
with emphasis on WWI and WWII uniforms and headgear,
particularly R.S.I. And colonial items. Please write or email
for a catalogue.

MIKE WARREN
PO Box 524, Amityville, NY 11701
Contact: Mike Warren
Tel: 516-731-0227
Fax: 516-731-0227
Email: MWDaggers@aol.com
Website: M.W.Daggers.com
Nazi, Japanese, Italian, Fascist, and other countries—
daggers, swords, medals, hat documents, standards, etc. I
buy collections, I'll come to you. Send $2 for large list.

WEB ANTIK
181 Route d'Oberhausbergen, 67200 Strasbourg, France
Tel: 03 88 26 32 90
Email: webantik@wanadoo.fr
Website: www.webantik.com
Specialising in ancient weapons and militaria on the web.

WESTERN FRONT MILITARIA
Email: thewesternfront@hotmail.com

WESTLAND MILITARIA
Email: info@westland.nl

WHAT PRICE GLORY
Email: wpglory@aol.com

WINCENTZEN SCULPTURES
126 Clarence Road, Horsham, W. Sussex RH13 5SG
Tel: 01403 242536

RON WOLIN
437 Bartell Drive, Chesapeake, VA 23322, USA
Contact: Ron Wolin
Tel: 757 547 2764
Email: RONWOLIN@home.com
Collector-dealer, specializing in Guaranteed original WWII
American and Third Reich military souvenirs of all types.

WOOD HARRIS
PO Box 50, Leatherhead, Surrey KT22 7RJ
Tel: 0372 362990
Fax: 0372 362920
Manufacturers of a wide assortment of military gear, from
tailored uniforms to hazard protection.

WORLD-MILITARIA
Email: sales@world-militaria.com

WORLD WIDE MILITARIA, INC
PO Box 522, Germantown, MD, 20875 USA
Contact: Robert Pitta
Tel: 301 972 3773
Fax: 301 972 3773
Email: bob@worldwidemilitaria.com
Website: www.worldwidemilitaria.com
Dealers in military and police uniforms, insignia, flags,
books, field manuals, field gear, WWII and Vietnam
reproductions, toys, armor, and all things military from all
countries and all periods.

WW2 GERMAN RE-ENACTMENT
Brian 01553 774543
Clothing, equipment, medals, awards etc bought, sold,
exchanged. Genuine Third Reich items also bought and
sold.

WW2HOMEFRONT.COM
Email: drpackrat@webtv.net

WOLFE-HARDIN
6490 Bixby Hill Road, Long Beach, CA 90815, USA
Contact: Stephen Wolfe
Tel: 562 596 6610
Fax: 562 596 0086
We buy, sell and trade in high-quality military antiques—
especially Third Reich. We have helmets, uniforms, daggers
and edged weapons, art medals and orders, badges,
gorgets, regimental embroidery flags, insignia, and
documents. We have 36 years experience in high end
investment grade militaria in exceptional condition with a
life time guarantee of authenticity.

W K OSMAN
5424 Elliot Ave. S, Minneapolis, MN 55417, USA
Contact: W.K. Osman5
Tel: 612 725 2430
Email: calirvine@aol.com
Military replicas, 1812–1865, including embroidered
insignia, sashes, mess equipment. Write for free catalog.

WARGAMING CLUBS

A G E M A
6 Studley Road, Linthorpe, Middlesbrough, Cleveland
Contact: I Moran

BATH WARGAMES CLUB
7 Heathfield Close, Upper Weston, Bath, Avon BA1 4NW
Contact: S Chasey
Established 1970. Meets every Sunday afternoon at Scout
HQ, Grove Street, Bath.

BIRMINGHAM WARGAMES SOCIETY
5c Calthorpe Mansions, Calthorpe Road, Birmingham,
W. Midlands B15 1QS
Contact: Martin Healey
Tel/Fax: 0121 242 6718
Meet alternate Sunday afternoons from 2 to 9pm at
Ladywood Community Centre, Ladywood Middleway,
Birmingham. All periods & all scales played, new members
welcome.

THE BRITISH HISTORICAL GAMES SOCIETY
The White Cottage, 8 Westhill Avenue, Epsom, Surrey KT19 8LE
Contact: F D McNeil
Tel: 01372 812132
Fax: 01372 817038
Email: 100523.547@compuserve.com
Website: http://members.aol.com/BritishHGS/index.htm.
The BHGS organise the UK National Wargames Tournament
and collate results from other competitions. We also
organise overseas tours for our members.

CENTRAL LONDON WARGAMERS
23 Rothay, Albany Street, London NW1 4DH
Contact: S Sola

CHICHESTER WARGAMES SOCIETY
7 Bellemeade Close, Woodgate, Chichester, W. Sussex
PO20 6YD
Contact: Andy Gilbert
Tel/Fax: 01243 544339
Meets Tuesday evenings and once a month for a whole
day. All periods covered, but specialise in 15mm Ancients,
naval wargaming, 5mm Napoleonic and ECW. Regular
entrants in national competitions and World Wargaming
Championships.

COLCHESTER WARGAMES ASSOCIATION
10 Golden Noble Hill, Colchester, Essex
Contact: Pete Anglish
Tel/Fax: 01206 563190
Most periods and scales covered. Meets weekly.

CORNWALL MINIATURE WARGAMERS ASSOC
17 Mitchell Hill Terrace, Truro, Cornwall TR1 1HY
Contact: Chris Kent
Tel/Fax: 01872 75171
All periods, Ancient to Sci-Fi, catered for. Meetings held fortnightly. Trips throughout year to conventions and museums.

CORNWALL WARGAMES SOCIETY
Women's Institute Hall, Cranstock Street, Newquay, Cornwall
Tel/Fax: 01209 212357
All periods catered for including fantasy. Membership fees per annum, £10.00 seniors, £5.00 juniors, £5.00 associated. £1.00 table fee per person per game. Meetings bimonthly.

DEVIZES & DISTRICT WARGAMERS
15 Chiltern Close, Warminster, Wiltshire BA12 8QU

DEVON WARGAMES GROUP
17 Lovelace Crescent, Exmouth, Devon EX8 3PP
Contact: Jonathan Jones
Meeting at Exeter Community Centre, 17 St. Davids Hill, Exeter, first Saturday every month. Membership16 and above. Periods: Napoleonic, WWII, ACW, Ancients, AWI, WWI Air.

DUKE OF YORK'S WARGAMES CLUB
Duke of York's Military School, Dover, Kent CT15 5EQ
Contact: Michael Carson

DURHAM WARGAMES GROUP
c/o Gilesgate Community Assoc, Vane Tempest Hall, Durham City, Co. Durham
Tel/Fax: 0191 384 7659
One of the longest established groups in the area now in its 23rd year. Annual conventions. All periods and scales including some SF and Fantasy. Weekly meetings.

EASTBOURNE MEN AT ARMS WARGAMES CLUB
49 Channel View Road, Eastbourne, E. Sussex BN22 7LN
Contact: Peter Helm
Tel/Fax: 01323 732801
'Men at Arms' have their own club premises where they play all kinds of wargames from ancient to modern. Come and join a friendly group.

ESSEX WARRIORS
67 Fourth Avenue, Chelmsford, Essex CM1 4EZ
Contact: Peter Grimwood
Tel/Fax:01245 265274
We play historical wargames, fantasy, Sci-fi and role-playing games, and meet at Writtle, near Chelmsford, alternate Sundays 9.30am-5pm. Contact for further details.

FORLORN HOPE WARGAMES CLUB
9 Brocklehurst Street, New Cross, London SE14 5QG
Contact: C Barrass
Tel/Fax: 020 7639 3240

THE FRENCH HORN
Oxford Road, Gerrards Cross, Buckinghamshire SL9 7DP
Contact: G Fordham

FRENCH-INDIAN WARGAMERS
55 Prestop Drive, Westfields, Ashby de la Zouch, Leicestershire LE65 2NA
Contact: Brian Betteridge
Tel/Fax: 01530 560164
French-Indian Wars wargamers exchange views, ideas, figures and information. Attend wargame shows with display games, or meet for private battles. Seek like-minded players, collectors, no fees, contact us for details.

HALIFAX WARGAMES SOCIETY
7 Brookeville Avenue, Hipperholme, Halifax, W. Yorkshire HX3 8DZ
Contact: Roger Greenwood
Tel/Fax: 01422 203169
Weekly meetings Wednesdays 7.30pm at Halifax Cricket Club, Thrum Hall, adjacent to Halifax Rugby League ground.

HARROGATE WARGAMERS CLUB
4 Birstwith Road, Harrogate, N. Yorkshire HG1 4TG
Contact: Andrew Baxter
Tel/Fax: 01423 54142-3
Email: ANDY@suc5.demom.co.uk
Organises the annual Sabre Wargames Show. Weekly meetings. Ring above number for further details. All are welcome.

I N D
9 Camp View Road, St Albans, Hertfordshire
Contact: M Scales

KINGSTON GAMES GROUP
The Swan, 22 High Street, Hampton Wick, Kingston, Surrey KT1 4DB
Contact: Ian Barnett
Tel/Fax: 020 8296 0369
The group meets every Tuesday, 6pm-11pm, and on Sundays 2pm-6pm at Wimbledon Community Centre, George Street. All games catered for.

KIRRIEMUIR & DISTRICT WARGAMES SOCIETY
7 Slade Road, Kirriemuir, Angus DD8 5HN, Scotland
Contact: Dale Smith
Tel/Fax: 01575 74128
All periods and scales covered; meet in Glengate Hall, Kirriemuir on alternate Saturday nights from 7.00pm.

MAILED FIST WARGAMES GROUP
Hyde Festival Theatre, Corporation Street, Hyde, Cheshire

MALTBY & DISTRICT WARGAMES SOCIETY
Church Hall, Church Lane, Maltby, Rotherham, S. Yorkshire S66 8JB
Contact: Russ Phillips
Tel/Fax: 01709 818425
We meet every other Sunday and are interested in most periods and scales. New members welcome, first meeting free. Ring Russ Phillips on 01709 818425.

MANCHESTER BOARD WARGAMERS
Sea Scouts Hut, Stockport Road, Romiley, Greater Manchester
Contact: Norman Lane
Tel/Fax: 0161 494 2604
Meetings first and third Saturdays monthly, 12am-6pm. All
board wargames played. The club is active in all areas of
the hobby and offers many services.

MANX WARGAMES GROUP
4 Wesley Terrace, Douglas, isle of Man IM1 3HF
Contact: David Sharpe
Tel/Fax: 01624 626642
Small, friendly group, regularly playing Ancients,
Napoleonics, world wars, Skirmish and Naval games, plus
mainly strategic boardgames. Anything considered. New
members, any age, welcome.

METHUSALENS
5 Fairfax Avenue, Oxford,
Oxfordshire OX3 0RP
Contact: M Goddard

MILTON KEYNES WARGAME SOCIETY
26 Swift Close, Newport Pagnell,
Buckinghamshire MK16 8PP
Contact: B Mills
Tel/Fax: 0 / 908 613558

RAGNAROCK WARGAMING CLUB
216 Powder Mill Lane, Twickenham, Middlesex IW2 6EJ
Contact: Christopher Poore
Tel/Fax: 020 8898 2950
Small wargaming club concentrating on Fantasy, Sci-Fi and
roleplaying games. We meet every Thursday and most
weekends.

RAWDONS ROUTERS
5 Shiplate Road, Bleadon Village, Weston Super Mare, Avon
BS24 0NG
Contact: D Aynsley

RED OCTOBER
19 Plants Brook Road, Walmley, Sutton Coldfield,
W. Midlands B76 8EX
Contact: R Boyles
Tel/Fax: 0121 313 1053

REIGATE WARGAMES GROUP
The White Cottage, 8 Westhill Avenue, Epsom, Surrey KT19 8LE
Contact: J D McNeil
Tel: 01372 812132
Fax: 01372 81 7038
Email: 100523.547@compuserve.com
Main interests are ancient, Napoleonics, other periods and
boardgames. Meetings on Thursday evenings and alternate
Sundays; contact club secretary above for further details.

S E ESSEX MILITARY SOCIETY
202 Westcliff Park Drive, Westcliff on Sea, Essex SS0 9LR
Contact: John Francis
Tel/Fax: 01702 431878
Historical wargaming with all periods covered. Produces
major demonstration game each year and runs annual
wargames show 'Present Arms'. Meets weekly.

S E LONDON WARGAMES GROUP
16 West Hallowes, Eltham, London SE9 4EX
Contact: Paul Greenwood
Tel/Fax: 020 8857 6107
The South East London Wargames Group (known as
SELWG) was formed in 1971 and has a membership of
over 100. A wide range of interests are catered for in the
wargaming field. The club also runs an annual open day.

S E SCOTLAND WARGAMES CLUB
182 Easter Road, Edinburgh, Lothian EH7 5QQ, Scotland

SOLO WARGAMERS ASSOCIATION
120 Great Stone Road, Firswood, Greater Manchester M16 0HD
Contact: Steve Moore
Founded 1976—quarterly magazine 'Lone Warrior' by
wargamers for wargamers, on solo aspects of wargaming.

SOUTH DORSET MILITARY SOCIETY
23 Monks Way, Bearwood, Bournemouth, Dorset BH11 9HT
Contact: B Tborburn
Tel/Fax: 01202 576443

STOCKTON WARGAMERS
c/o Elmwood Community Centre, Green Lane, Hartburn,
Stockton on Tees, Cleveland
Contact: Garry Harbottle-Johnson
Tel/Fax: 01642 580019
All periods including Ancient, plus Science Fiction and
Fantasy. Played in all scales and formats: tabletop, board
games, role playing. Frequent 'in club' campaigns, and day
trips to conventions, paintball, LRP etc. Annual weekend
camping trip; annual show. Miniumum age 12; annual
membership £2.00.

STORMIN NORMANS
26 South Norwood Hill, London SE25 6AB
Contact: N Scott

STOURBRIDGE DISTRICT WARGAMERS
72 Severn Road, Halesowen, W. Midlands B63 2NL
Contact: Ashley Hewitt
Tel/Fax: 01384 561389
Weekly meetings. Membership fee dependent on age. Most
wargames periods catered for, with role-playing and board
games.

STRATAGEM
The Sentry Box, 1835 10 Ave SW Calgary, Alberta, Canada
Tel/Fax: 403 245 2121
Website: http://www.cpsc.ucalgary.cal-vollman/strat.html
Calgary's stategy gaming club, promoting thinking skills
and historical study by playing strategy games.

TUNBRIDGE WELLS WARGAMES SOCIETY
83 Douglas Road, Tonbridge, Kent TN92UD
Contact: Andrew Finch
Tel/Fax: 01732 770811
Email: 113231.1344@compuserve.com
Wargames Society active in all periods. Meetings usually 1st Sunday in month and once per week. Contact Secretary for details of venues and dates.

ULSTER FREIKORPS LEVY
16 Marmont Park, Belfast, Co Antrim, N. Ireland BT4 2GR
Contact: D Taylor
Tel/Fax: 01232 760581

ULSTER WARGAMES SOCIETY
35 Kilmakee Park, Belfast, Co Antrim, N. Ireland BT5 7QY
Contact: Jeremy Dowd
Email: jdowd@dis.n-i.nhs.uk
The society specialises in wargaming, catering for most periods and scales, running multi-player games, campaigns and competitions. Meets monthly at Lough Moss Centre, Carryduff.

VIRGIN SOLDIERS
75 Woodford Green Road, Hall Green, Birmingham, W. Midlands
Contact: M McVeigb
Tel/Fax: 0121 778 5582

WARWAGER
37 Grove Road, Ilkley, W. Yorkshire LS29 9PF

WHITEHALL WARLORDS
2 Marsham Stree, London SWLP 3EB
Contact: Seamus Bradley
Tel/Fax: 020 7276 5586
Historical, Sci-Fi and Fantasy wargaming—miniatures, board games, map games—and role-playing. Annual membership £15.00; good facilities, no table charges- meets each Wednesday.

WILD GEESE 11
27 Kingsdale Croft, Stretton, Burton-on-Trent, Staffordshire
Contact: D McHugh

WARGAMING MODELS, EQUIPMENT & SERVICES

1ST CORPS SPIRIT OF WARGAMING
44 Cheverton Avenue, Withernsea, N. Humberside HU19 2HP
Contact: Rob Baker
Tel/Fax: 01964 613766
Progressive design in 25mm, featuring the American Civil War with the Mexican American War. With exciting new figures and ranges planned for 1995/6.

A & A GAME ENGINEERING
83 Douglas Road, Tonbridge, Kent TN9 2UD
Contact: Andrew Finch
Tel/Fax: 01732 7770811
Email: 113231.1344@compuserve.com
Produce wargames rules for Naval, Air and Science Fiction games with supporting data and scenario sets. Rules designed to give playable, satisfying games. Expanding range.

A B FIGURES/WARGAMES SOUTH
Ffos yr Eloig, Lianfynydd, Carmarthen SA32 7DD
Contact: Mike Hickling
Tel/Fax: 01558 6C)8771
Email: michael@ab-figures.demon.co.uk
Website: www.ab-figures.demon.co.uk
Manufacturers of the 15mm AB Figure range for wargamers and collectors; plus 10mm WW II and 19th century wargames figures. Mail order only, SAE for lists.

BASTION-WESSEX
36 St Mary's Road, Liss, Hants GU33 7AH
Contact: Andrew Rose
Tel/Fax: 01730 893478
Manufacturer and retailer of great quality 54mm traditional toy soldiers, covering Ameriacan Civil War, colonial wars, Boxer Uprising and WWI etc. Mail order only. Send SAE for lists or £22 for colour catalogues. C B G Mignot dealer.

BATTLEMENTS
Sextons, Wymondham Road, Bunwell, Norfolk NR16 1NB
Contact: James Main
Tel/Fax: 01953 789245
Email: battlements.modelmakers@virgin.net
Website: www.battlements.co.uk
We make quality hand-made buildings, fortifications and terrain with an excellent tradition of craftsmanship and attention to historic detail for wargamers, museums and collectors.

BEHIND THE LINES
Basement Unit, 18 Cambridge Street, Aylesbury, Buckinghamshire HP20 1RS
Contact: Graham Harrison
Tel/Fax: 01296 423118
Email: graham@sunjester.freeserve.co.uk
Shop with large stocks of secondhand military books, wargames figures and accessories. All scales and periods. Also stock paints, brushes and games. Open 10.30am-5.00pm.

BRITANNIA MINIATURES
33 St. Mary's Road, Halton Village, Runcorn, Cheshire WA7 2BJ
Contact: David Howitt
Tel/Fax: 01928 564906
Email: dave@homebase99.freeserve.co.uk
25mm wargame figures, Ancients, Colonial, Napoleonic, Crimea etc. 20mm Great War, early period Germans, British and equipment. Wargame accessories cast in resin. Mail order only. Callers by appointment. Non-illustrated listings available. Large SAE required.

CHART INTERNATIONAL LTD
Chart House, Littlehampton, W. Sussex BN16 3AG
Contact: John Reilly
Tel: 01903 773170
Fax: 0190,3 782152
Email: salesc@chartint.com
Website: http://www.chartint.com
UK importers and distributors of Avalon Hill and other conflict simulation games. Publishers of military simulation games distributed in hobby and games stores nationally.

COLLECTAIR 2000
32 West Hemming Street, Letham, Angus, Scotland DD8 2PU
Contact: Peter Fergusson
Tel/Fax: 01307 818494
Email: scotiagrendel@orangenet.co.uk
Makers of cast pewter scale model aircraft (200+ models), 1/300 and 1/200 scales, for collectors and wargamers. List available-, trade enquiries welcome. Available in USA from Simtac Inc, 15G Colton Road, East Lyme, CT 06333.

DEAN FOREST FIGURES
62 Grove Road, Berry Hill, Coleford, Gloucestershire GL16 8QX
Contact: Philip & Mark Beveridge
Tel: 01594 836130
Wargame figure painting, scratch-built trees, buildings and terrain features. Large scale figure painting and scratch-building to any scale. SAE for full lists.

DONNINGTON MINIATURES
15 Cromwell Road, Shaw, Newbury, Berkshire RG14 2HP
Contact: Graham &Maggie Hyland
Tel: 01635 46627
Fax: 07070 720712
Email: donningtonmins@btconnect.com
Manufacturer of 15mm wargaming figures/models. Worldwide mail order. Ancient, Medieval, pike & shot and ACW ranges covered. Figures sold singly, not in packets.

ELITE MINIATURES
26 Bowlease Gardens, Bessacarr, Doncaster, S. Yorkshire DN4 6AP
Contact: Peter Morbey
Tel: 01302 530038
Fax: 01302 530038 (24hrs)
Quality 25mm metal figures for wargamer and collector; Napoleonic, ACW, Seven Years and Punic wars covered. Send £1 and SAE for catalogue. Credit cards accepted.

ELLERBURN ARMIES
Boxtree, Thornton Dale, Pickering, N. Yorkshire YO18 7SD
Tel: 01751 474248
Fax: 01751 477298
Email: ellerburn@mcmail.com
Manufacturer of 25mm Hinchcliffe figures and equipments. Catalogue available of all 2,000 figures, from Ancient Assyrians to colonial Zulu wars. Mail order and painting service.

ESSEX MINIATURES
Unit 1, Shannon Centre, Shannon Square, Canvey Island, Essex SS8 9UD
Tel: 01268 682309
Fax: 01268 510151
Email: info@essexminiatures.co.uk
Manufacturer of 15mm & 25mm metal figures. Send SAE for catalogue. Figures supplied by mail order. All major credit cards accepted.

FRONT RANK FIGURINES
The Granary, Banbury Road, L.Boddington, Daventry, Northamptonshire NN11 6XY
Contact: Alec Brown
Tel: 01327 262720
Fax: 01327 200569
Manufacturers of 25mm figures.

THE GAMES ROOM
29A Elm Hill, Norwich, Norfolk
Tel/Fax: 01603 628140
Email: mike@gamesroom.fsnet.co.uk

THE GUARDROOM
38 West Street, Dunstable, Bedfordshire LU6 ITA
Tel/Fax: 01582 606041
Website: http://chilternweb.co.uk/guardroom
Wargames shop—wide range of figures and rules. Open Monday to Friday 9am-5.30pm, Saturday 9am-5pm. Two miles from junction 11 on the M1.

HOVELS LTD
18 Glebe Road, Scartho, Grimsby, S. Humberside DN33 2HL
Contact: Dennis Coleman
Tel/Fax: 01472 750552
Email: sales@hovelsltd.co.uk

IRREGULAR MINIATURES
3 Apollo Street, Heslington Road, York YO1 5AP
Contact: I Kay
Tel/Fax: 01904 671101
Ranges of white metal figures in following scales: 2mm; 6mm; l0mm, 15mm; 20mm; 25mm, 42mm, 54mm. Rules. accessories, award winning rapid mail order service.

KEEP WARGAMING
The Keep, Le Marchant Barracks, London Road, Devizes, Wiltshire SN10 2ER
Contact: Paul & Teresa Bailey
Tel/Fax: 01380 724558
Email: keepwarg@talk21.com
Shop and mail order service; stockists of wargames figures, books and equipment; some military models and plastic kits. Shop open Tues-Sat 10am to 6pm.

LANCASHIRE GAMES
20 Platting Road, Lydgate, Oldham, Greater Manchester
OL4 4DL
Contact: Allan Lumley
Tel/Fax: 01457 872212
Email: lancgames@lineone.net
15mm castings from Ancient to Colonial, 25mm Fantasy
and 20mm 1/1, available in standard and bargain packs.
Painting service available for figures from 5mm-25mm.

LEISURE GAMES
91 Ballard's Lane, Finchley, London N3 1XY
Tel: 020 8346 4327
Fax: 020 8343 3888
Email: shop@leisuregames.com
We stock the most comprehensive range of board war
games in London. Plus 'Minifigs' and a wide range of rulc
books, lists and Osprey publilcations.

MATCHLOCK MINIATURES
816–818 London Road, Leigh-on-Sea, Essex SS9 3NH
Contact: David Ryan
Tel/Fax: 01702 473986
Email: dave@caliverbooks.demon.co.uk or ask@caliverbooks.com
Website: www.caliverbooks.com
Wargames figures, all periods from Ancient to Modern.
Shop open seven days a week. Send five 1st class stamps
for sample.

MEDWAY GAMES CENTRE
294–296 High Street, Chatham, Kent
Tel: 01634 847809
Fax: 01634 814750

MNG GAMES & COLLECTIBLES
105 Dalrymple Way, Norwich, Norfolk BR6 6TR
Contact: Eamon Bloomfield
Tel/Fax: 01603 417 505
Email: diceman@games.u-net.com
Wargames, fantasy, general board games. secondhand
listing available by subscription. Trading card singles.
Visitors strictly by appointment only.

MUSEUM MINIATURES
28 Long Lane, Driffield, E. Yorkshire YO25 5HF
Contact: Dave Hoyles
Tel: 0137 7241010
Email: dave@museumminiatures.co.uk
Website: http://www.museumminiatures.co.uk
15mm wargaming figures. Ranges include Ancient, Dark
Ages, Medieval, Renaissance, ACW, Napoleonic. Equipment
includes wagons, carts, cannons, bombards, catapults. Mail
order service a speciality. Callers advised to ring first.

NAVWAR PRODUCTIONS LTD
11 Electric Parade, Seven Kings, Ilford, Essex IG3 8BY
Tel/Fax: 020 8590 6731
Manufacturers of 1/3000 and 1/1200 scale ships,
Roundway and Naismith 15mm figures; 1/300 figures,
tanks & aircraft. Closed Thursdays.

OLD GLORY CORPORATION
Institute House, New Kyo, Stanley, Co Durham DH9 7TJ
Contact: Andrew Copestake
Tel: 01207 283332
Fax: 01207 281902
UK and European agents for Old Glory Corp. PO Box 20,
Calumet, PA 15621 USA. Phone 724 423 3580, fax 724
423 6898. Manufacturers of a wide range of 25mm,
15mm and 20mm scale figures in a wide range of periods.
Trade enquiries welcome worldwide.

PETER PIG
Maebee, 36 Knightsdale Road, Weymouth, Dorset DT4 0HS
Contact: Martin Goddard
Tel/Fax: 01305 760384
Email: martin@peterpig.demon.co.uk
Website: www.peterpig.demon.co.uk
Makers of 15mm metal figures; 17 ranges including WMI,
ACW, SCW, Ancients, Renaissance, ACW Naval, Sci-Fi,
Vietnam. Send SAE for list and sampic.

PIREME PUBLISHING LTD
Suite 10, Wessex House, St Leonards Road, Bournemouth,
Dorset BH8 8QS
Contact: Iain Dickie
Tel: 01202 297344
Fax: 01202 297345
Email: iaindickie@freeuk.com
Publishers of 'Miniature Wargames magazine—covers all
periods of history and all theatres of conflict. Also the
Miniature Wargames Starter Packs for Ancients, Pirates,
Napoleonic and World War 11, plus inexpensive military
prints, booklets and 15mm Waterloo card buildings.

RAVENTHORPE MINIATURES
2 Bygot Lane, Cherry Burton, E. Yorkshire HU17 7RN
Tel/Fax: 01964 551027
Email: to come
20mm, 1/76th scale, figures and vehicles. Many unique
types: Zulu, Boer, Mexican Revolution, WW I, WW II, etc.
SAE and 2xlst class stamps for lists.

RICHARD NEWTH-GIBBS PAINTING SERVICES
59 Victor Close, Hornchurch, Essex RM12 4XH
Tel/Fax: 01708 448785
Any scale from 15mm up, single figures, groups, dioramas,
artillery pieces, mounted gun teams; British and Indian
Army specialist. Factual military work only. Callers by
appointment.

SPIRIT GAMES
98 Station Street, Burton-on-Trent, Staffordshire DE14 1BT
Tel/Fax: 01283 511293
Email: salnphil@spiritgames.u-net.com
Website: http://www.spiritgames.com
5mm, 15mm and 25mm figures, buildings and rules
stocked. Open Tues–Fri 10am-6pm, Sat 10am–5pm. Mail
order welcome.

TABLETOP GAMES
29 Beresford Avenue, Skegness, Lincolnshire PE25 JF
Contact: Robert Connor
Tel/Fax: 01754 767779
Established in 1976, we are a specialist mail order company serving the wargamer throughout the world. Please send an SAE (two IRCs) for our free catalogue.

TERENCE WISE
Pantiles, Garth Lane, Knighton, Powys, Wales LD7 1HH
Tel/Fax: 01547 529160
Wargames figures: mint castings and painted figures. Wide range of manufacturers, mostly 25mm, some 54mm, 20mm, 15mm. Free list from Terry Wise at above address.

VANDRAD
7 Marpool Hill, Exmouth, Devon EX8 2LJ
Contact: Rick Lawrence
Tel/Fax: 01395 278604
Email: vandrad@madasafish.com
20mm figures from 20:20 Miniatures, and Bataillonfeuer Miniatures. Painting service available. Various periods available.

WARGAMES HOLIDAY CENTRE
Enchanted Cottage, Folkton, Scarborough, N. Yorkshire YO11 3UH
Contact: Mike Ingham
Tel/Fax: 020 7890580
Email: gerryjelliott@aol.com

WARLORD GAMES SHOP (See CALIVER BOOKS)
818 London Road, Leigh on Sea, Southend, Essex SS9 1NQ
Contact: David Ryan
Tel/Fax: 017024 73986
Email: dave@caliverbooks.demon.co.uk
Retail outlet holding wide range of wargames figures, board games, rules, books etc. Open 7 days a week, one hour's drive/train from London.

WARRIOR MINIATURES
14 Tiverton Avenue, Glasgow, Strathclyde, Scotland G32 9NX
Contact: John Holt
Tel/Fax: 0141 7783426
Email: john@warriorminiatures.com
Over 1,600 wargaming figures, many periods, 10mm, 15mm, 20mm, 25mm. Catalogue £1.50, or overseas £5.00.

WEAPONS SUPPLIES

ALLEGHENY ARSENAL, INC.
PO Box 161, Custer City, PA 16725, USA
Contact: Greg Souchik
Tel: 814 362 2642
Fax: 814 362 7356
Email: Mg34@mg34.com
Website: www.mg34.com
We sell machine gun parts, parts kits and accessories. We also manufacture non-guns and replica arms suitable for re-enactments, displays or museum use. We carry rare and unusual parts for: MG-34, MAXIM, PPsh-41, RPD, PPS-43, Beretta, DP28 and many others. Watch our website, www.mg34.com for monthly specials and our newest offerings.

ANGLO LONGBOWS
No 1 Ol Wooth Farm, Pymore, Bridport, Dorset DT6 5LE
Contact: M and J Foote
Tel: 01308 458137
Website: www.anglolongbows.co.uk
Traditional hand crafted longbows—English, Saxon,/Viking and Native American bows, arrows and leather quivers.

ANNE FORD
Maytree House, Woodrow Lane,
Bromsgrove, Worcs B61 OPL
Contact: Alan Ford
Tel: 0121 453 6329
Suppliers to museums, gift and surplus shops—inert ammunition, all calibres. Bullet keyrings, souvenirs, replica grenades, de-activated weapons, MG belts, etc. Trade and retail lists available.

ARMOUR DISTRIBUTION/ACCURATE ARMOUR
Units 15–16, Kingston Industrial Estate, Port Glasgow, Inverclyde, Scotland PA14 5DG
Contact: David Farrell
Tel: 1475 743 955
Fax: 1475 743 746
Email: enquiries@accurate-armour.com
Website: www.accurate-armour.com

ARMS & ARCHERY
The Coach House, London Road, Ware, Herts SG12 9QU
Tel: 01920 460335
Fax: 01920 461044
Email: tgou104885@aol.com
Website: armaand archery.co.uk
Film and TV props and costumes. Makers of plate armour, chainmail and fighting swords (titanium) for stunt work only.

A S BOTTOMLEY
The Coach House, Huddersfield Road, Holmfirth, W. Yorkshire
HD7 2TT
Contact: Andrew Bottomley
Tel: 01484 685234
Fax: 01484 681551
Email: andrewbottomley@compuserve.com
Established 30 years with clients overseas and in the UK.
A fully illustrated mail order catalogue containing a large
range of antique weapons and military items despatched
world wide. Every item is guaranteed original. Full money
back if not satisfied. Deactivated weapons available.
Valuations for insurance and probate, interested in buying
weapons or taking items in part exchange. Business hours
Mon–Fri 9am–5pm. Mail order only. All major credit cards
welcome. Catalogue UK £5, Europe £7, rest of world £10.

AIR GUNNING TODAY INTERNATIONAL
2 Gleave Street, Standish Street, St
Helens, Merseyside WA10 1AU

ALBION SMALL ARMS
Unit 4, AMI. Industrial Estate, Rugeley Road, Hednesford,
Staffordshire WS12 5QW
Contact: Ron Curley
Tel: 01922 684964

ANTIQUES
Main Street, Durham-on-Trent, Nottinghamshire NG22 0TY
Contact: R G Barnett
Tel/Fax: 01777 228312
Antique flintlock and percussion pistols and long arms,
swords, daggers and armour our speciality. Also buy and
sell general antiques, furniture, etc.

APOLLO FIREARMS COMPANY LTD
PO Box 404, St Albans, Hertfordshire AH49YR
Tel: 020 7739 1616

ARIAN TRADING
1 The Monkery, Church Road, Great Milton, Oxfordshire
OX44 7PB
Tel: 01844 278139
Fax: 01844278790
Fine quality classic sporting and military firearms of all
kinds.

ASGARD ARMOURY
Asgard, 46 Haverhill Road, Stapleford, Cambridgeshire
CB2 5BX
Contact: Alex Talbam
Tel/Fax: 01223 842926
Email: asgard_armoury@compuserve.com
Certified hand-crafted replica swords and daggers of
carbon steel, hardened and tempered in accordance with
tests of the Department of Metallurgy, Cambridge
University.

AUX ARMES D'ANTAN
I Avenue Paul Deroulede, 75015 Paris, France
Contact: Maryse Raso
Tel: 1 47837142
Fax: 1 47344099
Expert and dealer in sabres, swords and ancient pistols
and other weapons from the 12th to the 19th centuries, for
25 years. Publishes a catalogue every three months,
available by post from the office. All pieces are sold along
with a guarantee.

BARTROP'S SHOOTING AND FISHING
206 Knutsford Road, Warrington, Cheshire WA4 1AU
Contact: Peter H Bartrop
Tel/Fax: 01925 572509

BATTLE ORDERS LTD
71A Eastbourne Road, Lower Willingdon, Eastbourne,
E. Sussex BN209NR
Contact: Graham Barton
Tel: 01323 485182
Fax: 013Z3 487309
Email: info@battleorders.co.uk
We specialise in Airsoft pistols, metal replica knives,
Japanese and European historic swords. Find us on the
A22 just two miles north of Eastbourne.

BENJAMIN WILD & SON
Price Street Works, Price Street, Birmingham, W. Midlands
B4 6JZ
Tel/Fax: 0121 359 4303

BULLITT MUNITIONS
11 Lime Road, Southam, Warwks CV33 0EQ
Contact: Steve McGregor
Tel/Fax: 01926 812972
Specialising in inert ammunition, grenades, bombs and
fuses.

BRIAN GREENHALGH
314 Central drive, Blackpool FY1 6LE
Tel: 01253 348272
Tel/Fax: 01253 348909
Email: BayonetKing@aol.com

C F SEIDLER
Stand G12, Grays Antique Mkt, 1–7
Davies Mews, Davies Street, London W1V 1AR
Contact: Christopher Seidler
Tel/Fax: 020 7029 2851
Email: tomus@tinyworld.co.uk
American, British, European, Oriental edged weapons,
antique firearms, orders and decorations, uniform items;
watercolours, prints; regimental histories, army lists; horse
furniture; etc. We purchase at competitive prices and will
sell on a consignment or commission basis. Valuations for
probate and insurance. Does not issue a catalogue but will
gladly receive clients' wants lists. Open Mon–Fri,
11.00am–6.00pm Nearest tube station Bond Street (Central
line).

CASTLE KEEP (WEAPONSMITH)
Uiginish Lodge, Dunvegan, Isle of Skye, Scotland IV55 8ZR
Contact: Rob Miller
Tel/Fax: 01478 612114
Email: robmiller@hotmail.com
Hand forged swords, knives, daggers and dirks. Damascus
steels, traditional Scottish weaponry. Catalogue available,
£2.

CENTRE VINE LTD
76 Stevensons Way, Formby Business Park, Formby,
Merseyside
Tel: 017048 70598
Fax: 017048 71613
Email: centrevineltd@aol.com

CHRIS BLYTHMAN
The Flat, Brook House Farm, Middleton, Ludlow, Shropshire
SY8 2DZ
Tel/Fax: 01584 878591
Quality hand-forged military and domestic ironwork, for
museums, re-enactment, TV and film.

COACH HARNESS
Haughley, Stowmarket, Suffolk IP14 3NS
Tel/Fax: 01449 673258
Mail order specialists; new books on antique and early
guns and Western artefacts. Suppliers of restoration parts
for flintlock and percussion guns. Gunsmithing service
available.

COLLECTABLE FIREARMS & EDGED WEAPONS
PO Box 8327, Fredericksburg, VA 22404, USA
Contact: Kristopher Gasior
Tel: 540 374 8124
Fax: 540 374 8124
Email: kristopher@collectablefirearms.com
Website: www.collectablefirearms.com
Dealers in collectable firearms, edged weapons, militaria,
and related books. We specialize in European military
firearms and edged weapons of all periods. We are an
importer of arms and armor books from Europe and
Australia.

CORRIDORS OF TIME (HISTORICAL PRESENTATIONS) LTD
22 Palace Street, Canterbury, Kent CT1 2DZ
Contact: Alan Jeffery
Tel: 01227 478990
Fax: 01227 478991
Email: corridors@argonet.co.uk
Website: www. corridors-of-time.co.uk
Retail outlet to provide genuine, antique, military, museum
quality and legendary artefacts, from swords to armour,
buttons to badges. Gifts, souvenirs, momento's all linked to
British history, including organisers of major centenial and
commemorative events. 35 years exeperience and still
enthislastic.

DELTA ARMS UK
Contact: Ian Varley
Tel/Fax: 01159831506
Mobile: 0802414433
Email: deltaarms@aol.com
Website: www.deltaarms.co.uk
Ordnance supplies.

DRAGON FORGE
Y Bryn, Llaneilian Road, Amlwch, Anglesey, Wales LL68 9HU
Contact: T K M Craddock
Tel/Fax: U1407831070
Manufacture of fully researched weaponry, iron work and
furniture for re-enactment or the collector. Sword blades,
spring steel, predominantly 9th/10th centuries catered for.

EAGLE CLASSIC ARCHERY
41 Spring Walk, Worksop, Nottinghamshire S80 1XQ
Contact: Roy Simpson
Tel: 01909 478935
Fax: 01909 488115
Longbows & replica Mongol bows, any poundage; arrows and
replica medieval arrow heads. Telephone or fax anytime.

ENGLISH ARMOURIE
Department 10, 1 Walsall Street, Willenhall, W. Midlands
NW13 2EX
Contact: Alan Jones
Tel/Fax: 01902 870579
Website: www.englisharmourie.fsnet.co.uk
Armour manufacturers from Roman to English Civil War.
Also makers of muzzle loading muskets. Deactivated guns.
General militaria dealers covering all periods.

FINE ARMS
PO Box 86D, New Malden, Surrey KT3 6NJ
Contact: R D Cockerill
Tel/Fax: 020 8942 59 50
International Small Arms Company. All leading makes of
firearms and accessories supplied and repaired.

*LES FRÈRES D'ARMES
16 Rue Lakanal, 38000 Grenobles, France

FREDERICK'S ANTIQUE SWORDS
6919 Westview Drive, Oak Forest, IL 60452, USA
Contact: Fredérick Coluzzi
Tel: 708 687 3647
Fax: 708 687 3695
Email: coluzzi113@aol.com
Website: Fredericksantiqueswords.com
Original antique edge weapons. All countries, all periods.
Many Damascus.

GAUNT D'OR (WEAPONSMITH)
58 Springfield Road, Wolverhampton, W. Midlands
WV10 0LJ
Tel/Fax: 01902 683875
Email: gauntdor@compuserve.com
For authentic reproduction swords, daggers and other
weapons from the Dark Ages through to Renaissance.
Suitable for re-enactment or wall-hangings.

HENRY KRANK
100/102 Lowton, Pudsey, W. Yorkshire LS28 9AY
Tel: 0113 2569163
Fax: 0113 2574962

HISTORICAL BREECHLOADING SMALLARMS ASSOC
PO Box 12778, London SE 6XB
Contact: David Penn
Tel: 020 7416 5270
Fax: 020 7416 5274
For serious students or collectors. Publishes an annual journal and approx. four newsletters a year. Regular monthly meetings in London. Range practices April-October. Active in monitoring legislation affecting small-arms and ammunition. Occasional national or international symposia. Corresponding membership available for non-UK residents.

HISTORICALWEAPONS.COM
Markoviceva 27, Krizevci, 48260 Croatia
Contact: Kruno Kovacic
Tel: 91 529 5040
Fax: 48 712 390
Email: webmaster@historicalweapons.com
Website: http://www.historicalweapons.com
Online store selling antique and replica arms and armour dating from Roman times through the present day, swords, military sabres, daggers, knives, guns, cannons, medieval shields, suits of armour, books, art prints and articles with tips for edged weapons collectors.

LE HUSSARD
BP 69, 38353 La Tour du Pin Cedex, France
Contact: Jacques Buigne
Tel: 474 97 45 6,3
Fax: 474 97 62 88
Old weapons. Firearms from 18th and 19th centuries, edged weapons: sabres, bayonets, halberds, swords, from all ages. Illustrated free catalogue on request (in French).

IAN D WIGGINS RFD
Mulsanne, Hadlow Road East, Tonbridge, Kent TN11 0AE
Tel: 01732 850296 or 851627
Mobile: 0836 714140
Firearms consultant.

INTERKNIFE
PO Box 107, Wymondham NR18 9EQ
Tel: 01953 606457
Fax: 01603 748570
Email: See Website
Website: www.interknife.co.uk
Authentic knives and daggers made by Rod Matless. From Dark Age to Tudor—museum quality, as supplied to the Mary Rose Trust and other organisations. See our travelling stall at all major battles and re-enactment markets.

INTER-MEDIEVAL INTERNATIONAL MEDIEVAL ALLIANCE
c/o 18 Asgate Valley Road, Ashgate, Chesterfield, Derbyshire S40 4AX
Contact: Roger Lankford
Tel: 01246 270090
Email: roger@lancaster-armry.demon.co.uk
Website: england@intermedieval.org
International Medieval Alliance is a dream—a new born babe weened to bring together all the true knights and merry medieval re-enactors from all over the world. A brotherhood bound by honour and commitment to promote our heritages for all.

JACK GREENE LONGBOWS
Oldwood Pits, Tanhouse Lane, Yate, Bristol BS 17 5PZ
Contact: Jack Greene
Tel/Fax: 01454 227164
Utility English longbows in degame/hickory or yew. Varied for different periods, e.g. plain or horn nocks etc. Linen strings. Visitors welcome by appointment.

THE JELLING DRAGON
Flat 4, The George Centre, 30 North Parade, Matlock Bath, Derbyshire DE4 3NS
Contact: RobertTaylor.
Tel: 01629 760120 or 07714 088132
Email: admin@jelldragon.com
Website: www.jelldragon.com
Manufacturer and supplier of weapons, armour & crafts from Roman, Viking & Medieval times. Battle ready and museum replica swords, leather craft, horn craft, iron work and Viking jewellery.

JEREMY TENNISWOOD
PO Box 73, Aldershot, Hampshire GU11 1UJ
Contact: Jeremy Tenniswood
Tel: 01452 319791
Fax: 01252 342339
Email: 100307.1735@compuserve
Established 1966, dealing in collectable firearms civil and Military, de-activated and for shooters; also swords, bayonets, medals, badges, insignia, buttons, headdress, ethnographica; and books. Regular lists of Firearms and Accessories, Medals, Edged Weapons, Headdress, Headdress Badges and Insignia; comprehensive lists Specialist and Technical Books. Office open 9am-5pm, closed all day Sunday. Medal mounting service.

JOHNSON REFERENCE BOOKS & MILITARIA
403 Chatham Square Office Park, Fredericksburg, VA 22405, USA
Contact: LTC (Ret.) Thomas M. Johnson
Tel: 540-373-9150
Fax: 540-373-0087
Email: ww2daggers@aol.com
Website: johnsonreferencebooks.com, ww2daggers.com
Specializing in WWI and WWII German edged weapons, uniforms, medals, decorations, insignia, accouterments, parts, and reference publications (new and out-of-print). Our sales catalog includes over 2,100 original items. The cost per catalog (airmail, overseas & Canada) is $15.00, domestic (U.S.) is $10.00. On-line catalog is available at JohnsonReferenceBooks.com.

LANCASTER'S ARMOURIE

18 Ashgate Road, Ashgate, Chesterfield S40 4AX
Contact: Roger Lankford
Tel: 01246 270090
Email: roger@lancasters-armry.demon.co.uk
Website: lancasters-armry.demon.co.uk
Manufacturer's of medieval weapons and armour for full
contact medieval combat and martial arts specialists.

MACDONALD ARMOURIES

At the Sign of the Cross and Sword, Brunswick St Lane,
Edinburgh
Contact: Paul Macdonald
Email: macarmouries@aol.com
Website: http://users.ox.ac.uk/~zoo10328/macdonald.html
Macdonald Armouries manufactures functional reproduction
historical edged weaponry, specialising in accurate
weight/balance swords and daggers for the historical
fencing market. Weapons are made individually to order,
recreating original examples or catering to customer speci-
fications. All styles of European weaponry from Celtic to
C19th can be created.

MANTON INTERNATIONAI ARMS

140 Bromsgrove Street, Birmingham, W. Midlands B5 6RG
Tel: 0121 666 6066
Fax: 0121 622 5002
Email: sales@firearms.co.uk
We sell a wide range of de-activated weapons, swords and
bayonets. Export and retail enquiries welcomed. Shop open
Mon–Fri 9am–5pm; Sat 10am–4pm.

*MARCHT SERPETTE

Allee 1, Stand 8, 110 Rue des Rosiers, 93400 Saint Ouen, France
Contact: Jean-Pierre Maury

MARK P JONES

1064 N. Main St, PMB 111 Bowling Green OH 43402-1346,
USA
Contact: Mark P Jones
Tel: 419 283 0941
Email: nixe@bright.net
Website: www.bright.net/~nixe/
Japanese sword collector interested in buying Japanese
swords and samurai related items.

*MARS

5 Rue Jean-Marie Michel, 69410 Champagne au Mont d'Or,
France

*MICHAEL REAPE—HISTORIC ARCHERY

Fortshaus Strasse 4, 65606 Langhecke, Germany
Contact: Michael Reape
Authentic medieval archery equipment for the re-enactor
historian. Warbows or longbows of self yew or elm. High
quality arrows made to order. Hand forged war points. Free
catalogue.

MOUNTAINSTONE FORGE & ARMOURY

8 Fairfield Road, Morecambe, Lancashire LA3 1ER
Contact: Peter Constantine
Tel/Fax: 01524 401292
Viking, Norman, Medieval and fantasy swords, daggers,
scrams, axes, helmets, shields, polearms, hearth furniture
and fittings. All weapons made to order. Blacksmith
products, ironwork etc. Museums etc supplied.

NATIONAL PISTOL ASSOCIATION (NPA)

21 Letchworth Gate Centre, Protea Way, Pixmore Avenue,
Letchworth,
Hertfordshire SG6 1JT
The NPA promotes the sport of pistol shooting in the UK. It
organises shooting meetings, sells merchandise, advises
members on shooting problems, etc.

NATIONAL SMALL BORE RIFLE ASSOC (NSRA)

Lord Roberts House, Bisley Camp, Brookwood, Woking, Surrey
GU24 0NP
Contact: J D Hoare
Tel: 01483 476969
Fax: 01483 476392
Email: NSRA@dialpipex.com
National governing body for small-bore, airgun and cross-
how shooting. For details of local clubs please write
enclosing SAE.

THE OLD BRIGADE

10A Harborough Road, Kingsthorpe, Northampton,
Northamptonshire NN2 7A7
Contact: Stewart Wilson
Tel: 01604 719369
Fax: 01604 712489
Email: theoldbrigade@easynet.co.uk
Website: www.theoldbrigade.co.uk
Specialist dealer in Third Reich militaria, daggers, uniforms,
medals, badges, flags, helmets, etc also a good selection
of Imperial German items and militaria from other coun-
trys.Please visit our web site or visit our shop in
person,visitors by appointment only please.

PERIOD CROSSBOWS

7 Alexandra Close, Milton Regis, Sittingbourne, Kent
ME10 2JP
Contact: Robin Knight
Tel: 01795 427461
Manufacturers of crossbows and stonebows of all periods.
Repair services offered to museums and collectors of origi-
nal pieces. Seminars and lectures offered.

REDHEADS

PO Box 107, Wymondham NR18 9EQ
Tel: 01953 606457
Fax: 01603 748570
Email: See Website
Website: www.interknife.co.uk
Protective arrowheads designed especially foe re-enactors.
Safety rubber arrowheads especially designed to shoot fur-
ther and more accurately. With extra rubber to deter shaft
penetration. All at a bargain price!

R R T
26 Lomas Drive, Northfield, Birmingham, W. Midlands
B31 5LR
Contact: Ray Thorne
Tel/Fax: 0121 4769078
Specialised metallic/shotgun cartridge display cases.
Collections made up. Trade supplied. Send SAE for details.
Personal callers by appointment only.

RELICS
20 St Wilfrid's Green, Hailsham, E. Sussex BN27 1DR
Contact: C Hodgson
Tel: 01323 846 007
Fax: 01323 842 234
Email: relicsarms@hotmail.com
Website: www.relics.org.uk
Replica weaponry from WWI and II to the present day war
theatres—and into the future! Hand built, full size accurate
copies of guns, grenades, mines and missiles. Illustrated
catalogue available £4. 'Auld Arms' catalogue £5—includes
Wild West guns, flintlock pistols and muskets, crossbows,
swords and daggers. We supply worldwide maiol order
only.

RICHARD WELLS SPORTING GUNS
The Gunshop, Haslemere, Surrey
Tel/Fax: 01428 651913

ROD AKEROYD & SON
101-103 New Hall Lane, Preston,
Lancashire PRI 5PB
Tel: 01772 794947
Fax: 01772 654535
Email: info@firearmscollector.com
Extensive stock of British, Continental, and Japanese guns,
swords, helmets and armour. Callers welcome.

RODING ARMOURY
Silver Street, Market Place, Abridge, nr. Romford, Essex
Tel/Fax: 01992 813570 or 813005

ROY KING HISTORICAL REPRODUCTIONS
Sussex Farm Museum, Manor Farm, Horam, nr. Heathfield, E.
Sussex TN21 0JB
Reproduction armour, helmets, edged weapons and some
associated goods. Theatrical and film props, cannons, siege
engines etc. Pyrotechnic service for simulated battles
available. Mail order, limited catalogue available—most
items made to order. Visitors by appointment only.
Surrounding fields and Farm Museum available for location
hire.

RYTON ARMS
RFD 65, PO Box 7, retford, Notts DN22 7XH
Tel: 01777 860222

SABRE SALES
85–87 Castle Road, Southsea, Portsmouth, Hampshire PO5 3AY
Contact: Nick Hall
Tel: 01 705 833394
Fax: 01 705 837394
Open six days a week near D-Day Museum; we have an
extensive stock at our shops and warehouse, specialising
in @l memorabilia, and all collectables.

SERVICE ARMS (UK)
PO Box 21, Llandeilo, Carmarthenshire SA19 6YE, Wales
Contact: Brian C Knapp
Tel/Fax: 01558 823010
Email: servicearmsuk@freeserve.co.uk
Leading specialists in 18th and 19th century military
firearms. Send SAE for free catalogue.

SHERWOOD ARMOURY
34 Lambs Walk, Whitstable, Kent CT5 4PJ
Contact: David Lee
Tel/Fax: 01227 262217
Reasonably priced, de-ctivated weapons and ancilliary
equipment bought and sold. Part-exchange considered.
Anything goes: artillery, field-guns, aircraft guns, machine
guns, rifles and pistols.

SHOOTERS RIGHTS ASSOCIATION
PO Box 3, Cardigan, Dyfed SA43 1BN, Wales
Contact: Richard Law
Tel: 01239 698607
Fax: 01239 698614
Email: RichardLaw@btinternet.com
Membership Organisation for collectors and shooters specialis-
ing in dealing with legal and licensing problems. Members are
insured for public liability and legal costs for £24.

SOLDIER OF FORTUNE
Unit 18, Tyn y Llidiart Ind Estate, Corwen, Clwyd, Wales LL21 9RR
Contact: Peter Kabluczenko
Tel: 01490 412225
Fax: 01490 412205
Email: sof@chesternet.co.uk
Website: www.sofmilitary.co.uk
Specialising in reproduction 2nd WW clothing and equip-
ment. British, German and the USA. Catalogue available.

TASCO SPORTING GOODS
2 Tewin Court, Tewin Road, Welwyn Garden City,
Hertfordshire AL7 1AU
Tel: 01256 374700
Fax: 01707373013
Email: sales@hama.co.uk

THE TREBUCHET SOCIETY
23 Viewside Close, Corfe Mullen, Dorset BH21 3ST
Contact: R Barton
Tel/Fax: 01202 090224
Email: richardbarton@msn.com
Research into the trebuchet and other siege weaponry.
Design, construction and experimentation with working
reproduction weapons, using authentic materials, and in
further modern technological evolution.

TRENCHART
PO Box 3887, Bromsgrove, Hereford & Worcester B61 ONL
Tel/Fax: 0121 453 6329
Suppliers to museums, gift and surplus shops. Inert
ammunition, all calibres; bullet keyrings, ringtags, souvenirs,
replica grenades, de-activated weapons, MG belts and clips,
large cartridge cases, etc. Trade only supplied.

VIKING CRAFTS
20 Snowbell Square, Ecton Brook, Northampton NN3 5HH
Contact: Mike Haywood
Tel/Fax: 01604 412672
Email: mike@vikingcrafts.co.uk
Website: www.vikingcrafts.co.uk
We supply replicas, 'in the style', and copies of historical
artefacts and games from the Dark and Viking ages. These
include: pewter, bronze and silver, pendants, mythological
figures and belt fittings, leatherwork, weapons, helmets,
shields, woodwork and horn and games such as: Hnefatafl,
Nine Mans Morris, chess, Runes etc.

WOLFE-HARDIN
6490 Bixby Hill Road, Long Beach CA 90815 USA
Contact: Stephen Wolfe
Tel: 562 596 6610
Fax: 562 596 0086
We buy, sell and trade in high-quality military antiques—
especially Third Reich. We have helmets, uniforms, daggers
and edged weapons, art medals and orders, badges,
gorgets, regimental embroidery flags, insignia, and documents. We have 36 years experience in high end investment grade militaria in exceptional condition with a life
time guarantee of authenticity.

WHITEROSE
Unit 59 Clock Tower Business Centre, Works Road,
Hollingwood, Chesterfield S43 2PE
Tel: 01246 475 782
Fax: 01246 471 123
Website: www.white-rose-armourys.co.uk or
www.white-rose-castings.com
Arms and armour from Ancient Greek to Civil War. Brass
and bronze castings.

EVENTS & SHOWS

AVONCRAFT FAYRE
AVONCRAFT MUSEUM OF HISTORIC BUILDINGS
Stoke Heath, Bromsgrove, Worcs B60 4JR
Tel: 01527 831363 or 831886
Fax: 01527 876934
Email: avoncraft1@compuserve.com
Website: www.avoncraft.org.uk
Avoncraft is a fascinating world of historic buildings cover-
ing seven centuries, rescued and rebuilt on a beautiful
open-air site in the heart of the Worcestershire country-
side. The Fayre is held from 14–15 September 2002.
Merchants of all periods, displays, food and beer tent.

CERS—UNION OF EUROPEAN HISTORICAL COMPANIES
San Polo 2322, 30125 Venice, Italy
Contact: Massimo Andreoli
Tel/Fax: 041 524 1243
Email: martinelli@radiovenezia.it
Historical events all round Europe with the support of more
than 80 groups covering 13th–16th centuries.

ARMS FAIRS LTD (PM)
PO Box 2654, Lewes, E. Sussex BN71BF
Tel/Fax: 01773 475959
Organisers of London Antique Arms & Military Fairs held in
April and September each year. Both fairs open for two
days—140 tables.

ENGLISH HERITAGE'S EVENTS
Tel: 020 7973 3434

GALLOWAY COACH TRAVEL
Denters Hill, Mendlesham, Stowmarket, Suffolk IP14 5RR
Contact: Glen Foremen
Tel: 01449 767778
Fax: 01499 766241
Email: coach@galloway-travel.co.uk
Specialising in battlefield tour especially for school parties .

HANDS MILITARIA FAIRS
PO Box 254, Marden, Tonbridge, Kent TN12 9ZQ
Contact: Gary Howard
Tel/Fax: 01892 730233
Email: ghq1uk@aol.com
Website: www.militaria-fairs.com
Militaria and collectors fairs held at Barnhill, Cheshunt,
Didcot, Dorking, farnham, Guildford and Midhurst. Held on
Sundays 10am–2pm. Dealers selling: uniforms, equipment,
books, paintings, ephemera, helmets, hats, swords, de-acti-
vated weapons and firearms etc. Tables to be booked in
advance. Public entry £1.50. Refreshments available.
Contact us for dates.

HERSTMONCEUX CASTLE MEDIEVAL FESTIVAL
Tel: 09068 172902
Wmail: info@mgel.com
Website: www.mgel.com
Now in its 10th year. Britain's largest celebration of the
Middle Ages. Hundreds of combatants with cannon support
will siege the castle. Mounted knights will joust. Europe's
finest archers compete. The Medieval art of falconry from
horseback is recreated. Living history village and Kids
Kingdom. In this magical setting history will come to life.

HISTORICAL TOURS
PO Box 3241, Parklands, Gauteng, South Africa 2121
Contact: Mike Hardisty
Tel: 2711 447 8574
Fax: 2711 442 3479
Email: marleneh@medscheme.co.za
Anglo-Boer War Centenary. South African programme of
events and commemorations. Customised tours. Research
undertaken foe regimental associations.

HISTORICAL PROMOTIONS
Bulstone Business Centre, Petrockstowe, Okehampton, Devon
EX20 3ET
Contact: Rob Butler
Tel/Fax: 01837 811243
Website: www.historicalpromotions@aol.com
Planning, management, promotion and delivery of historical
re-enactments and events for councils, historic properties,
museums, show organisers and heritage bodies. We undertake costumed interpretation, living history and multi-period
spectaculars throughout the UK and abroad. We provide
service to film and television production companies including historical extras, location services and vehicles.

INTERNATIONAL ARMS & MILITARIAFAIR
Rosenheckhalle, Ebernhahn, D-56424 Germany
Organizer and Information:
Geschichtsverein Siershahn e.V.
Contact: Christoph Schaefer
Im Tonfeld 1
D-56427 Siershahn
Tel: 26235651
Fax: 2623951729
Mobile: 1752728684
eMail: geschichtsverein@gmx.de
Internet: http://www.militariafair.de

INVICTA MILITARY VEHICLE PRESERVATION TRUST SHOW
The Old Rectory, Sandwich Road, Ash, Canterbury, Kent CT3 2AF
Contact: Rex Cadnam
Tel: 01304 813128
Fax: 01304 812422
Email: rex@warandpwace.uk.com
Website: www.warandpeace.uk.com
Invicta military vehicle preservation society show at
Beltring.

LA GLEIZE BOURSE INTERNATIONAL MILITARIA
Rue de l'Eglise, 25-B-4987, La Gleize, Belgium
Contact: Y Gabriel
Tel: 00320 80 78 61 83
Fax: 00320 80 78 66 06
Huge summer militaria show.

MILITARY ODYSSEY
PO Box 254, Marden, Tonbridge, Kent TN12 9ZQ
Contact: Gary Howard
Tel/Fax: 01892 730233
Email: militaryodyssey@aol.com
Website: www.military-odyssey.com
The country's largest multi-period historical living history
extravaganza. Over 400+ trade stalls, over 400 military
vehicles. Displays and dioramas; battle re-creations;
children's sactivities. A packed weekend for all—too much
to be seen in one day. Historical 'In Camp' Talks—from the
Romans through to the Gulf War.

PLANTAGENET EVENTS
10 Sydney Street, HoddlesdenVillage, Nr Darwen,
LancashireBB3 3LZ
Contact: Mark Johnson
Tel: 01254 762050
Email: mark@kolshanks.freeserve.co.uk
Organisers of events covering all periods.

SCHEDULE OF EUROPEAN ARMS & MILITARIA FAIRS
Email: geschichtsverein@gmx.de

SOLDIERS III
Brent
Tel: 01342 835669 0860 236291
Blank firing. De-Act. Air Soft. Replica weapons.

THE TEMPLARS FAYRE
Cressing Temple Barns, Nr Braintree, Essex
Tel: 01304 381699 or 01603 414045
Email: morgan@plantagenetshoes.freeserce.co.uk
Fayres take place at least twice a year—phone or email for
details. Merchants covering Roman to 1600. Food, wines,
ales and entertainment!

TEWKESBURY MEDIEVAL FESTIVAL
c/o 5 Kings Lane, Norton, Evesham, Worcs WR11 11TJ
Contact: Jane Baalam
Tel: 01386 871908
Email: battle.tewkesbury@bigfoot.com
Living history encampment depicting aspects of Medieval
life. Displays include: archery, woodcarving, pewter casting,
limining, candlemaking, cookery.

U K M S
90-92 King Street, Maidstone, Kent ME14 1BH
Tel: 01622 763987
Fax: 01622 763995
Military show organisers.

W D MODEL FAIRS
c/o Garden Flat, 75 Bouverie Street West, Folkestone, Kent
CT20 2RL
Contact: Richard Windrow
Tel/Fax: 01303 240006 (evenings)
Organisers of International Toy Soldier Fair held annually on
a Saturday in March at a venue on The Lees, Folkestone.
All trade stands (from @30), toy soldier manufacturers
and dealers; open to public. Enquire for up-to-date details.